REGULATING
HEALTH FACILITIES
CONSTRUCTION

A conference sponsored by
American Enterprise Institute for Public Policy Research
and the Committee on Legal Issues in Health Care
Duke University School of Law

REGULATING HEALTH FACILITIES CONSTRUCTION

Proceedings of a Conference on Health Planning,
Certificates of Need, and Market Entry

Edited by Clark C. Havighurst

American Enterprise Institute for Public Policy Research
Washington, D.C.

ISBN 0-8447-2043-7 (Paper)
ISBN 0-8447-2044-5 (Cloth)

Library of Congress Catalog Card Number L.C. 73-93825

Printed in the United States of America

MAJOR CONTRIBUTORS

Jan P. Acton
The Rand Corporation

Rick J. Carlson
Health Services Research Center, Institute for Interdisciplinary Studies
American Rehabilitation Foundation

William J. Curran
Frances Glessner Lee Professor of Legal Medicine
School of Public Health, Harvard University

Symond R. Gottlieb
Executive Director, Greater Detroit Area Hospital Council

Robert N. Grosse
Professor of Health Planning, School of Public Health
University of Michigan

Clark C. Havighurst
Professor of Law, Duke University School of Law

Judith R. Lave
Associate Professor of Economics and Urban Affairs
School of Urban and Public Affairs, Carnegie-Mellon University

Lester B. Lave
Chairman, Department of Economics, Graduate School of
Industrial Administration, Carnegie-Mellon University

J. Joel May
Director, Graduate Program in Hospital Administration
Center for Health Administration Studies, University of Chicago

Duncan Neuhauser
Assistant Professor of Health Services Administration
School of Public Health, Harvard University

Joseph P. Newhouse
The Rand Corporation

Patrick O'Donoghue
Health Services Research Center, Institute for Interdisciplinary Studies
American Rehabilitation Foundation

Mark V. Pauly
Associate Professor, Department of Economics, Northwestern University

Richard A. Posner
Professor of Law, University of Chicago Law School

Laurens H. Silver
Director, National Health and Environmental Law Program, School of Law
University of California, Los Angeles

FOREWORD

In June of 1972 the American Enterprise Institute for Public Policy Research and the Committee on Legal Issues in Health Care, centered at the Duke University School of Law, jointly sponsored a conference in Washington, D.C., on Regulating Health Facilities Construction. This volume contains the papers and proceedings of that conference.

In recent years there has been a growing trend to limit competition in the delivery of health care and to increase government regulation in the health care sector. This trend has been evidenced in the passage of certificate-of-need laws in a number of states. A major purpose of the conference was to examine this trend as it would affect future health care delivery. Experts of various disciplines and with widely ranging views examined many aspects of this trend that could affect the public's access to medical care in the future, as well as the quality of that care and its cost.

It is hoped that the distribution of these proceedings will contribute to increased public understanding of some of the issues involved in medical care delivery. In addition to those who presented papers or were discussants of papers, some seventy experts participated.

The volume is organized into four parts, each covering a session of the conference and including papers prepared for that session and discussion of participants.

We are indebted to Professor Clark C. Havighurst of the Duke University School of Law, who is director of the Committee on Legal Issues in Health Care, for organizing the conference and editing the proceedings.

THOMAS F. JOHNSON
Director of Research
American Enterprise Institute
for Public Policy Research

CONTENTS

PART TWO

Health Facilities Planning with "Teeth":
Certificate-of-Need Laws

PART THREE

Nonprofit Monopolies in Health Care:
Controlling the Progeny of Certificate-of-Need Laws

PART FOUR
National Health Policy Directions:
The Future of Certificate-of-Need Laws and Health Planning

INTRODUCTION

Clark C. Havighurst

The conference memorialized in this volume was convened to examine the strong trend toward enactment of state laws prohibiting construction or expansion of medical facilities without a prior certification of the "need" therefor by a state agency. Known as certificate-of-need laws, these measures—adopted in twenty states at the latest count—are widely hailed as a solution to certain problems relating to the cost of medical care. Until the conference, they had occasioned very little critical comment. As appears herein, criticism can be mounted on several levels, and a central purpose of the conference was to provide the skeptics with a forum in which to confront the issues and the advocates.

Much of the skepticism originates in recognition of the similarity between the "certificate of public convenience and necessity," which is widely employed as a device in regulating public utilities and transportation companies, and the certificate of need. Many persons, particularly economists, who are familiar with experience in these regulated industries, find it difficult to share the optimism of many experts in the health world concerning the operation of certificate-of-need laws. In their view, restrictions on growth and new entry in other industries have eliminated important competitive pressures and opportunities for consumer choice, created privileged market positions for certain interests, weakened guarantees of efficiency and high-quality performance, retarded certain kinds of innovation while over-stimulating others, raised prices, and generally misallocated resources—all with only debatable public benefits, though clear private ones. Moreover, recent economic literature has purported to document the case that regulation's failures are not mere aberrations, produced by sinister influences or by regulators' lack of dedication to the public interest, but are inherent in the political economy of regulation itself. In view of the widespread innocence on these matters in the health world, a conference seemed an appropriate way to give certificate-of-need proponents and the skeptics a chance to explore each other's concerns. The result was a lively and at times highly charged discussion.

The arguments in favor of controlling expansion of facilities and new entry in the health care industry may be substantially stronger than the arguments for such controls in those other industries where they are widely discredited. The tendency of the voluntary nonprofit hospitals to accumulate discretionary funds, to consult nonmarket factors in their investment decisions, and to compete for doctors' favor

1

by expansion of facilities suggests the need for controls over the most important class of hospitals. Moreover, hospital utilization is widely thought to be in large measure a function of bed availability rather than of patients' medical needs, as a consequence of fee-for-service payment; decision making is placed largely in providers' hands and financing is available largely from third-party "deep pockets" on a cost reimbursement basis. Finally, competition by profit-seeking new entrants could jeopardize hospital revenues which are badly needed to support important community services, particularly medical care for the indigent population. These arguments suggest that the usual presumptions about market forces may not hold, at least not as the medical care industry is now organized. The conference was called upon to grapple with these phenomena as well as with the appropriateness of a particular regulatory response.

The certificate-of-need issue, affecting as it does the fundamental resource allocation mechanisms in health care, has very broad ramifications. The conference prospectus, which is printed herewith, reveals the intention to examine as many of these as possible. The meeting began with a discussion of the experience with various kinds of health planning, from which came the movement to put regulatory "teeth" behind planners' recommendations. After the legislative developments were presented and the skeptics' position had been voiced and examined, the consequences of restricting growth and new entry in the hospital world were reviewed. This discussion noted the tendency of such laws to strengthen the monopoly position of hospitals and reviewed the problems of predicting and influencing the behavior of "nonprofit monopolies" and of imposing various nonmarket mechanisms of social control. The conference then branched out more widely to examine the bearing of national health policy trends on the need for regulatory controls. National health insurance, health maintenance organizations, foundations for medical care, proprietary institutions, and comprehensive health planning all received attention. The broader context for these discussions was consideration of the prospects for restoring market forces which would work well enough to obviate the more comprehensive kinds of regulatory intervention. As so often occurs, the attempt to focus attention on a narrow issue of health policy—certificate-of-need laws—led naturally to consideration of a broad spectrum of related problems.

The conference reached no consensus, and much of the debate reflected disagreement over fundamental principles, premises, and values. Nonetheless, the dissenting voices warned that the regulatory "solutions" of the past have produced a heritage of protectionism, special interests, resource misallocation, and systematic neglect of consumer interests. This warning might suggest that health care experts should examine the experience outside the health field and address themselves to demonstrating how the health care industry might be immune from the fundamental afflictions attending other regulatory efforts. Even though the case for certificate-of-need laws would seem to be highly plausible, not much work has been done to establish that direct regulation of growth and new market entry is the *best* remedy public policy has to offer for the problems being addressed. It is to be hoped that the questions raised sharply at the conference will be regarded as provocative only in this constructive sense.

The conference was held in Washington, D.C., on June 15-16, 1972. Most of the papers and remarks have undergone significant revision by the participants since then, and I have myself undertaken substantial reorganization of the proceedings, mostly by grouping related remarks under headings. I have also composed at leisure a few of the moderator-like questions and remarks appearing under my name to clarify the issues being discussed at various points and have added explanatory "Reporter's notes" at other points. Thus, although what we have here is of only slight value as a historical record of what transpired on two particular days in June, it is a more useful document than a verbatim record would have been.

I am personally grateful to the American Enterprise Institute for Public Policy Research for supporting the conference financially and logistically. The titular co-sponsor of the conference with AEI was the Committee on Legal Issues in Health Care, of which I am director and which is supported under contract HSM 110-69-214 between the National Center for Health Services Research and Development (Department of Health, Education, and Welfare) and Duke University. Seven members of the committee participated actively in the conference—on all sides of the issue, I might note. My appreciation to them and to the other participants is very great indeed.

December 1972

PART ONE

Health Planning and Health Planners: Forerunners of Certificates of Need

REPORTER'S NOTE: This session of the conference was designed to fill in the historical and other background of certificate-of-need laws and proposals. The need for health facilities planning is widely accepted, and the trend toward its expansion is likely to prove inexorable. One purpose of the first session was to allow persons knowledgeable about planning to present the case for it. Others were invited to supply the skeptical point of view.

Although certificate-of-need laws relate primarily to new health facilities and to the identity of the providers of new services, the functions of health planning were seen to extend well beyond this range of concerns. For this reason, health planning proved difficult to sum up, and differences arose over its purposes and the criteria to be applied in judging its success. Much discussion was prompted by what some perceived as aspersions on planning in the May paper, but the main point that emerged was the difficulty of making a firm demonstration for or against planning as a real-world activity. The more important job of the conference was clearly to focus on the asserted need to control growth and market entry.

In the view not only of the skeptics but of most others, facilities planning—and, a fortiori, *regulation of entry by certificate-of-need requirements—must be defended by distinguishing hospital care in some meaningful way from those numerous industries in which free entry and decentralized private decision making in response to market signals are usually regarded as desirable features. The proponents of planning convincingly distinguished hospital care from other industries on two grounds: first, the preponderance of nonprofit providers and, second, the impact of third-party cost reimbursement, which is the primary means of paying for hospital care, on the supply and consumption of health services. Once this case was presented, the issues seemed to become (1) whether the showing was strong enough to overcome the pro-market presumption or required, in addition, an affirmative demonstration of effectiveness; (2) whether the tendency of all human enterprises to deviate from the ideal model might render planning and regulation, even though attractive in theory, no better as instruments of social control than the imperfect market; and, finally, (3) whether the market and institutional conditions cited as justifying a planning approach might themselves be correctable in such a way as to obviate or minimize the need for regulatory measures inspired by planning. The first two of these issues received the most attention in this session of the conference, and all of them were to reappear in later sessions.*

A BRIEF HISTORY OF HEALTH PLANNING IN THE UNITED STATES

Symond R. Gottlieb

In developing plans for today's conference, it must have seemed logical to devote part of the opening session to a discussion of the history of health planning in the United States. After all, the past is a prelude to the future, and we should know where we have been if we are going to discuss intelligently the current scene and where we are heading.

But on sober reflection, I am not so sure that this is the most logical time slot for a historical review. The reason is simply that it is extremely difficult, if not impossible, to discuss the development of health planning in a vacuum and before a heterogeneous audience. A proper interpretation of the history of health planning should be based upon some common understanding of the assumptions on which health planning is based and some common appreciation of the characteristics of effective health planning. A cursory examination of the topics to be covered in this conference and the preeminence of the other program participants suggests that the rest of us will be better able to understand the history of health planning at the conclusion of these sessions than we are this morning. But the program is set, and I am here before you to interpret the brief history of this movement.

Context and Background

Fortunately, I need not say much to place health planning in historical context. Most of you are aware of the rapid changes in our health system during the past fifty years and of the forces that brought them about: rapidly advancing medical technology; the shift in emphasis in technological development from the prevention of disease to curative medicine; the growing lag between scientific development and its application; the rising health expectations of the American people and the uneven rate at which those expectations are fulfilled; the growing disparity in the quality and quantity of health services accessible to diverse segments of the population; the rapid growth of third-party financing of health care and the concomitant increase in their influence; the substantial reduction in the number of direct purchasers of health services and the increasing sophistication of the largest purchasers; the growing significance of health benefits in labor-management negotiations; the inevitable increase in government involvement in financing health care

7

and in influencing the supply and organization of resources; the apparent shortage of health manpower; and, of course, steadily rising costs, brought about by all of the other factors and a generally inflationary economy.

I am sure that you are equally aware of the way in which the forces affecting health system development interacted with other forces operating in our society: the rising levels of education in most of our society, creating more sophisticated health expectations; the severe imbalance between the supply of and demand for health services created by fifteen years of depression and war at a time when technology was advancing most rapidly; the growing urban and suburban sprawl and the exodus from rural to urban life that required, among other things, massive redistribution of health resources; the growing complexity of urban life that increases health hazards exponentially; the generally prosperous economy since 1946 to feed the apparently inexhaustible demand for capital and operating dollars, which resulted, however inadvertently, in a growing disparity in the effective demand for health services among different segments of society; the growing restlessness of large segments of society as they seek greater dignity, more control over the institutions that affect their lives, and a greater share of the resources that contribute to the quality of life; and the increasing competition for scarce resources to meet conflicting demands for better health, better housing, better education, more jobs, and so forth, as well as the conflict between these demands and the demands for military expenditure.

If it were not beyond the purview of my assignment, it might be fruitful to list the forces affecting health system development more completely and to delve into them more deeply. For today's purposes, this brief description gives us at least some sense of the milieu in which health planning was spawned and has developed. Perhaps even more important, it provides some insight into the assumptions upon which health planning is based. It seems to me that there are three such assumptions:

(1) Because of the overriding importance of health to human well-being and because ours is a society of scarce resources, optimum value must be obtained from the resources allocated to health care.

(2) The health system reflects the society in which it operates, but the requirement that it serve primarily a social purpose transcends economic and other values of society.

(3) Public accountability is the cornerstone of an effective health system, and responsiveness to the economic, social, cultural, professional, and political forces that operate in each community is the measure of the health system's accountability.

To some extent these assumptions, usually poorly articulated, have been at the roots of health planning since its earliest days. Experience and the continuing interaction of forces affecting the health system have helped us to understand the parameters of these assumptions more clearly, determining to some extent subsequent development of health planning activities. In my opinion, the fact that these concepts are still insufficiently understood and accepted probably accounts for much of our current confusion about the nature and role of health planning in the United States.

The current confusion is most apparent when we try to develop a generally accepted statement concerning the goals of health planning, or when we try to define health planning and the characteristics of the health planning function. Whenever such statements are attempted it is clear that we are dealing with the proverbial elephant as perceived by a posse of blind men. But I will never get around to a discussion of the history of health planning if I try to describe and analyze all of the current perceptions and misconceptions of the nature and goals of health planning. For the purpose of today's assignment, I will use a very simple definition of planning (with apologies for its brevity to Bob Sigmond and Steve Sieverts, from whom I borrowed some of my best ideas). In my view, planning is the process of thinking before you act. It is reciprocally related to action, but planning in itself is not action.

I realize that a definition of planning as the process of thinking before you act may be so simple as to be unfathomable—although I am not always sure that clarity is assured by lengthening a statement. What is important about this definition is that it is equally applicable to any organization—whether it is an institutional provider, a community planning agency, a state agency, or the federal government (assuming that the federal government ever thinks before it acts). This definition is also useful because it clearly implies that planning is always voluntary—I know of no way to require anybody to think before action is taken. And the definition is helpful in providing insight into the fact that the planning role is always advisory to those who have the responsibility to make decisions or take action.

If I were to lengthen that simple definition as a backdrop for the remainder of this paper, I would still try to keep it simple. I would add that effective planning requires that thinking be done systematically; that it is enhanced by the use of all available tools, including data, that provide insight into the problems that must be resolved; that it is done by a number of people, interacting with each other, under the direction of a responsible individual; that it is done in conjunction with other organizations and individuals who have related responsibilities; that its purpose is to advise those responsible for making decisions or taking action; and that it is a continuous major function of every organization.

And so my prologue ends. Having suggested that health planning is a product of its times and the complex forces that affect health system development, having described the assumptions on which health planning is based, and having established a simple definition of health planning, I have now clearly exposed my biases, and we can turn to an examination of the history of health planning in the United States.

The literature on some aspects of health planning goes back at least to 1920, as one group or another or some advanced thinker discussed either the methodology or the need for health planning. I am not going to provide a detailed review of all of this literature for you—nothing would be more boring and unproductive, and I am not as good a researcher as Joel May. In general, most of the early literature described methods of determining hospital bed needs and the importance of doing so. Beginning in the early 1930s, discussion of the need for coordination of health facilities and services began to creep into the printed page. These two aspects came together briefly in the mid-1940s and were discussed with higher frequency throughout the 1950s. In the early 1960s, the development of so-called "voluntary" area-wide health planning agencies was urged repeatedly, and some cookbooks were published. After a few earlier pronouncements that "voluntary" planning would never work and that planning should have more "teeth," by the mid-1960s an increasing number of writers confused planning with regulation and advocated certificate-of-need or franchising legislation.

Concurrently, a growing body of literature after 1965 began to discuss the importance of a broader approach to health planning and to deplore its concentration upon health facilities and general hospital beds. In the past ten years, the crescendo of demand in the literature for more and better health planning has increased to a flood—although, as I have already suggested, it has not always been easy to discern a common motivation for such demands or a common understanding of the nature of health planning. And, of course, all of this literature about health planning was imbedded in an impressive body of material describing health problems, advancing technology, rising costs, and the many forces that were affecting the developing health system.

Early Development, Local Initiatives

In the real world—and I don't mean to imply that the literature does not reflect and influence the real world—health planning outside of the individual health care institution or agency began to develop at the local level immediately after the First World War and began to develop at the federal level immediately after the Second World War. Because the two levels of health planning development were quite distinct and operated with relatively little interaction in a parallel fashion for many years, it is useful to trace their development separately until the two sets of activities began to converge in the mid-1960s.

Parenthetically, I should note that I will not trace the development of health planning at the state level separately unless there is some particularly pertinent point to be made. In general, the states have been part of federal health planning programs—usually dragged kicking and screaming into them to operate as the agent of the federal government in the years after 1946. Needless to say, that has not engendered the universal, whole-hearted cooperation of the states and has contributed very little to the capacity of state government to resolve its own problems.

The real genesis of health planning outside of the individual institution or agency in a variety of local communities around the country concerned only voluntary health and welfare agencies. Councils of social agencies, which had emerged in the years after World War I, were succeeded by health and welfare federations. Their formats and sponsorship varied somewhat, but they were all impelled by substantially the same motivations—professional concern to have a forum to exchange information and the concern of community leaders to coordinate the activities of these diverse but related agencies.

When joint fund raising was introduced with the development of community chests in the late 1920s and throughout the 1930s, the other ingredients of planning began to emerge. The establishment of fund-raising goals and allocation of the funds required a planning arm that could provide insight into community needs and help to determine priorities. As the major source of contributed dollars shifted from the individual wealthy family to the corporation and the foundation, these joint fund-raising and related planning activities were refined substantially with the introduction of the concept of the United Foundation in Detroit in 1949.

The rate at which these local organizations developed and their specific characteristics varied considerably around the country as they adapted themselves to local conditions and local demands. Certain of their common characteristics are especially relevant to this discussion. First, they were concerned primarily with resource allocations, with strong overtones of concern for the effective delivery of service. Second, they were concerned almost exclusively with the allocation of charity dollars. Third, they were dominated and controlled by the principal contributors of charitable dollars, with carefully built-in interaction with the agency professionals and board members. And, fourth, they seldom included any of the community's hospitals in their planning or fund raising.

The last characteristic is especially relevant to this discussion. There are many reasons for the omission of hospitals, but only one need be mentioned at this point. As the requirements of the voluntary health and welfare agencies for operating funds from charitable sources increased, the operating requirements of community hospitals were being met in increasing amounts by noncharitable sources—until the need for charitable funds began to approach zero in the period after 1946. Conversely, the cost of hospital construction increased dramatically as scientific medicine advanced; and the pent-up demand for hospital construction after fifteen years of depression and war made their capital requirements seem almost limitless. The attention of potential contributors was therefore focused on the capital needs of hospitals. The amount of each capital fund campaign was so large that it dwarfed the problems of funding the operations of the voluntary health and welfare agencies, and most communities gradually developed separate and special mechanisms to take care of capital fund requirements.

It is not surprising that the principal contributors, especially the corporate contributors, should begin to ask the same kinds of questions regarding hospital capital funds that they had already been asking about other charitable dollars. How could they be sure that all of those capital funds were really needed? How could they satisfy themselves that such funds were being used as efficiently and as effectively as possible? But the scope and complexity of the problem were so different from the problems of the voluntary health and welfare agencies that in most communities these business leaders concluded that a different organization and different techniques were needed. And so, beginning in the early 1940s in New York City, Columbus, Rochester, Detroit, Chicago, Pittsburgh, and other cities, they launched hospital or health facilities planning agencies. By 1964 there were thirty-three such independent agencies in major metropolitan areas across the country.

To some extent these agencies had many characteristics similar to those of their forebears, but they also had some distinguishing features. There was more diversity in their organization and operation among the several communities. Some included the health professionals in their planning and decision-making process from the outset; others did not. A few communities tried joint capital fund-raising campaigns that were directly related to the planning activity (some still do), but the size of such an undertaking in a large metropolitan area and the strength of the competitors for such funds deterred other communities from such an approach. Thus, the planning and the decision making concerning contributed capital were gradually separated, and the method by which planning influenced such decision making became more subtle and substantially more diluted.

In their early stages almost all of these metropolitan hospital planning agencies were dominated by representatives of major corporate contributors and their peers who were primarily interested in bricks and mortar developments that were to be financed by contributed capital. The symbol and the basic unit of measurement became the general hospital bed—as the writers had long advocated in the literature—and the basic purpose was to restrict construction as much as possible. When that was not possible, the purpose was to delay construction and to space the demand for contributed capital as much as possible. Staff hired for these agencies had a largely technocratic orientation and viewed themselves as serving a control function—although their motivation was usually not consistent with the motivations of their governing boards, since most of them were dedicated health professionals. In most of these communities, at the time of the organization of such agencies, there was no established precedent for their role with respect to hospitals. Accordingly, hospital administrators, their boards, and their medical staffs tended to be suspicious, uncooperative, and resentful of the planning agencies, and the hospitals and planning agencies usually developed an adversary relationship.

But times were changing, and experience was being gained. As capital funds were sought increasingly from other than contributed funds, the relationship between capital and operating funds was clarified. As health insurance became a major factor and its cost increased, management and organized labor began to be more concerned with hospital operating costs. It was gradually becoming apparent that the programs operated in hospitals were more important than the construction of a physical facility. It was also becoming apparent that alternatives to general hospital care were needed if costs were going to be contained and that unnecessary duplication of services was a serious villain on the metropolitan scene. The effect of the shortage of manpower on the costs of care and on the capacity to deliver care was becoming apparent. Interaction between the planning agency and others in the community—inevitable because of the complexity of the basic task—brought to the consciousness of the planning agency some understanding of serious gaps in the availability and accessibility of certain kinds of services. And, most importantly, it was becoming apparent that the confrontation approach between the planning agency and its community's hospitals did not work very well.

At different rates, and in different ways because of the diverse nature of their communities, the hospital planning agencies began a slow but inexorable change in their organization, role conceptions, and methodology. Membership on their governing boards gradually expanded to include more kinds of people; their scope of concern began to include long-term care, mental health, ambulatory care, home care, health manpower and related programs; they began to focus on program planning rather than construction planning; they began to develop constructive relationships with providers of care; they began to demonstrate some concern with the organization of the delivery system; and they began to focus upon strengthening the quality of institutional planning. Coincidentally with this kind of evolution, many of the area-wide health facilities planning agencies (as they came to be called) expanded their sphere of influence through the establishment of relationships with Blue Cross, insurance companies, banks, investment firms, and a variety of public and private agencies at the local and state levels.

In 1964, after federal grants became available to assist in financing area-wide health facilities planning agencies, a host of new agencies was formed; by 1967, there were about seventy-five such agencies in the country, most of them in metropolitan areas. In general, the new agencies learned from their predecessors and developed a somewhat broader base from the outset. But both the old and the new agencies suffered from the same problems. They moved slowly and results were hard to demonstrate; they were underfinanced for their broadening role; they were still dominated on all important issues by the representatives of the corporate community in spite of changing societal attitudes; their basic goal, often unarticulated, was still to improve the management of community resources; and their efforts to improve the quality of institutional planning were often frustrated by the rigidity of institutional traditions and organization.

Moreover, the expansion of their scope of concern brought them into increasing conflict with other community organizations—such as the United Fund and its

13

related planning arm—and new categorical planning agencies sprang up in many communities to promote or protect special interests. Concurrently, local governments were beginning to get into the planning act with the establishment of regional planning commissions or councils of government. Most importantly, the local nature of these health facilities planning agencies—each using a different methodology and progressing at a different rate—made it impossible to discern a national pattern of health planning development at a time when health care and its financing were becoming major national issues. Because performance and results were uneven, the entire movement was extremely vulnerable to attack.

Federal Impact

Hill-Burton. Meanwhile, beginning in 1946, the federal government began to have an increasingly important impact on health planning. The Hospital Survey and Construction Act (the Hill-Burton Act) was a landmark piece of legislation, unique in many respects when it was passed in 1946. It was primarily a program to finance the construction of community hospitals and related health facilities to fill the huge backlog of demand that had grown since 1929. But grants were to be provided in accordance with a state plan developed by a designated state agency under the close scrutiny of the federal authority. The especially pertinent features of the planning aspect of the Hill-Burton program were that it attempted to inventory health facilities needs and resources, to project needs, to determine priorities in each state, and to bring about coordination of health facilities of different capacities and different types. Concurrently, the Hill-Burton program sought to establish and improve construction standards, to maintain close surveillance over construction costs, and to influence the states to improve the operating standards for health care institutions. The planning was closely related to decision making since the federal grants were to be dispensed only in accordance with the state plan.

It is easy, with the 20/20 vision of hindsight, to criticize some of the results and methodology of the Hill-Burton program. In my opinion, however, it has been one of the most effective federal programs yet devised, coming closer to achieving its purposes than any other of which I am aware. Its thrust has been positive rather than restrictive, and the program has had much to do with improving the standards of hospital care as well as making adequate facilities available and accessible throughout the nation. The pork barrel attitude that might have been expected in such a massive program has largely been avoided. And, in the course of its twenty-five years of operation, the Hill-Burton program has contributed much to the methodology of planning.

In spite of its general excellence, the Hill-Burton program has had several serious flaws. Its planning aspect has been highly technocratic, with almost complete

14

reliance on quantitative methods and little interaction with providers or consumers in the planning phase. Until very recent years, the Hill-Burton program operated alongside local health planning activities with little formal interaction between them in most states. The high degree of centralized administration made adaptation to the conditions in each state very difficult. The inability to influence any developments for which federal funds were not available or could not be used severely limited the scope of its impact. And the relative inflexibility of the regulations and practices that have developed over these twenty-five years has severely limited the ability of the program to adjust to the changing scene.

It was, of course, through the Hill-Burton program that the federal government first became involved with local health planning agencies in a structured manner. Beginning in 1962, some of the research and demonstration funds allocated in these programs were used to foster the development of new local agencies and to augment the financing of existing agencies. Then, in the 1964 extension of the Hill-Burton Act, funds were specifically earmarked for grants to area-wide health facilities planning agencies, and federal stimulation of local health planning began in earnest. Interestingly, these funds were administered directly from Washington, and the state agencies were not involved in the process. The federal authority provided limited technical assistance for the development and operation of such agencies, but almost no effort was made to guide their operations. No attempt was made to tie together the state and local planning or decision-making activities, and it seldom evolved in any structured relationship. The local agencies were treated as what they were—locally developed and operated autonomous agencies with federal financial assistance that indirectly helped to carry out a federal purpose.

Forerunners of Comprehensive Health Planning. It is too often assumed that the next major step by the federal government in the health planning field was the passage of the comprehensive health planning (CHP) legislation. But a substantial amount of legislation was passed in the intervening years that was part of the evolutionary process leading to its passage and our current health planning scene. Three pieces of legislation are seldom remembered these days—because of inadequate funding—but were quite important to the process. The Community Mental Health Center Act of 1963, the Community Mental Retardation Center Act of 1964, and the Comprehensive Rehabilitation Act of 1965 were all significant. They were important because each of them delegated planning and administrative responsibilities to the states; each of them provided not only construction funds but also staffing funds for the operation of such centers; each of them emphasized a coordinated system of services; and each of them required "comprehensive" statewide program planning as distinguished from facilities planning or service planning. They were also important because they further fragmented health planning, intensified the rivalry and competition among state governmental units, and gave local special interest groups a direct pipeline and a wedge to avoid coordination of health activities at the local level.

Regional Medical Programs. Another piece of federal legislation was passed in 1965 that has considerable significance for the health planning field. Federal funds were provided to establish regional medical programs to combat the killer diseases, namely, heart disease, cancer, and stroke. Although this act was later expanded to remove most of the categorical disease limitations, there is a remarkable lack of unanimity about why it was passed in that form, what it is supposed to accomplish, how it is to be organized, or how it is to function. I cannot dwell on it too long, but the act seems to suggest that regional medical programs would develop regional arrangements between medical schools or other centers of excellence and other hospitals and clinical facilities for the purpose of increasing the rate of application of advancing medical technology.

Some of the regional medical programs established under the act seem to be working along those lines; but many of them seem to have other agendas. We could get into quite an argument about them, and I don't propose to contribute to the conflict any more than I must. For purposes of today's discussion, the Regional Medical Program legislation is important because it attempted to bring medical schools into more active concern with the delivery of care and made federal funds available specifically to achieve operational coordination designed to enhance the quality of care. It is also significant because state government was given no role to play in the formation of regional medical programs or in their subsequent operation.

Although they were only partly concerned with health, two other pieces of federal legislation are especially relevant to our history of health planning. The programs funded by the Office of Economic Opportunity (OEO) after its establishment in 1964 had great experimental value. They significantly and purposely bypassed state government for all practical purposes, and they generally bypassed all of the established institutional structures in local communities, including local political bodies. They stimulated a broad array of new developments in the health field, including the concept of neighborhood health centers and new types of health workers. But, perhaps, the greatest long-range impact of the OEO programs comes from their insistence upon "maximum feasible participation" in the development and operation of programs by the people being served by those programs. For the first time in our history the federal government was mandating the concept that even disadvantaged and minority people should have some direct control over the institutions that affected their lives. It was the forerunner of a change in the decision-making structure of our society that has not yet reached its peak and that has tremendously influenced the current nature of health planning.

The other related piece of federal legislation that is significant to the current health planning scene was the Metropolitan Development Act of 1965 which in-

16

cluded, among other things, the Model Cities program. This act promoted the concept of regional comprehensive planning for all community subsystems, including health. It also promoted greater coordination in the awarding of federal grant funds and encouraged, to some extent indirectly, the development and strengthening of governmentally based regional planning commissions and councils of governments.

The Model Cities program segment of the act (originally called "demonstration cities" until somebody noted the unpleasant connotations of the term "demonstration") had several features of significance to the states. It represented an attempt to develop a coordinated attack on several systems simultaneously in a clearly defined neighborhood, including health as one of the components of the program. This program also bypassed state government, but it sought to increase the role of local government and to strengthen the mayor's office. Concurrently the legislation seemed to suggest that local government and the mayors could not be trusted, and it sought to give substantial control over the program to the people living in the target area. The lessons learned by both local governments and the community people through this artificially created conflict will haunt health planning for many years to come. And, of course, the Model Cities program had an extensive planning component that, among other things, further fragmented community health planning.

Comprehensive Health Planning Legislation

P.L. 89-749. The flurry of federal legislative activity in the mid-1960s included a rather innocuous piece of legislation that was casually adopted in the closing days of the 89th Congress. Known as the Comprehensive Health Planning and Public Health Services Amendment of 1966, the new law had all of the "motherhood" characteristics that appeal to congressmen, and, since it required almost no additional money, there seemed to be little reason to vote against it. It seemed to give the states some role in the nation's health activity, but the role was largely undefined. It paid lip-service to some sort of planning role at the area-wide or metropolitan levels within states by speaking vaguely of some sort of "coordination of existing and planned health services." It provided a little additional money to train health planners and to stimulate experimental and demonstration health services delivery programs. And it provided that the categorical funds for public health services made available to the states would be given to them in block grants instead.

The legislative history of P.L. 89-749 provides little insight into why it was passed or what Congress hoped to accomplish with it. If the hearings and reports were to be taken at their face value, it would appear that very few major interest groups advocated the legislation and almost none opposed it or saw much reason

17

to alter it. It would appear from the reports that the chief purpose of the legislation was to give state health departments more freedom in determining how they would use federal funds for public health services by combining federal categorical programs into a block grant. Special recognition was given to mental health interests in the funding mechanism for the block grants. Some of the fragmentation of existing health planning activities was noted, and the desirability of bringing some of them together was given its proper emphasis.

With respect to area-wide or metropolitan health planning, Congress apparently intended to build on the experience of existing agencies and to effect an expansion of their scope of concern and their health planning activities. Funding of area-wide planning agencies for health facilities under the Hill-Burton Act was to be replaced by funding under the comprehensive health planning program. Except with respect to the expenditure of the block grant funds for state public health services, there was no indication that planning would be tied to decision making. And little was said about how area-wide comprehensive health planning agencies should be organized or what functions they should have.

Going behind the written history, several groups seemed to be interested in the legislation at that time for a variety of reasons. State and territorial health officers were obviously interested in block grants for public health services which would give them more freedom and power within their own states. Many of them were also concerned with the steady erosion in the role of the states with respect to health, as federal programs seemed to bypass them with increasing regularity.

Others who played a role in the development and passage of P.L. 89-749 were primarily concerned with what they viewed as an overemphasis on curative medicine, since they viewed this legislation as a method of bringing about a greater emphasis on preventive medicine, including environmental health. Then there were those who worked for this legislation as a method of reversing the trend to overemphasize the role of hospitals in the economics and delivery of health services. Some of the people advocating the legislation believed that it was the first in a series of steps that could be used to contain or reduce costs of health care, and that comprehensive health planning could later be tied directly into the decision-making process with respect to the allocation of funds and regulation. A few of the more far-seeing strategists viewed this legislation as a means of establishing a structure that would provide a useful instrument for major change in the organization of the health care delivery system. And then, of course, there were a few dewy-eyed dreamers who really believed in the esoteric concept of bringing everybody together in a coordinated and comprehensive approach to improving the health status of all of the American people.

A few of us who had been engaged in area-wide health facilities planning saw some real possibilities in this new legislation, even though most of us were not involved in promoting it and were not consulted about it. The additional funds to operate health planning agencies, the federal commitment to planning that seemed

18

to be implied, the mandate to have a broader scope of concern, and the absence of any implication that planning would be a regulatory mechanism were all consistent with the directions in which we had been moving in our own communities. We felt that this legislation, properly implemented, would strengthen us and speed the rate at which we could broaden our service to our communities.

We also generally agreed that the involvement of state government and federal support implied did provide an opportunity for an effective partnership between the public and private sectors that would considerably enhance our ability to help our communities cope with their health problems. And some of us believed that the delineation of a health planning role for the federal government, the state government, and regional or local planning bodies—however vaguely those roles were defined—offered a tremendous opportunity to demonstrate how national policy could be developed and effectively adapted to the problems, to the institutions, and to the realities faced by each state and each diverse segment of each state. We knew from experience that because every community is different, its problems are not susceptible to uniform national or statewide solutions; therefore the concept of a federal-state-local partnership with mutual interaction but equal rights, privileges, duties, and obligations was very appealing. We recognized how difficult it would be to implement such a concept, but at least this legislation suggested that it might be tried.

Federal Implementation of the CHP Concept. The administration and implementation of the comprehensive health planning legislation at the federal level since November 1966 has been largely opportunistic and somewhat ambivalent. The current characteristics of comprehensive health planning were largely created by federal administration of the program during its first two or three years—a period when it became apparent that there was no really strong congressional support for the program and very little commitment to the program by the administration or by the Department of Health, Education, and Welfare (HEW). Into this vacuum stepped a few individuals who, with relatively little support or direction from their superiors, created the structure within which comprehensive health planning currently functions. It is a tribute to them that they accomplished so much with so little help and such limited financing.

The early administration of the comprehensive health planning program (and to some extent its current administration) was characterized by an inordinate amount of attention to the organizational structures that were to be created at the local level. Limited attention was devoted to such structure at the state level. Almost no attention was paid to the activities that were to be conducted by such agencies, the goals of health planning, the methodologies of health planning, or the results that were to be sought through the comprehensive health planning process. Lack of internal coordination within the health arm of the Department of Health, Education, and Welfare enabled or required comprehensive health planning to be developed in a vacuum, with little or no awareness of the current or past operation of other related programs.

Since the law itself was so vague, early administration of the program sought to adapt several aspects of federal policy inherent in other legislation to provide guidance for the organization of comprehensive health planning. It was concluded that area-wide comprehensive health planning agencies should be new institutional structures that provided a new approach to decision making in local communities. It was determined that such agencies should be controlled by consumers (no reference had been made to the organizational pattern of such agencies in P.L. 89-749) broadly reflecting the total population to be served by the agency and representing "an appropriate balance between the previously influential and the hitherto unheard" (to quote an early statement in the federal guidelines). It was also decided that because of the broad scope of concern of such agencies, all of the 200 or more kinds of health care providers should be given some kind of voice in the operation of such agencies. And it was decided that effective health planning could not be accomplished unless local governments were involved in the policy-making role of the area-wide comprehensive health planning agency.

The early administration of the federal program was complicated by a lack of articulation of the goals of comprehensive health planning and some internal conflict within the federal bureaucracy as to those goals. There were those who believed that the basic purpose was to develop a broad planning process in which the local planning agency basically provided a forum in which a wide range of interest groups could exchange opinions and eventually reach consensus on the directions that should be taken to solve some community health problems. This was the dominant view in the earliest stages of the program which pervaded federal directives concerning the organization of area-wide comprehensive health planning agencies. An initially less important view that gradually grew to a dominant position was the belief of some that these planning agencies should be mechanisms to assist in controlling or containing costs and in reorganizing the delivery system in a manner that would be acceptable to their communities. Unfortunately in some respects, by the time this view became dominant most of the local agencies had already been organized around the consensus concept.

Local Organization Efforts. The directions having been charted by the federal administration of the program, it was not surprising—indeed, it was absolutely inevitable—that the process of organizing area-wide comprehensive health planning agencies in most communities became a horrendous task. The area-wide health facilities agency, if one existed, was set up for attack by all of its formerly vocal and latent critics—the better the job it had done, the more ripe it was for such attack. All major and many minor interest groups were forced into the fray either to promote their own interests or because they perceived the need to protect their interests. Very few had any real commitment to health planning or any of its possible

20

goals, but, partly because of its vague threat and partly because of its vague promise, all of them saw something of value in it to their own interests. The larger and more complex the community, the greater the conflict became because of the number of interest groups and the complexity of their interaction.

Whether the approach to organizing these area-wide agencies was effective cannot be determined until they have had a chance to operate for a while. At least 150 such agencies have been organized through this difficult process and are somehow in operation. At this writing we can only observe that it took two to four years just to organize each agency; and even though they are currently in operation, some of them are still going through the throes of organization. In the meantime local health planning almost came to a standstill in most parts of the country—there was no time to carry on the organizational task and also do health planning. One by one the existing area-wide health facilities planning agencies were forced out of business or quietly dropped from the scene. Usually their chief executives and staffs sought other kinds of employment, leaving their communities totally devoid of experienced health planners. Many of their enemies and a few federal officials do not find their disappearance from the scene to be a disadvantage.

But it takes time to develop qualified new people to staff the new agencies and assume these broad responsibilities. This task was made even more difficult by the underfinancing of the new planning agencies as they developed. Federal funding was far too limited for the scope of the program envisioned, even on a fifty-fifty matching basis; and the lack of commitment to planning with which most interest groups became a part of the local planning agency, coupled with the wounds created by the battles surrounding its organization and the continuing vagueness of the goals, has made local financing extremely difficult. In spite of these early problems, many of the new agencies are showing signs of solid accomplishment and the ability to work together as cohesive units. The number of those agencies that are beginning to become effective units seems to be increasing every year.

State Level Developments. The development of effective state comprehensive health planning agencies since 1967 has encountered a different set of problems. Apparently because they had an even less clear-cut sense of direction about what they wanted from state agencies, federal bureaucrats paid substantially less attention to them. Their timidity with respect to the state agencies probably also stemmed from traditional reluctance on the part of federal officials to interfere directly with the operation of state government. As a result the states have been given almost no direction, little guidance, and only limited help in organizing their programs and developing their roles.

The governor of each state has been required to designate a single state agency to conduct comprehensive health planning if he wants any federal funds for public health services. All of them have done so—most of them within the first two years of the program. Since little additional money was made available for

21

planning, since it was not really a state program, since the program's goals were vague and unclear, and since it was not a results-oriented program of political significance, the initial compliance in most states was merely technical. Under the misconception that it was merely a program to dispense federal funds for public health services—a misconception that state health officers did little to dispel—most governors designated their state health departments for this purpose. As the parameters of the program became a little more clear, some of the later designations went to interdepartmental commissions, or to the larger state department of administration, or to the executive office of the governor. Initial designations of state health departments were subsequently changed in a few states to reflect the broader role imputed to comprehensive health planning.

In most states, the comprehensive health planning function was established by executive order of the governor, and only a few states have in the intervening years provided a statutory basis for the function. As directed by P.L. 89-749, the governors have appointed state advisory health planning councils to the designated state agency, including a majority of consumers as required by the federal law. But since these were gubernatorial appointments, federal officials made no attempt until the last year or two to tell the states what kind of balance of consumers or of providers they should have on such councils. Hence, most of them were appointed in accordance with the usual political considerations taken into account by any governor in appointing public advisory bodies.

In a very few states, the statewide comprehensive health planning agency is beginning to define its role and carve out a series of effective functions and activities. This seems to occur when the governor has a special interest in health problems, when health represents a major local political issue, when there is an unusually strong public administrator involved, or when the governor is seeking to increase the power of his office by strengthening the department of administration or developing a planning department that includes health as one of its fields of interest.

Recent Developments

Developments since P.L. 89-749 was enacted begin to give us some clues as to future directions of health planning. The basic federal legislation has been amended twice. In 1967 it was changed to give congressional support to the concept that the interest of local government must be represented on the governing board of area-wide health planning agencies. Having been stirred up by the federal approach to administration of the program, groups representing cities and counties brought about this change through effective lobbying. This legislative change and the federal regulations subsequently adopted often made local government the dominant partner in the organization of such agencies and gave some impetus to the move to

22

make health planning a governmental function at the local level. In spite of that thrust, most of the area-wide planning agencies are still nonprofit corporations.

In 1970 the comprehensive health planning legislation was renewed for another three years (P.L. 91-515); for the first time the administration of the program was legitimized by including provisions concerning the broad composition of the governing boards and advisory councils of area-wide health planning agencies. Additional funds were authorized for grants to such agencies for their operations, and some attempt was made to tie comprehensive health planning a little more closely to the regional medical programs. The program was also upgraded slightly in terms of its apparent importance in the federal hierarchy by the establishment of a National Advisory Council on Comprehensive Health Programs to the secretary of HEW.

The real signs of change are in other federal legislation and in other administrative mechanisms that have been developed. There has been a gradual increase in the review and comment functions assigned to the area-wide health planning agencies and, to a lesser extent, to the state health planning agencies. By statute, any grants requested from the regional medical programs and any grants or loans requested from the Hill-Burton agency must be first submitted to the appropriate area-wide health planning agencies for review and comment. Their decisions are not officially binding on the granting authority, but they carry great weight. Administratively, HEW has been gradually increasing the number and kinds of other federal grant programs in which applicants must first submit their proposals to the appropriate area-wide health planning agency for review and comment. The word is out that a negative comment from such an agency will kill a proposal, but a positive comment does not guarantee that an applicant will get the money.

Currently in the hopper are two types of legislation that will have important implications for the future of comprehensive health planning. Section 221 of H.R. 1, the amendments to the Social Security Act, would provide that in order to obtain reimbursement for its capital expenses under any federal reimbursement program (Medicare, Medicaid, et cetera), health facilities must submit their proposals prior to construction for review by area-wide and state comprehensive health planning agencies. Favorable recommendations would guarantee reimbursement; negative recommendations would be subject to review by the secretary. This legislation is quite likely to pass whenever the holdup concerning its welfare provisions is resolved; a more far-reaching administration proposal, not yet ready to be acted on, would go so far as to deny all payment for services rendered in unapproved facilities. In addition, each of the several versions of legislation to assist in funding health maintenance organizations contains a provision that requests for federal funds must be submitted first to the area-wide health planning agency for review and comment.

There seems to be a fairly clear trend to relate comprehensive health planning directly to the decision-making process. When coupled with the review role being assigned to such area-wide agencies in the administration of state certificate-of-need laws, it seems likely that these agencies will come to have substantial influence on the allocation of resources for health. In our results-oriented society, it seemed inevitable that they should be assigned such a role; indeed, most of them are seeking such a role. Whether they can carry out such an assignment effectively remains to be seen. Whether they can do it with their current organizational patterns and as nonprofit, private corporations is also a question for the future. Whether they can assume this quasi-regulatory role and still serve their purpose as planning agencies, as I define planning, is perhaps the most significant long-range question of all.

Epilogue

That is my interpretation of some of the history of health planning. But an epilogue is in order. As part of my charge from your chairman I was also asked to evaluate the results of health planning in this country. This I cannot do. The only way that I know to evaluate any operation is in terms of its goals and objectives. But the goals of health planning are the subject of so much conflict and are still so indefinite that I could only serve my biases in an additional way by attempting such an evaluation.

Is the goal of health planning to improve the health status of the American people? If so, such a goal has not really been enunciated, and it would be bound up with all of the other activities in our pluralistic society. Is the goal to contain costs or to save money? Before we could begin to evaluate progress toward that goal we would have to decide the answer to the question, costs for what? The tools for such a complex evaluation are not available for analysis, even if we could agree on that goal. Is the goal to develop new institutional structures designed to carry on the planning process without concern about the results of the process? Even if I agreed with that goal, and I don't, we could not get much agreement on the definition of a "planning process," and the concept is too new to evaluate. The perceived need for more "clout" by most of the new planning agencies seems to suggest to me that the planning process is not working very well.

If the goal of health planning is to improve the management of community health resources, as I believe, depending upon the subordinate objectives selected to define movement toward that goal, I think there is some evidence of progress. Unfortunately, most of the progress occurred under the old area-wide health facilities planning agencies—most of which are now defunct. Some of the new agencies are also beginning to demonstrate some progress in improving the management of community resources, but experience is still too limited for any meaningful evaluation.

I do not see any real value in adding to the length of this paper by examining the entire problem of evaluation of the results of planning. What seems important to me is that as a nation we accept the assumptions upon which health planning is based and that we begin to define and agree on a realistic set of goals for the activity. Having done that, we can establish a mechanism for evaluating results and holding the planners and their constituencies accountable for their performance. Inherent in such a suggestion is the cautionary note that effective health planning requires hard work and a long time to produce results. We cannot continue to indulge ourselves in our national propensity for flitting from one mechanism to another to get results if we really want the planning function to achieve its defined goals. After all, it is easy to make a decision or to take an action. But thinking takes time, and for most of us it is hard work.

THE NEED FOR HEALTH PLANNING

Robert N. Grosse

To address the question of the need for planning in the health field raises a series of interrelated questions—planning about what, by whom, and for whom? What types of planning? What are the alternatives to planning? And perhaps most confusing of all, just what is planning? In the context of this meeting, insofar as I have understood the program and some of the preliminary conversations (dare I call *them* planning?), the issue is community planning of health services, especially as supported by existing or future federal and state legislation.

Cost and Efficiency Objectives

The need for the planning of health services by representatives of community interests is based in large part upon the fact that most of the costs of hospital and physician services are paid for not directly by the patient or his family to the provider, but rather by federal, state, and local governments and by private health insurance. In the last fiscal year (1970-71), 86 percent of the costs of hospital care and 61 percent of the payments for physicians' services in the nation were covered by either government or insurance. Because health care costs are widely shared through these mechanisms, decisions on the type, location, and quantity of hospital and physician services directly affect the broad community, both as taxpayers and as purchasers of insurance. Thus, in the most direct sense, the community has an interest in and responsibility for the cost, efficiency, availability, accessibility, and quality of care.

In the health care industry perhaps more than in any other, the volume and nature of the services rendered are principally determined by the primary provider of those services—the physician. Physicians largely decide the volume of visits and the frequency of use of surgical or other therapeutic techniques. Their judgments chiefly determine the admissions and length of stay in hospitals. Their decisions with respect to hospitalization in turn are affected by the availability of hospital beds and of insurance to pay the cost. With some exceptions, such as maternity, the creation of hospital beds leads inexorably to their utilization, either by increased admissions or by longer stays—especially if there is no substantial financial inhibition because of insurance or government payments.

27

The growth of government and insurance payment for health services has certainly reduced the resistance to cost increases that might otherwise have limited utilization. Without the apparent blank check, hospital administrations would probably have been slower to introduce cost-generating services or hospital beds for which no clear need existed. Because, to the individual family, the use of many expensive health services comes largely prepaid, limitation of use has only modest financial benefits. To the providers of care, government and insurers ask only that services be performed and that the charges be based on cost or community practice. Expensive decisions of physicians to specialize and expensive decisions of hospitals to add resources result in costs to the community which few individual consumers have any interest in fighting at the time when they have a perceived need for service. The citizens can fight back only collectively, seeking to reduce total costs, as reflected in insurance premiums and taxes, by organizing cooperatives or by political action through government or voluntary associations.

Both private insurance and government have been slow to grasp the concept that collective responsibility should cover more than transferring funds to cover costs or charges for services rendered. Both have generally taken the attitude that some unseen hand—a now diminishing play of market forces perhaps—has appropriately determined costs and that the insurer or government need only write checks.

The philosophy of planning which is gaining ground today argues that the community, through governmental power or interest group bargaining, must intervene to assure that the products and costs of health services are more subject to social decision making. To some extent the interest of the community is to avoid unnecessary costs, whether they be paying for more services than are needed, paying excessive prices, or using more expensive services when less costly ones could have met the need. This interest, in the economist's jargon, is termed a concern with efficiency—getting the most out of available resources or getting the desired jobs done with the least expenditure of resources.

One of the ways movements toward efficiency may be achieved is for the community to control the quantities of the various health care services which will be permitted or encouraged to function in that community. Planning—some hopefully rational manner of understanding the cost and benefit implications of various feasible combinations and scales of health services and community decisions which can be implemented to control supplies—is, in the absence of market forces to bring about the desired efficiency, what many see as a critical need now and in the future. Whether the appropriate information can be collected and analyzed and whether workable specifications for change can be designed, agreed upon, and implemented is a key question. Without these, the planning is likely to be very bad indeed, and our need is for good planning, not bad.

Community Control

But the efficiency of health services is just one dimension of the goals of planning. A second is for a community to assure that the distribution of health services reflects social values. Communities and societies are concerned that appropriate and acceptable health services be available to the various groups in society. Here the concern is less with efficiency in its usual sense than with assurance of equity—that is, that the resources are accessible to all age groups, ethnic groups, and income groups and in all locations. Concerns with respect to locations, hours, and cultural attitudes of staff are strong. Because the economic and political power of many subgroups has been weak, community health planning frequently has as its goal the correction of this condition or change from the situation which developed as a result. Again, simply relying on governmental or private insurance to pay for services may not produce the desired result, and community information development, analysis, design, agreement, and implementation may be required.

Communities may desire health services which differ from those that private suppliers, supported by community taxes and premiums, would provide. If the community strongly wants comprehensive care, mental health clinics, family planning services, and so forth, and wants them organized in an integrated fashion, they will need to engage in planning to bring about the kinds of services desired.

Communities may see a need for planning to provide the feeling—or even the reality—that they are the masters of their own environment of health services. Satisfying this need—assuring that each community makes its own decision and assures the participation of its citizens in decisions about the nature and quantity of health services—may be a stronger requirement than any other, more important even than analytical approaches to the planning of health services.

Apart from immunizations, birth control, sanitation, and nutrition, there is little hard evidence that any particular configuration or volume of hospital, physician, or other health services has a predictably greater beneficial impact on the health status of populations. If you believe this, then perhaps the appropriate health services for a community should be a matter for its own decision, independent of technical or professional knowledge. The need for health care is then a cultural phenomenon: we want to talk with physicians when we fear we are ill, and we want hospitals and nurses to take care of us when we are incapacitated or undergo serious therapeutic processes. These wants can be satisfied either through the market or through political decision making. Since the market appears to have failed, political decision making is an alternative which may have some promise of giving communities greater assurance of getting what they desire.

For several years now, the term "comprehensive health planning" has been tossed about in every setting from legislation to cocktail conversations. While there are many definitions and applications of the phrase, one aspect might be emphasized here. If we look at some significant health problems from the perspective of the problem rather than from that of the health service industry, we find that the array of services necessary to cope include many that are now public in nature and that the organization of these and private resources to address the total problem requires health planning which is comprehensive in that it includes many different ingredients. Common examples might be the control of motor vehicle injuries, which would include planning of emergency rooms, ambulance and communication services, vehicle design and regulation, street and highway design, changes in law, law enforcement, licensing, control of alcoholism, driver and pedestrian training, and so on. Another example is how to address the problem of mental retardation, which would include prenatal care, screening, diagnosis, treatment, education, recreation, vocational training, job placement, and more besides.

The problem orientation makes the idea of each family struggling with an unplanned system a horrible alternative. While planning in a comprehensive fashion to ameliorate these problems may be difficult and may be done poorly, we certainly need to plan and plan as best we can to deal with such major social problems as accidents, mental retardation, alcoholism, drug addiction, suicide, venereal disease, population control, and aging. It is most unlikely that individual physicians and hospitals could or would get on with these pressing jobs without community planning.

What Needs to Be Done?

I have used the word planning to describe many different kinds of activities, including cost control, problem solving, consensus formation, and community decision making. These are the objectives, and it is clear that they have yet to be fully and satisfactorily achieved. The obstacles to their accomplishment are numerous but they are now being recognized and gradually overcome.

At present, good information about the basic production functions in health services are in short supply, the input-output relations are obscure, even basic cost information about services is unreliable, and we know little about the effects of medical services on the health of populations. Representative community health planning organizations are in almost a fetal state, and the mechanisms for carrying out community decisions are lacking except for some limited negative authority.

The health planning field, which is widely looked to to put order into our fragmented health care systems, is itself badly fragmented. If I may quote from a speech by former HEW Secretary Richardson to the Institute of Medicine:

> Thus we see a planning system in which, as with its operational counterpart, interrelationships among functions are very poorly thought out—if any real thought has even been given to the possibility of interrelationships—and which is thus hopelessly confusing and sometimes duplicative and overlapping.

It is, again, a "non-system" incapable of either rationally identifying shortfall or gaps in performance, or of rationally addressing needs.

Ignorance and political weakness characterize the fragmented health planning field today. Our need, as I have tried to stress, is for good planning. This will take political will and effectiveness and the development of insights into relationships which we are just beginning to sketch.

To conclude: The community has and should have an interest in collective action to determine the priority health problems and to organize their amelioration and the distribution, volume, and nature of health services to address them. Planning, done reasonably well, is an essential ingredient in determining what services are desired, given their costs, feasibilities, and benefits. Planning must include not only the analysis and specification of health programs and services but also the development of strategies and tactics to bring the health system decisions under community control.

Who represents the community is a complex question, but we have seen from Mr. Gottlieb's historical review that the voluntary agencies have in the past been largely dominated by selected establishment interests. Attempts are being made today to broaden the composition of planning bodies, but I doubt that anything short of community government will achieve acceptance as representative.

COMMENTARY ON THE PAPERS

Reuben Kessel

The question I asked myself when I read these papers is: Why does health planning exist? In Mr. Gottlieb's paper, I got the impression that planning developed because some of the resources going into the medical sector were charitable and gift-giving had to be coordinated in order to achieve the most efficient use of these gifts. Subsequently the government came in as a "sugar daddy," and its contributions had to dovetail with private giving.

In Mr. Grosse's paper the emphasis is a little different. The explanation for why health planning exists is—you will excuse the expression—market failure. In this context, market failure means the presence of third-party payers, the development of insurance companies, and the special characteristics of the medical profession, specifically the view that in some mysterious way supply creates its own demand.

With respect to the coordination of sugar daddies, I think there is no doubt planning is bound to fail. Anyone associated with private universities has learned that sugar daddies tend to be very willful people who have their own ideas as to how money is to be spent and often they don't take kindly to suggestions.

With respect to the government as a sugar daddy, the principal vehicle seems to be the Hill-Burton Act, which Mr. Gottlieb regards as a great success. Suppose for the sake of discussion and analysis that I assert it is a great failure. What tests exist? How do you measure success here? How is the Hill-Burton Act evaluated? I really don't know. Moreover, I can't find out from Mr. Gottlieb's paper.

I had trouble with Mr. Gottlieb's narrative because I was looking for a thesis that made the facts he presented hang together. I found his definition of planning no help, since it encompasses a wide range of activities which are not normally regarded as planning. Indeed, his definition encompasses all thinking activity. Gottlieb asserts that health planning is a product of its times and of the complex forces that affect health system development. That really threw me for a loop, for I don't know what it means nor how it helps us to understand why planning exists.

Turning to Professor Grosse's paper, I thought a great deal about his point regarding third-party payments and his argument that they lead to laxity with respect to cost control. I thought about automobile insurance where you have many third-party payers. It is my general impression that, in the case of automobile insurance, Allstate does better in dealing with a garage than I do, and if anything, I would guess that the effect of having Allstate handle a claim would be just the opposite of the one that Professor Grosse imputes to the presence of third-party payers. Possibly this is because Allstate is a profit-seeking organization, and we have an important class of third-party payers that are nonprofit, such as Blue Cross.

If third-party payers are really a serious problem, it seems to me the market would develop prepaid groups where the insurance company and the supplier of medical care would be one and the same. I believe we would have had much greater development of prepaid groups if there had not been important constraints on their formation; I think that they are still illegal in about one-third of the states. A prepaid group breaks the coalition between a patient and a physician to defraud the insurance company. If such a coalition is really a serious problem, you would have much lower costs for prepaid groups than for third-party payers with cash indemnity. The public would be free to choose between higher-cost insurance, with more opportunities for coalitions with physicians to obtain extra services, on the one hand, and lower costs in the form of these prepaid groups, on the other.

Another point that Professor Grosse raises is that supply creates its own demand. I have heard that view before, as I am sure many of you have .The point of view is that somehow or other Marshall Field controls what I buy there rather than that I control what I buy at Marshall Field. Yet I am sympathetic to this view. As a description of what does occur in reality, I think there is something to it. The question is, why?

It certainly is not true, as I say, in the case of department store sales. Suppose we produced a lot more rabbis. Would I go to the synagogue more often? I suppose if many more rabbis were produced, the cost of rabbi services would fall and, insofar as this happened, the extent to which I bought those services would be influenced. Presumably this argument goes for priests also. (I meant this to be nonsectarian.)

But this is not what Grosse means. He is referring to a shift in demand, not a movement along a demand curve. More concretely, if we increase the output of physicians, there are many people who are prepared to say that there will be more surgery and more use of physicians' services. The market will take more physician services at all the old prices.

This view seems to be analogous to a problem that is discussed in quite a different context. In a discussion of fisheries it is asserted that the oceans contain a certain number of whales who reproduce at a given rate and that, if we have more whaling ships going out, each ship is going to come back with fewer whales. The analogy with medicine is that if we start producing more physicians, and particularly surgeons, we will have more surgery going on, and these surgeons will be elbowing each other at the operating table. In other words, they will be fighting with one another to get at our organs, and since we have a finite number of organs, which correspond to the finite number of whales in the ocean, we are going to have more and more organs removed.

This sounds as though I am poking fun at the idea. Yet I at least half believe that it is right. And I really do not know why it should be so. But if this is really a problem, then health planning is doing nothing for us, because if anything is sacrosanct in health planning, it is that you must not interfere with the intimate relationship of the physician to his patient. All the health planning literature that I have read takes a very noninterventionist attitude towards this relationship.

Suppose Grosse is right. What ought to be done about it? My feeling is that a part of the problem is the constraints upon the way medical services can be purveyed. The recommendation by a physician for a surgical procedure has an important economic content; it is not completely God's will or nature which determines whether an organ is regarded as malfunctioning and is to be repaired or removed. Such a recommendation has an important economic content, and the economic welfare of the physician who makes such a recommendation is at stake. A physician making such a recommendation has a conflict of interest. He is paid both for the diagnosis and then for the implementation of that diagnosis. Yet we have the same situation in dealing with our automobile repairman. When he says, "Your brakes are shot. You need new brakes," we receive both diagnosis and treatment.

The market provides many such analogies with medicine. The one thing that is quite different is, I think, the absence of free entry into the medical profession. I think there has been a tremendous bottleneck, ever since the work of Flexner, in providing opportunities to become physicians for those who wish to study medicine and who ostensibly are qualified for the study of medicine.

In addition, there seem to be great barriers affecting how physicians' services are marketed. Constraints on options available for marketing medical services have often been enacted into laws. Marketing medical services in nonapproved ways has led to great problems, if not martyrdom, for the few who have been innovative. Probably the most interesting example is the harassment of prepaid groups. Advertising is highly frowned upon. There are a number of other marketing practices that have been disapproved, and physicians have had difficulties in maintaining their licenses to practice if they adopted these disapproved methods.

If the problem exists—if supply creates its own demand—would it disappear if there were more commercial methods in purveying medical services? Maybe it would be worse. My own guess is that more openly commercial methods of marketing medical care would break down the myth of the priest-healer. Going to a physician ought not to be a strange amalgam of a commercial and a religious experience.

Unless these are the problems that health planners are addressing themselves to, then I would say, when we look at what has been done, they have really not addressed themselves to the need at all.

Daniel Zwick

I will be talking mostly about the political institutions engaged in health planning and the mechanisms for holding them accountable to the public. As the planning agencies assume broader roles, the concepts and the forms of accountability become a good deal more important.

Recent history has been a complicated period of development. As Mr. Gottlieb indicated, the federal government has played a major role in stimulating and supporting the evolution of state and local planning agencies. Separate support was provided to the state and local agencies. The Comprehensive Health Planning Act made available direct federal aid to local agencies; while some link to the state agencies is required, it is usually not very strong.

The federal law provides that grants for local health planning can be made to both public and private nonprofit agencies; in fact, not just a majority but almost all of the existing local agencies are private, nonprofit bodies. This situation did not just happen. Evidently the development and organization of the agencies were biased in this direction, probably purposefully.

Federal legislation has focused some attention on the issue of public accountability. Requirements for extensive consumer participation were included in the Hill-Burton Act and were broadened in the Comprehensive Health Planning Act. In the 1967 amendments, a requirement for a role for local elected officials was introduced; thus began a movement toward closer relationships between local health planning and general-purpose government, but it was a relatively modest step. Perhaps, though, these forms of accountability were quite commensurate with the rather limited powers actually exercised by the developing agencies.

Within this framework one might view the search for "consensus" discussed in Mr. Gottlieb's paper. The efforts to achieve voluntary agreement might be viewed as a search for local legitimacy in the absence of formal endorsements through the established state and local political processes.

More recently, however, we have seen many interesting developments in state legislatures. About twenty states have now enacted laws establishing comprehensive health planning as an appropriate and desirable function of state and local government. More recently, there has been much stronger state action relating to certificate of need. Within a framework of state law legitimacy and accountability are being developed, supplementing and giving a firmer structure at that level to the activities that federal funds helped initiate. These actions are consistent with the expanded authorities and roles being assigned the agencies.

The potential enactment of a federal law (H.R. 1) requiring state certification of a need as a condition of certain payments under Medicare has, it seems, helped to inspire additional state legislation along these lines. An intergovernmental system of checks and balances may be developing, involving local, state, and national participation. A local agency would review and comment; decision making would rest with a public body at the state level; and there would be an administrative mechanism for appeal to a federal authority. The system would include all three levels of government in the process, acting as checks upon each other. Such an approach would be well within our constitutional tradition. It will tend to multiply, if not to maximize, visibility, disclosure, and scrutiny. Whether it will provide all the necessary forms of accountability is up to history—and the courts.

I would like to comment further on state government, because there is a general tendency to underestimate the states' role in many of these activities. As we review the last five or so years, it is interesting to note that, in the administration of Medicare as well as in Medicaid, state agencies have had significant parts. As we move toward a time of national health insurance, it is possible that the state role will be diminished, but this is by no means a certainty. There are a number of noteworthy developments.

One such development is in that remarkable state institution known as the state university, particularly the state university medical school. About forty-five states will have state university medical schools before long. Perhaps the most influential agency of state government in the future will be the state university; it is likely to have a significant impact on health care delivery and health care planning, especially with respect to the development of manpower and the advancement of quality.

Another state institution of potentially increased importance is the department of human resources. Over twenty states now have established departments of human resources or similar agencies; these reorganizations may be one of the most important developments in American government in this period. We see some movement of state health planning activities into these offices. As state health departments become parts of these consolidations, their responsibilities for licensure and certification of need are set in a broader framework.

My final point concerns the relationship of health planning to other forms of human services planning. During recent years, there has been a rather substantial expansion of other forms of human services planning, largely through metropolitan planning agencies, with increasing support from the Department of Housing and Urban Development. While very few local health planning agencies are sponsored by metropolitan planning agencies, all of them have to come to terms with such related activities, including transportation and land-use planning. As we consider the best ways of determining what is needed in health, it will be useful to keep in mind the essential relationship of health and health services to the other human services that contribute to the style and quality of life.

The 1960s were a lively period of institution building. Justice Holmes reminded us years ago that we live in a country with a "living Constitution." It used to be said that each generation had a responsibility to "rewrite" the Constitution of the United States to meet its needs and conditions. Nowadays, change seems to occur even more rapidly.

The development of many new health programs in the last decade, including the expansion of comprehensive health planning, was part of this ferment. Some view these developments as part of the vital process of social change. Others characterize them as the beginning of chaos. Whether the critics or the friends are more accurate, the future will tell us. We do know that, while there is no necessary relationship between the quality of the child and the nature of the birth pains, the process of birth is a necessary, if not by itself a sufficient condition for human development.

DISCUSSION

Planning's Role in Relation to the Market

PROFESSOR GROSSE: First, let me address several points that Professor Kessel raised.

While I did not address myself to the problem of the automobile repair industry, I would think it is one which is ripe for planning and intervention on the part of communities in several senses. It would seem to me, for example, that a systematic approach by communities to the transportation problem would include, among other things, pressures for the development of both mass and individual vehicles which would not be so subject to the horrendous time, trouble, and cost that we currently have, and I think a utilization and tissue review committee of some sort on the repair industry might help. As I mentioned, one could also view the whole question of automobile accidents as something requiring a kind of systematic view.

More seriously, Professor Kessel suggested that health planners have not addressed the problem of the supply of manpower. I think this is an incorrect historical interpretation. It is true that there have been only limited attempts to do this—for very good reasons, I think—on the part of area-wide agencies and on the part of American planning institutions. But if one were to look at health planning activities in the United Kingdom, for example, I think one would find that their central purpose is to determine the number and types of health professionals, and specifically types of physicians, who will be permitted to practice both generally in the nation and in any particular community. There is a very definite attempt to restrict the number of specialists and to promote the number of general practitioners.

Next, there is the question of the third-party payer. I was not really raising the question, at least not in the context of my speech, of whether the unit price for a particular service would be cheaper or more expensive with or without an insurer or governmental intervention. What I was addressing instead was the nature of the services that were offered, both in terms of the quantities of these services and the types. And I felt that there was a responsibility to look at them.

With regard to the broad concept of planning, it would seem to me that implementation of some of Professor Kessel's suggestions with respect to the supply problem—for example, the promotion of prepaid group practice—would be part of the planning activity.

GUIDO CALABRESI, Yale Law School: I am a little puzzled by Professor Grosse's comment about systematic views and the auto industry. If planning means just looking at an activity systematically, then I do not think anybody has any argument. And I take it that was what Mr. Gottlieb's definition was. Obviously you need it, and you have gotten some of it in the auto industry. And you need it in the health industry.

The issue becomes whether you then, as a result of this systematic view, decide to let essentially decentralized market forces work or whether you decide to establish tissue committees, licensure, and things of that sort. Now, it is far from clear that, with all the waste which does exist in the auto repair industry, we would have less waste if we had tissue committees, licensure, and so on. Far from clear.

All I would suggest is that, while there is probably more waste in a private-enterprise type of health care system than there is even in the automobile industry, I haven't heard anyone address himself to the question of whether the same kinds of things which create waste in health care when it is privately organized would not also create waste—and would not create even more waste to the extent that they are more centralized—in a highly planned and regulated system or whether there are other factors which would make a centralized, licensing, tissue-committee type of approach preferable.

There may well be things which make that an improvement. But this seems in fact to be the issue. The question is not whether we can point to an area and say there is waste. Obviously there is. There is a great deal of waste in free enterprise generally, of course. But the question is, is it less wasteful than something else? And that is what I would like to see the discussion turn to.

PROFESSOR GROSSE: I cannot answer your question directly. I agree with the question. But it would seem to me that planning, at least as I think of it, would attempt to address that question rather than to assume that, because a number of economists writing in the 19th century concluded that competition and free enterprise were the most efficient system under a set of assumptions which do not exist in our society, we are therefore justified in surrendering public and collective control.

I think all I would argue at this moment is that the points you raise require investigation, that it is extremely difficult to conduct this investigation with the data of the past. We need both experimentation and testing, but all of these things involve what I see as planning, by means of which I would assume offhand that the current system could be improved upon.

The question is, what improvements? Now, it may be that the improvement would be—and I think this was the thrust of Professor Kessel's suggestions—a move in the direction of making the medical care industry, in terms of market entry and such, more competitive. I am not at all sure that this is correct. But the planning activity would be the application of intelligence to the problems that you have posed.

I certainly would not argue that any given alternative is demonstrably preferable. What I am suggesting is that there is, I believe, a social responsibility to look at the problems and to look hard and to seize what powers are necessary to make sure that the collective will is articulated and implemented.

PROFESSOR HAVIGHURST: Professor Calabresi's question is very helpful. It recalls a phenomenon that seems to be almost universal—namely, that in taking up a problem of this kind, it is customary to start out by saying why the free market does not work and then giving four or five reasons why the particular market is different from the classical model. This is a natural enough starting point, but too often the conclusion then is: the market does not work, and therefore we should scrap it and go to some other system, in this case a planned system.

But, of course, that conclusion follows only because the wrong question was asked. What one should ask is whether the market can be made to work tolerably, and whether, if you worked on it from that standpoint, the market might be, though still imperfect, nevertheless workable and less imperfect than the alternatives—because planning, though it sounds on paper as good as the economists' models, is certainly not perfect.

If one approaches both the working of the market (perhaps as one might fix it up by legislation) and regulation or planning (whatever name you want to give it) with the same degree of skepticism—namely, that which is so often brought to looking at the market as it functions—then maybe you would have a completely different set of questions. The calculus becomes much harder, of course. But the choices, then, are clear, and one has to weigh whether this set of imperfect solutions is better than that set.

There is, I regret to say, a great tendency to treat someone who suggests the possible desirability of a market-oriented solution as an ideologue, but nothing could be more pragmatic and less ideological than approaching problems as I have suggested. I happen to believe that the true victims of ideology are those who reject market-oriented solutions too quickly.

PROFESSOR GROSSE: Professor Havighurst, I think perhaps, if I understand you, you are taking too narrow a cut at what planning is. For example, economic development planning in many societies follows the pattern of introducing free enterprise and creating markets where markets previously did not exist. I think I would distinguish not between a market system, however constructed, and a planned system but between planning and the mindless approach. The latter lets whatever forces—political, planning, market—move ahead without the application of a social conscience and a community decision and without the application of that thinking in decision making which might lead to the building of a market or improvement of a market. And I would say that that total activity is what I would think of as planning.

PROFESSOR HAVIGHURST: Your point is clear. And, indeed, in your remarks you noted a number of kinds of planning—for example, emergency care and the viewing of automobile accidents as a total problem—which it seems to me are not in any way inconsistent with having a basically market-oriented system. And I think you are right, that there is no dichotomy between planning and the market if planning is characterized as the attempt to discover whether there are ways of mixing the market and regulation to achieve a system in which we can have confidence.

But, of course, we are concerned in this conference specifically with entry restrictions designed to keep out new hospital beds or new entrepreneurs who want to build them, and that is a much narrower question than planning as a global concept. Certificate-of-need laws are very clearly an attempt to displace the market with a regulatory model derived from the precepts of health planning. I hope we can address these laws as I have suggested.

Pragmatic Appraisals of Planning

STUART ALTMAN, deputy assistant secretary for planning and evaluation, Department of Health, Education, and Welfare: I cannot quite decide, Professor Grosse, whether it is because you left the federal government a couple of years ago and cannot remember back that far, or because of a much stronger series of biases, but I think you are too sanguine.

In my new position, which is one Professor Grosse once held, we try to look at planning at both the federal and local level. We look at the federal government and try to keep track of all the programs that exist—I carry around in my vest pocket a card which tells me all the federal health programs that exist. If anything, the pressure now to introduce an expanded CHP is an admission on the part of the federal government that we have failed in our ability at the federal level to plan, and we are somehow hoping that at the local level someone can bring some semblance of rationality to the chaos that we have created. But we are pretty smart and the people that my predecessor put together in the previous administration were very capable people, too; it is hard to believe that you are going to be able to duplicate that level of talent all over the country. Then you have to say to yourself, Why, if we cannot put a degree of rationality in our own house, will there be a rational system when it gets to the local level?

The reasons are many: You are dealing with a bureaucracy which is very large and cumbersome; you are dealing with individuals and their individual fiefdoms and bureaus; you are dealing with a Congress that allocates money by limited categorical programs—and try to break that! You know—many of you have been in that position—that you can't. So you say to yourself, Okay, we know that at the federal level we have this series of categorical programs. But can we expect that at the local level order will come out of chaos? I, for one, am skeptical.

I have to ask myself the question which I was hoping Professor Kessel would go further to answer. He asked the question, and then he didn't answer it very well. Maybe because there is no answer. I cannot answer it either. And that is, what is going to happen when strong comprehensive health planning is put in place? What are the new forces that will be created in that marketplace? For there will be a market! It will have new incentives and new forces. What are those forces going to be, especially when all federal dollars funnel through a single comprehensive health planning unit?

What I am really asking and what I would hope that, as this conference progresses, we would give serious thought to, is what kind of incentives will we be creating with these local planning agencies, and, in fact, what kind of a new system will we have? I do not have the answer, but I hope we can find out before we put it in place.

PROFESSOR KESSEL: I think we are getting close to a very critical issue, and that is: Just what have we accomplished by the interventions that we have already undertaken? And it seems to me there is no point in asking why people want to have the government intervene. It is always to accomplish some good. So we know that already, and we can set that aside. The gut issue is: What have we achieved? And does it have any relation at all to what we set out to do? I think on that point we know relatively little.

Bob Grosse said that we really have to do something about helping health maintenance organizations—HMOs—get started. Those of us who have looked at the record have found that there have been great efforts to start HMOs in the past. (They used to have a different name, of course. They were called prepaid medical groups, but some advertising genius has relabeled them.) Many would-be prepaid groups have been aborted in many states in the United States, including my own. In Chicago a group that tried to get started many years ago was harassed out of existence by organized medicine. The point is that the existing establishment has done the planning, and their planning has consisted of making it impossible in many states for these HMOs to come into being. And I regard this as an important form of planning which has been done for us through this kind of intervention.

Another form of health planning, if we look at the history, has been planning with respect to medical schools. At one time medical education looked very chaotic. There were night medical schools turning out large numbers of graduates. And the planners came in, in the form of the Carnegie Foundation and the patron saint of the medical profession, Abraham Flexner. As a result, what we now have is a very restricted set of opportunities for people who want to study medicine.

Students who were well qualified for the study of medicine—some have won Nobel prizes—have been thwarted in their desire to become physicians.

What we forget is that planning is a mechanism by which the establishment entrenches itself in such a way that would-be newcomers cannot budge them. What the establishment needs in this ball game is a patsy, like Flexner, to front for them, and then, once the laws are passed that the insiders desire, these dupes are kicked out and the hardheaded, entrenched establishment is left running the show. If we would just sit down and look at what has been accomplished by the planning that we have already done, we would find out that it has so far been a device by which the establishment has entrenched itself. Planning is a vehicle by which the establishment has feathered its own nest.

Planning or Politics?

PROFESSOR HAVIGHURST: Some of the descriptions of planning we have heard seem to me to suggest that planning merely provides a forum for political bargaining, and, if that is what it is, "planning" would seem to be the wrong name for it. One interpretation, which incidentally seems to me consistent with both Professor Kessel's views and those of the "health radicals" as expressed in the book *The American Health Empire,* is that planning began as a sort of cartel in which the providers got together for bargaining out their conflicting interests, saying, "This is your empire, and this is mine, and let's limit output so as not to depress our respective earnings." Gradually there was increased pressure to bring consumers in, and that meant that new interests became involved in the bargaining. But the political character of the cartel did not change, although a new set of interests had to be accommodated.

What you have now may be seen as a political forum, a place to work out the conflicts in the community. But somehow to call that "planning" is inaccurate. That term implies that there is some scientific and rational process going on in which data are collected and used and some optimal result is reached. That may be a misrepresentation.

PROFESSOR GROSSE: I think what you are trying to do is to make too sharp a line between what Mr. Gottlieb called thinking before action and the implementation of that action. What I am talking about—and I do not care whether you call it planning or not; I choose to because they fund things called planning—involves an interchange. If you want to look at it from the planner's point of view, one of the things to take into account is the kinds of information about health problems, either in terms of disability, mortality, morbidity, or in terms of—as someone very appropriately pointed out—the need for human care and the reduction of suffering.

44

But one of the other informational inputs beyond what you might call technical inputs is what the community perceives as its needs. If the community feels that its major psychiatric need is counseling of teachers towards the better adjustment of kids in school as distinct from the more conventional psychiatric services of the medical model, then it seems to me that that is an informational point that is an essential ingredient in helping decide what to do. And I see planning as providing these inputs into a decision process which produces, at least in the context that I have described it, a political decision.

STEVEN SIEVERTS, executive director, Hospital Planning Association of Allegheny County, Pennsylvania: It seems to me that this use of the word "planning" and arguing about what it means is a useless exercise. Sometimes, to make a point in my own work, I say that what my agency is doing is not planning: we help *you* —whomever we are talking to—to plan. I suppose even that activity of helping somebody else to plan could be called planning.

The analogy I would draw for area-wide health planning agencies is not so much to a governmental planning office, because a governmental planning office tends to be staffed by people who are fundamentally decision makers, who are actually drawing up the plans for decisions to be made by their bosses. The analogy that I would rather use would be to the planning division of the industrial corporation, because it seems to me that the role that we as planning agencies (and there aren't very many of us here today—an interesting omission, I note) play in our communities is more directly analogous to the role that the planning department of, say, Westinghouse Electric plays for Westinghouse Electric.

Part of what the planning agency is concerned with is simply getting the decision makers to think better. Another part is making sure they understand the technologies of those problems which are largely technological. What we do is very similar to what the planning division of Westinghouse Electric or General Motors or U.S. Steel does, which is to try to stimulate good decision making and work out difficult and highly technical problems in intensely human situations. The "planners" have to learn how to deal with the competing forces in an environment and how to bring them together into rational decisions, especially in the long haul. In our case it happens to be a total community, as it relates to decision making that affects the health of people. It may be an impossible job, but it is the one that we try to fulfill.

Now, coming to the question of whether the people who are responsible for that process should be given "teeth," I think you have first got to give them jaws to put the teeth in. I think a great many of us in the field of area-wide health planning who see ourselves staffing, if you will, a community decision-making process would greatly prefer to see "teeth" exercised not by our jaws but by the jaws of proper regulatory bodies at the governmental level. We are perfectly prepared to be advisory and helpful to them. But many of us do not want delegation of regulatory power to our agencies, because the minute *we* become the decision makers we can no longer be the planning office; we are then no longer the group which can lead the hospitals, public health agencies, and neighborhood groups to better decision making and planning.

PROFESSOR GROSSE: Dan Zwick and Sy Gottlieb both commented on consensus formation as a thrust in area-wide health planning. I don't think, if my recollection is correct, that the emphasis on achieving consensus arose because that was the decision of the area-wide agencies, individually or even collectively. I think very clearly this was the federal agency's policy even before they gave out their first grant. I remember getting involved in a series of papers—I was at HEW at the time—protesting against what I thought was the lack of leadership, the lack of planning, the lack of technical assistance, the lack of addressing health problems, upon the part of the comprehensive health planning activities, which were then in the office of the Surgeon General. I was replied to with a white paper which announced that I had misunderstood the whole concept of the legislation and that what they were after was the establishment of forums for consensus. I don't know if that white paper has ever been published, but I have a copy in my files.

THE PLANNING AND LICENSING AGENCIES

J. Joel May

Health planning as an institution is a complex social-economic-political phenomenon which could, with high expectations of payoff, be studied by political scientists, organization theorists, social psychologists, industrial psychologists, economists, industrial engineers, and many others. I write this paper from the point of view of my training in economics and statistics, and in a role of "interested observer" of health planning and health planners over a period of six years. The idea that all people can be relied upon to make decisions and act in their own self-interest appeals to me as a paradigm useful in both describing and predicting behavior. I am therefore dubious about the viability of any effort to "change the world" which fails to take this idea into account.

D. J. Reynolds, in *Economics, Town Planning, and Traffic*, says: "One may respect and sympathize with the aims of planning, but unless the plans are related to people's wants and the economy's resources, they will not meet the claims which are made for them and will, more often than not, never be realized." [1] It is from this viewpoint that this paper describes, analyzes, and interprets health planning.

Planning and Its Goals

It is quite common and, indeed, fashionable to assert that the prevailing methods of delivery of health services constitute a "nonsystem" in the sense that the existing arrangements do not result in a sensible or "rational" whole. Given this assumption, it follows that this "nonsystem" is less efficient, more disorganized, more expensive, and less productive than it might be.

Many conclude, therefore, that if a "system" could be developed and the arrangements for provision of health services "rationalized," facilities and services of higher quality would be more easily and more nearly equally available at a smaller cost per service, duplication of costly equipment would be reduced or eliminated, "gaps" in the services available would be closed, and so forth.

This *weltanschauung* provides the single most important justification for health planning. Ever since the 1932 Report of the Committee on the Costs of

---

[1] D.J. Reynolds, *Economics, Town Planning and Traffic* (Levittown, N.Y.: Transatlantic Art, Inc., 1967).

Medical Care first made these arguments, they have enjoyed a good deal of popularity. These assertions appear in the early attempts at creating a "regional" health care system, in the voluminous literature on the Hill-Burton Act, in the deliberations of the Joint Committee on Areawide Planning of the American Hospital Association and the United States Public Health Service, and, more recently, in the language of the regional medical programs and comprehensive health planning laws. There is disorder, there is inefficiency, there is no "system"—goes the argument. Therefore, there must be planning.

Public Law 89-749, the Comprehensive Health Planning Act, has as its purpose

> promoting and assuring the highest level of health attainable for every person, in an environment which contributes positively to healthful individual and family living; [through] an effective partnership, involving close intergovernmental collaboration, official and voluntary efforts, and participation of individuals and organizations; [using] federal financial assistance . . . directed to support the marshaling of all health resources—national, State and local—to assure comprehensive health services of high quality for every person, but without interference with existing patterns of private professional practice of medicine, dentistry, and related healing arts.

Given this purpose and the supply of federal money available for its encouragement, numerous agencies of various sorts sprang up around the country. Many new positions were created and a large number of these positions were filled by persons already engaged in public health activities of one sort or another who had new and broader ideas about what should be included in the purview of an agency responsible for planning "an environment which contributes positively to healthful individual and family living." It seemed to them obvious that this included more than illness episode-related therapeutic treatment represented by hospital and physicians' services. In addition they typically included more than general preventive care, prenatal care, well-baby care, immunization programs, and all other programs which fall under the rubric of *personal* health services. They were at least as concerned with problems of social and personal environment including sanitation, air and water pollution, housing, nutrition, and, more recently, radioactive contamination, highway safety and accident prevention, industrial health programs, and so forth. Naturally they came to their new positions equipped with a definition of "health" somewhat broader than that used by the "traditional" health planners. (Marvin Strauss makes a case for an almost unlimited definition in the 1969 "Administrative Reviews" issue of *Hospitals* magazine.) What, then, was to be included and/or excluded at each level of the new health planning mechanism?

This question has not yet been resolved; nor, I expect, will it be in the foreseeable future—except in the breach. However, though no definition of "comprehensive health care" which excludes very much has been promulgated to date, the behavior of planners, particularly at the area-wide and local level, tends to indicate that they consider personal health care, including but certainly not limited to that provided by hospitals or other health facilities, their top-priority concern. The reason for this is that either (1) there is a history and tradition of planning in that area or (2) they believe that that is where they can realize the most results from their efforts. A nearly correct generalization is that the closer the agency is to the point of actual implementation of the plans being made, the more restrictive is their working definition of what is within their area of concern. It may very well be that the appropriate definition of the variety of an agency's concern is a function of the geographic scope of its activities.

It is not clear whether the broad definition alluded to above is a useful one in the sense that it can be developed, used, and implemented. Yet it is also unclear that the use of the more restrictive definition of health will make it possible to move as far in the direction of the original purposes of the act as some desire. It is, however, perfectly clear that, whatever definition is chosen, it must be explicitly stated in the form of a goal or goals in such a way that measurement of progress on the part of the agency toward the goals is possible.

The Appropriate Role of the Agency

There are actually three classes of agencies involved in the system for health planning. They are the "a" agency, or state comprehensive health planning agency, which is by law a part of the state governmental structure; the "b" agency, or area-wide health planning agency, which may be either a private or public agency; and, finally, a wide variety of other agencies which specialize in a particular area of data collection or type of planning or which have had some sort of planning or decision-making responsibility vested in them either by law or by default.

Though the legislation does set some criteria and/or tasks for the "a" agency, it is completely silent on the appropriate role to be played by the "b" agency. Insofar as functions are concerned, the Comprehensive Health Planning Act says that, in addition to establishing an agency to administer the state's health planning system and to function as an advisory council to assist it, the "a" agency must

> set forth policies and procedures for the expenditure of funds under the plan which . . . are designed to provide for comprehensive State planning for health services (both public and private . . .), including the facilities and persons required for the provision of such services, to meet the health needs of the people of the State . . . .
>
> provide for encouraging cooperative efforts among governmental or nongovernmental agencies, organizations and groups concerned with health services, facilities, or manpower, and for cooperative efforts between such agencies, organizations, and groups and similar agencies,

organizations, and groups in the fields of education, welfare, and rehabilitation.

In addition to these provisions there are a number which deal with administrative procedures and handling of federal funds.

Thus, the official health planning agency at the state level is responsible for (1) making a health plan, (2) allocating funds to elements of the system in a way consistent with this plan, and (3) setting up communication channels among all concerned.

In "Information and Policies on Grants for Comprehensive Area-wide Health Planning," Section 314(b), which was developed by the Department of Health, Education, and Welfare to supplement the legislation, the following guidelines for area-wide health planning agencies (or "b" agencies) are given:

> The organization conducting a comprehensive area-wide health planning program should engage in a variety of study, informational, consultative, promotional, and technical assistance activities. It should undertake the collection, organization, and dissemination of data pursuant to its own planning activities and those of many other groups in the area. It should provide a means of relating available services to eliminate duplication and to realize the full potential of health resources. It should serve as a major focus for relating health planning activities to other planning programs operative in the area.

There follows, in the "information and policies" statement, a rather long list of activities which such an agency, when applying for federal funds, "should, as a minimum, be prepared to do." For the most part these elaborate and expand on the functions delineated in the quotation above. All of these functions are to be accomplished without interference with current arrangements in the private sector, that is, the private practice of medicine.

Since federal funding became available in 1967, in addition to the fifty-six states and territories which have received grants to do health planning under section 314(a) of the act, more than 100 agencies around the country are supported by funds from section 314(b) of the act. Thus upwards of 150 agencies, the majority of which have been in existence for only a very few years, are wrestling with their responsibilities to society under the act which finances them and, at the same time, are attempting to develop a useful set of relationships with one another.

In principle, the job of the area-wide agency in a particular region is to develop a consensus of all interested parties in the public, voluntary, and private sectors with respect to a particular plan or development and to submit it to the state agency for approval. In the quest for this consensus, the area-wide agency is to be responsive to the wishes and/or needs of all concerned. The state agency, based on the priority system it has established for the state as a whole, then either approves or disapproves a particular application from the area-wide agency for funds which has been developed on the basis of some amalgamation of these wishes and needs.

Because of the difficulties inherent in the process of comparing and evaluating various preference structures in reaching a decision, one quickly realizes that the decision-making processes involved at both the area-wide and state agency levels are not likely to be based on very precise rules and criteria, but rather will probably be based on ad hoc criteria—probably of a subjective and/or political nature— and on the size of the budget of the funding agency. While little can be said as yet about the relative roles of the various agencies, it is probable that they will develop *ipso facto* as a result of these forces.

In passing, it is interesting to note that a number of the area-wide health *facility* planning agencies which existed and were funded by the federal government under the program which preceded the Comprehensive Health Planning Act have unilaterally decided not to apply for section 314(b) money—that is, not to attempt to do comprehensive planning but rather to restrict their concern to their traditional scope of facilities only. In many cases, these agencies, while eminently qualified to contract with the new area-wide comprehensive health planning agency to do *facility* planning, will not do comprehensive health planning, or are not interested in doing it. Other such agencies (four of the six in Ohio, for example) have decided to make the transition to becoming comprehensive health planning agencies. An examination of the logic behind these two types of decisions would be interesting and enlightening, but such an examination has not been attempted.

Manifestations of the Agencies' Role

Useful information and data on the composition, policies, attitudes, and activities (to say nothing of the impact) of health planning agencies are scarce. The bulk of the literature on the subject consists of "conventional wisdom" and exhortation, along with articles on "how we did it in Podunk." I have found only three studies which deal more substantively and on a broad basis with the questions of organization and purpose, and only two (one a duplicate from the former list) which deal with effect or impact of those agencies. The studies are those of James Cavanaugh,[2] Douglas Brown,[3] Darvin Palmiere,[4] and my own done in 1967.[5] The

---

[2] James H. Cavanaugh "Areawide Planning for Hospitals and Related Health Facilities" (Ph.D. dissertation, University of Iowa, 1964).

[3] Douglas R. Brown, "The Health Planning Process: A Study of Areawide Hospital and Health Facility Planning Agencies in the United States" (Ph.D. dissertation, Syracuse University, 1968).

[4] Darvin Palmiere, "Health Facility Planning Councils Evaluation Project," mimeographed (School of Public Health, University of Michigan, 1970).

[5] J. Joel May, "Health Planning—Its Past and Potential," Health Administration Perspectives No. A5 (Chicago: Center for Health Administration Studies, University of Chicago, 1967).

most complete—as well as the most recent—is the work by Palmiere and his staff. In what follows, I rely most heavily on his work.

The questions with which we must now deal involve how the health planning agencies see their purpose with respect to controlling, restricting, or rationalizing entry into the market and how successfully they have played the role. To answer these questions we will look at (1) formal statements of purpose in their bylaws, constitutions, et cetera; (2) the process by which decisions are made and the composition of the decision-making bodies—that is, who calls the shots; and (3) some evidence on the impact the health planning agencies have had upon the health services system.

Stated Purposes of the Agency. Palmiere, in a study of forty-five health planning agencies—the universe of those which were staffed and in operation on June 30, 1967—classified formal statements of purpose on several dimensions. One category included those activities considered to "aid various community groups . . . to allocate human and financial resources for the development and operation of health facilities and services." Twenty-two of the forty-five agencies were judged to have one or more purpose statements in this category, a substantial proportion of which related to priorities and allocation of resources for construction of health facilities. By contrast, only two councils had purpose statements dealing with allocation of operating funds and only a few had statements dealing with resources for health manpower.

His analysis of the agencies' activities showed a similar concentration related to the establishment of priorities and the allocation of capital funds for construction of various health facilities. For example, thirty-three were reported to have developed a general area-wide plan for the future development of short-term general hospitals. Nineteen had reportedly developed a similar plan related to nursing homes and extended care facilities.

Twenty-four of the forty-five agencies reported having developed a general set of priority standards on which recommendations could be made to corporations, local governments, the general public, et cetera, concerning proposed construction by various health facilities. Thirty-seven reportedly had developed a formal written process for review of construction proposals of general hospitals, while all the rest reported reviewing such proposals without a formal written process. Thirty-two reported a formal written process for review of nursing home construction proposals; twenty-five had a similar formal procedure for ambulatory care facility construction; and twenty-three for rehabilitation facility construction. In fifteen of these agencies, one general, formally written procedure was used for reviewing all health facility construction proposals.

Despite all this, few agencies were able to provide information about the numbers of construction proposals reviewed, the purposes of proposed construction, number of beds involved, and the impact of recommendations on sources of capital funds and implementation of the proposals.

It is difficult to sort out how much of the emphasis on priority setting and resource allocation questions is real and how much represents "good works." Certainly there is a long history of interest (associated with very little progress) in this area. In 1931, Arthur Bachmeyer, later the author of the report of the Committee on the Costs of Medical Care, made a speech to the Colorado Hospital Association on hospital planning.[6] Thirty-six years later, Secretary of Health, Education, and Welfare John W. Gardner reported to President Lyndon Johnson on medical care prices.[7] A juxtaposition of selected quotations from these two sources makes this point:

Bachmeyer (1931): "Hospitals have usually been developed as independent entities without sufficient consideration of all existing conditions and circumstances. Not infrequently they have been located in close proximity to existing institutions without regard for community need, or for type, quantity, variety or extent of service which each institution offered."

Gardner (1967): "Most communities have no mechanism for health planning. There is nothing to prevent . . . the construction of a hospital or nursing home in an area already well served, or the perpetuation of several inefficient facilities where replacement with a modern health center would be preferable."

Bachmeyer (1931): "Planning should be done on a broad and comprehensive basis, duplication of special and unusual equipment and services should be eliminated. Careful study and coordination of effort . . . are necessary if a well-balanced program for service is to be obtained."

Gardner (1967): "P.L. 89-749 is intended to coordinate existing and planned health services, to reduce overhead costs by increasing utilization rates, to prevent unnecessary expansion of hospital beds, and to encourage expansion of less costly services and facilities. It will also encourage the development of needed facilities which are not now available and improve the quality of medical care."

Apparently little progress toward the goal of an orderly, coordinated health services system had been made in the intervening years, despite these statements of intent.

How the Decisions Are Made. Again, in Palmiere's study, agency directors were asked whether at any time a general, area-wide plan had been developed which projected population characteristics and bed needs of the community.

---

[6] Arthur Bachmeyer, quoted in *The Modern Hospital*, April 1966.
[7] Department of Health, Education, and Welfare, *Medical Care Prices: A Report to the President,* February 1967.

Thirty-three directors reported that their agencies had developed a general, area-wide plan for the future development of short-term general hospitals. Two other directors reported that they made projections of population and bed need but did not consider that they had an area-wide plan. Another director commented that "such data are not published because I don't believe in it; however they are kept on hand in the office." Finally, two additional agencies were reportedly developing such plans.

Twenty of the thirty-three agencies reporting an area-wide plan for general hospitals stated that such plans included recommendations related to specific existing institutions. However, one of these also reported that a study planned for the current year (1968) would not include recommendations for specific hospitals. Twelve councils also reported that their plans included an estimate of the total capital costs of replacement of all obsolescent facilities in their areas.

Agencies were asked whether a general set of standards had been developed on which priority recommendations could be made to the community on construction proposals of general hospitals, nursing homes, and other health facilities.

Twenty-four of the forty-five agencies reported having such standards for general hospitals. Seventeen had such standards for nursing homes and/or extended care facilities. Eleven had developed standards for other types of health facilities, four of which related to community mental health centers.

Another question dealt with the formal review process (if any) undertaken. Thirty-seven of the agencies reported the existence of a formal, written review process for proposals from short-term, general and special hospitals, and a smaller number reported a formal process for other types of health facilities.

Regardless of whether they had a formal written process for review of construction proposals, each was asked to indicate which of seven specific activities were included in the review of construction proposals of general hospitals and nursing homes. They were encouraged also to specify additional types of review activities not designated on the questionnaire. The frequency of application was measured along a three-point scale of "always," "sometimes," and "never."

Table 1, taken directly from Palmiere's paper, shows the frequency with which selected review activities were reported by the agencies in connection with construction proposals submitted by general hospitals. The table also shows that all but one agency compared construction proposals of general hospitals with written criteria concerning community need and general location as determined by the councils. Staffs of all councils at least sometimes engaged in site visits while board members of eight out of ten councils made site visits at least some of the time. Nine out of ten sometimes or always compared construction proposals of one hospital with written plans submitted by other hospitals. However, somewhat fewer (eight out of every ten) provided for review of a proposal by representatives of other hospitals and about one-half of these agencies performed these activities only some of the time. Finally, about six out of ten provided a priority ranking of con-

Table 1

REVIEW ACTIVITIES OF COUNCILS WITH RESPECT TO
CONSTRUCTION PROPOSALS OF GENERAL HOSPITALS

Type of Review Activities	Number of Councils Reporting Each Type of Activity (N = 45)		
	Always	Sometimes	Never
Comparison of proposal with written criteria relative to community need and general location as determined by the health facility planning council	38	5	1
Comparison of proposal with written plans submitted by other institutions	28	14	2
Review of proposal by representatives of other institutions	17	18	10
Site visits made by health facility planning council staff	36	9	0
Site visits made by members of health facility planning council board	16	20	9
Review of proposal by individual members of a committee of the health facility planning council board	38	5	2
Priority ranking of proposals beyond general recommendation of endorsement or discouragement	10	17	18

Source: Palmiere, "Health Facility Planning Councils Evaluation Project."

struction proposals which went beyond a general recommendation of endorsement or discouragement, though about two-thirds of these councils performed this activity only some of the time.

Various materials published by the agencies appeared to contain occasional value judgments concerning the operation of general hospitals under different types of sponsorship. As a result, the study attempted to determine whether agencies had an "official position" or an "operational approach" which favored, was neutral, or opposed each of four types of sponsorship of general hospitals.

Thirty-nine of the forty-five agencies were found to favor, either officially or informally, the operation of general hospitals under community nonprofit, nonreligious sponsorship. None reported opposing this type of sponsorship. Thirty reported that they favored sponsorship of general hospitals by religious organizations, either officially or informally, while only one opposed such sponsorship informally.

In contrast, fourteen agencies favored government sponsorship of general hospitals while six opposed it. Only three reported favoring proprietary operation of general hospitals while thirty-three opposed such sponsorship.

55

Those Who Make the Decisions. Since the passage of the Comprehensive Health Planning Act, there is a legal mandate requiring "consumer representation" on the boards of health planning agencies. A consumer is defined as an individual who is not involved in producing, financing, or delivering health care. Thus, physicians and other health professionals, hospital board members and employees, and representatives of insurers, among other groups, are excluded. The regulations attendant to the act require a majority of consumers, and those associated with the 1967 and 1970 amendments imply representation roughly proportional to the ethnic and racial composition of the area served. B. C. French of the Institute for the Study of Health and Society, in a recent unpublished study, suggests another dimension of representation—that of high- versus low-income consumers.[8]

No data exist on the extent to which this change in the composition of agency boards has effected corresponding change in the decision-making process. In the late 1960s there was a good deal of furor about it. Some existing agencies chose not to become "comprehensive" to avoid the requirement; some established advisory boards, parallel to but separate from the decision-making group; in some extreme cases, when consumers were added to the board—particularly if they were not "establishment types"—the power structure which the agency had carefully built up disintegrated as the result of resignations and/or factional struggles.

Since then, most of the field has seemingly settled down to live and work with this new arrangement. None of the studies mentioned earlier is recent enough to reflect this development, and no similar national study has been done. French's 1970 study presents data on board membership in fifteen state health planning councils selected at random. In all but three of the states, consumers hold majority representation although in four of the cases it was a majority of one. Altogether a total of 222 consumers of a total of 395 board members are included in his sample. Their occupations break down as recorded in Table 2.

Among the questions that remain unanswered with respect to consumer representation in the health planning process are: What unique insights do consumers bring to bear on the planning process? Do they represent a constituency? If so, is the representation adequate? If not, what role should they play? Unfortunately a great deal of smoke surrounds an apparently tiny fire in the area.

One final point on the general question of the role of consumers in the decision-making process: It is not at all obvious that involving consumers will necessarily result in a superior process or produce better or more quickly arrived-at decisions. Kenneth Boulding has said,

> If we want to navigate a satellite, or produce a new drug or a hybrid, or even explode a nuclear weapon, we do not call in the old wives. In social systems the old wives, or at least their husbands, are called in all the time. Creating a peaceful world, abolishing slums, solving the race

---

[8] "Who Are the Consumers on the State Health Planning Councils?" (1970).

Table 2

OCCUPATIONS OF CONSUMERS ON THE BOARDS OF
FIFTEEN STATE HEALTH PLANNING COUNCILS
(N = 222)

Occupation	Number	Percent
Secretary	1	0.5
Allied health, et cetera	16	7.2
Publisher	2	0.9
Architect/Engineer	3	1.3
Businessman	28	12.6
Rancher	4	1.8
Housewife	33	14.9
Junior League	3	1.3
Legislator	27	12.2
Attorney/Judge	13	5.9
Union	8	3.6
State government agency	18	8.1
Local government agency	17	7.7
Insurance	15	6.7
Teacher	16	7.2
Clergy	8	3.6
"Low-income consumer"	4	1.8
Other	6	2.7
Total	222	100

Source: Palmiere, "Health Facility Planning Councils Evaluation Project."

problem, or overcoming crime and so on, are not regarded as suitable subjects for scientific technology but are regarded as fields where a pure heart and a little common sense will do all that is really necessary.[9]

Although Palmiere's study was done prior to the requirement that consumers be on hospital boards, it is useful to look at his findings with respect to representation of various groups on the agency boards since, at the regional level which he studies (as contrasted to the state-level agencies discussed above), it is likely that his findings still hold.

As a part of his study, board members of local agencies and state agency directors were asked to judge whether there was an adequate balance of representation of community interests or whether they were dominated by specific interest groups. Seventy-three percent of the responses from board members and 49 per-

[9] K. E. Boulding, "Dare We Take the Social Sciences Seriously?" *American Psychologist*, July 1968.

cent of those from state agency directors judged the individual agencies to maintain an adequate balance of representation. Eleven percent and 19 percent of the two groups respectively believed that agencies were dominated by health care institutions in their respective areas. However, 14 percent and 15 percent of each group believed that there was domination by business-industrial interests. Only one agency was considered by both groups to be dominated by the medical profession.

Board members and hospital administrators were asked whether, in their opinions, membership on agency boards of directors by hospital trustees and administrators resulted in favoritism toward related hospitals. In contrast with the general agreement on other questions, there was a marked difference of opinion between two respondent groups on this one. While 64 percent of board members believed that the fact that their boards of directors included hospital trustees did not affect their judgments, only 22 percent of the board members and 30 percent of hospital administrators believed that the interests of hospitals represented by trustees were influential in the decisions made. The remainder of the respondents in each group either did not express an opinion or reported that no hospital trustees served on the board of directors of their planning agency.

Membership of hospital administrators on agencies' boards of directors was considered not to have affected judgments by 50 percent of board members and 24 percent of hospital administrators. Seventeen percent and 37 percent of the respective respondent groups believed that the interests of hospitals represented by administrators had been influential. The remainder of respondents in each group had no opinion.

Palmiere presents no data on inputs or influence of other occupational groups. What he does present provides little support for the contention that the planning and regulation activities have been, or are in danger of being, captured by the industry.

Impact on the Health Services System. Given the structure, purposes, representation, and activities described, a final task is to examine the impact of health planning upon the health care system.

How are we to measure the performance of an area-wide health facility planning agency? We can look at quantitative measures of the "state of the system"; but we could argue that the true impact of such an agency is upon attitudes of people both within and without the system rather than upon "things," and cannot be observed (or at least measured) by counting hospitals, beds, et cetera. We could argue that activities are designed to fill gaps in the system rather than to change the system and that the effect is manifested in coordination and comprehensiveness rather than in numbers. In fact, unless we know why and under what circumstances agencies are organized, it is difficult to assess, or even to make intelligent statements about, their effectiveness.

Suppose that the amount or rate of change is related to what the area had to start with, and that an area that is already "well off" with respect to health services is less likely to change (other things being equal) than one that is not. Then, if planning agencies tend to be established by community leaders who are desperate about an existing (bad) situation in the community, rather than by people who know they already have a satisfactory situation with respect to health services, one would expect to see a "successful" agency bringing about large changes in the system. If the reverse is true, that is, that agencies tend to be established in communities which already have well-functioning health service systems as a result of the activities of a community leadership which sees planning as a positive force, one would expect to see little change occurring as a result of the establishment of a formal planning agency.

Unless and until we can be sure, or come to an agreement about, why planning agencies get started and what they explicitly set out to accomplish, measurement of their effectiveness will remain in the realm of the intelligent guess. There are also problems associated with how to describe the existing system and how to evaluate in a qualitative way the direction and magnitude of changes observed. But the most serious problem involves the scarcity and poor quality of the data available.

It seems apparent, under the circumstances, that an attempt to evaluate the area-wide planning movement based on what the planners state as their goals will not bear fruit. How, then, are we to determine whether or not planning has been useful and effective?

There are some measures of effectiveness of medical services which, though crude, provide at least a point of departure for looking at the question in an objective fashion. Though the very word "effectiveness" is at least as ambiguous as some of the statements referred to, I believe there is sufficient consensus about the validity of certain broad criteria for measuring the adequacy of the health services in an area to make the present undertaking more than a semantic exercise. Among such measures are (1) number and type of hospitals, (2) supply of beds, (3) availability of services and programs, (4) utilization patterns, and (5) costs. Two things must be said concerning the measures listed. First, they are interrelated. A look at any one of them, without attention to the others, will provide few useful answers. Second, each is subject, at least in theory, to influence by the planning agency, either through its activities involving the allocation of funds and the approval of construction projects or through its data dissemination and public education activities.

Palmiere examined the question of performance of the planning agency by looking at trends in several of these measures over a twenty-year period (1948-1968). His analysis involved an inspection of changes in trends during the "pre-agency," "post-agency," and total periods of time. He selected eight characteristics of the system for analysis covering the measures of ownership and type of hospitals, supply of beds, utilization, and availability of services and programs.

He concluded that none of the eight selected characteristics showed consistent or extensive changes in direction which could be associated with creation of the health planning agencies. However, changes in trend for admission rates and average occupancy offered modest support for an interpretation of some impact.

In twenty-three of the forty-five areas he studied, trends in the bed/population ratio continued in the same direction both before and after creation of the agency. In ten other areas, changes in this trend tended to support an interpretation of control of the supply of short-term hospital beds. However, in six other areas, a reversal in trend was evident.

The percentage of short-term hospital beds in proprietary facilities was above 10 percent in only thirteen of the areas. No consistent pattern was observed in these areas. During the entire twenty-year period, proprietary beds increased as a percentage of all beds in five areas; they decreased in eight others. Creation of the agency appeared to be unrelated to this trend.

Special hospital beds represented more than 10 percent of all short-term hospital beds in only seven agency areas during the period 1948-68. In three of these seven areas, such beds increased as a percentage of the total; they decreased in the other four areas. The trend analysis before and after creation of the planning agency showed no pattern which would suggest impact on this characteristic.

Admission rates to short-term hospitals showed an overall increase in thirty-seven of the forty-five areas between 1948 and 1968. However, in twenty-two of these areas, admission rates showed a relative decrease (seventeen areas) or remained relatively stable (five areas) after the agency was established. These comparisons, Palmiere reasoned, offer modest support for the possibility that the councils may have had a moderating effect on the consistently increasing trend in admission rates.

The twenty-year analysis of trends in average occupancy of short-term hospitals showed that the minimum level increased from 52 to 67 percent overall. However, the median and maximum levels increased by 1 and 3 percent respectively during the same period of time. The comparison of trends in periods before and after agency creation showed that average occupancy rates increased after agency creation in more areas than would have been expected.

Trends in the percentage of short-term hospitals having therapeutic x-rays and/or radioisotope therapy appeared to have no relationship to the creation of the councils.

It should additionally be noted that health planning activities may have exerted an effect on other characteristics of short-term hospitals. They may not have affected the total supply of beds available in their respective areas, but they may have affected the types of hospital services to which the beds were allocated. They also may have affected the geographic location of such beds and the choice of specific hospitals for expansion and development of selected services. Thus, the effectiveness and efficiency of the system of short-term general and special hospitals may have been enhanced by the involvement of the councils. More sensitive types of analysis for which data are not yet available will be required to determine the nature and degree of such impacts.

In my own earlier study, I compared the trends observed in four Standard Metropolitan Statistical Areas (SMSA) which had had active planning agencies for at least five years with those observed in four other (matched) SMSAs without planning agencies. These areas are subsequently referred to as "planned" and "unplanned." Despite the fact that the data are somewhat antiquated and the scope of the study universe small, the study remains the only one of its kind and, as such, it provides inferential evidence on the impact of health planning activities. The findings are summarized below.

Number and type of hospitals. Table 3 presents the findings with respect to the number of hospitals and beds classified by ownership and services offered. The total number of hospitals remained unchanged in number in the areas with planning agencies and decreased by 1.8 percent in the unplanned, but the total number of beds increased by 23.8 percent in the planned and decreased by 2.6 percent in the unplanned. Since the unplanned areas began with significantly more beds, it is difficult to evaluate these figures.

With respect to proprietary hospitals, there was a decrease in number (68.8 percent) and beds (54.0 percent) in the planned areas; in the unplanned areas the number of such hospitals decreased 42.9 percent while the number of beds more than tripled. (If large proprietary hospitals are better than small ones, this situation may not be as bad as it would appear.)

Planned areas experienced a decrease in the number of specialty hospitals (28.5 percent) but an increase in the number of such beds (37.5 percent); the unplanned areas had a similar decrease in number of specialty hospitals (29.4 percent) coupled with a decrease of 0.8 percent in the number of specialty hospital beds. Here, too, the relationship between size and quality would seem to be an important consideration.

From these observations, it would seem that planning activities have a very slight, positive effect upon the number of hospitals and hospital beds in an area.

An interesting aspect of Table 3, however, is the measure of average size of hospitals. To begin with, hospitals (except proprietary) in the planned areas were of a somewhat smaller size on the average than were those in the unplanned areas. During the course of the twelve-year period in question, the average size of hospitals in the planned areas increased from this smaller base, while in the unplanned areas both voluntary and governmental hospitals decreased in size from a large base. One would expect that, with control of funds for construction and with general agreement on the fact that larger hospitals are superior to smaller ones, partic-

61

Table 3
HOSPITALS AND BEDS: EIGHT SMSAs

	Planned Area			Unplanned Area		
	1952	1963	Percentage change	1952	1963	Percentage change
Hospitals:						
Total	113	113	—	112	110	−1.8
Voluntary	84	95	13.1	99	98	−1.0
Proprietary	16	5	−68.8	7	4	−42.9
Governmental	13	13	—	6	8	33.3
General	99	103	4.1	95	98	3.2
Special	14	10	−28.5	17	12	−29.4
Average Size:						
Voluntary	166.3	196.2	17.9	193.8	186.9	−3.6
Proprietary	25.8	38.0	8.5	19.1	107.8	464.4
Governmental	306.9	318.8	3.9	724.0	539.5	−25.5
Adult Beds:						
Total	18,373	22,971	23.8	23,664	23,065	−2.6
Voluntary	13,970	18,637	33.4	19,186	18,318	−4.5
Proprietary	413	190	−54.0	134	431	221.6
Governmental	3,990	4,144	3.9	4,344	4,316	−0.6
General	17,496	21,765	24.4	22,309	21,722	−2.7
Special	877	1,206	37.5	1,355	1,343	−0.8

Source: May, "Health Planning—Its Past and Potential."

ularly in a metropolitan area such as those being considered, planning agencies would be very active and interested in increasing the average size of the hospitals.

Bed/population ratios. Table 4 presents data on the bed/population ratios for both total general and special hospital beds and for general hospital beds alone. During the period covered by the study, the planned areas decreased their bed/population ratios by 0.1 percent for total hospital beds, and 1.2 percent with respect to general hospital beds. The unplanned areas show decreases of 19.9 percent and 11.4 percent, respectively.

Services and programs. In this section only selected services and programs which can be, however tenuously, associated with the ideas of quality of care and duplication of facilities are examined.

Quality of care is an extremely elusive concept, and nowhere in the literature is there a definition which is susceptible to measurement. The measures which have been suggested, such as tissue committee reports, medical audit reports, eval-

Table 4

BED/POPULATION RATIOS: EIGHT SMSAs

	Planned Area			Unplanned Area		
	1952	1963	Percentage change	1952	1963	Percentage change
General and Special Hospital Adult Beds (per 1000 population)	3.80	3.78	−0.1	4.30	3.48	−19.9
General Hospital Beds (per 1000 population)	3.63	3.59	−1.2	4.05	3.59	−11.4
General Hospital Admissions (per 1000 population)	121.3	135.5	11.7	121.5	133.2	9.6

Source: May, "Health Planning—Its Past and Potential."

uation of a panel of physicians of the performance of an individual physician, et cetera, are not available to us in this study. Thus, as a very crude approximation, three factors are examined: the percentage of hospitals with internship programs, the percentage with residency programs, and the percentage offering rehabilitation services. Table 5 reports the data for the areas with respect to these factors.

It is sometimes argued that the existence of internship and residency programs enhance the quality of care in a hospital primarily in two ways. First, the fact that a number of reasonably (and sometimes highly) competent physicians are on the premises or available at all times makes it possible for the voluntary hospital to provide more intensive medical care for its patients than is normally possible with

Table 5

SELECTED HOSPITAL PROGRAMS AND SERVICES: EIGHT SMSAs

	Planned Area			Unplanned Area		
	1952	1963	Percentage change	1952	1963	Percentage change
Percentage of General and Special Hospitals						
Internships	32	39	21.9	40	38	−5
Residencies	35	32	−8.6	39	42	7.6
Rehabilitation services	—	17	—	—	18	—
Isotope therapy	—	33	—	—	33	—
Schools of nursing	30	28	−6.7	40	30	−25.0

Source: May, "Health Planning—Its Past and Potential."

a non-full-time staff. Second, the presence of interns and residents is said to challenge the staff physicians to keep up with the latest developments and to interest them in their own continued growth. The percentage of hospitals with internship programs increased 21.9 percent in the planned areas and decreased 5.0 percent in the unplanned, while the percentage with residency programs decreased 8.6 percent in the former and increased 7.6 percent in the latter.

The availability of rehabilitation services can be considered an indication of higher quality of care in the sense that, if the role of the hospital as a medical center for the community implies availability of a complete range of services, a hospital must have a rehabilitation facility to fit this definition. In 1963, 17 percent of the hospitals in the planned areas and 18 percent of the hospitals in the unplanned areas were operating rehabilitation programs. These figures would seem to indicate little significant difference between the areas with planning and the areas without it with respect to these extremely crude measures of the quality of care rendered.

With respect to duplication of services, the most hackneyed example is the "cobalt bomb." Presumably, in a highly populated metropolitan area, transportation facilities are such that infrequently used treatment facilities could (or should) be centralized in a few large hospitals; hence, the smaller the percentage of hospitals offering such services (down to a point) the better. Planning agencies themselves have frequently used isotope therapy in their literature as an example of "unnecessary duplication."

The available data refer to "all radioisotope therapy" in 1952 and only cobalt therapy in 1963, so between-years comparisons are not meaningful. It is interesting to note, however, that cobalt therapy was available at one-third of the hospitals in the planned areas and also at one-third of the hospitals in the unplanned. If "unnecessary duplication" were taking place in the absence of planning activities, one should observe a higher percentage in the unplanned areas.

Also presented is the percentage of hospitals with diploma schools of nursing. Leaders in the field of nursing education have expressed a desire to reduce the number of such schools in the interest of improving the quality of nursing education. One might assume, then, that the fewer of these in a community the better. On the other hand, one of the reasons hospitals continue to operate them is to provide themselves with a supply of graduate nurses, a very scarce commodity. As a result, planning agencies might not exert much pressure to rid the community of them, given a shortage of available nurses.

Utilization patterns. A decrease of 2.8 percent in the average length of stay occurred in the planned areas and a 3.5 percent increase in the unplanned. These changes are small, and probably do not indicate any differences between the areas.

With respect to occupancy levels, it is probably safe to assume that, within limits, the higher the percentage of occupancy the better, since typically, for a hospital of a given size, the average per-unit cost of hospital care is minimized at an occupancy level of between 70 and 90 percent. Thus, increases in occupancy levels represent a desirable trend. Furthermore, the shape of the distribution of levels of occupancy in various hospitals is an important consideration. The more hospitals which a community has operating at high levels of occupancy, and the fewer at low levels, the more effective the system is likely to be. Table 6 presents, along with average percentage of occupancy for the areas, the percentage of hospitals operating at levels equal to or greater than 75 percent and the percentage of hospitals operating at levels less than 50 percent during each of the two years in question. With respect to the area averages, in the planned areas percentage occupancy for all hospitals increased by 8.7 percent during the period and in the unplanned areas by 15.0 percent. In the planned areas, the percentage of hospitals with "high" occupancy increased 21.7 percent, while in the unplanned areas there was a much larger increase (42.8 percent). With respect to "low" occupancy hospitals, planned areas experienced a 42.6 percent decrease and the unplanned areas an 80 percent increase.

This means that the hospitals in planned areas are becoming much more homogeneous with respect to occupancy levels and no hospitals have particularly high or low levels. Meanwhile, hospitals in the unplanned areas are becoming more heterogeneous—some are real standouts and others are not. There is no ready explanation for this phenomenon.

Another measure used is a concentration ratio with respect to beds and admissions. This is expressed in the following way: "The largest _____ percent of the hospitals account for 20 (50) percent of the beds." It is interpreted to mean that if, for example, the largest 50 percent of the hospitals account for 50 percent of the beds, all hospitals are of relatively equal size. If, on the other hand, 10 percent of the hospitals account for 50 percent of the beds, there are a few very large and many very small hospitals. Thus, the smaller the first number shown in relation to the second, the greater the concentration. It is usually assumed that concentration of both beds and admissions is "good" based on our earlier discussion of the relation between size and quality.

During the twelve years in question, the percentage of hospitals accounting for 50 percent of the beds increased by 4.8 percent in the planned areas and by an almost identical amount (5 percent) in the unplanned. The percentage of hospitals accounting for 50 percent of the admissions, however, increased 9.1 percent in the planned areas and decreased by 9.5 percent in the unplanned. With respect to beds, then, it would appear that there is no difference between planned and unplanned areas, and with respect to admissions a superior pattern exists in the unplanned areas insofar as concentration is concerned.

Costs. Cost per admission increased by 97 percent in the planned area and by 100 percent in the unplanned (Table 7). Cost per patient day increased 98.4 per-

Table 6

PATTERNS OF UTILIZATION IN
GENERAL AND SPECIAL HOSPITALS: EIGHT SMSAs

	Planned Area			Unplanned Area		
	1952	1963	Percent-age Change	1952	1963	Percent-age Change
Hospital Admissions (per 1000 population)	121.3	135.5	11.7	121.5	133.2	9.6
Average Length of Stay	8.54	8.3	−2.8	8.46	8.76	3.5
Percentage of Occupancy	72.6	78.9	8.7	79.9	91.9	15.0
Percentage of Hospitals with Less than 50 Percent Occupancy	12	7	−42.6	5	9	80.0
Percentage of Hospitals with More than 75 Percent Occupancy	46	56	21.7	42	60	42.8
Bed Concentration						
20 Percent	8	8	—	8	9	12.5
50 Percent	21	22	4.8	20	21	5.0
Admission Concentration						
20 Percent	9	10	11.1	8	9	12.5
50 Percent	22	24	9.1	21	19	−9.5

Source: May, "Health Planning—Its Past and Potential."

cent in the planned area and 94.1 percent in the unplanned. There was an increase in operating cost per bed of 154.2 percent in the planned area and 168.7 percent in the unplanned.

Presumably one of the purposes of health planning is to create a more efficient system. To the extent that percentage costs stand as a proxy for efficiency, health planning has not had significant impact.

Summary and Conclusions

What does all this mean for the future of health planning? Can we reasonably assume, for example, that although health planning activities cannot be unambiguously shown to have reduced medical costs, improved distribution of services, and so forth, for whatever reasons we may choose to offer, is it still possible that they will become demonstrably effective in the future? Is it possible that statements

Table 7

GENERAL AND SPECIAL HOSPITALS' OPERATING
COSTS: EIGHT SMSAs

	Planned Area			Unplanned Area		
	1952	1963	Percent-age change	1952	1963	Percent-age change
Hospital Cost per Admission	$ 180.54	$ 355.72	97.0	$ 173.65	$ 347.39	100.0
Hospital Cost per Patient Day	21.63	42.92	98.4	20.59	39.98	94.1
Hospital Cost per Adult Bed	4,231.00	10,754.00	154.2	4,914.00	13,204.12	168.7

Source: May, "Health Planning—Its Past and Potential."

such as those by John Gardner and those quoted from the Comprehensive Health Planning Act have led us to expect more from health planning than we have a right to expect? Is it worth the price we are paying for the effort? Let me attempt to answer these questions one at a time.

Can we reasonably assume that health planning will, in the future, become demonstrably effective in reducing medical costs, improving distribution of services, equalizing access thereto, and improving the overall quality of the system? No, not as health planning is presently carried on. The system out of which these problems arise, the strategies being used by the planners, the apparent aversion to the idea of making sanctions available to them all conspire to make it most unlikely that health planning activities, as now constituted, will engender any significant change in the physical or statistical attributes of the system. Coupled with these more or less logistical or systemic problems is the fact that planners find it difficult to agree with one another, or with the operators, or with the "public" on priorities.

Is it possible that we have been led to expect more from health planning than we ought to? I believe so. It is a tradition in the voluntary sector, and a part of our Protestant ethic, that if the goal we have chosen is a "good" one, and if we try hard enough, we will succeed. The language of the Comprehensive Health Planning Act and the implications in the literature on health planning assume that the health field is peopled mostly with "men of goodwill" who are not quite well enough informed (or smart enough) to do what they would be doing if they knew more (or better). The implied function of health planning activities is, therefore, to inform them or help them to inform themselves and guide them in the "right" direction. Once this is done, the health system will, it is thought, become all that is desired of it. This set of assumptions, which is accepted by a surprisingly large

67

number of people in and out of public life, leads to the unrealistically high expectations for health planning which we have accepted as a fact of life.

The final question raised above is this: Is planning worth the price? This is a difficult question. One could glibly answer, "If I have a program with a positive cost and if I find no measurable benefit (return) from the program, I should not undertake it." But this is not quite a complete answer despite what we have said above. Some would associate a positive benefit with doing something—anything—about the problems faced in the health field. Many would argue that better data, advice, counsel, and so forth are not without value. The value of the benefits depends on one's own assessments and judgments.

A minimum estimate of the annual cost of health planning nationally is $52,500,000. Of this, at least $15 million is expended at the level of the states for comprehensive health planning activities, $15 million of federal funds and a matching amount of local funds for area-wide health planning, and $7.5 million for educational programs for health planners. These figures are based on federal allotments for the 1970 fiscal year and do not include private funds (other than matching funds) which are spent for health planning. Health planning is not a small undertaking. Furthermore, it is most improbable that we, as a nation, will ever realize anything like a dollar in savings or in reduced costs for each dollar spent on health planning. The answer to the question of whether planning is worth the price depends (1) on the value of the long-run benefits of coordination and cooperation among hospitals which cannot be measured at all unless some common measure of benefit can be devised and agreed upon, and (2) a necessarily very subjective assessment of the likelihood of these benefits being realized.

COMMENTARY ON THE PAPER

Frank P. Grad

Professor May's paper on planning and licensing agencies is interesting, but I am sorry that he omitted something in oral presentation. In the original draft of his paper he started out with a quote to the effect that the common good will be served by the balance of individual greeds. And that, of course, is a classical statement of the nineteenth century view of the free market system.

Now, Mr. May focuses on the faults of planning, and the faults of planning are many. It is perfectly clear from his presentation, however, that we have only planned in a systematic, professional sense for relatively few years. It is actually a very new kind of approach. We have always done some planning, of course; we have not invented planning in this generation. But professional planning is a relatively new phenomenon of the past thirty years or so.

In addition, planning thus far has served several masters, as he points out. It has served professional needs; there has been professional emphasis. It has also tried to serve the needs of consumers. The entire consumer emphasis, which is a recent arrival upon the scene, has to some extent skewed some of the original planning aims.

Now, I resented his description of the consumer groups as "the old wives." Obviously, we don't call in the old wives when we want to go to the moon, and we shouldn't call in the old wives when we try to determine what is an appropriate catchment area for a general hospital, for instance. That is not what we call in the old wives for.

But I would suggest that the old wives in community control, if you want to call it that, have a great deal to contribute when it comes to such matters as, for instance, whether or not we should have appointment systems for visits to clinics or whether we should just let people sit day after day until they happen to be reached—unless they drop dead before they are reached, of course. The old wives may also have some useful ideas on the times and places where services will be most conveniently utilized, and they may also have a useful notion or two about taking medical histories in Spanish rather than in inadequate English.

It seems that even the old wives may have a certain amount of useful input. And if you have ever had to utilize clinic services, you will know that this kind of input is rather important. In New York it has been rather difficult to convince the voluntary hospital establishment which provides clinic services under contracts with the city, as well as the public hospitals, to institute an appointment system, until the community representatives have said that is the way it is going to be, that you had damn well better institute an appointment system because patients are no longer willing to sit with their kids in a waiting room for six to eight hours at a time.

So there are certain instances when the community does know its needs. A community may not know exactly how many beds there ought to be in a hospital and how many of these beds ought to be devoted to the care of narcotics addicts, or whether or not you should have a cobalt machine. But the community does know where the shoe pinches, where they have been mishandled and hurt and where their very real human concerns have not been taken care of.

Besides, there is nothing new in the idea that a board which regulates professional conduct and the like should not consist exclusively of professionals and that the agency which determines who ought to enter the field should also have members who represent the public interest. We have this in all kinds of regulatory agencies. This should be good enough reason to have consumers on boards involving entry into the field in the health services area, too. They may not have technical contributions to make, but they certainly may make some other useful, even unique, contributions.

The other aspect of Joel May's paper that I would like to comment on is his review of the results of planning—particularly of the Palmiere study. That study covers a twenty-year span. May tells us that the outcome, on various tests of health outcome, in the planned areas does not differ significantly from the outcome in some of the unplanned areas. Well, I think that is certainly so, if you believe Palmiere's findings, and I certainly have no reason to distrust them.

But I would like to know more about the particular areas covered. It is quite possible that the areas selected were atypical; it may also be that in some of the planned areas considerably greater changes, population gains or population losses or the like, were taking place which were not occurring in the unplanned areas. In other words, this covers a twenty-year span, and the outcomes are reported without any correlation with other developments in the same areas over that twenty-year period.

Conceivably the results of planning may have been considerably better than Palmiere indicates. There may have been any number of adverse factors working in either kind of these areas. Conceivably these adverse factors or these correlative factors may have had no impact at all. But we do not know that. All we have is the bare output, and to me the bare output is insufficiently convincing to discount planning altogether.

Also, I think that Mr. May sits a bit on the fence in his conclusion. Does planning pay off? Well, he makes the point that the decision on this issue involves value judgments, and that is perfectly true. But I would like to add one other factor. Maybe planning pays off in a way which has not as yet been mentioned. As the old travel ads used to say: Getting there is half the fun.

In the process of planning we learn a great deal about the field. As a matter of fact, it is perhaps not amiss to remark that what has gone on today right here on this platform is in a sense a planning effort. A critical evaluation of what planning has or has not produced is itself an input into planning, and we cannot have that unless we at least undertake the effort.

True enough, we do not know enough about planning to do it very effectively thus far, but unless we try to do more planning, we are not going to find out any more about the system than we know, and we certainly do not know anywhere nearly enough.

DISCUSSION

The 1967 May Study

PROFESSOR MAY: Let me mention the data sources used in my 1967 study, since I think I can clear that up pretty quickly. The criterion for selection of the SMSAs was that the planning agency had to have been in existence for at least five years as of 1963. There were seven such areas in the country. Three of them were too large to find matches for, namely Chicago, New York, and Los Angeles. The four which I used were Rochester, Detroit, Columbus, and Kansas City. And they were matched as to level of population, population change, immigration, emigration, median income, white collar percentages, education—and so forth.

FROM THE AUDIENCE: What were the communities that matched those?

PROFESSOR MAY: Hartford was matched with Rochester, Philadelphia with Detroit, Dayton with Columbus, and Cincinnati with Kansas City.

PROFESSOR KESSEL: In Professor Grad's evaluation of some of the empirical work on the effect of planning, the burden of his argument was that he could conceive of interpretations other than the ones offered or that—to use his words—the interpretations offered might be false. But he never really got down to saying that he thought there was a misinterpretation and to specifying an alternative interpretation.

Now, any time you have a substantive hypothesis, it is conceivable that it is wrong. In fact, that is a necessary condition that must be met for a hypothesis to be substantive. Only in the world of logic can you make statements that are not conceivably wrong. It is conceivably wrong that if I throw a ball out the window, the ball is going to fall to the ground. That statement is conceivably false because the ball could have risen. This illustrates the character of the argument being made. There was nowhere an attempt to say that the evaluation of the effect of planning was incorrect or that it was incorrect because the evidence was misinterpreted in particular ways.

Professor Grad also contends that a reason we ought to plan is to learn more about planning. It seems to me that you can learn about the planning we have already done by studying what its effects have been. Implicit in his view is the abandonment of all hope of learning anything from our experience thus far.

He also contends that the reason we have planning is failure of the market. In at least two important respects in the health field I believe that is a false statement. One is with respect to planning for medical education. It seems to me that the planning that has arisen there was at the instigation of professional groups for their own parochial interests. I see no evidence that this was the fault of the market or that this planning was of great public benefit. Those of you who have deigned to read Flexner will find that Flexner says we can find instances of miserable small towns of 500 people which have six doctors; moreover, only three doctors can make a living in this tiny town, and towns like this one can be found all over the United States—too many doctors for the population. This is the failure of the market that led to the Flexner report and the planning of medical education.

Similar arguments can be made about HMOs. Why haven't we had more HMOs? The planners have made them illegal. But Professor Grad regards that as a failure of the market.

PROFESSOR GRAD: All I really said was that I wanted to know more about the particular areas chosen and that alternative explanations were possible. I did not think that the burden was upon me in my brief comment to duplicate the study to determine exactly what it did or did not produce, nor did I think the burden was upon me to present detailed alternative resolutions of the particular problem. All I was to do was to raise the question. It seems to me that the question is properly raised by saying that if, in a particular study, the results are consistent with other interpretations, then other interpretations may well be made. I did not proceed to draw these alternative conclusions because I simply did not have enough of the facts. I simply asked the question whether or not more must be known about the particular circumstances before we can accurately appraise the particular conclusions.

As for your other comment, I agree with you completely that you cannot consider HMO experience in any way as a market failure. You are perfectly right, of course, that this was a situation where the law prevented certain kinds of experience from being acquired. But it is perfectly clear, too, that the law was not created at the instance of the consumers, but was enacted at the instance of the free professionals, the physicians, who generally were against group practice. So, while I do not regard it as a failure of the market system, I do regard it as evidence of the hazards of the market system, because the physicians who could do this once to the market system can do it again.

KAREN DAVIS, The Brookings Institution: Since there has been discussion of Professor May's results, I would like to comment on those briefly. I might say first that my own biases are that I would expect to get the type of results that May got, namely that planning does not make that much difference.

The measures of effectiveness of hospital planning which he proposes are reasonable ones since we do expect planning agencies to have some effect upon hospital utilization, upon rates of increase in hospital costs, and upon duplication of specialized hospital facilities.

But I do not feel that May's study in any way constitutes a rigorous test of the effectiveness of planning. It is difficult to base strong statistical tests upon four observations, and I do not really have much faith in the technique of paired cities. I can think of over a dozen determinants of just hospital utilization alone, and I find it hard to believe that even in paired cities you are going to have the same trends in prices, insurance coverage, incomes, demographic composition, and all the things that affect hospital use. The data he presents are interesting, but they do not constitute a test of the hypothesis that planning has made a difference.

PETER WRIGHT, Governor's Health Policy and Planning Task Force, Wisconsin: I approach what Joel May did much more neutrally than some others, and I feel we have a very limited privilege to attack what he did, since, as he pointed out, almost nothing else has been done. I think that is the alarming thing. His study was completed in 1967, and that is five years ago!

It is fairly obvious that, while the measures he used may be imperfect and at most can only suggest one side of planning and try to evaluate one part of it, they are at least plausible expectations of the outcomes of good planning. Even though those agencies may not have established his measures as objectives—in other words, raising the occupancy, lowering the average daily bed cost, and so on—I think it was a reasonable approach. It evidently has not been replicated, but I think that any community in which planning activities are going on could easily copy it, starting with where they are at that moment, waiting five years before looking again, and doing this examination periodically.

I think the whole question of evaluation of planning activities is sadly ignored. We pursue planning endlessly as if it were self-justifying, as if you did not have to justify yourself further than to say that planning is a good end in itself. And it certainly is not. It cannot be.

JOHN GENTRY, School of Public Health, University of North Carolina: As a former trustee of the Syracuse Regional Hospital Council, I would like to speak to the validity of the interpretations that Mr. May has drawn from his study findings. Although the various New York State regional hospital councils have been categorized as planning bodies, at the time of this study they did not have either formal planning responsibilities or plan-implementation authority. It is most inappropriate, therefore, to use these data as a basis for evaluating the effectiveness of planning agencies. The conclusions drawn have no basis in fact and can be considered erroneous.

During the era described, the councils were primarily responsible for responding to applications by community hospitals for Hill-Burton construction funds. The obvious ineffectiveness of application denial to deter unnecessary and costly duplication of neighboring facilities actually led New York State to enact the first hospital franchising legislation in the United States.

I have had an opportunity to discuss this matter with Mr. May and in so doing have identified major differences in our perceptions of the responsibilities and authorities of planning agencies and how the performance of such agencies can be evaluated. It would thus appear that we have a need to define our terms more precisely and recognize that each of us may be imputing different meanings to the same word.

Evaluating Health Planning

EUGENE GUTHRIE, executive director, Maryland Comprehensive Health Planning Agency: I would like to express my concern over Mr. May's comments on planning—that is, whether or not we should continue to do planning. I think it would be very wrong to reach a conclusion on the basis of the data that he surveyed and the references that he made.

Even though some have implied that we have had a lot of experience in health planning, I say we have had very limited experience in health planning in the United States. The planning that has been done, particularly in the last twenty years, is really bits and pieces of planning. The experience we have had with it should only serve as a limited experience and should not be the basis for a decision as to whether or not we expand or develop planning programs in the health field in the future. I believe May's conclusions seem to indicate that we ought to toss planning out the window and proceed with other kinds of activities. I wouldn't want to rest the case on that.

RICHARD A. POSNER, University of Chicago Law School: I am amused by your comment. It is what I regard as the Vietnam approach: If you have failed in what you have done, the answer is to expand the scope of your activity.

DR. GUTHRIE: That's not what I said.

PROFESSOR POSNER: You said that planning has failed because it has been piecemeal, and because it hasn't been sufficiently comprehensive, and that, if it is expanded, maybe it will succeed.

DR. GUTHRIE: I didn't mean that we should use the same things which did not work. Under the rubric of planning there are many things that have gone on, and certainly I would hope we would not take the same models that we have used in the last twenty years and apply them in the next twenty years.

MR. SIEVERTS: I run an area-wide health planning agency, and I feel a little like the patient on the operating table surrounded by the surgeons here. I feel very much alone, undergoing surgery and wondering how come there was never a history and physical done.

I have been in area-wide health planning for seven years, involved in the running of an agency. It is one of those that Joel May purports to have studied, even

76

though we do not meet a basic criterion in that we were founded in 1960, halfway through his study period, and therefore did not have any impact on the years before 1960.

The main point I would like to make, though, is that I hope we are not all too glib and quick in assuming that the health planning efforts of the last decade or twelve or thirteen years can be dismissed out of hand as a failure. I don't think they can.

I think that one thing which is clearly true is that the area-wide health planning experience is remarkably unstudied. In the seven years that I have been with the Hospital Planning Association in Pittsburgh we have never once been visited by a scholar or researcher who was interested in making observations or getting facts and figures on what we were doing, nor by a federal official who was paying us, never once. The only federal officials we ever saw in Pittsburgh were auditors to make sure we were not cheating. They have never once caught us cheating and presumably we will therefore continue to get federal money. And we are very grateful to you all.

But it seems to me that if we are going to evaluate the effectiveness of the area-wide health planning effort in the past and in the present and in the future, we have got to develop some hypotheses about what we think we want the area-wide health planning agency to accomplish. And let's debate those hypotheses and see if we can agree on what those hypotheses should be. I don't agree, for example, that the job of the area-wide health planning agency is to stop the growth in the number of hospital beds. I never heard it defined that way until Joel May wrote his essay quite a few years ago. And I severely criticized it at the time.

We don't see that as our role. If we ended up not achieving a "goal" of freezing the bed supply in the 1960s, if we did not in fact stop the growth in hospital beds, we don't consider that as a sign of failure. There are certain *other* goals that we did have and certain other hypotheses upon which we based our programs. We would be delighted to discuss them. Area-wide health planners used to discuss them a great deal when they got together, and they still do to some extent. It is interesting that neither the scholars nor the federal officials were paying much attention.

It is also true that area-wide health planners tend to be pragmatic, hard-working guys with insufficient resources to cope; therefore we are not taking sabbaticals to write up our results. I think maybe some of us should, because the public agencies that pay us aren't examining our activities and because the universities and research houses by and large are not paying attention—not even those that purport to be training health planners.

My feeling is that we have made a lot of mistakes in the last ten or twelve years. We are continuing to make mistakes, but, as a new human endeavor, area-wide health planning in this country has a lot to show in the way of results. Come ask us, take a look.

PROFESSOR POSNER: What kind of self-evaluation program do you have?

PROFESSOR KESSEL: What should we look at to determine whether you are doing a good job or not?

MR. SIEVERTS: I am not sure this is the place for the kind of lengthy answer that would call for. I can give you some examples though.

As a beginning: Did the area-wide health planning process—not just the agency, but the process in which it is involved—identify and decide upon areas of unmet need in the community, and were effective actions implemented to meet those needs? I am willing to have my agency and the CHP agency over us judged on that score. Examples of those "needs" could be, say, poor people in urban neighborhoods not getting primary health services. A "need" could be the problem of patients hospitalized in obsolescent, unsafe facilities. Another unmet "need" might well be for high-quality ambulance services, mobile intensive care units. Progress in the community in defining and solving problems of unmet need is one large parameter upon which I think we could be looked at. And not in the space of two or four years while an agency was getting organized, but in a space of five or ten years while it was working.

Did change take place in the community's health service delivery system? No one has ever looked at us in that way that I am aware of. I am prepared to suggest some additional broad parameters of planning agency achievement if called upon.

EUGENE FEINGOLD, School of Public Health, University of Michigan: I would like to add a different dimension to this exchange that has just been taking place, because it seems to me that Professor May's study, as valuable and interesting as it is, is really not a study of planning. Rather, it is a study of planning agencies' activities.

I would argue that planning agencies—both in the period which he studied and to a large extent still today—did not and do not plan. Rather, the agencies are a vehicle for bringing people together to exchange ideas and information. This, I would argue, is not planning.

Accountability and Standards of Assessment

ERIC PFEIFFER, Department of Psychiatry, Duke University Medical Center: I think a number of the speakers have raised the question of accountability. Mr. Gottlieb has, Professor Grosse has. I think the missing piece in talking about accountability is the fact that we really do not have an adequate system of assessing the impact of interventions in the health care field. Unless some sort of crash program is developed to assess such impacts, there really can be no system of accountability. At present there is no way of categorizng the impact of any dollar amount or bed amount that you do or do not put into a community, whether it is in an HMO or in a new hospital that is or is not going to be built.

And I think the problem here is that doctors individually have not been terribly interested in doing anything else but assessing what happens to their own individual patients. And the methodology even for that has been extremely sloppy. I speak as a physician. This is not one of the major aspects of what is taught in medical school. And the diversity of diagnostic categories in medicine makes it hair-raising to try to implement some kind of systematic assessment of impact of intervention. Some moves in the direction of creating, say, functional levels of health—of physical functioning or of mental health functioning—are, I think, moves in that direction.

Instead of just proceeding with planning, however, I think that accountability is an utterly empty word unless a methodology for assessing impact of intervention can be developed through interaction of measurement people, systems people and medical people.

I would be interested in hearing the two of you who talked about accountability respond to that.

PROFESSOR HAVIGHURST: I wonder if Mr. Gottlieb could say something about how perfect is the art of determining how many beds there ought to be in a community. When one speaks of planning, of course one gets a good feeling all over. But does it really work? Is there any way of knowing how many beds a community should have? Is there any hope that we will ever have a rational way of working that out?

MR. GOTTLIEB: We have been talking about how to count beds and how to measure and project bed needs and so on for about fifty years. I think it's time we stopped worrying about it. There is so much overemphasis on it that we have forgotten to look at, and to develop a methodology for evaluating, all the kinds of alternative approaches to delivering care and organizing care that we should be looking at. Even in that area, of course, we don't really measure need. We try to anticipate demand in short stretches of time, and, at best, we are using a substitute for need.

I don't think that we have very much in the way of a methodology that is useful for the kinds of things Dr. Pfeiffer is talking about. I think we have to develop it. I think that is part of what planning is supposed to be doing, too. But if we start out with the idea that we are in fact trying to identify some goals and some alternative methods of getting there and if we acknowledge in advance that this requires us to evaluate those alternatives and to bring all available information, quantitative and otherwise, to this evaluation, then we can begin to effect a more rational decision-making process. The weakness in the past has been that we didn't start out with that point of view.

Of course we have a long way to go. The important thing that is currently going on is not that planning programs have or don't have teeth, but rather that planning is being mandated. We are at a stage of stimulation and pressure, where the task is to get all the people involved in health care—those who are delivering care, those who have other kinds of responsibilities external to that, or those who are using care—to accept the concept of beginning to develop goals and evaluate alternatives. I think that is the most useful thing that the federal government has done to us so far.

On the question of accountability, sure, we all talk about that. (I wasn't going to say this, but you got me started.) My concern runs something like this. I know—because I have worked on that side, too—that government isn't particularly accountable in the usual sense of the term most of the time. I remember when I was director of a state Hill-Burton agency that I was really accountable to only about three people when you came right down to it, and yet I had one heck of a lot of influence on what happened in the development of health facilities in that state. And any real accountability to the public was, at best, very indirect. Working in the private sector in a sense, in a nonprofit corporation, I am now accountable, of course, to my board and membership; probably more people have access to me and can pressure me now than was the case when I worked for a state government.

One of the values of the whole comprehensive health planning approach as envisioned in that particular law—one that I hope doesn't get eroded too quickly before it has had a chance to work—was the opportunity to identify and develop respective roles at the federal, state, and local levels that are interrelated but different, and to develop the interrelations between them so as to begin to identify, in a complex way, the accountability at each level for a given kind of activity. The value of the mix is clearest to me, of course, at the local level—not because we have so much expertise down there, but because it provides the closest opportunity to have the mixture of viewpoints revolving around the conditions that dictate how action will really occur. The federal government's job is one of mixing that local activity with the respective political roles of the state and other governments to achieve the greatest possible accountability. But I am looking to these wise people here, since we don't have much expertise at the local level, to tell me how that is going to be done.

MR. ZWICK: On the subject of accountability and intervention, I would like to add, that it is important to keep in mind the standard against which you are holding people accountable. An important development over the last ten years in the development of institutions has been the political process in which there is a growing consensus on what the goals may be. Reference has been made by a number of the speakers to the collective will and to the goals of the country in terms of health care. Well, certainly over the past ten years we have seen, I would suggest, an important evolution in thinking on this process.

Now, federal law hasn't done a very good job, as has been noted, in clarifying this issue, because it is perhaps more likely that the federal law will reflect that national consensus than provide leadership in developing it. But certainly the country's expectations and the country's feelings about what health care should be are developing a standard that is bound to affect this whole process fundamentally.

PAUL GERTMAN, Office of Science and Technology: I think many people interested in health care are going at cross purposes, because, first, we don't have definite measures of effectiveness of a personal health services system and, second, there is a difference between measures of efficiency of a process—talking about dollars, beds, and so forth—and measures of effectiveness in terms of mortality or people made well. I think there is widespread disagreement about what the measures of effectiveness are.

Next, I think health planners and the types of people in this room tend to focus on measures of effectiveness in terms of mortality, cure of disease, and so forth, while the traditional role for medicine until about thirty years ago was primarily the alleviation of pain, suffering, and discomfort. And I think those are still very important measures of what a personal health services system does.

I think if you take a look, for example, at some of the differences, in OEO-sponsored centers, between consumer-controlled and provider-controlled planning, you will find greater effectiveness in dealing with what the people want in terms of alleviation of anxiety, pain, discomfort, and so forth, in a consumer-controlled system than in a provider-controlled system, where measures of effectiveness are different.

PART TWO

Health Facilities Planning with "Teeth": Certificate-of-Need Laws

REPORTER'S NOTE: Certificate-of-need laws strengthen the planners' ability to control events by giving them either an absolute veto or a strategic role as advisers to the ultimate regulatory authority with respect to new health facilities construction. The first panelist in this session was asked to review the current status of proposals for certificate-of-need legislation, the second to explore the ramifications of the laws and proposals from the standpoint of experience with similar laws in other settings. The session was successful in opening up a vigorous discussion of the appropriateness of regulatory approaches to the health industry's problems.

The session revealed both the deep skepticism in the audience about the "public utility" approach and the widespread concern that a market system could not be expected to work well where nonprofit hospitals, third-party payment, and provider control of demand are the dominant influences. It proved difficult, however, to focus on the need to choose between two highly imperfect devices and the possibilities of improving either, and most of the discussion dealt with the weaknesses of regulation. Thus, the last two sessions were left to explore the prospects for obtaining good performance from either a planned, noncompetitive system or a substantially restructured marketplace.

Concentrating on state law, Professor Curran did not discuss developments at the federal level which have an important bearing on the certificate-of-need issue. H.R. 1, which was pending at the time of the conference, eventually passed under the name Social Security Amendments of 1972 (P.L. 92-603); it contained a provision (section 221) reducing federal Medicare payments to health facilities and health maintenance organizations (HMOs) to the extent that they represent recovery of depreciation and other costs connected with capital investments in facilities costing more than $100,000 which are constructed without approval of state planning agencies. Thus, the health planners are conceded the power effectively to control all new major public and private investments in health facilities, including HMOs, and to prevent all new

83

construction for which they are not satisfied that a "need," as they define it, exists.

An even more draconian proposal appears in the administration's proposed National Health Insurance Partnership Act. This bill would not only affect reimbursement of funds used for capital improvements but would deny reimbursement from federal funds for all services rendered in facilities not approved by the local certificate-of-need agency. Under both H.R. 1 and the later proposal there would be an opportunity for appealing any denial at the local level to the secretary of health, education and welfare. This would at least permit relief to a party which felt it had been conspired against by local providers, but the effect is clearly to create an extra hurdle for any would-be entrant. Heretofore these proposals have not been deemed particularly controversial.

For the record, this session of the conference originally included the May and Neuhauser papers, but these are published elsewhere to sharpen the focus here. Professor Grad's original remarks were directed to the four papers, a fact which may clarify some statements in the discussion.

A NATIONAL SURVEY AND ANALYSIS OF STATE CERTIFICATE-OF-NEED LAWS FOR HEALTH FACILITIES

William J. Curran *

The Legislative Initiative

There is still debate in academic circles about whether the health care industry should be regulated by law in the same manner as the so-called public utilities. The debate has largely ended in the hospital industry itslf where public regulation now seems to be accepted as inevitable, if not desirable. The battles are now being fought in the state legislatures and courts, and they involve the content and extent of the regulatory systems enactd by these law-making bodies in recent years.

The legal campaigns for certificate-of-need legislation began in the states in the mid-1960s. There can be no doubt of the political thrust of the laws: it has been a response to the vastly increased cost of medical care in the United States during the past two decades. In particular, hospital bed-care charges are the focus of attention of these programs. It is widely believed that uncontrolled growth and expansion of hospitals, particularly general hospitals, are in large part responsible for the skyrocketing costs of hospital care. Many of the legislative enactments contain preambles or statements of purpose expressing such views, as in the laws of California, Florida, Minnesota, New Jersey, North Dakota, and Washington. The language of the Minnesota law of 1971 is exemplary:

> The legislature finds that unnecessary construction or modification of health care facilities increases the cost of care and threatens the financial ability of the public to obtain necessary medical services. The purposes of this act are to promote comprehensive health planning; to assist in providing the highest quality of health care at the lowest possible cost; to avoid unnecessary duplication by ensuring that only those health care facilities which are needed will be built; and to provide an orderly method of resolving questions concerning the necessity for construction or modification of health care facilities.[1]

The Enacted Laws. As of the end of the legislative year of 1972, there were certificate-of-need laws covering some category of health care facilities in twenty states:

---

* I must express my particular thanks to Jay Hedgepeth, general counsel of the American Hospital Association, and to Peter J. Elsasser and Thomas P. Galinski of the Division of Planning of the American Hospital Association for allowing me to examine their extensive collection of legislative bills and other materials on certificate-of-need legislation.
[1] Minnesota Statutes, 1971, Chapter 628, Section 1.

Arizona (1971, 1972), California (1969, 1971), Connecticut (1969), Florida (1972), Kansas (1972), Kentucky (1972), Maryland (1968, 1972), Massachusetts (1971, 1972), Michigan (1972), Minnesota (1971), Nevada (1971), New Jersey (1971), New York (1964, 1969), North Carolina (1971), North Dakota (1971), Oklahoma (1971), Oregon (1971), Rhode Island (1968), South Carolina (1971), and Washington (1971). The year of enactment is given for each state, though the effective date of the legislation was often delayed for six months to over one year. Where two dates are given, both years contained important legislative action. In Massachusetts, the 1972 legislation completely replaced the previous temporary law. In all states the later amendments strengthened and broadened the original scope of the programs. Table 1 catalogs legislative action in all of the states and indicates states from which I have received copies of adopted or proposed administrative regulations intended to interpret and to implement the programs.

Catalog of Other Legislative Activity. Proponents of certificate-of-need laws have not won all the legislative battles. Proposals for similar regulatory programs for health care facilities have either been defeated or are still within the legislative process in nineteen additional states: Alaska (defeated in 1972), Georgia (defeated in 1971, refiling expected in 1973), Hawaii (defeated in 1971), Idaho (defeated in 1971), Illinois (defeated in 1972), Indiana (defeated in 1971, refiling expected in 1973), Iowa (defeated in 1972), Mississippi (defeated in 1971 and 1972), Montana (defeated in 1971), New Hampshire (defeated in 1972), New Mexico (defeated in 1971), Pennsylvania (defeated in 1971 and 1972), South Dakota (defeated in 1971), Tennessee (did not pass in 1972, but may go to study), Texas (did not pass in 1971, refiling expected in 1973), Vermont (defeated in 1972), Virginia (defeated in 1972), West Virginia (defeated in 1971), and Wisconsin (defeated in 1971, refiling expected in 1973).

According to the information available to me, no legislation of this type has as yet been filed in the remaining eleven states.

Legislative History and Political Trends. It is always dangerous to attempt to identify the origins of any particular legislative program. The significant antecedents are generally much earlier than any contemporary observer would notice. This is characteristic of all law. Here we are considering industrial regulation. The beginnings of public control of business can be traced back to Roman times. Regulatory mechanisms for public utilities in the form of royal charters have medieval origins. With this historical apology, I will attempt only to trace the more immediate precedents for the current legislative movement.

Serious discussion of some form of public control over growth of health care facilities actually began with a series of meetings held by the United States Public

Table 1
LEGISLATIVE AND REGULATORY ACTION

State	Law Enacted	Regulations Adopted	Bill Defeated	No Action
Alabama				X
Alaska			1972	
Arizona	1971, 1972	1972		
Arkansas				X
California	1969, 1971	1971		
Colorado				X
Connecticut	1969			
Delaware				X
Florida	1972			
Georgia			1971	
Hawaii			1971	
Idaho			1971	
Illinois			1972	
Indiana			1971	
Iowa			1972	
Kansas	1972			
Kentucky	1972			
Louisiana				X
Maine				X
Maryland	1968, 1972	1970		
Massachusetts	1971, 1972	1972		
Michigan	1972			
Minnesota	1971	1971		
Mississippi			1971, 1972	
Missouri				X
Montana			1971	
Nebraska				X
Nevada	1971	1972		
New Hampshire			1972	
New Jersey	1971			
New Mexico			1971	
New York	1964, 1969	1965		
North Carolina	1971	1971		
North Dakota	1971	1971		
Ohio				X
Oklahoma	1971			
Oregon	1971	1972		
Pennsylvania			1971, 1972	
Rhode Island	1968			
South Carolina	1971	1972		
South Dakota			1971	
Tennessee			1972	
Texas			1971	
Utah				X
Vermont			1972	
Virginia			1972	
Washington	1971	1971		
West Virginia			1971	
Wisconsin			1971	
Wyoming				X

Health Service and the American Hospital Association in 1959.[2] The occasion for the meeting was a portent of all the "crises" to come: it was the first major denial of a Blue Cross rate increase by a state insurance commissioner. The early 1960s also saw the establishment of hospital planning councils throughout the country.[3] The first legislative proposal came from an exhaustive study by a legislative committee in New York State examining hospital costs and health insurance rates.[4] The result was the Metcalf-McCloskey Act of 1964, a truly seminal piece of legislation, which contained most of the basic features of what have come to be known as certificate-of-need laws in the health care field. The statute controlled both new facilities and the expansion of old ones, and it set as the criterion for approval the public "need." It established a state-level hospital review and planning council and provided for the recognition of regional hospital councils in an integrated system of facilities planning.

In the middle 1960s two important pieces of federal legislation gave further impetus to the movement for more adequate health planning. These were the Regional Medical Program (RMP)[5] and the Comprehensive Health Planning Program (CHP).[6] The latter in particular brought consumers into a prominent role in health planning on the local level. The original legislation for CHP, however, had its problems. As I noted at the time in another publication,[7] the law provided no political status or authority for the planning agencies on the state or local levels. Also, the area-wide agencies were required to raise half of their funds locally. This often forced the agencies to rely on the local hospitals for financial support. Close identification with hospital affairs was inevitable, and many "comprehensive" planning agencies became virtually technical consultants to the hospitals to aid them in carrying out their own plans. The lack of effective coordination between hospitals became more and more serious and charges to patients continued to rise in an uncontrolled fashion. Spiraling Blue Cross rates made the worsening conditions painfully obvious to the public and the legislatures. It was clear to the politicians that "something" had to be done. When the federal and state lawmakers began to search frantically for a vehicle to represent the public in regulating the health care industry, the CHP agencies, like Mount Everest, were just "there" as lonely symbols of consumer-provider cooperative enterprises in planning, if not in regulation. Reluctantly in some cases, but quite willingly in most, the CHP agen-

---

[2] *Principles for Planning the Future Hospital System,* U.S. Public Health Service Pub. No. 721 (Washington, D.C.: Government Printing Office, 1960); Ray E. Brown, "Let the Public Control Utilization Through Planning," *Hospitals,* vol. 33 (1959) pp. 34-39.
[3] J. H. Cavanaugh, "The Rise of the Areawide Planning Agency: A Survey Report," *Hospitals,* vol. 38 (1965), pp. 52-59.
[4] Report of the Joint Legislation Committee on Health Insurance Plans, *N.Y. Legislative Documents,* no. 39 (1964).
[5] Public Law 89-239 (1965).
[6] Public Law 89-749 (1966).
[7] William J. Curran, "Comprehensive Health Planning: Audacious Lawmaking," *American Journal of Public Health,* vol. 58 (June 1968), pp. 1100-1101.

cies were preempted first into roles as reviewers and commentators on federal funding programs in their own jurisdictions. Planning with "teeth," or "clout," had begun.

The national drive for certificate-of-need laws got under way in 1968 and 1969 with the support of the American Hospital Association and its affiliates in the states. The hospital groups had accepted the necessity for public regulation and had decided to join the campaign and to contribute their own ideas to it rather than be dragged along into something they might consider unworkable at a later time. Speech after speech was made and article after article was published in the voluminous literature of the hospital field in this country supporting the idea of hospitals, particularly voluntary, general, community hospitals, as "public utilities" subject to "franchising" control by the government.[8]

The AHA indicated its support for such legislation in 1968 as a part of its general endorsement of comprehensive health planning. In the statement, the national hospital group still saw the hospital as the "major institutional participant in planning personal health services and a key participant in other facets of community health planning."[9] As far as controls over hospitals were concerned, the AHA then described certificate-of-need authorization by government agencies as the fourth, and last-listed, method in its scheme of things. Ranked ahead of governmental regulation were voluntary agreements among health care providers and professional associations, contractual reimbursement for patient services, and the provision of construction capital. Since 1968, however, the general evidence of the failure of voluntary controls has been so great that the mechanism of legally enforced controls, with participation by providers of services, has moved quickly to the front position among most hospital organization people.

The certificate-of-need legislation in the states has generally been supported by the comprehensive health planning programs and by the state health departments with their health care facilities licensing units and their Hill-Burton program funding units. The state insurance commissioners have also supported the proposals as a means of controlling health insurance premium rates. The bills have generally gained support from both labor unions and business groups as they moved through the legislative process.

The first new provisions enacted at this time came in Maryland and Rhode Island in 1968 and in California and Connecticut in 1969. California in particular gave extensive legal recognition and responsibility to its voluntary, area-wide health planning agencies. Activities increased in 1970, but no additional states passed laws. The peak year in both activity and successful enactments was 1971 when twenty-nine states considered bills and eleven new laws were passed. In 1972 the

---

[8] See a collection of such references in Paul D. Ward, "Health Care Regulation," *Hospitals*, vol. 46 (1972), pp. 101-105.
[9] American Hospital Association, "Statement on Planning," Document S51r (1969), p. 2 (approved by the AHA, May 8-10, 1968; revised September 15-16, 1970).

campaigns continued, but the opposition had stiffened and only four more states joined the roles of the enacted regulatory programs for health care facilities.

The reasons for defeat or failure to pass legislation are always more difficult to analyze than those for success. In some cases failure was attributed simply to inept handling of the bills in the committee process or to the brevity of the legislative session itself. In these situations, no substantive opposition became visible. In at least one state, Iowa, it was reported that the comprehensive health planning agencies were opposed to being forced into becoming state regulatory agencies. In West Virginia, it was said that "the state of the art" in health planning just was not sufficiently advanced to warrant moving into a regulatory program dependent upon strong and effective planning agencies. In Delaware it seemed that the state was laying aside consideration of such legislation until it could be combined with a system of hospital rate regulation. In Ohio it was said that priority was being given to a new hospital licensing law.

In some states, however, the cause of defeat or inaction could be found in more fundamental objection to government regulation in the health care field. In these states, the opposition has consisted of powerful groups such as the state medical societies, proprietary hospitals, or nursing home operators. The basis of the medical society objection is not always simple to determine. The members seem to see such legislation as inevitably leading to hospital rate regulation and then on to control of personnel costs, including physicians' fees. Also, the societies are generally opposed to persons who are not physicians having regulatory or planning powers over essentially medical and health care services. Lastly, there may be some state-level rivalry involved within the medical field itself. Since hospital groups are often seen actively in support of these bills, the medical societies may be opposed because they fear the hospitals will obtain a legally supported power base in the regulatory bodies and the comprehensive health planning councils. Some evidence of compromise with the medical professional groups can be seen in enacted legislation in this field. Some of the laws, such as those in North Carolina, Kentucky, and New Jersey, specifically exempt physicians' services or construction of private physicians' offices from regulation.

It should be observed, however, that the medical societies have not become open and obvious objectors to certificate-of-need bills in all of the states. They may not have led the parade in their favor, but they have not organized significant opposition. Neither have the nursing home groups opposed the bills in all states, we should note.

The major additional push which may bring the remaining states into line with certificate-of-need legislation would be federal law tying the receipt of federal funds or eligibility for certain federal programs to approval by a state certificate-of-need process or its equivalent established by federal guidelines.

90

Constitutional Foundation for Regulation

Governmental controls over business operations in this country have generally been fought out bitterly and unflaggingly in the legislatures and then in the courts on fundamental constitutional grounds. This has not as yet been the case with the certificate-of-need legislation, even though these statutes as a whole are the most concerted and far-reaching legal regulation ever imposed on the health industry in our nation's history. There is really no argument about this observation. It seems to be fully realized by both proponents and opponents of the bills.

No less a leading figure in the public utilities bar than A. J. G. Priest has no trouble at all upholding the constitutionality of both state and federal regulation of health care facilities.[10] He sees no significant legal difference in governmental controls in this field than in others long under broad regulation and surveillance. In his characteristically clear and pithy style, Priest put the question and answered it directly:

> Why would regulation of the health care industry be analogous to the fixing of public utility rates and practices? Basically, because the business of health care is deeply and intimately affected with a public interest, because hospitals and like institutions have the power of exploitation in some measure even though it is not frequently exercised, and because such instrumentalities carry on what is in some respects a natural monopoly. And, as has long been recognized as a matter of economics as well as law, when a necessity of life is provided by a monopoly or quasi-monopoly, effective regulation of that enterprise is required to protect the public interest.[11]

There have been very few challenges in the courts to the constitutionality of certificate-of-need laws. Two cases are important, however, since they involved two of the most important of the early laws in the field from our two largest states. Also, the issues raised were quite fundamental to the programs. The first case, *Attoma* v. *State Department of Social Welfare*,[12] occurred in New York and questioned the basic constitutionality of the Metcalf-McCloskey Act as it applied to nursing homes and hospitals. The Appellate Division of the Supreme Court held unanimously that the law was a reasonable exercise of the police power of the state in the field of health. The Appellate Division had no real difficulty with the question. Only two not very applicable cases, both in New York, were cited as authority to support the court's refusal to substitute its own judgments for that of the legislature that such a regulatory program was needed. This portion of the opinion took only two paragraphs or twenty-six lines in the printed decision which also examined other aspects of the law.

---

[10] A. J. G. Priest, "Possible Adaptation of Public Utility Concepts in the Health Care Field," *Law and Contemporary Problems,* vol. 35 (1970), pp. 839-848.
[11] Ibid., p. 840.
[12] 270 New York Supplement 2d 167 (1966).

The other case involved the California law and was again brought by a nursing home operator. The case was heard in the U. S. District Court for the Central District of California. In *Simon* v. *Cameron* [13] the plaintiff sought declaratory relief challenging the constitutionality of the regulatory law and also the delegation of approving authority to private groups, that is, the area-wide comprehensive health planning agencies, all of which were private, nonprofit corporations. Judge Curtis disposed of the first issue quickly. He ruled: "There can be little question that health planning is a necessary and proper function of the State Legislature." [14] His sole authority for this emphatic determination was the aforementioned *Attoma* case in New York.

The judge took more time with the second challenge. He first observed that the voluntary planning agencies were specifically authorized by the legislature in regard to their composition and functions and were operating under federal financing. Thus, Judge Curtis held that the connections of the agencies with the state were so close as to make them public administrative bodies, even though they were privately incorporated. He also noted that the local agencies had only an initial decision-making authority and that the final decision was made by the state-level health planning council which was entirely composed of state officials and appointees of the governor and hence was clearly a state government unit. This discussion would have been enough to dispose of the case, but the judge went on to point out that California law had long recognized that private groups, even without the quasi-governmental character of these planning agencies, could be utilized to carry out state purposes. He also cited opinions of the United States Supreme Court upholding delegation of decision-making authority to private groups in business-regulation programs.

Lastly, the Court found that the statutory standard of "community need and desirability" was not overly vague or unclear. Judge Curtis held that assessment of need was "a definite and reviewable delegation." He noted that the agencies were required to seek certain specific information from applicants which provided further criteria for determinations of need. These were the geographic area to be served, the population to be served, the anticipated demands for the health care services to be provided, descriptions of services, utilization of existing programs within the area, the benefit to be derived by the community from the new facility, and the impact of the new services upon existing institutions in the area.

In upholding this standard, Judge Curtis cited no previous authority whatsoever. As a final irony, no analogy was made to certificate-of-need regulatory programs in the public utilities or in any other business or communications fields.

---

[13] No. 70-1790-JWC (D.C. Cal., October 9, 1970).
[14] Ibid., p. 3.

92

Coverage of the Laws

There would seem to be general agreement that the broader the scope of the facilities covered, the more effective the planning and regulatory programs because of the interrelationship of the services offered. For example, where only hospitals are controlled, laboratory and other ancillary services may be added to clinic operations or to outpatient "surgicenters," thus resulting in the same undesirable growth of facilities in the community. Table 2 describes the coverage of the legislation in each of the twenty states.

Among the existing laws, the great majority include in their scope the wide range of all health care facilities. In only a few states are there obviously limited programs. Michigan, Oregon, and Rhode Island cover only hospitals, while Oklahoma reverses the situation and controls only nursing homes. Maryland did not include proprietary nursing homes until an amendment enacted in 1972. California does not seem to include intermediate care facilities, though nursing homes are covered, and does not include boarding facilities not offering medical or nursing services.

In the states with generally broad coverage most of the statutory schemes merely include all "hospitals" and "nursing homes" as defined in their licensing laws without any effort to redefine the terms.

If a model were being sought for a wholly new, comprehensive-coverage regulatory program, I would suggest the Kentucky and New Jersey laws. Both states define in great detail both health care facilities and health care services, and they regulate both. They are also the only states which specifically include "health maintenance organizations" fully under their scope. However, both states were forced to modify their great breadth with specific exemptions for the services of physicians in their private offices. The Kentucky law exempts the private offices of physicians, dentists, and other healing arts practitioners where patients are not kept overnight and are not given general anesthetic. This could exempt many types of clinics and related programs. North Carolina has a similar exclusion and specifically excludes surgical, emergency, and other free-standing outpatient services.

Construction and Services Necessitating Certification. After the question of the type of facilities regulated, the next most important issue of coverage in the laws is the area of operations actually controlled. Here we find somewhat greater diversity in the laws, largely because of the lack of clear standards among the planners in the states as to what they can handle and effectively review at the present time and what the hospital and nursing groups feel should be controlled.

There is not so much variety of operational coverage in the laws actually passed as there is in the total number of bills filed and considered. Surprisingly enough, the bills enacted into law are generally simpler in language and broader in coverage than many of the bills considered but not passed. This may well be due

Table 2

COVERAGE OF CERTIFICATION PROGRAM

State	Type of Facility	Minimum Capital Expenditure	Minimum Change in Number of Beds	Change in Service
Arizona	All health care facilities; broad definition		1+	x
California	Hospitals and related health facilities, nursing homes		1+	
Connecticut	Hospitals and other licensed health and nursing facilities	$250,000		
Florida	Hospitals and nursing homes	$100,000 hospitals $50,000 nursing homes	1+	Substantial
Kansas	All licensed health facilities	5 percent of operating expenses or $350,000	1+	
Kentucky	All health facilities; broad definition including HMOs	$100,000	1+ or 1−	x
Maryland	Hospitals and nursing homes		1+	
Massachusetts	All health care facilities	$100,000	4+	Substantial
Michigan	Hospitals	To be established (if any) by director of department of public health	1+	
Minnesota	Health care facilities	$50,000	1+	x
Nevada	Licensed health facilities		1+	x
New Jersey	All health care facilities, broad definition including HMOs			Broad definition
New York	Hospitals, nursing homes, other medical care institutions	$10,000 by regulations		

94

Table 2 *(Continued)*

State	Type of Facility	Minimum Capital Expenditure	Minimum Change in Number of Beds	Change in Service
North Carolina	Licensed medical care facilities		1+[a]	
North Dakota	Medical care facilities		1+	x
Oklahoma	Nursing home facilities			
Oregon	Hospitals		1+	x
Rhode Island	Hospitals			x
South Carolina	Hospitals, nursing homes, and so forth, all defined as "hospitals"		1+ or 1−	Except simple modernization
Washington	Hospitals and nursing homes			

[a] Except outpatient or emergency beds.

to the fact that many of the laws enacted were passed in smaller states where there was little, if any, significant opposition; thus the proposals did not undergo very complex analysis or require much change or compromise.

All of the enacted laws are tied to review of plans for construction changes in the facilities covered by the program. Most are also interrelated with the licensing laws and require certification of need for new facilities, new management, or a change of classification of the license. A few, such as Arizona, have made their licensure provisions essentially the same as a certification of need, that is, the facility license is specifically limited to the type of program in operation at the time of licensing, including the specific number of beds utilized. Twelve of the states have no minimum dollar amount attached to the construction plans reveiwed. A minimum capital expenditure is included in the laws of Connecticut ($250,000), Florida ($100,000 for hospitals, $50,000 for nursing homes), Kansas (5 percent of annual operating expenses or $350,000), Kentucky ($100,000), Massachusetts ($100,000), Minnesota ($50,000), and Washington ($100,000). New York imposes a $10,000 minimum by regulation. The law which was most recently passed, that in Michigan, has no statutory minimum, but allows the director of the state public health department to set such a minimum with the concurrence of the newly created state Health Facilities Commission.

Many of the states were able to get language into their laws providing for more sophisticated surveillance of facilities expansion than simple approval of construction plans. One technique has been to establish control over any addition of beds, while another has been to require approval of any significant change in the service programs of the institutions. No dollar figures were attached as minimums to either of these functional changes in operation. Twelve of the states require certification of need for any expansion of bed capacity (Arizona, Florida, Kansas, Kentucky, Maryland, Michigan, Minnesota, Nevada, North Carolina [inpatient], North Dakota, Oregon, and South Carolina). In Kentucky and South Carolina certification is required for any *decrease* in number of beds as well.

In eight of the states, the law specifically requires certification of need where changes in services are planned (Arizona, Kentucky, Massachusetts, Minnesota, Nevada, New Jersey, North Dakota, and South Carolina). Problems of interpretation are most apt to occur in the area of changes of services, particularly when no appreciable capital expenditures are involved for construction changes. Some of the states, such as Kentucky and New Jersey, have taken great pains to define the types of services covered. North Dakota and Massachusetts leave the definition of "services" to administrative regulations. It can be expected that many of the states will use their regulations and guidelines to define further the scope of controls they wish to exert over changes in services. Most of the laws are not clear as to whether *reduction* of services as well as expansion will require legal sanction. In the Kentucky law, for example, the term "modification" is used, which may or may not include reductions. In the otherwise highly comprehensive New Jersey law, only *new* health care services are controlled. The California program is also unclear about coverage of service changes. Decreases in beds do not seem to be controlled in California.

The South Carolina law is one of the few which deals in detail with these issues. It provides:

> The type of change requiring certification of needs [sic] is defined as anything which would either expand or reduce the scope or type of health services rendered; such as construction of any facility, the major modernization of an existing facility, or the modification of an existing facility or program. Simple modernization to improve care does not require certification of need.[15]

The effort at clarity here may have gotten the South Carolina draftsmen in trouble. The exclusion of "simple modernization" may be intended as a *de minimus* rule based on amount expended, such as for purchase of new furniture to replace old, broken, or uncomfortable chairs and tables. This may have been thought necessary where the law contains no minimum on capital expenditures to be reviewed. However, the language refers only to construction and ties "modernization" to *improving care,* implying that each construction or purchase of equipment is directly related to quality of care. It might have been more advisable

---

[15] Laws of South Carolina, 1971, Chapter 395, Section 48.

96

to exclude only those simple and inexpensive purchases which have *no significant effect* on patient care and are not apt to be in any way reflected in charges to the patient for his care and treatment.

Administration of the Programs
And Relationship to Comprehensive Health Planning

Up to this point, it does not seem to me that the regulatory programs examined in this paper have been basically different in character from any of the other established programs of public control over public utilities and certain other enterprises such as radio and television station franchises. Matters will begin to change, however, as we come to the issues of who is doing the regulating and the content of the questions raised in the review process.

In nearly all of the other publicly controlled fields noted above, the structure of the regulating agency is fairly simple. It is a board or commission exercising quasi-judicial and rule-making authority. Generally there is one board covering the federal level or covering an entire state, though the commissioners may be augmented by hearing examiners directly responsible to the single board. Even in the licensing field, including health facilities and manpower licensing boards, the same pattern prevails with nearly all such licensing being a state-level function by a single special board or by a separate unit of the state health department.

The field of certification of need for health care facilities is developing differently, however, and the reason for the difference is quite clear. It is because of the fact that nearly all of these regulatory programs for health facilities development are being grafted upon the comprehensive health planning (CHP) programs in the various states. As a result, the certificate-of-need programs have gained certain further dimensions. First, they have automatically involved a large number of consumers and providers of health care on the local and state levels. Second, they have effectively broadened the review process itself to a "planning" viewpoint where multiple factors of community need may be taken into consideration. It is much too early in the development of the certificate-of-need programs to assess the impact of these planning elements in the system, but they are probably the dominant features of the programs as we see them now.

Nearly all of the enacted laws and filed (not passed) legislation in a total of thirty-nine states involved area-wide health planning councils in the review process. Most have also involved their state-level health planning councils. Nevertheless, the administration of the programs and the final decision on the granting or denial of a certificate is generally placed in the regular, traditional, governmental agency for health, the state health department. This is the case in fourteen of the twenty states. Only three states (California, Nevada, and Oregon) vest the final decision in the state CHP agency. Connecticut and Kentucky vest authority in new state

97

agencies created for the purpose. Kansas, Michigan, Minnesota and Massachusetts create new appeal boards to review decisions by the health departments.

In the great majority of states where administrative control has been placed in the state health departments, it has been done as a result of a very practical decision to seek governmental experience and expertise and the necessary staff to carry out the huge number of investigations of facilities required under the program. A great deal of data must be collected and analyzed. The health departments, because of their Hill-Burton planning and construction experience and their general licensing and inspection experience, have the expertise and the readily available staff already on salary and part of the state budget. These may require augmentation, but nothing like the expense and time necessary to set up an entirely new operation.

In New Jersey, the failure of the legislature to place the certificate-of-need program in the health department resulted in the only gubernatorial veto of any of the legislation in this field. In early 1971, Governor Cahill vetoed a comprehensive bill on certification of need because it was to be administered by the Department of Institutions and Agencies, a state unit responsible for the state mental hospitals, chronic disease hospitals, and prisons. The legislature amended the bill by transferring authority to the state Department of Health. The governor signed this bill in late April 1971, and it became effective sixteen weeks later.

In California, one of the few states to place the program under the state Comprehensive Health Planning Agency, a recent executive order by Governor Reagan moved the state CHP under a new "super agency" called the Office of Health. The effective date on the order is July 1, 1972.

The Review Process. For most people, the certificate-of-need system begins and ends, quite literally, with the process of review of individual applications for certification. If the applications are handled fairly and equitably, the participants and the public will consider the system itself to be properly administered. If the review is unfair, if politics prevail, the grumbling will grow and destroy the system.

There is great variety in the enacted laws in the twenty states. Some major themes can be noted, however. In the majority of states there is a system of review involving consideration of the views of the sub-state-level health or hospital planning groups composed of providers and consumers. Only in Arizona and Kentucky is the decision of the area-wide CHP agency on disapproval binding upon the state. In all of the other states the local review is advisory to the state level where it may be examined once or twice again. These states are California, Florida, Kansas, Massachusetts, Michigan, Minnesota, Nevada, New York, North Carolina, North Dakota, South Carolina, and Washington. In California, the first appeal from a local review is to the consumer members of another area-wide health planning council before the application reaches the state level.

98

The intention to utilize a local-level review of applications is spelled out in the statement of purpose in the Minnesota law: "It is the policy of this Act that decisions regarding the construction or modification of health care facilities should be based on the maximum possible participation on the local level by consumers of health care and elected officials, as well as providers directly concerned." [16] The Minnesota law is as good as its rhetoric. Its review provisions are among the best, if not the very best, of those I have examined. For example, the Minnesota law requires that the directors of facilities "intending to embark on a program of construction or modification of a health care facility" [17] notify the appropriate area-wide health planning agency of such an intention before engaging architects, or professional consultation, or any fund-raising services. The local planning group must in turn notify the state board of health and the state CHP agency. If the facility *fails* to give this notice, the local "b" agency may refuse even to consider a later proposal for a certificate of need. Obviously, the notice is intended as a means of beginning consultation with, and involvement of, the local planning agency at the earliest possible time. The 1972 Massachusetts law also requires notification before public solicitation of funds for construction, but is not so all-inclusive as the Minnesota law.

The Minnesota law goes on to provide a well-detailed set of procedures for the local review of applications. A public hearing is required, whether requested by the applicant or not. Notice is required to the community, and "any interested person" [18] is given an opportunity to be heard, to be represented by counsel, to present oral and written evidence, and to cross-examine witnesses at the hearing. A transcript is required and the agency must make findings of fact and present its recommendations and conclusions in writing. The review must conform in all respects to the Minnesota Administrative Procedure Act.

The California, Florida, and Kansas statutes are also well drawn in regard to procedural safeguards at the local level. All require hearings, the taking of evidence, and the making of findings and conclusions.

The great bulk of the states, however, give little or no attention to procedural or substantive matters concerning local review. In five states (Connecticut, Maryland, New Jersey, Oklahoma, and Rhode Island) there is no local review at all. Review is contemplated, but no hearing and no formal requirements for local review are imposed in eleven states (Arizona, Kentucky, Massachusetts, Michigan, Nevada, New York, North Carolina, North Dakota, Oregon, South Carolina, and Washington).

Procedural matters improve somewhat when the state level is reached, but most of the statutes are loosely drawn and unclear on issues which most lawyers in

---

[16] Minnesota Statutes, 1971, Chapter 628, Section 1.
[17] Ibid., Section 6.
[18] Ibid., Section 8(3).

the administrative law field would consider fundamental. It is presumed that administrative regulations will spell out procedural steps regarding the processing of applications. The adopted regulations which I have seen do attempt just such clarification.

None of the laws provides guidance on the weight to be given recommendations from the sub-state level. Twelve of the states require that the local area review of an application be conducted and completed before any consideration is given to the case on the state level. In five other states the review at the local level is simultaneous with consideration at the state level. It seems to me that initial review at the local level is much the preferable system. It provides greater assurance that the local views will receive full consideration at the state level, even if the local decision is only advisory and can be overturned by the state. A few laws refer to the state-level consideration as an "appeal" from the decision below (California and Kansas). Many merely require the state agency to consider the comments or recommendations of the local agency (Massachusetts, Michigan, New York, North Dakota, South Carolina, and Washington). It would seem clear that review in all of these states is *de novo,* that is, that the state agency hears the entire case and makes its own decision on the evidence. In the states where the local agency makes findings of fact and prepares a written opinion or conclusion supported by reasons, it can be hoped that the state agency will give some weight to these determinations.

The laws with regard to hearing requirements at the state level are diverse. The majority require a hearing only where there is a preliminary intention expressed to deny the certificate, or where the hearing is requested by the applicant, the local planning agency, or the state CHP agency. Some of the statutes seem to allow a request for a hearing by one of these interested parties but not by others, with no very clear reasons for the discrimination.

In New Jersey, for example, certificates are issued by the commissioner of health. However, he cannot deny a certificate without the "approval" of a health care administration (HCA) board, which has a number of functions in the state regarding health matters. The implication of this provision would seem to be that the commissioner can grant a certificate with or without board approval and with or without a hearing in his own discretion. The HCA board in New Jersey is, by the same section, required to hold a hearing on request of the applicant. In another provision, the HCA board itself cannot make a decision contrary to the recommendations of the state CHP council without giving the council or the applicant an opportunity for a hearing. The New Jersey law makes no mention of a local health planning agency review, and a local agency has no opportunity to request a hearing if its recommendations, if they are even considered, are not followed. Despite these omissions, there is a mention in the section on definitions of "referral" by the commissioner of applications for certificates of need to the area-wide planning agencies. The only hope for making sense out of the New Jersey law seems to me to be good administrative regulations.

An example of another odd discrimination is the North Dakota law. In that state there are three separate reviews by the area-wide CHP council, the state CHP council, and the state health department's health council with clear periods of time for consideration at each level. At the third level, we find the first statutory requirement of a hearing on the application. The hearing can be granted only *after* a decision has been rendered by the state health council approving or denying the application. In effect, it is a request for reconsideration. The hearing can be requested by the applicant, any other person who has filed an appearance in the case, or by the area-wide health planning agency involved. The state CHP council, on the other hand, is *not* allowed to request a hearing, the reverse of the situation in New Jersey.

Perhaps the strangest system of all is that of Kentucky. This state set up a special new board to be concerned with the issuance of certificates of need at the state level. It is called the Kentucky Health Facilities and Health Services Certificate of Need and Licensure Board. Its duties, as implied in its title, combine concern for initial licenses and certificates of need. It is a fifteen-member board composed of ten providers and five consumers. Certificates are issued by the board, which is also empowered to adopt and enforce criteria and procedures for determinations of need. This may sound like impressive authority, but the remainder of the 1972 law seems to circumscribe these powers considerably. Kentucky is one of the two states in the twenty which gives the area-wide agencies, called regional health planning councils, veto power over all certificates of need. The approval of the application on the regional level is required before it can be considered by the board. In addition, the decision of the regional body goes first to the state CHP council which is empowered to "ratify" the decision. Again, it would seem that a failure on the part of the state CHP council to ratify would stop the application and cause its disapproval. The law contains no details whatever on the requirements, substantive or procedural, for review of applications at any one of these three levels. All standards are left to adoption by the board itself. However, the criteria and procedures for certification of need must be "as developed by the State Health Planning Council. . . ." [19] It would seem, therefore, that it is the state CHP agency which actually prepares the "standards, rules and regulations" adopted and enforced by the board. This interpretation is reinforced by a section of the law describing the duties of the state and regional CHP groups as relating to the carrying out of such duties.[20] Again, the puzzling statutory structure can be greatly clarified by good administrative standards, although the statutory distribution of powers cannot be contradicted by interpretive regulations.

When it comes to administrative appeals and court review, the enacted certificate-of-need laws are again quite loose and unclear. Administrative procedure acts

---

[19] Senate Bill No. 283, Section 4(6) (1972).
[20] Ibid., Section 5(2).

in the various states may help to clarify these issues, but no particular guidance is given in most of the statutes.

As examples of unusual appeals mechanisms, those in California, Kansas, Minnesota, and Nevada are worthy of examination. California, as noted earlier, allows an initial appeal by an aggrieved applicant to an "appeals body" composed of the consumer members of an area-wide health planning council on the same level and previously designated by the state CHP agency. Area-wide boards cannot be "appeals bodies" for each other, but otherwise the state CHP agency can assign as it determines. The California law also allows one-third or more of the area-wide board to appeal the decision of its own majority. This appeal, however, goes directly to the state CHP council. The state CHP council is the final reviewer after a decision by an "appeals body." The law allows the use of a three-member hearing committee by the council with a majority of consumers. The ultimate decision, however, must be made by the full council.

The Kansas law also has a unique system of review. Appeals from decisions of the regional health planning agency are made directly to an "appeals panel." There is no other statutory review by any state agency and the certificate is issued or denied dependent upon the decision of the appeals panel. The panel is defined in the law as a board made up of two representatives designated by the state CHP agency and one representative designated by each of the approved regional health planning agencies in the state exclusive of the agency involved in the appeal. Each of the regional agencies receives a number. When an even-numbered region is involved in the appeal, all other even-numbered regions must name providers as their representatives on the appeal panel with the odd-numbered regions sending consumer representatives. For odd-numbered regions involved in an appeal, the selection procedure is reversed. The Kansas law provides specifically for a *de novo* review in the district court of the decisions of the appeals panel. It is the only certificate-of-need law among the twenty specifically providing for *de novo* judicial review, though it can probably be implied in many of the others. No state specifically denies court review of certificate-of-need determinations.

One other recently enacted law deserves mention at this point in regard to review procedures. This is the law passed in Florida during early May 1972 to become effective on July 1, 1973. Its provisions have caused concern among Floridians interested in a stronger law. The law establishes a so-called "advisory certificate of need." It is defined in the law as "a written advisory statement issued by an areawide council evidencing community need or lack of need for a new, converted, expanded, or otherwise significantly modified health facility." [21] The advisory statement is sent to the state Bureau of Community Medical Services Planning. This bureau has the authority to issue or deny a certificate of need after considering the advisory statement and apparently after conducting its own review.

---

[21] Combined Senate-House Bill No. 3152, Section 3(4).

The statute goes on to provide that the decision of the bureau "shall be final when all rights of appeal have been exhausted." [22] The statute provides no methods of appeal, however. The next section of the law then asserts that the Division of Health of the state of Florida in exercising its authority to issue licenses to health care facilities "shall duly consider the advisory certificate-of-need study required by this act, although the recommendation in said study shall not be binding upon the division." [23] This section is most puzzling. It has been viewed by some Florida authorities as making the entire certificate-of-need system merely advisory on the Division of Health. This may be the case, but the law as written does not make this clear. First, the statement of legislative intent in the Florida law asserts that its purpose is to provide that "health care facilities shall not change the scope of those services without the *approval* and *authorization of the health planning agency*" (emphasis supplied). Second, the only *advisory* certificate of need is issued at the local level. The state-level bureau issues a full certificate which is specifically designated a *final decision* according to the law unless reversed upon appeal. The state's Division of Health is allowed to override only the *advisory* certificate-of-need *study,* not the certificate actually issued by the bureau. Also, this power of overriding is applicable only in a license-issuance case. Apparently, where the facility aleady has a license to operate and is seeking merely to modify its facilities or services, it would be required to seek the certificate from the bureau and could not take action without it. The fact that the local-level determination of need is only advisory is not unusual, as noted earlier. Only two of the twenty states, Arizona and Kentucky, give veto power to the local health planning agencies.

I am concerned that so many states allow appeals from decisions on certificates of need only where the certificate is *denied*. This is an example of rather myopic legalistic thinking. It assumes that grievances can only arise out of the facilities applicant's own loss of a financial interest in construction or expansion of his property. Actually the central theme in this legislation is the public interest in stopping unnecessary construction. It is when a certificate is granted, not when it is denied, that this interest could be compromised. Therefore, avenues of appeal from decisions to *grant* certificates should be opened up and made available to groups representing the public interest such as the state CHP agency or other community groups or individuals.

Health Planning and Standards of Review. The certificate-of-need programs are too fresh in all states to provide any measure of how the reviews will actually be made, what additional standards will be worked out and applied, and what the effect will be of integrating the process with comprehensive health planning.

---

[22] Ibid., Section 6(7).
[23] Ibid., Section 7.

The statutes themselves are not of any great help in answering these questions. All of the systems except those in Connecticut, New York, and Rhode Island are interlocked with the health planning programs. In New York State, the certificate-of-need program preceded CHP by some years and has not as yet been fully integrated with it. However, the New York program is linked with local hospital planning groups. The situation is similar in Rhode Island where there are no area-wide CHP agencies.

Despite their ties to health planning, all of the certification systems are essentially reactive; that is, they come into operation only on the initiative of a local facility which contemplates a change in its structures, services, or programs. If the review process itself is also passive, the handling of applications will be no different than any other quasi-judicial decision making. Determinations will be made on the basis of the evidence presented by the applicant and what little independent evidence is produced by the agency itself. No local agencies have large staffs. Their capacity to conduct independent investigations may be quite limited unless they can mobilize other community resources to join in the process and unless the general health planning programs and priority setting of the agencies can be related directly to the review process on individual certification.

In the legislation itself, a largely passive review system at the local level is implied in many, if not most, of the laws. This posture is characterized in the laws where the information must be furnished by the applicants themselves. There is frequently a long list of requirements, not merely concerning the facility itself, but its impact upon the community and other facilities, and on the community's need for new construction, service, or program. In some of the laws, the criteria to be applied by the reviewing groups are no more comprehensive than the information required to be furnished by the applicant. In a few states the term "public need" is left undefined with only the expectation that administrative regulations may spell it out.

In some of the states, the law which established the certificate-of-need program also constituted the first official recognition of the comprehensive health planning agencies under state law. Where this was the case, the law was more apt to integrate the certification program and the planning functions by such devices as requiring the applicant to conform to the "state plan" for comprehensive health, or to the local plan, or to the general objectives of health planning. The Arizona law, for example, requires applicants to conform to the "state plan." [24] The plan is defined in the law as "the plan for construction and modernization of health care institutions formulated by the Department in conformity with the State Comprehensive Health Plan. . . ." [25] The Michigan law has a similar provision. Oregon, Maryland, and Washington have provisions requiring applicants to conform to

---

[24] Laws of Arizona, 1971, Chapter 196, Article 2, Section 36-421 (A) (f).
[25] Ibid., Section 36-401(21).

area-wide plans. The Michigan law does not mention compliance with the area-wide plan, but uses much broader language requiring the state in reviewing applications to consider "rules, regulations and standards adopted by appropriate local and regional areawide comprehensive planning agencies which reflect the conditions, problems and resources of the various areas represented by these agencies. . . ." [26]

The standards in the Oregon law are particularly comprehensive and give specific notice to planning factors. The state-level health planning authority is required when reviewing an application for a certificate of need to take into consideration the following:

(a) Recommendations of the areawide health planning authorities.

(b) The relationship of the proposal to the areawide health plan.

(c) The need for health care services in the area or the requirements of the defined population.

(d) The availability and adequacy of health care services in facilities which are currently serving the defined population and which conform to state standards.

(e) The need for special equipment and services in the area which are not reasonably and economically accessible to the defined population.

(f) The need for research and educational facilities.

(g) The probable economies and improvement in service that may be derived from the operation of joint central services or from joint, cooperative, or shared health resources which are accessible to the defined population.

(h) The availability of sufficient manpower in the professional disciplines required to maintain the facility.

(i) The plans for and development of comprehensive health services and facilities for the defined population to be served. Such services may be either direct or indirect through formal affiliation with other health programs in the area and shall include preventive diagnostic treatment and rehabilitation services.

(j) Whether or not the applicant has obtained all relevant approvals, licenses or consents required by law for its incorporation or establishment.

(k) The needs of members, subscribers and enrollees of institutions and health care plans which operate or support particular hospitals for the purpose of rendering health care to such members, subscribers, and enrollees.

(l) In the case of an application by a hospital established or operated by a religious body or denomination, the needs of the members of such religious body or denomination for care and treatment in accordance with their religious or ethical convictions may be considered to be public need.

(m) The proposed facility will be adequately funded. [27]

---

[26] Michigan House Bill No. 4949, Section 5a(j).
[27] Laws of Oregon, 1971, Chapter 730, Section 16(1).

In the opinion of this examiner, the Oregon law quoted above provides the best set of review criteria in any of the laws of the twenty states. It ranks consideration of the recommendations of the area-wide agency and conformity to the area-wide health plan even before an independent consideration of the "need" for the services in the area. Also, the Oregon list contains factors not specifically mentioned in the law of any other state, such as the need for research and educational facilities and the needs of subscribers to health care plans.

A question might be raised about the advisability of providing detailed statutory criteria for review of applications for certificates of need. I believe that the laws are at a particular stage of development where the articulation of standards can be very helpful to the entire certification process. If public regulation is to be imposed on the health care industry, as these laws so provide, then the statutes ought to contain safeguards to require open consideration of different views and interests. This is the aim of the formalities. The procedures are intended to create the appearance and the reality of fundamental fairness in the process.

I believe that the careful articulation and ranking of criteria to be used in considering applications for construction or expansion of health care facilities is a necessary step in making the entire system workable. There are a number of reasons for taking special pains to develop criteria in this field. First, the system is intended to involve *consumers* at all levels in the determinations of need. These consumers will not be trained or experienced in the health field, and most will not be trained or experienced in law either. They will be aided in participating in the process and their voices will be heard more effectively if the basis for the decisions —the criteria for review—are fully articulated and ranked. Second, the criteria are the main mechanisms for requiring an *integration of the health planning process and the certification process*. Otherwise, the decisions may deteriorate into the passive review of evidence submitted by the applicants as indicated earlier. The criteria set forth in the Oregon law militate against myopic, individualized, decision making. Third, it is most important to spell out criteria for review in full when the new regulatory program is intended to accomplish *basic reform* in the practices of the field and where the special interests will be exerting heavy pressure to be allowed to follow their traditional methods of operation. For example, hospitals and other health care facilities are not in the habit of cooperating or of sharing their facilities with each other. These new laws are intended to foster and sometimes to force cooperation and sharing. The criteria for review spell out these objectives, which are mentioned nowhere else in the law.

The last reason I would mention for taking special care in formulating review criteria is the fact that the local administering agencies, the area-wide health planning councils, were not created as public regulatory agencies. They were not organized along the lines of licensing or review bodies. They are not groups of lawyers with fact-finding bodies or investigational staffs. They are broadly conceived planning organizations, policy-making boards, composed of a consumer (nonprovider) majority and a provider minority. The interest of these boards is in the health of the community viewed in very wide terms. These agencies are generally staffed by personnel trained in social work, social and behavioral science, or public health. Rarely have these staffs any training in law or in decision making and investigatory methods in public regulatory systems. It is therefore advisable to provide these councils and their staffs with more structure, more procedural safeguards, more articulated criteria for decision making than might be necessary in the average regulatory agency organized and manned by attorneys, hearing officers, and trained regulatory personnel.

Some Concluding Comments

The above pages may have contained more information on certificate-of-need laws for health care facilities than most readers really wanted to know. Nevertheless, it seems to me that the catalog needed to be completed. Emphasis was placed upon the actual language of the laws and upon the skill in draftsmanship, or lack of it, in the hope that the analysis may be helpful to the many remaining states where legislation has yet to be enacted.

In a general way, it can be said that nearly all of the enacted laws are basically adequate for their purposes. None of them is, however, a wholly satisfactory model for other states without such laws to follow. The best provisions on the different aspects of the law, as indicated in earlier pages, would have to be selected from among at least seven or eight states. Some of the laws give evidence of hasty preparation. Some of the laws, such as those in New York, Rhode Island, and Connecticut, do not integrate comprehensive health planning into their operations.

It may be useful to provide a brief listing of some general issues which seem to me to continue to present difficulties of a legal nature to the development of certificate-of-need programs. I would suggest the following:

(1) The laws enacted give very little evidence of having benefited from the experience of other certificate-of-need regulatory programs in other industries. The laws and what few commentaries I have seen seem to start at "year one" in a new field as if no other program provides any guidance. Is this actually the case? Is the matter of health care so much more complex, or simpler, than utilities regulation or insurance regulation?

(2) The laws present a great variety of "threshold" or jurisdictional issues of coverage. Are there areas of the health care facilities environment which should *not* be controlled? Should all doctors' offices and clinics be included? Should federal and state institutions be controlled in the same way and under the same system as private facilities? Does any minimum capital limitation make sense, particularly when linked with a requirement, as in most states, that certificates be obtained when even a single bed is added?

(3) Can the roles of "health planner" and "government regulator" be reconciled in the CHP program, particularly at the local level? Will the pressure of numbers of applications to review warp the local programs toward a regulatory posture and toward concern only for facilities planning to the detriment of other health issues in the communities?

(4) Will the local and state health planning agencies, with their consumer and provider boards and with their nonlegally trained professional staffs handle applications fairly and with due process of law, particularly under the loosely drawn laws now on the books? The habit of many of the professionals in the health field is for decision making behind closed doors and without much demand to hear witnesses or to prepare justifications for their determinations. The NIH review system for scientific grants is the process most familiar to the field. It has served its purposes extremely well and has been greatly respected. However, it is not an open system and does not involve consumer interests. Social and behavioral scientists and social welfare personnel generally are not trained in the requirements of due process of law and open decision making. Most of the staffs of the comprehensive health planning programs are drawn from these fields.

(5) All of the certificate-of-need legislation has passed through the legislatures on the constantly reiterated promise that they will reduce the costs of hospitalization and other health and nursing care and will bring rational planning to the health care facilities field. Can these objectives be met under the current laws? Can costs and charges be reduced *solely* by controlling growth in the supply of facilities and the capital invested in facilities? Must not other aspects of health costs also be controlled? Even in regard to construction and services, can rational planning succeed, or even be called "planning," if it is merely reactive to the institutions' own plans to increase facilities or services? If, on the other hand, the health planners are given a more aggressive role to change the health care delivery systems in their areas, how will this be accomplished by law, particularly by due process of law? For example, can a planning agency refuse to allow a private hospital to *reduce* beds, even though it has a good financial reason for doing so, because the community "needs" the beds? On the other side of the coin, could the planners force the closing of what they assert are unnecessary facilities or services without being required to compensate the private institution for its property loss?

(6) I indicated earlier that the certificate-of-need laws show little evidence of having gained from the experience in other similar regulatory programs for other industries. One could make the same observation about learning from experience with other legal decision-making systems. I commented earlier on the lack of procedural safeguards for fairness in most of the laws. I have also noticed some confusing systems of review and appeal in the statutes. The general trend, however, is to treat all applications alike and to start at the area-wide CHP level in all cases. This may be simple and it may encourage local participation most clearly, but some applications may not fit this pattern. Not every facility serves only the geo-

graphical area covered by the health planning council in which its facility is located. The area served, or that which it could or should serve, may be quite different. It may be that on some applications, two or more area-wide councils should be involved in the initial review. There may also be some facilities which serve a very wide geographic area, or the entire state, or a multi-state region, or they may have national significance. Should such applications receive a local review by one area-wide council? What issues should that council consider? Can it use its power to force a state or nationally oriented institution to give a much higher percentage of its services to the local community? In terms of criteria for review, should the state level be allowed to reverse a local determination, or to ignore its recommendations, on grounds not considered by the local groups?

(7) Notice was taken earlier of the fact that these laws have been strongly supported in most states by the hospital organizations themselves. Such a situation may make some people suspicious about the impact of the program when it is so clearly influenced by the groups most directly affected by it. Will this quickly become another of the regulatory programs dominated by the very industry it was intended to regulate? Will the program become the tool of the established health care providers to prevent change and competition in the field? These are serious issues. Yet, all outward appearances seem to indicate a genuine desire on the part of the health care institutions to cooperate and to allow this regulatory system to work. The participation of consumers in the review process should help to avoid co-opting by the industry also. Perhaps most serious, however, is the problem of continuing financial support for the CHP programs on the sub-state level. The raising of voluntary dollars in local communities can be a serious problem for the planning agencies if they take an aggressive role in regulatory programs. A more secure method of financing CHP at the local level and also of covering the entire state with such agencies with a certain minimum staff and technical support seems to me a necessary part of the future planning for certificate-of-need programs and other regulatory systems which may follow in the health care field.

Summary

This paper has been a review of the certificate-of-need laws for health care facilities now on the books of twenty states: Arizona, California, Connecticut, Florida, Kansas, Kentucky, Maryland, Massachusetts, Michigan, Minnesota, Nevada, New Jersey, New York, North Carolina, North Dakota, Oklahoma, Oregon, Rhode Island, South Carolina, and Washington. There have also been similar bills filed but not enacted in an additional nineteen states.

The political trend of these laws was examined in some detail. The basic purpose of the laws would seem to be the same in all jurisdictions, that is, to help to control the costs of health care and to bring orderly planning to the development of health care facilities and services in the future. The backers of the laws have been hospital groups, comprehensive health planning organizations, and state health and insurance departments. Opposition in some states has come from medical professional groups, proprietary hospitals, and nursing home organizations.

The constitutional foundation for certificate-of-need laws was also examined. There seems to be little doubt that regulation can be imposed on the health care industry as it has been upon other fields over the decades of this century. Analogies to the public utilities field are common in the literature. Two lower court opinions in New York and California were examined which upheld regulation in the health facilities field through certificate-of-need laws.

The remainder of the paper provided an analysis of certain major features in the programs enacted in each of the states. The first feature examined was the coverage of different types of facilities. It was found that most of the laws attempt to cover all health care facilities. Michigan, Oregon and Rhode Island cover only hospitals while Oklahoma covers only nursing homes. North Carolina exempts many outpatient types of facilities.

The next aspect of the laws discussed was the coverage of types of construction and services requiring certification. Much variation was found. All laws are tied to construction plans of the facilities. Thirteen states have no statutory minimum capital amount for required review. The other seven states have limits ranging from $50,000 to $350,000. Many of the states apply controls when there is any contemplated increase in bed capacity, no matter what the construction cost. Kentucky and South Carolina require certification for decreases as well as increases in bed capacity. In eight states the law specifically requires certification where there is a change in services.

Administration of the programs is also examined. A key feature in most states is the interrelationship of the certification process with the state's comprehensive health planning programs.

The next major feature of the laws which was examined was the process of review of individual applications. This was found to be a very complex and often unclear area which will require administrative regulations to sort out and clarify. Most of the laws provide for an initial review of applications at the local level, and, in the case of Arizona and Kentucky, denial at the local level is final. In five states (Connecticut, Maryland, New Jersey, Oklahoma, and Rhode Island) there is no provision for local review.

The last aspect of the laws examined was the criteria for review. It was found that most states do provide some statutory standards, but many are basically passive reviews of the applications and the evidence presented by the petitioning facility. In some states, however, a broader role as a health planner is contemplated for the reviewers on both the local and state levels, particularly where the certificate-of-need law is also the same law which recognizes and establishes the state's comprehensive health planning program.

In a concluding section some overall comments and queries are put about the system as a whole. As is typical of most such papers, the questions are left largely unanswered, but are hopefully provocative of further study.

CERTIFICATES OF NEED FOR HEALTH CARE FACILITIES: A DISSENTING VIEW

Richard A. Posner

As Professor Curran's useful survey in the previous chapter reveals, many states have recently enacted and others are considering the enactment of statutes that require that a certificate of need be obtained from a state health agency, normally the state department of health, as a prerequisite to the construction or expansion of hospitals or other health care facilities. The standard governing the granting of such certificates is whether the public need or, in some formulations, the public necessity and convenience would be served by the construction or expansion. The procedures used to decide the question are those generally employed in administrative adjudication.

As Curran suggests, the concept and often the very language of certificate-of-need laws are borrowed from public utility regulation and are an aspect of a broader movement to classify institutional providers of health care as public utilities. The people who propose the imposition of public utility controls in the health care field are typically quite ignorant of experience with those controls in their traditional settings. Part of the function of this paper is simply to report on that experience. Elsewhere I have argued that the general proposal to treat health care providers as public utilities is unsound because it ignores both the failure of public utility regulation in its traditional settings and the differences between those settings and the health care field that make such regulation even less likely to succeed in the latter setting.[1] Here I shall focus on the appropriateness of importing one feature of public utility regulation, control over new construction, into the health care field. I discuss first the experience with such controls in traditional public utility settings, and second which way the differences between those settings and the health care field appear to cut.

Construction Controls in Public Utility Industries

A natural gas pipeline company may not extend its line and a telephone company may not lay a new coaxial cable unless each first obtains from the relevant regulatory agency a certificate of public convenience and necessity. The rationale for im-

---

[1] See Richard A. Posner, "Regulatory Aspects of National Health Insurance Plans," *University of Chicago Law Review,* vol. 39, no. 1 (Fall 1971), pp. 8-12.

posing such a requirement is that it is necessary to prevent overbuilding. The rationale would be unconvincing as applied to the usual, nonregulated firm. Whether it is a monopolist or has competitors, it can only lose money by building facilities that are not cost justified; and it is likely to have much better cost information than any regulatory agency. Regulation, however, introduces various distortions into the incentive structure of firms that weaken the presumption that they will act to minimize their costs.[2] An important example arises from the policy that many regulatory agencies follow of fostering internal subsidization, whereby some services are priced below cost and the resulting deficit is recouped by pricing other services above cost. Such a pricing system, which I have elsewhere characterized as "taxation by regulation,"[3] creates an incentive for other firms to initiate or expand service in the high-price markets even though their costs are higher than those of existing firms or facilities. To illustrate, if the cost to an existing firm is $5 per unit but it charges $10 in order to defray a subsidy elsewhere, another firm would be attracted to the market even if its cost were $6 per unit. Given this incentive to construct uneconomical facilities, there is an argument for subjecting construction proposals to public scrutiny in order to prevent "cream-skimming," which not only is uneconomical, if the cream skimmer's costs are higher, but also subverts the system of internal subsidies by reducing the profits that can be obtained in the lucrative markets.

Quite apart from any genuine danger of wasteful duplication of facilities, construction controls in the regulated industries often serve to reinforce cartelization among the regulated firms. In the absence of such controls, members of the cartel would be tempted to cheat by expanding output beyond the quota fixed for each, and if any of them yielded to this temptation the cartel could eventually collapse. Control of construction can be used to limit expansion of output. If the cartel dominates the regulatory agency, as is unfortunately often the case, construction will not be permitted where the result would be overcapacity from the standpoint of maximizing cartel profits.

The "dark" side of construction controls helps to explain why claims of "overbuilding" are so common in regulated industries and provides a plausible, although spurious basis for construction controls. Any industry that desires cartelization believes as a corollary that it has excess capacity, for the optimum output (and hence capacity) under cartelization is smaller than that under competition. Furthermore, in the short run, cartelization does create excess capacity. The capacity that was appropriate to a competitive output is too large for a monopolistic output. Eventually capacity will be reduced to the level appropriate to the smaller

---

[2] For a detailed discussion of the incentive effects of regulation, see Richard A. Posner, "Natural Monopoly and Its Regulation," *Stanford Law Review*, vol. 21 (1969), pp. 548, 597-606.
[3] Richard A. Posner, "Taxation by Regulation," *Bell Journal of Economics and Management Science*, vol. 2 (1971), p. 22.

output but there will be a transitional period in which the industry appears plagued with excess capacity.

I have thus far assumed that construction controls are applied to firms already in the business which wish to expand their output. An even more important anticompetitive consequence of construction controls is that they provide a means of barring new entry into the cartelized industry. The monopoly price established by a cartel makes entry highly profitable. New firms are attracted which, in their efforts to gain a foothold in the market, enlarge the output of the market, with the result that the monopoly price can no longer be obtained. This problem can be eliminated if entry is barred. Entry can be barred by an obliging regulatory agency that equates public need to the private greed of the existing firms in the market.[4]

Even if the regulatory agency is not a captive of the regulated firms, construction controls reduce the likelihood of new entry by increasing the costs of entry. The costs, both in direct outlays and in time, of persuading even a well-meaning agency to grant a certificate of public convenience and necessity to a new firm are often very substantial.[5]

Application of Construction Controls to Hospitals

To what extent may the foregoing analysis be applicable to the health care field? The "cream-skimming" rationale of construction controls has at least some application, in view of the competition between charitable and public institutions, on the one hand, and proprietary institutions on the other. The typical charitable or public hospital is compelled or assumes an obligation to provide unremunerative services; it attempts to recoup at least part of the costs by charging very high prices to more affluent patients. This situation creates an attractive market opportunity for the proprietary hospital. By offering only remunerative services at a price slightly below that charged by its "full service" competitors, it can attract profitable business from those competitors. Such a practice may, however, be wasteful. The proprietary's costs may be higher than those of the full service institution, even after allowing for the artificial cost difference created by public and charitable institutions' privileged tax status.

Whether this is a serious problem or not is unclear; without further information, however, my instinct is to reject this basis for imposing construction controls. By hypothesis, the controls would bear more heavily on proprietary institutions; they are the potential "cream skimmers," whose proposals for construction would

---

[4] The literature on the use of control over new facilities or entry to limit competition is extensive. For some examples, see Posner, "Natural Monopoly and Its Regulation," p. 612, footnote 125.

[5] See Robert W. Gerwitz, "Natural Gas Production: A Study of Costs of Regulation," *Journal of Law and Economics,* vol. 5 (1962), p. 69.

be scrutinized with a hostile eye.[6] In view of the widespread charges that the hospital industry is permeated with inefficient managerial practices, there are grave risks in limiting the competition of profit maximizers. They may point the way toward more efficient methods of hospital management. If this is a serious possibility, it seems foolish to discourage their entry by subjecting them to the costs involved in procuring permission to build a facility from a public agency which is concerned with the effect of cream-skimming on the revenues of charitable and public institutions.

The cartel theory of construction controls may also have some relevance in the health facility context. The practice of medicine is riddled with monopolistic restrictions, and it is at least possible that one method of effectuating physicians' cartels is by limiting the number of hospital beds. This would prevent a physician from expanding output by treating more patients than the local medical society believed optimal in terms of maximizing physicians' income. I do not suggest that this is in fact a motivation behind the drive for construction controls; but it is a possibility. I may be unduly suspicious, but I am also troubled by the fact that the American Hospital Association supports construction controls.

To all this, the proponent of certificate-of-need laws will answer that there are special, and especially compelling, reasons to fear that without such laws immense resources will be squandered on unneeded hospital and other health care facilities. There are two arguments. The first is that the way in which health care services increasingly are sold in this country undermines incentives to refrain from creating excess capacity. Health care services are normally sold not to the consumer but to an insurer, whether Blue Cross-Blue Shield, a private insurance company, or the federal government, and these third parties seem to lack either the incentive or ability to minimize the price they pay.

The second argument is that most hospitals are nonprofit institutions and hence lack the incentives to minimize costs that profit maximizers have. This argument is easily overstated. In order to build a hospital, the sponsors must convince either wealthy donors or some public agency to advance the necessary funds. It is not obvious to me that the competition for such funds is less intense than, say, the competition among ordinary commercial enterprises for construction capital. Moreover, nonpublic hospitals, at least, rarely raise from donors, public or private, funds sufficient for maintenance and operating costs as well as construction. They thus remain dependent to a significant degree on fees from patients and, if patients paid, competition among hospitals would squeeze out the least efficient. So we are back to the first argument.

The first argument is a bit odd, for it runs counter to the normal assumption that a large, knowledgeable purchaser can drive a better bargain than a single indi-

---

[6] It is relevant here to recollect Joel May's finding that health agencies are generally hostile to proprietary hospitals. See above, Part I.

vidual. In any event it is only an argument. Although many people consider it almost axiomatic that there is substantial excess capacity in the hospital industry today, there appear to be serious difficulties involved in deciding when capacity is excess. Of course examples can be adduced, but it is with central tendencies that we should be concerned. A typical allegation of overbuilding is that there are too many intensive-care centers and many of them are underutilized. Suppose an intensive-care center located in a rural hospital is "underutilized" in the sense that, on average, only one of its ten beds is occupied. Does it follow that the intensive-care center should not have been built? Surely not. The value of the center to those who utilize it is very great. Is it clear that the center should only have been built with a capacity for two beds, or one? Again no. The marginal cost of the additional beds may be slight. And those beds have some value, either as standby facilities in the event of a public disaster or as peak-load facilities; perhaps once a year, on average, the intensive-care unit is fully occupied.

Determining optimal capacity is probably more difficult in the hospital industry than in the typical regulated industry. In both contexts, the difficulty lies in the fact (mentioned above) that the existence of unused capacity cannot be equated with the existence of excess capacity, given that the optimal amount of standby or peak-load capacity must be greater than zero. In the medical context it may be much greater than zero due to the value that people place on immediate availability of medical services and to the difficulty of predicting when the need for immediate access to hospital facilities will arise.

Even if it were unquestioned that there was a serious problem of excess capacity in the hospital industry, it would not follow that construction controls are the answer. From what we know of experience with them in the public utility industries, they should be viewed as a last resort, after all alternatives have been considered and rejected. In the present context, there is an obvious alternative, and that is to change the methods of pricing health care services that foster excess capacity. Medical insurance provides greater benefits for institutional than for ambulatory care, thereby creating an incentive to substitute institutional care even when ambulatory care would be more economical; this disincentive feature of medical insurance, public or private, can and should be changed. Another example: fee-for-service pricing by physicians creates an incentive for the physician to advise the patient to undergo costly procedures, often involving hospitalization. This incentive can be reduced by fostering the competition of those alternative systems of pricing medical services, such as that used by prepaid group practice, whose development is at present deterred by state laws regulating the practice of medicine. This is not the place to review the range of inexpensive alternatives that are available for reducing the incentive to overuse hospital facilities, which in turn creates an incentive to build unnecessary facilities. Suffice it to say that the case for construction controls has not been made.

COMMENTARY ON THE PAPERS

Frank P. Grad

I have a sense that the battle lines have been rather clearly drawn. Essentially the agenda of this conference consists of the entire problem of planning and regulation as against the free market.

Of course, planning and regulation are in bad repute right now. Basically it is the plaint of the disappointed lover, I would say: We have done so much planning, and we have tried so hard, but the probelms are still here. I have encountered this attitude in just about every one of the fields that I have touched on recently. You can hear it repeatedly in the field of housing; we have planned so hard, but we have still got the slums. You can hear it in the field of health; we have poured so much money into planning, but the health problems are still with us. In the field of the environment, all of the regulations do not do us any good; we have still got the dirty rivers and the dirty air, and we should move from direct regulation toward institution of effluent charges, because market forces are going to solve it all for us.

And thus, having been so thoroughly disappointed in planning and in regulation, we have in this year of our Lord 1972 rediscovered the wisdom of the nineteenth century, and we have welcomed the return of the invisible hand. I find myself totally surounded by members of the "Chicago School," and I wish I were somewhere else.

But let me continue. Let me start by pointing out the general technique of downgrading planning and regulation. First, you take an imperfect, messy, troublesome, but extremely "real" system; you examine the system of regulations, and you examine the system of planning; you find that it is messy—nobody ever said it was not. You find that its problems are really troublesome, infrangible, and difficult to deal with; answers are not easy to come by.

And then you take this real and difficult and messy system and you juxtapose it, compare it with a smooth, logical, theoretical, and neat market system; of course the theoretical system invariably comes out on top. The technique is used regularly, and it is with this blunt and very general analysis in the background that I would like to review the papers that we have heard.

Let me say first that these papers—and my reference includes the May and Neuhauser papers as well—are excellent, informative and sensitive; I enjoyed reading them very much, though I do not agree with a great deal of what I have read. Obviously, you cannot disagree with facts. We have a full truckload of factual information, of useful compilations and compendia of factual data. I do strongly disagree, however, with quite a few of the conclusions drawn from them.

I agree, on the whole, with Professor Curran's paper. I think he has done us all an enormous service by delivering a discerning and acute analysis of the state certificate-of-need legislation, or franchising as it has been called. And I think before you deal with this field, you ought to know what the legislation is all about. It is a legislative field, and it is significant that there is legislation on the books which tries to articulate criteria of public need. This is in and of itself a considerable step forward and indicates that this legislation, though it is as yet fragmentary and rudimentary, is beginning to grow in sophistication, and in the recognition of the realities of the field. Professor Curran properly views certificate-of-need legislation as part of the total health delivery planning effort.

Now, I think there is no question that if we need planning, then we need more and better planning. Obviously much of the planning that we have had thus far has not been very effective. The next question to be asked is do we therefore give up the whole effort and pour out the baby with the bath water? Or do we say instead that the planning we have had thus far has not been effective enough and therefore we ought to do better, different, more informed, more sophisticated kinds of planning?

Actually, while I follow the logic of Professor Havighurst's argument that blames the intrusions of the regulatory system for causing distortions in an otherwise free market system, I nonetheless have a sense that it is the basically unplanned system we have had thus far that has gotten us where we are. In effect, planning is an attempt to get us out of the mess. And, indeed, that we are in a mess is not subject to any great doubt.

There cannot be any significant disagreement with the contention that there is need for government money in health care—and it is inconceivable as a political matter that government will support a health care system without controls and without insisting on a rational application of the funds. And the rational application of funds, by whatever name you call it, is planning. And planning, as the next corollary, also involves some regulation, some controls on entry into the system. Whether you like the particular franchising laws that are currently on the books or whether you agree with the older licensure laws, there are very few regulatory systems that do not have some kind of provisions regarding entry into the system. Indeed, it would be difficult to think of a regulatory system that does not provide for licensure or registration or for some other way of finding out who in the regulated field is doing what, with what and to whom.

I am not all that happy about disagreeing with Professor Posner, who is also a law professor and who calls his paper "A Dissenting View." One thing is clear to me, Professor Posner. Yours is not a dissenting view; it is the new orthodoxy which you are espousing—because the new orthodoxy has it that utility regulation has been a failure. I would like to take Professor Posner's course on this. I know that the criticism of utility regulation is rampant right now, and that nobody is very happy with the way things are being run. But the question I would like to raise is, what is the cure? What are the alternatives?

It is an area which is very difficult to get at. We agree that the present system leaves much to be desired, but we have not heard much about alternatives. I would like to hear something about alternatives not only in the utility field, of course, but also in the health field.

One of the questions which Professor Posner's paper raises is the risk of cartelization which is enhanced by regulation of entry. Obviously cream-skimming is a problem in any oligopolistic system, in any cartel system, and franchising may well contribute to this. I also agree that the concept of excess capacity is a very troublesome one to deal with. But I do not believe that we are really talking about excess capacity. I think that we are talking about maldistributions of capacity, capacity which is excessive in some places and inadequate in other places; in effect, entry regulations try to equalize capacity rather than merely to cut down on excess capacity.

By doing away with planning, by doing away with entry regulations, we set the stage for the free-market alternative. But experience has shown that the free markets steadfastly and traditionally have refused to remain free or pure. It takes quite some doing by way of regulation—including antitrust regulation, regulation of unfair competition, regulations to make sure that the consumer is adequately informed, regulations to make sure that there are no built-in subsidies in other parts of the system—to make free markets work. In other words, by the time you get all done, the machinery to keep that market pure is likely to be quite as ponderous as the regulatory machinery which it seeks to displace. And, with that in mind, I would think that the regulatory system we have going, though it is not very good, is the best we have been able to accomplish at the present time, and I think that we ought to try to improve it, rather than abandon it altogether.

As a matter of political realities, the states that are presently going in the direction of entry and franchising legislation are not doing so because they have been duped by some peculiar combination of oligopolistic health providers. They are doing so in response to a real need. I think that to the extent that problems in the health field will persist, to the extent that public funds will continue to be poured into the health care system, regulation of and entry regulations into the health field will certainly follow the pouring in of public money.

The question is not so much, shall we plan or shall we not plan?—because the allocation of public monies involves planning decisions. The question is quite simply, how shall we plan most effectively?

DISCUSSION

On Professor Grad's Comments

PROFESSOR POSNER: I would like to make a few comments on Professor Grad's comments, which I thought set back discussion of the problem by quite a bit. Pavlov trained a dog to salivate when he rang a bell, and somebody trained Professor Grad to foam at the mouth when the word "Chicago" is mentioned.

To begin with, he could not have read the papers—because in none of the papers as written nor in anything said by anyone today was there any suggestion that the proper comparison is between a perfectly functioning market and a set of imperfect real-world health planning institutions. As Professor Calabresi said earlier, the proper comparison is between an imperfect market and imperfect alternative arrangements; or, more realistically, between varying degrees of public control and private choice.

If you strip Professor Grad's comments of their endearing jocular tone, there is no logical or factual core. For example, he says that, sure, excess capacity is hard to define, but the problem is not excess capacity; it is maldistribution—excess capacity some places, inadequate capacity other places—and the function of social control is to eliminate the imbalance. But obviously, in order to eliminate the imbalance, you have to be able to identify the areas that have excess capacity. And in order to identify the areas with excess capacity, you would have to have a working, operational definition of excess capacity. And I have said—and he has not disagreed—that coming up with such a definition is extremely difficult.

Let me also comment on the question of alternatives. It is odd that Professor Grad should have faulted the participants for not proposing alternatives when he began by saying that they all had this pat alternative, which is the perfect market.

In fact, as I have suggested in my paper but did not mention in the oral summary, it seems to me that there are alternative methods of trying to avoid problems of mislocation of facilities; in particular, one can alter the incentive structure in the indstury. There are methods of pricing medical services that create incentives to economize, which total fee-for-service pricing does not seem to do. Prepaid group practice schemes are, however, inhibited by various state laws and the customs of the medical profession, and quite probably by a certain amount of collusion among physicians. These impediments to giving prepaid group practice a fair chance ought to be eliminated.

If you want to facilitate the introduction of new alternatives into the medical profession—forms of providing service that might provide superior incentives to economize, such as prepaid group practice or health maintenance organizations— one thing you would want to do is to relax the traditional prohibition against advertising because, whatever the field, a new firm or a firm with a new service is going to find it very difficult to attract customers if it is not permitted to communicate information and persuasion.

So, I think there are alternatives which would be more attractive than the importation of a device from the regulated industries, the certificate-of-need device, which has a history of failure. What Professor Grad describes as the new orthodoxy can also be described as a growing consensus among people who study the regulated industries that construction control has been a substantial failure in that setting.

PROFESSOR CALABRESI: First, I should thank Professor Grad because his paper resulted in Dick Posner's citing me favorably. I think that is something new. Still, I was troubled by some of the things he said. And specifically there was a tendency to view regulation as all of a piece. Certificate of need, which is what we are talking about today, is a very particular type of regulation which has very particular types of dangers. It may have some benefits, but the dangers of that kind of regulation are very different from regulation of, say, the prices in the telephone industry. They are much more like the dangers of deciding how many builders to have in a particular town. And if we concentrated on that, we might get somewhat further.

I was especially troubled because, after talking about regulation as if it was all of a piece, Professor Grad said something about how people now are suggesting effluent charges as a sort of invisible hand. Well, effluent charges are a very visible hand. And that is just the point—that it is a form of regulation which uses some market incentives to try to accomplish some things because of a judgment that an uninfluenced market and an invisible hand are not working properly.

Now, I would suggest that this discussion might be furthered if people would talk about the kinds of incentives which might be useful in this area as alternatives to certificates of need, if they see dangers in certificates of need.

I do not believe that simply because the government pours out money, a specific form of regulation need follow—that is another statement which I think Professor Grad made. Quite the opposite; very often the type of regulation which follows when the government gives out money uses up more money than if all of the money were wasted. One ought instead to ask, can the money be given in a way that does not require other forms of ineffective regulation or other forms of more dangerous regulation? Let us give the money in a way which intervenes, if that is what we want to do, or which regulates, if that is what we want to do, but in the least destructive way possible.

PROFESSOR GRAD: Let me say this, Professor Calabresi. I do not disagree at all. As a matter of fact, the generality of my response was essentially engendered by the generality of the attack on planning per se. I quite agree that we are dealing with rather specialized aspects of legislation here, that each of these matters must be considered separately. But to me many of the papers appeared to represent broadsides against any kind of planning or regulation or any planning activity with teeth.

If issue had been joined on some more particular matters, I would be perfectly happy to comment on them in those terms. I think your comment is very well taken. I do think that entry into the field is a rather special problem and one which requires all kinds of considerations which are unique to that particular problem. But let me remind you, if I may, that the papers were not all that pure in their concentration.

The Role of the AHA

PROFESSOR HAVIGHURST: Both Professor Posner and Professor Curran have noted the central role of the hospital establishment, particularly the American Hospital Association, in the movement for certificate-of-need laws. It is no secret among those who study the regulated industries that this kind of economic regulation has usually been imposed only after major elements of the regulated industry itself have embraced the idea of regulation and actively sought legislation to accomplish it. For example, American Telephone and Telegraph invited the federal government and the state governments to step into regulation of telephone service in the early part of the century after they had discovered that independent telephone companies were quite capable of competing effectively with the Bell System once its basic patents had expired. Professor Posner, you stated in your prepared paper that you were "troubled by the fact that the AHA supports construction controls." Could you elaborate a bit on your suspicions?

PROFESSOR POSNER: Yes. I do not want to cast stones at the AHA—I do not really know much about it. But when an industry supports legislation which on its face is restrictive you wonder whether the effect of that legislation is actually going to be restrictive in the sense in which it is intended to be.

Every industry, I think, believes that it has excess capacity, which is another way of saying it would like to reduce output and charge higher prices. (I really do not think it makes much difference whether we are talking about an industry composed largely of what are formally nonprofit firms or ordinary profit maximizers. Both are interested in pretty much the same thing.) As I indicated in my prepared remarks, very often what regulators do is to support a cartel of the regulated firms or to supply controls very much like those the cartel would like to implement among its members. I do not think industries generally support government regulation unless they think it will be in their pecuniary interest to do so.

PROFESSOR CURRAN: I pointed out the AHA's role in my paper, of course, and in fact asked the question whether or not this was a "suspicious feature" that should be examined. I think it should be.

The hospital industry is a very large one and has much that is good and much that is not good about it. I think that the major supporters of certificate of need are those hospitals which consider themselves the best; they would like the regulatory system in the hospital industry, as in so many other industries, to support those who consider themselves the best and to force out those whom they consider to be either hurting the good name or holding back the fulfillment of various purposes of the industry.

THOMAS GALINSKI, director, Division of Planning, AHA: I would like to respond to this question about the reason for the AHA's interest in and support of certificate-of-need laws. This position of our member hospitals is a result of some fifteen years of thinking and policy formulation on the subject of health planning on the part of the association. In the early 1960s the AHA published a statement to the effect that joint planning on the part of hospitals was an extreme necessity. Although not specifically stated, it was implied that the appropriate structure for this joint planning would be the area-wide health planning agency. There was no mention at that time of the question of "controls" or putting "teeth" in planning. Throughout the late 1960s, the association formulated several policies in its continuing effort to define the role of the area-wide planning agency and to stress the necessity for long-range planning on the part of each hospital. In 1968 for the first time, the association published a "Statement on Planning," which formally cited the necessity for controls in the planning process. The statement very clearly defined the role of the area-wide planning agency as an adviser and working partner with the hospital as opposed to the agency having approval or disapproval authority over hospital expansion plans. The document stated that controls might be exercised through (1) voluntary agreements among health care providers and professional associations, (2) contractual reimbursement for patient services, (3) provision of construction capital, and (4) licensing or franchising. This was the first time that the association publicly stated that to assure participation in the planning process, controls would be needed.

The association then went on to apply one of these methods of control in its 1969 "Statement on Financial Requirements," which effectively stated that in order for an institution to receive its demonstrable capital financial needs, third-party payers would have the right to seek the advice of the area-wide health planning agency prior to reimbursing the hospital for those needs.

In late 1969, concurrent with the development of the association's "Policy Statement on the Provision of Health Services," which, by the way, is embodied in

126

the Ullman national health insurance bill (H.R. 14140), the association changed its fourth example of planning controls from licensing or franchising to "governmental authorization to change scope of services," which, in our parlance, would be certificate-of-need laws.

From this discussion of controls in our 1968 "Statement on Planning" grew a more definitive set of guidelines (adopted by the AHA on February 6, 1972) on the subject of the establishment of a certificate-of-need process in a state. This position on certification of need fits very well with the franchising function of the state health commission provided for in the Ullman bill.

Finally, I am concerned that the participants and the audience in this program represent only a very narrow viewpoint of the certificate-of-need process. Based upon a survey the American Hospital Association conducted a short time ago, roughly 3,000 hospitals come under the purview of certificate-of-need laws in eighteen states. In addition, there are approximately 185 funded, area-wide, comprehensive health planning "b" agencies in this country. I feel we would have gotten a much better picture had we invited a "b" agency director and a hospital administrator, since both represent institutions which are an integral part of any certificate-of-need process.

REPORTER'S NOTE: The program for the meeting contemplated the appearance of a prominent official of a state hospital association as a commentator on the papers in this session. At the last minute an emergency prevented his appearance.

The Public Utility Model

DR. GUTHRIE: When Professor Posner started out by saying he thought it would be a bad idea to take the public utility model and transplant it into the health system, I agreed, and I thought we were off to a good presentation. But the more he talked, the worse he got. For one thing, I think that to say the public utility models with which we have had experience have been complete failures is a very controversial statement. Truly, they have not been perfect by any means, and there are difficulties with them, not so much in principle as perhaps in methodology.

In certificate-of-need programs I think we are looking to considerably new and different methodologies in the application of the principles of public utility models. I have heard a number of people discuss the use of a public utility model in the health system as a direct transfer, and I think that would indeed lead us into difficulty. But there are many different ways to apply some of the principles in public utility franchising in certification of need in the health system. I believe the condition of the personal health care system today calls for the application of these principles through reasonable methods which can be correlated with comprehensive health planning objectives. Indeed, I believe certificate-of-need models are very much worthy of further utilization and adaptation in the health field at this time.

PROFESSOR POSNER: I am still struck by the fact that, having failed in the more traditional mode of planning, the planners now look to the public utility industries for their model. It is extraordinary to someone like myself, who is particularly interested in the public utility and common carrier fields, to see people blithely propose the extension of public utility regulation to new industries without knowing anything about how that regulation has functioned in its traditional settings. This is not the first time this has been done. The same proposals are being made in areas like auto repairs and cable television—people blithely pull out the public utility model and say this is how the problem should be taken care of.

REPORTER'S NOTE: It is appropriate to note, at this point, that some are proposing the "franchising" of hospitals as a further step beyond mere entry restrictions in the direction of public utility regulation. Franchising would involve not only limiting entry but assigning affirmative responsibilities to hospitals, and one argument for it is that certificate-of-need laws are merely reactive, requiring an agency to say yes or no to a project brought before it, but giving it little opportunity to direct resources where they are most "needed." Although presumably some negotiating power accompanies certificate-of-need requirements and planners do influence decisions in their advisory roles, giving regulators power to designate specific responsibilities has a certain added attractiveness. The notion is similar to that reflected in the common carrier's responsibility to carry all tendered traffic at the listed price or the public utility's "duty to serve." The regulated firm's acceptance of these "public" responsibilities is often regarded as a sort of quid pro quo for the protection against competition provided by regulatory restrictions on growth and market entry.

The delineation of the hospital's responsibilities would not carry with it, however, the funds with which to carry them out, and therefore the hospital would have to raise the needed revenue by pricing its other services above cost. Such discriminatory pricing is a common phenomenon in regulated industries of other kinds and is already widely practiced in the hospital world. Franchising proposals, however, suggest even more complete acceptance of this covert type of health care financing (called "taxation by regulation" by Professor Posner) and even greater reliance on it in the future. The results of reliance on such internal subsidization in other regulated industries has been excessive growth as the regulators, influenced by various obscure forces, have sponsored numerous "good works" to absorb the excess revenues made possible by restricting entry. This experience, coupled with the hospital industry's ability to absorb

unlimited amounts of money for arguably, but not clearly, worthwhile
purposes, should give pause to anyone concerned about how public util-
*ity regulation might affect health care costs.**

Can Excess Capacity Be Identified?

PROFESSOR HAVIGHURST: The planners, I believe, have studied the problems of excess capacity, about which Professor Posner spoke, for a long time. I
would like first to ask Professor Posner if he believes the task of determining the
"right" number of hospital beds is so difficult that it should not even be attempted
and then to ask some of the planners in the audience to respond to the same question, perhaps enlightening us on how they do the job.

PROFESSOR POSNER: The concept of "excess capacity" seems to me to be almost completely devoid of operational content, especially in an industry like health
care where there is obviously a need for substantial standby capacity. Clearly, it
would be disastrous if every hospital bed were occupied, because then there would
be no reserve capacity to deal with public disaster or fluctuating demands for
health care. People attach a great deal of value to instant access to health care facilities. If a person has a heart attack, he would like to have an intensive-care center—assuming it does some good (I do not know whether it does)—in his vicinity,
not two hours away.

So, although everyone seems to assume that there is an enormous overcapacity in the hospital industry, it is not obvious to me that this is so; nor is it clear how
you go about deciding what is an optimum amount of standby capacity or
optimum proximity of people to various types of therapy. Even with treatments
like radiation therapy, there would be substantial costs involved if people had to
travel long distances for daily treatments, quite apart from any emergency aspect.

The fact that excess capacity is so elusive a concept suggests some of the difficulties that an agency implementing a certificate-of-need law would face. If you
look at the criteria in the statutes that Professor Curran reviewed, you will see that
they are absurdly ambitious. There is one—I think it is Oregon—which has thirteen criteria; that law seems to require that the agency do all kinds of things that
are virtually impossible, such as determining the demand for health care facilities.
I view these certificate-of-need laws—unless they are cynically designed, as someone suggested, simply to freeze future hospital construction—as requiring the
agency to perform analytically intractable tasks.

---

* This line of argument is more fully developed in Clark C. Havighurst, *Public Utility Regula-*
tion for Hospitals: The Relevance of Experience in Other Regulated Industries, Reprint No.
17 (Washington, D.C.: American Enterprise Institute, 1973).

The prospects for successful implementation of these laws become even more dismal if you look to experience from other industries. If you look into the literature of public utility regulation, you find that the one type of public utility control which nearly everyone agrees has been a flop is precisely the control of new construction, which entails control of new entry. This is a type of regulation that is, by and large, perversely applied. Few who have studied the Federal Communications Commission or the Federal Power Commission, the other federal agencies, or their state counterparts think that what these agencies are really doing when they pass on requests to build a new pipeline or to provide service to a new market is determining whether permission would result in overcapacity. They do not have the skills to make these impossible judgments about demand and cost and the like. What they are really doing is something quite different, either supporting a cartel of the regulated firms, or supporting methods of pricing that involve the subsidization of some services by others, that is, preventing cream-skimming.

So, if you consider importing this rather stale and discredited mode of public control into the health industry, the prospects, using history and experience in other industries as a guide, are that entry control will be used either (1) to foster cartelization in the health care industry, of which one would have thought we have had enough, or (2) to maintain and perpetuate a system of internal subsidies in the health care industry, which does not seem to be a desirable alternative either. And, because the determination of optimum capacity is probably more difficult in the health care industry than in the usual public utility industries, a probable side effect of the certificate-of-need laws would simply be unsound decisions on whether new facilities are needed and a definition of excess capacity that is neither economically nor socially meaningful but one which implies that the less standby capacity, the better.

Professor Curran seems to admire the Oregon certificate-of-need law because it provides the longest list of criteria and the most formal procedures. These do not seem to me to be adequate bases for endorsing a certificate-of-need law. The essential question is whether there is a real problem to which such a law is responsive. Is there a meaningful concept of excess capacity that such a law would embody? What has been the experience with virtually identical statutory schemes at the state and federal levels over a long period of years in a variety of other industries? And is there any basis for thinking that the people in the health care field have so much greater competence, probity, vigilance, and determination that they can make workable what has seemed to be an unworkable method of public control?

PROFESSOR HAVIGHURST: In other words, I take it you are saying that other agencies assigned similar tasks in other fields are often just faking it or worse, and you see no reason to expect any better performance in planning for hospital construction, where you think the job is probably harder. I would like the planners who are here to respond to those thoughts, particularly the question as to whether they can, in fact, engage in scientific determinations of the need for hospital beds.

DR. GUTHRIE: I have had almost two years experience of everyday immersion in a certificate-of-need program, and one result I see from the experience is an evolving program building better planning principles into the health facility development in our state.

In our state, if we look at the individual institutions which have been required to participate in the program, what do we find has actually happened? The level of sophistication with which an institution goes about deciding what it is, what it is going to do, and how it relates in its sphere of influence with other institutions demonstrates marked changes as you are exposed to what they said the first time around and what they say when they have completed the certificate-of-need process. It is really quite a surprise. I would certainly agree with Mr. Posner that the determination of supply and demand in this health game is a very difficult thing. I do not know how it is in the electrical industry and the air carriers and the rest. In health it is difficult, but it is not impossible.

In my locality we are making progress by using the vehicle of certificate of need in combination with some old methods, some new methods, and a routine fact-gathering effort. We are making progress in the institutions through helping them achieve a better understanding of their own operations and of how they relate to one another. We are bringing about communication among the providers in the health industry which we never had before. We are producing some factual information on the tough problems and getting on with solutions to some of these problems in manpower, in financing, in questions about future regulation.

This combination of methods has proved immensely helpful as a backdoor approach to more comprehensive facility planning. We could have talked about the principles of planning until we were blue in the face—and made little headway. But now when an institution sees that it must perform in a certificate-of-need process, it is going to have some incentive to get its program into acceptable shape, approved, and financed.

And I do not know what will ultimately develop in planning and regulation, but, so far, we see a lot of opportunity in the certificate-of-need process. Of course, we can misuse it, and this may be what ultimately happens to it. But after experience with it for two years, I think that use of it has resulted in more advantages than disadvantages.

PROFESSOR POSNER: Well, let us be concrete. How do you measure demands? Suppose someone comes in and wants to put in a radiation machine or build a hospital wing. You can name your example. How do you decide whether there is demand for this additional facility?

DR. GUTHRIE: In the cardiovascular field right now there is a whole series of technical reports that have just been produced under the auspices of the American

Heart Association and a number of other organizations in the cardiovascular field. They spell out in very specific terms the elements needed for a determination of need for specialized cardiovascular services, such as open-heart surgical services and intensive coronary care units, so that one can apply these specifically to a given community. You can set parameters by which you can judge where these services should be provided, when they should be provided, what their utilization is going to be, and what their expectations of cost, manpower, and the rest will be. You can do this in some areas fairly accurately, quite accurately; you can do it in others with medium accuracy; and in some we have only elementary tools. But we can do it.

PROFESSOR KESSEL: How do you know whether you are doing it accurately or not?

DR. GUTHRIE: Well, even if we do it poorly, it is better than not doing it at all.

PROFESSOR KESSEL: Yes, but how do you know whether you are doing it well or poorly?

DR. GUTHRIE: Well, you measure it by established methodologies that are acceptable to those who are regulating and being regulated.

PROFESSOR GROSSE: I would like to try to change the question that is being asked by Professors Posner and Kessel and some others. I do not think the question ought to be, how do you know whether a particular act being proposed by a hospital board or somebody else is good or bad in and of itself? I think there is a broader concern at stake and that is, generally speaking, that if there is a limit to what can be done with the resources that might be made available for health in the community, then doing certain things precludes doing others, and a decision has to be made at some level by some mechanism as to what will be done. If the community feels that its crying need is outpatient services of a particular type for a particular subset of that population, it does not want to bury all of its resources in building a hospital regardless of whether the level of demand for that hospital is "a," "b," or "c."

Now, one can convert that, if you like—and I am not proposing that we do it —into numerical form by adding and subtracting dollars and lives and the like. But I think that those who argue for planning do so on the grounds that a decision regarding facilities should be made on the basis of community need and not left to a particular group which perceives only its own need, its own clientele, and its own professional constituency.

So what I am suggesting here is that you must take into account many elements of the community if you are to make these choices fairly. I do not see how that can be done reasonably except through some sort of mechanism which we defined as planning. The certificate of need comes in not as just one function of

132

planning, but I would rather put it another way. I see it as one possible tool to try to get the community decision into being.

PROFESSOR POSNER: That is an extraordinary definition of planning, because what you are saying is that planning is taking a poll of the residents of the community and giving them the choice of emphasis in service.

PROFESSOR GROSSE: I can think of worse things.

The Effects of Third-Party Payment

RITA CAMPBELL, Hoover Institution on War, Revolution and Peace, Stanford University: I would like to ask Professor Kessel to comment in respect to the basic problem that if you do not have planning, then price or some other factor has to be the allocator of resources. In view of the historical development of cost reimbursement, multi-pricing, and sometimes even no price for a given item, price does not usually work to allocate resources in the health industry. A hospital may receive cost reimbursement under Medicare by the federal government or a different level of cost reimbursement under Medicaid administered by state government. A hospital also may have charges or prices paid at a rate of 100 percent by commercial insurers or at a lower percentage of that rate—or even prospective cost reimbursement—by Blue Cross-Blue Shield. In cases where a hospital has all its patients covered by third-party reimbursement of costs incurred, there is no price for many items, just a total dollar cost per diem covering many items. Given this situation of cost reimbursement, multi-pricing, and sometimes no specific price, can it be said that prices today allocate resources in the health area in the fashion that they do in other sectors of our largely capitalistic economy? And, if they do not, can you see any way of restructuring the socioeconomic framework so that the function of price is strengthened?

PROFESSOR HAVIGHURST: Let us not try to answer that at great length, but the panelists might outline the nature of their answer. This question of restructuring the system to make it more responsive to market signals will come up in a number of other ways as we go along in the next day and a half.

PROFESSOR KESSEL: Your question raises very complex issues. It is my view that having the government go directly into the business of reimbursement rather than providing people with insurance policies or the wherewithal to pay for medical care—that is, the class of people you are referring to who are covered by Medicare or Medicaid—has probably led to effects in the product market that are socially undesirable; I think that movement in the direction of getting the government out as a buyer would have desirable allocative effects. I have already spoken about prepaid groups as one possible solution to the problem you describe. They would give consumers a chance to register their concerns with price.

RITA CAMPBELL: Whether the government or private third-party insurers, such as Blue Cross, do the paying on a cost-reimbursement basis is immaterial to the distortion effect on resource allocation. I feel that reimbursement insurance encourages greater utilization than does indemnity insurance where the consumer can identify actual prices or charges. Health indemnity policies, however, do not provide the consumer with cash to use to shop for health services as automobile collision policies do. The individual has to have received health services before he or the provider receives the cash. All health insurance acts, therefore, to reduce the net price to the consumer and thus increase demand and induce more resources into the health area than otherwise would occur.

MARK PAULY, Department of Economics, Northwestern University: Bob Grosse made that point this morning, namely, that under customary forms of health insurance, overuse of care tends to occur either because people do not consider its costs or perhaps because they are not well informed anyway.

I am not sure that planning is the only solution to that, but it is certainly one possible solution. You are then led to ask what kind of principles you would want to have used in planning. And it seems to me that the obvious kind of principle would be that the decisions made would be those that fully informed consumers would make if they were aware of the costs. That is the kind of principle one would want to guide the awarding of certificates of need. Would this addition to capital or addition to personnel be justified on that basis?

The difficulty I have, having dipped into this literature a bit, is that I fail to find any kind of consideration of that question. First of all, the discussion is usually in terms of "needs" in the abstract rather than of a comparison of costs and benefits; this seems to me absolutely wrong. And, secondly, there does not seem to be even an implicit recognition of the notion of trying to provide consumers with what they would choose if they were fully informed.

And I suppose this absence of rational principles explains why I tend to be somewhat squeamish about proposals to further extend planning and certificates of need; maybe that is behind some of Joel May's bad feelings about planning as well.

RICK CARLSON, Institute for Interdisciplinary Studies, American Rehabilitation Foundation: When we talk about certificates of need, I assume we are talking about a resource allocation device. We are talking about somebody making decisions as to how resources will be allocated. It seems to me that many of you are saying that in the perfect market or relatively perfect market, the consumers ought to express preferences and thereby make those decisions. In the imperfect market which has prevailed in health it is not true. Largely because of third-party insurance, the producers have generally made the resource allocation decisions. Professors Kessel and Posner seem to be against having bureaucrats make those decisions, but—without expressing my own preferences—if you are against bureaucrats making the decisions and are also against producers making those decisions, as you must be if in fact you want to move this system towards the market approach, then what specific measures would you advocate to give consumers more power to make rational decisions?

PROFESSOR POSNER: A number of these have been mentioned. One is to remove from the medical industry the type of restraints on competition that have limited the emergence of a real market—the restriction on advertising, the restriction on the provision of medical services by nonphysicians, the restriction on the flow of private (nonmedical) capital into the medical industry, restrictions on the methods of pricing that physicians are permitted to use, restrictions on who may become a doctor, all restraints that limit the supply and raise the price of medical services.

Now, after all these reforms have been implemented, there may still be serious problems resulting from the uncertainty of the service—our lack of knowledge about which medical procedures really work. But there is so much to be done in making the market more competitive that the steps I have suggested should be taken before increased reliance is placed on rather dubious methods of governmental control.

MR. CARLSON: We had that once. We had such an uncontrolled system, and quality went to hell. And the reason all the controls were introduced—and I am not saying they did not go too far—was to try to establish quality. And then came the scientific explosion, which further reinforced the need for quality-oriented restrictions.

PROFESSOR POSNER: I suggest you read Professor Kessel's article on the Flexner Report for another view.

More Particularized Arguments for Restricted Entry

REPORTER'S NOTE: Surprisingly, the discussion in this session, being concerned primarily with the shortcomings of regulatory solutions, got no closer to the main affirmative lines of argument for certificate-of-need laws than in the foregoing discussion of third-party payment. Of course, these arguments had been presented in general terms in discussing health planning, but rigorous examination did not occur until the last session, when the papers attempted to account for the appeal of the laws and to suggest alternatives to the regulatory solution. In that session, too, Professor Herman Somers supplied a good summary statement of the arguments in his commentary. Here, however, some important quality considerations were mentioned for the first time.

PROFESSOR CALABRESI: There are at least some areas where useful things can be said about the need for restricting entry. I am told by transplant surgeons, for example, that unless a team does a certain number of some types of procedure —open-heart surgery or kidney transplants—their failure rate goes up very sharply. If that is so—and I am in no position to argue with them and have never heard the point denied with respect to these procedures—there is a very real problem. If in each of several hospitals in, say Seattle, which was a case given, there are eight teams in different places doing this procedure with the result that none of them can do a good enough job just in terms of mortality, then this is an area where one can speak with some clarity about the need to regulate entry. It is not just a matter of saying some people will choose to have a poorer surgeon, presumably at a lower price. Rather, everybody is forced to have a poor surgeon as a result of there being too many parties in the field.

Now, what I have not heard is an argument of the same sort with respect to hospitals and certificates of need in general. What I would like to know, in other words, is this: When can arguments of this sort be made, and at what point does it become less and less likely that such problems exist, so that the dangers of certification become greater than the possible benefits?

PROFESSOR HAVIGHURST: We have a transplant surgeon with us who can speak to the considerations in implementing highly sophisticated programs of the sort referred to.

DELFORD L. STICKEL, Duke University Medical Center: In the development of such new, expensive programs as open-heart surgery, kidney transplantation, and the artificial kidney, three points would be cause for concern and attention in connection with any certification of need; and these three points are clearly evident in such diverse institutional settings as university medical centers, private and non-governmental, nonuniversity hospitals, and the VA hospital system.

First, wasteful duplication of expensive programs occurs not simply from lack of planning and coordination but also from positive forces of pride, prestige, and status which drive institutions and communities to seek to establish all of the new, sophisticated programs.

Second, it is not enough to establish need. Resources devoted to establishing a much needed program will be wasted if one or more of the essential elements of the program is weak or missing—for example, adequately trained manpower to use the facility. A proposal to establish a kidney transplant program at an institution, for instance, needs an in-depth review by experts in the field to judge whether the institution has available all of the necessary staff, equipment, space, and ancillary support services.

Third, there may be unquestioned need and the necessary resources to fill it, but there may be an inadequate market—that is, too few of the patients in need willing or prepared to pay the cost of the service.

136

Multiple Criteria and Formalized Procedures in a Certificate-of-Need Law

PROFESSOR HAVIGHURST: Professors Curran and Posner have both alluded to the Oregon statute, which incorporates thirteen criteria for the planners to use in assessing need. Professor Curran appears to regard the Oregon statute as a model, and Professor Posner called it "absurdly overambitious." I wonder if we could explore the desirability of such a statute a little further.

PROFESSOR GRAD: I disagree with Professor Posner that the thirteen criteria which the Oregon statute set up are useless or beside the point. Nor would I criticize the state of Oregon for having thirteen criteria in its certificate-of-need legislation. The state of New York is no better because it has only one criterion—public need, which is, on the whole, undefined and probably susceptible to any number of interpretations.

At least in Oregon one would hope that the legislature has gone through a rather discrete, rather careful process of analysis. We may not agree with all thirteen criteria, but at least there was an attempt in the Oregon legislature to state a range of priorities, to emphasize certain aspects of choice, and to articulate what the standards for access to the field ought to be.

I believe that any articulation of standards in a piece of legislation is invariably better than none. It gives the reviewing court or agency an opportunity to trace the various steps which the initiating agency took; it provides a chance to check the evidence presented against the requirements and criteria of the law. In short, it enables the reviewing authority to follow the decision process of the agency below it. From that point of view, while thirteen criteria may not be better than twelve or even six, the mere fact that criteria have been articulated is important.

PROFESSOR POSNER: Enthusiasm for such a specification of criteria illustrates the tendency in this field to refuse to consult experience. For example, Professor Grad states that a statute with multiple criteria facilitates judicial review. Well, no one who studies the regulated industries thinks that is true. The opposite is true. That is, in the case of statutes like the Civil Aeronautics Act or with the rules that the FCC has developed for awarding television licenses, it turns out that when the statute or rule contains multiple criteria the agency can justify any decision it reaches by picking out whichever criterion is consistent with its preference. So if you have a whole list of criteria that include serving the needs of a religious denomination, meeting demand, minimizing cost, and so forth, all the agency has to do is pick out one that meets its view of the circumstances and write a review-proof decision.

Professor Curran, in addition to admiring the thirteen criteria of the Oregon law, complained that most certificate-of-need laws provide for insufficiently formalized procedures. No more cumbersome method of controlling the construction of hospitals could be imagined than to apply multiple criteria in the context of formal

137

administrative proceedings, with cross-examination, appeals, and all the other paraphernalia of the legal adversary process. Past experience with similar controls in the regulated industries suggests that there is a very high probability that the impeccable criteria and formalities will be fig leaves concealing the monopolistic organization of the regulated activity.

Integrating the Planning and Certificating Functions

PROFESSOR POSNER: Professor Curran has also entered a plea for integration of planning with the certificating function. This also is nothing new. There is plenty of experience in the other public utility industries with the combination of planning and certificating. The Federal Communications Commission (FCC), for example, has long had master plans for the allocation of television licenses that guide policy on licensing individual applicants. But people who have studied the FCC think the efforts to plan are at least as unsuccessful and basically misconceived as the efforts to regulate on a case-by-case basis. Their master plan for the television industry is a lousy plan; they have acknowledged this by frequent changes of direction.

As Professor Kessel pointed out this morning, the history of planning in the health care industry itself is an unpromising one, one of its major features having been the drastic reduction in the number of medical schools following the Flexner Report. Thus, not only do planning and certificating separately have dismal histories in a variety of contexts, but the combination in particular agencies like the FCC has not improved the functioning of either part.

PROFESSOR CURRAN: I also believe we in the health field may have a good deal to learn from the successes and failures of regulation in other industries. The important feature in this regulatory picture which could distinguish it from some others, however, is the emphasis on "comprehensive health planning." On the local level at least, these agencies should be able to expand consideration of problems and priorities beyond the needs for or against hospital beds, the immediate needs of the particular industry. This could force an examination of the overall health demands of the people, with hospitals only one contribution to the system. Whether this type of regulatory program will succeed depends greatly on whether we continue to support the planning effort on a local level to provide some effective approach at comprehensiveness in the review of the needs of the people.

MR. ZWICK: In considering planning and particularly planning with "teeth" and regularized procedures, it is important to discuss the contribution of simple "visibility" in the process. It may no longer be possible to make decisions of broad public impact in private. This condition we hope will cause the initiators as well as the reviewers to take into account a broader range of factors.

138

I am more and more convinced that disclosure may be the most significant means of influence, especially among powerful groups. It can substantially affect both the behavior of the participants and the content of the decision, both in its formulation and in its evolution.

The greatest contribution of planning and certificate-of-need laws may be that they extend and regularize the "disclosure" process.

Composition and Behavior of the Certificating Agencies

PROFESSOR HAVIGHURST: We earlier heard Professor May describe the planning agencies as they are currently constituted, and several people have indicated the desire for heavy consumer representation. I wonder if Professor Posner thinks the composition of the agencies would make any difference in the administration of certificate-of-need laws.

PROFESSOR POSNER: The notion of somehow merging a regulatory function of deciding when a facility may be built with a planning function carried out by groups which are dominated by "consumers" seems to me to be a very odd way indeed of doing business.

I would predict that such an agency would produce one of two results. First, paralysis: no construction certificates would be granted because the people who make up this agency (doctors and consumers) are wholly incompatible, warring groups. Appointed precisely to provide a balance of warring factions, they cannot agree on what the public interest requires in the health field. Maybe that is the intention. Perhaps some people have decided that there are too many hospitals, so in order to hold down the visible costs of hospitals we will create a new class of invisible, queuing costs by freezing hospitals at their present capacity.

The second possible result is that the consumers will not prove to have a durable interest in or commitment to these agencies and the agencies will lapse into the control of some special interest group, such as the medical profession or the voluntary hospital establishment. The assumption here would be that the large economic interests in the health care field will outlast the impulses which led consumers to get involved.

REPORTER'S NOTE: At this point in the discussion, Professor Pauly anticipated some of the points regarding the behavior of bureaucracies which appear below under the Models of Bureaucracies section of his prepared paper, Part III.

PART THREE

Nonprofit Monopolies in Health Care: Controlling the Progeny of Certificate-of-Need Laws

REPORTER'S NOTE: Having established the inevitable thrust of certificate-of-need laws toward a further reduction of competition in the delivery of hospital services, the conference proceeded to an evaluation of the consequences of such a development. Monopoly in hospital care may be less objectionable than in other fields because the hospitals are predominantly nonprofit enterprises whose assets, including any excessive earnings, are presumably dedicated to the public interest; indeed, the redistributive effects of a nonprofit hospital monopoly appear on balance to favor the poor rather than the rich, although undoubtedly some of the "excess" earnings of hospitals are absorbed in perquisites or used indirectly to augment physician incomes. Nevertheless, it would seem that objections to nonprofit hospital monopolies must relate to their effects not on the distribution of wealth but on resource allocation, efficiency, the quality of care, and consumer interests. This session of the conference was to consider the possibly pernicious effects of hospital monopolies and some of the techniques for controlling them. The issues here were obviously too broad for comprehensive treatment, and emphasis was necessarily placed on the benefits or costs of preserving entry possibilities as a means of subjecting hospital monopolies to the bracing influence of both actual and potential competition.

A completely different response to the problem of hospital monopolies is represented by the consumer movement in health care. Pressure from organized consumers, particularly the poor, has been directed primarily toward obtaining legal recognition of providers' obligations to render free care to indigents, toward widening recognition of patients' rights in the health care system, and toward obtaining a greater role for consumers, particularly disadvantaged ones, in the system's decision-making processes. In addition to revealing the outrage of certain groups confronted with what they deem an unresponsive and establishment-dominated monopoly, this movement represents a classic instance of the exercise of what J. Kenneth Galbraith calls "countervailing power," the

141

spontaneous development of a new power center to resist the depredations of monopoly wherever they appear. The organizers of the power blocs engaged in this enterprise seem to have accepted the presence of the hospital monopoly and to have invested little faith or effort in the restoration of consumer choice in a competitive market setting as an alternative means of subverting provider sovereignty. One of the purposes of the third conference session was to call attention to consumer complaints about nonprofit monopoly and to consider the possibility of its control by countervailing power, but time permitted little more than an acknowledgment of this added dimension of the problem of restricted market entry.

THE BEHAVIOR OF NONPROFIT HOSPITAL MONOPOLIES: ALTERNATIVE MODELS OF THE HOSPITAL

Mark V. Pauly

Unless the consequences of monopolization by nonprofit hospitals and health care facilities are known, it is obviously impossible to determine what social and legal arrangements are desirable. There are good economic reasons to fear a for-profit monopoly. But is not the nonprofit monopoly benevolent, almost by definition, and therefore not to be feared? In this paper I will indicate that there *are* grounds for fearing not-for-profit monopolies, although they are not always the same grounds as those on which the case for regulating or prohibiting for-profit monopolies is based; in a way, this analysis provides a description of what might be expected to happen should control over the process of granting certificates of need be entirely captured by the industry. I will also discuss at the close, in considerably less detail, what some models of the bureaucratic decision process suggest as the expected behavior of individuals or groups who pass on certificate-of-need applications or who do health planning generally.

If all producers of health care were profit or income maximizers, this paper could be only a few paragraphs long. It would say that unregulated health care monopolists would equate marginal revenue and marginal cost. It would say that regulation of health care monopolists could follow the same principles as regulation of for-profit monopolists. If marginal cost is equal to or above average cost when costs are minimized (both in the sense of maximum output from inputs and of least-cost combination of inputs), price is to be set equal to that cost-minimizing level of marginal cost. If marginal cost is below average cost, price is to be set equal to average cost (including a return on equity capital just equal to its opportunity cost), unless a subsidy permits marginal-cost pricing. Practical problems arise in the implementation of these rules, problems not only in determining the opportunity cost of capital but also in determining the theoretical cost-minimizing level of marginal or average cost. Inability to accomplish the latter can lead to the "Averch-Johnson" effect, involving relative overuse of capital,[1] or to the presence of "slack" expended on emoluments, staff, or other executive perquisites. Indeed, in the opinion of many critics these practical problems have left much of the regulation of public utilities seriously deficient. But at least in principle we know what

---

[1] See Harvey Averch and Leland L. Johnson, "The Firm Under Regulatory Constraint," *American Economic Review,* vol. 53, no. 5 (December 1962), pp. 1052-69.

should be done, or at least what we want to have done. Set the appropriate price, and profit maximization will do the rest. For hospitals there might be the additional problem of defining quality, it being harder to measure care than amperes of electricity, but that again would be "only" a technical problem.

But most hospitals in the United States are not run for ostensible profit. They are owned either by governments or by not-for-profit corporations. The consequences of monopoly, and hence the appropriate regulatory measures, if any, would presumably be different in these cases. The main theme of this paper will be the extent to which positive and normative conclusions about the effects of monopoly depend on the model chosen. In what follows, I shall set out several potential objectives for the hospital, usually considered to be not-for-profit, and will examine the implications of each set of objectives with regard to monopoly. Throughout, I shall be using two sorts of benchmarks. First, I shall be comparing the not-for-profit hospital with a for-profit firm confronted with similar market and production considerations. Second, I shall be measuring the predicted performance of the hospital system against that standard of efficiency and optimality which characterizes a perfectly competitive system of profit-maximizing firms.

Why Monopoly Exists in Health Care

Before beginning to consider alternative models of nonprofit monopolies, one should first look at the basis of the emergence of for-profit monopolies to see whether, and to what extent, such a basis exists in the market for medical care, and to consider the efficiency aspects, broadly defined, of for-profit monopoly under alternative rationales for its existence. Here I shall be thinking of monopoly as any situation in which the number of firms is not "large," so that firms do not behave as if the price is given. But in many cases the clearest monopoly model to analyze is that of a single firm.

Natural Monopoly. The most common justification for, and explanation of the presence of, monopoly is decreasing costs, in the sense that the cost-minimizing size for the producing unit is large relative to the size of market demand. This means both that the larger firm will have a cost advantage over the smaller one, and so might be expected to capture the market, and that a single firm can produce ideal industry output at a lower cost than can a system of many firms. Thus, monopoly should be encouraged, but its price must be regulated to make sure that it does permit ideal output to be sold.

Do hospitals exhibit such decreasing costs? The most generous comment about the empirical evidence on costs is that it is confusing; much of it is nonsensical. It is confusing because one can find empirical studies which show decreasing costs, increasing costs, constant costs, or all three of these at once for different

144

types of hospitals. If scientific questions were to be answered by majority vote, mildly increasing returns to scale might receive the nod, but there are equally reputable studies finding different conclusions. The evidence is nonsensical, in my view, not only because it ignores quality deterioration but, more importantly, because the physician input has largely been left out of studies done of United States or Canadian hospitals. One of the inputs in producing hospital services is certainly provided by physicians; yet most of this is not a component of the hospital costs which have been studied. My best judgment is that, except for some very sophisticated kinds of facilities and personnel, which are unlikely to be relatively important, and except for some spreading of the overhead of the very small hospital, costs are probably pretty nearly constant over a reasonably long run. Except for isolated rural areas and a few sophisticated research centers, the bulk of hospital care is probably rendered under conditions of approximately constant costs. While there may be some economies of scale for sophisticated equipment, and while duplication or excess capacity here is likely to be painfully obvious, it is unlikely to be of major importance in its contribution to the overall level of hospital costs. I should add that, although this is my best judgment, it is not one based on very good evidence one way or the other.

Monopoly by Legislative Fiat. Patents, franchises, favorable tax treatment, and other legal devices are means by which the state makes its resources available to a firm to prevent or inhibit the emergence of competitors. There need be no presumption in such cases that monopoly is justified by lower costs, for lower costs would in many cases themselves be sufficient for the attainment of monopoly.

Such legal barriers to entry do exist in the hospital industry. The tax-free status of not-for-profit firms also gives them an advantage. Some states now have the power to regulate the entry and expansion of hospitals.

Lack of Consumer Price and Product-Characteristic Information. Where consumers are less than perfectly informed about the prices charged by the lowest-priced entrant, or where they are prevented from being informed, some firms could charge higher prices than others and still continue to sell something. Where consumers are not fully informed about the characteristics of outputs, misinformation may create a monopoly.

Of course, it is not really necessary for *all* consumers to possess perfect information in order for competition to exist. If there are only enough marginal consumers who are aware of the characteristics of different producers and who are willing to seek out the producer who produces that output they like most efficiently and at lowest cost or price, competitive results can be approximated. For example, I know even less about the works of a movie camera than I know about my own organs; yet I feel fairly confident in purchasing a camera for a given price as long as I know that there are at least a few experts in the market who are keeping all sellers reasonably honest. Thus, the extent to which lack of consumer information causes the medical marketplace to depart from the competitive point can be over-emphasized. It is probably undeniable, however, that both the characteristics mentioned above do exist in the hospital industry.

They arise in part from the lack of information to the consumer on hospital prices and quality. Part of this lack is no doubt attributable to the peculiar characteristics of the product; hospital care is consumed only rarely, has few objective standards against which it can be measured, and yields an outcome which is itself delayed and uncertain. Perhaps more importantly, the typical insurance policy provides no incentives for the consumer to find out about prices or costs, since within wide limits it will pay any price in full.

Why Regulate Entry or Expansion?

In an ordinary, monopolistic market, it is not really necessary to regulate *entry* for efficiency (although entrants may be regulated). If costs decrease with size, new entrants will not be able to earn profits. Indeed, the threat of entry may be a useful accompaniment to and check on public regulation. For example, railroads and regulated trucking companies probably are prevented from raising prices as much by the existence of unregulated surface transportation as by the lawyers and the accountants of the Interstate Commerce Commission. If costs do not decrease, new entrants motivated by profits are efficient. If costs do decrease, it is true that regulation of entry may help to prevent the waste associated with entry by a firm that cannot be viable, and may shield an existing monopoly from dog-in-the-manger strategies of potential entrants.

In the health care industry, except for those rural areas in which economies of scale are likely to be important, regulation of entry does not have productive efficiency as a justification. Instead, it is a roundabout way of dealing with potential inefficiencies on the *demand* side. These inefficiencies arise from the way in which demand is expressed. Typical hospital insurance reduces the user price for care, and the quantity demanded would be expected to increase. This increase can be prevented if the quantity supplied is not permitted to increase; if no new facilities are built, they cannot be used. That this can be done is evidenced by the experience in the United Kingdom. No new hospitals were built for many years after World War II; as a result, the percentage of gross national product devoted to medical care was lower for a country which ostensibly provided free medical care than for countries like the United States which continued to charge for it.[2]

Monopolization is not therefore the goal of regulation of expansion of supply. But it may be and is likely to be an incidental effect. If individual health care in-

---

[2] This point is made most forcibly by James Buchanan, *The Inconsistencies of the National Health Service* (London: Institute of Economic Affairs, 1964).

stitutions desire to expand to satisfy excess demand, one way to prevent them from doing so is to have some centralized control. Uniting them in a single organization or in an area-wide organization may achieve this goal, but at the cost of providing an instrument also usable for monopolization. Other devices are available, for example, taxing hospital capital expansion, but these do not have the specific impact of direct controls; nor do they provide jobs and power for planners. The price of getting hospitals to agree to supply restriction may be to give them a fillip of monopoly power.

It is true that if care is provided free but facilities are insufficient to satisfy the demand at a zero price, then excess demand will occur. Some form of rationing other than price must be instituted to determine whose demands will be satisfied. As compared to a situation in which prices equal to cost could and would be charged, nonprice rationing may well be inefficient. For example, suppose access to care is rationed by the use of a queue in the waiting room. Such a queue may even induce people to get the amount of care they would have purchased had they paid prices exactly equal to real cost, although differences in individuals' ability to pay the "time cost" lead us to doubt even this result; the wealthy dowager may get more care than the busy common laborer. But even if ideal output could be achieved, there is inefficiency involved. For not only must social costs be incurred to produce the output, but the time wasted by those in the queue is also a reduction in output and satisfaction. Thus, rationing by time is in general more costly than rationing by price or by any other device which does not require the people to wait in order to receive care. Appointment systems and other schemes to obviate the need of wasting time would represent improvements, but it is still unclear exactly how rationing will occur under such devices. There may be other kinds of costs that people have to undergo to make sure they get an appointment, and the mere inconvenience of having to wait, whether at home or in the office, is a real cost. Moreover, as noted above, the use of devices other than price may produce rather odd and undesirable distributions of care among individuals, since the ability to pay a time cost or to outguess the system is not necessarily related to benefits received from care.

With these qualifications in mind, we must still recognize that we are not comparing an ideal price mechanism in which people actually do pay prices related to cost with the system of controlling demand by restricting supply. Instead, we are comparing two "second-best" alternatives—restriction of supply and potential overuse under typical forms of insurance. Thus, conclusions probably will depend on quantitative information and not on qualitative speculation obtainable from theoretical rumination. The real question is whether the system of entry control and planning is more efficient than some feasible alternative, such as health maintenance organizations or alternative insurance devices—indemnities or deductible coinsurance combinations—which avoid to some extent the inefficiencies associated with customary insurance.

Models of Hospitals: In General

There are several ways of characterizing hospital models. The first sort of model looks at the hospital as a single entity, facing ordinary markets for factor inputs, which pursues a single goal or set of goals.[3] Most published models fall into this category. The goal is usually output maximization, with variation occurring as alternative weights (prestige, labor and capital input, price, average cost) are placed on the components of output and as constraints (no loss, minimum level of service) are varied. All of these models identify the hospital's price as the one relevant to the demand for its output.

Although insurance is usually introduced, it is necessary to assume that there is less than complete coverage, for otherwise there would be no demand constraint on the hospital's actions. It seems reasonable to assume that insurance coverage is less than full, and I shall do so. It also seems reasonable to assume that greater insurance coverage lowers demand elasticity, and in this sense contributes to the possibility of monopolization. Although, as Martin Feldstein notes, there is no theoretical case for this assumption if insurance covers a constant proportion of hospital costs, insurance coverage usually spreads by providing more and more people with full coverage.[4] Unless the elasticity increases very rapidly with reduction in net price for non-full-covered demand, the insensitivity of full-covered patients to price tends to make demand relatively more price inelastic as coverage increases.

The second sort of model is different. It notes that the price which is most relevant to the patient is the *total* price he pays, the sum of the physician and hospital prices. Moreover, physician services, though clearly productive of output, are not included in the hospital price nor need they be purchased from the same seller as other hospital services. The relationship of the hospital, its physician, and the consumer are investigated here.

Models of Hospitals: Hospital Price Relevance

Initially I shall assume that there is a single hospital or, equivalently, a cartel that behaves as a single hospital, and costs will be assumed to have the traditional U-shape. Insurance will be assumed to cover some, but not necessarily all, of the total price for every purchaser, and the introduction of monopoly will be assumed

---

[3] See Martin S. Feldstein, "Hospital Cost Inflation: A Study of Nonprofit Price Dynamics," *American Economic Review,* vol. 61, no. 5 (December 1971), pp. 853-872; Maw Lin Lee, "A Conspicuous Production Theory of Hospital Behavior" (Paper presented at Western Economic Association meeting, August 1970); Joseph P. Newhouse, "Toward a Theory of Nonprofit Institutions: An Economic Model of a Hospital," *American Economic Review,* vol. 60, no. 1 (March 1970), pp. 64-73; and Melvin W. Reder, "Some Problems in the Economics of Hospitals," *American Economic Review,* vol. 55, no. 2 (May 1965), pp. 472-480.
[4] Martin Feldstein, "A New Approach to National Health Insurance," *Public Interest,* Spring 1971, pp. 93-105.

not to affect insurance coverage. The price which affects the quantity of hospital care demanded will be assumed to be the hospital price. Although I shall be discussing the "entry" of new firms, it should be kept in mind that this entry will often take the form not of new hospitals but of expansion of smaller firms or hospitals which formerly provided other kinds or types of care, or expansion of smaller similar hospitals.

Profit Maximization. As a benchmark, we assume that the hospital maximizes profit. Equilibrium occurs at point M. It will choose output OG, and sell it at a price of OP. As compared to the competitive solution of price equals marginal cost, point C, output will be too small and price too high. Should C be to the right of R, R would be chosen unless a subsidy could be paid. (It is also possible for the firm not to achieve lowest costs, to take some of its profit in the form of non-cost-minimizing behavior. This would not occur in the profit-maximizing unconstrained world, but it is more likely to occur as the effect of additional costs is reduced, as by a "cost plus" regulatory scheme.) Point C is the competitive solution if the number of firms is fixed. For prices below C, firms will choose to produce outputs whose total is too small to satisfy market demand. For prices above C, industry output will be larger than the quantity demanded at that price. We ask, in effect, what is the price at which industry demand is just satisfied and all firms are of profit-maximizing size? When entry is possible, there is an alternative competitive solution. Firms will enter as long as positive profits are earned. Equilibrium will then be at point E if $Q_D = 2X_E$.

Constrained Output Maximization. Assume as before that the hospital produces a single output. Under competition, output maximization subject to a no-loss constraint would lead to equilibrium at point R in Figure 1. This is the only point at which the firm can just sell all the output it wishes to produce. If there were only one firm facing the market demand curve, the same result would still be obtained. Point R is the maximum output at which average costs are covered. Thus, holding all else constant, including number of firms, *there is no difference between the output-maximizing competitor and the output-maximizing monopolist.* But if new hospitals are always willing to enter as long as they can sell some output, then there will be a difference. Equilibrium will occur at E (if $Q_D = 2X_E$), for at that price no new firm can enter, sell output, and still break even.

Point E is also the equilibrium of profit-maximizing competition under free entry. Entry works to achieve the efficient result even in the absence of profit maximization. But if the number of firms is fixed, the output-maximizing output will be greater than either the profit-maximizing monopoly output M or the efficient output C. Price will be lower as well.

As Joseph Newhouse has noted, output maximization as a motive for entry is even less convincing than output maximization as a goal for established hospitals.[5] Although he offers no good alternative explanation, his point seems well taken. There is no really strong explanation for entry by output-maximizing firms.

Constrained Utility Maximization. Hospitals can produce more than one kind of output. What determines the type of output they produce? One suggested answer to this question is that hospitals be assumed to maximize, subject to a no-loss constraint, a utility function in which both homogeneous output (patient days or cases) and the quality of output enter. Feldstein suggests that hospital labor inputs and materials and supplies per unit of output might be a measure of quality, while Newhouse uses average total cost.

The monopolist can produce various combinations of output and "quality." Suppose, in Figure 1, that demanders consider all qualities of care to be the same. Suppliers, however, produce what they regard as high-quality care at higher prices. The average cost curve AC_1 is associated with the quality of care most acceptable to consumers, given its price, while the curve AC_2 is associated with a higher quality of care by the hospital. As the hospital increases quality, it raises cost and zero loss price, and hence reduces quantity. It chooses, from the set of feasible quality-quantity combinations available to it, that one which maximizes its utility. It will tend to produce a level of quality higher than and a quantity smaller than that which would maximize consumers' utility. Monopolistic equilibrium would be at point Z if the hospital maximized its utility by choosing the quality-quantity combination associated with AC_2.

If there is competition betweeen a given number of firms, hospitals that offer higher-quality care than consumers want to buy will lose customers to hospitals producing more and lower-quality care. Price, cost, and quality level will be bid down to R. Thus, competition does produce a difference.

If new hospitals can enter, and if they are willing to enter as long as they can produce any output, even at a minimum quality level, then equilibrium will be again at E. Price will fall to minimum average cost, the same solution as the optimal one and the competitive free-entry one under profit maximization. Whether this will happen depends in part upon whether hospitals might be willing to enter and produce low-quality care, whether their "utility level" upon entry is greater than if they did not exist. If it is not, not only may new entrants fail to enter, but existing hospitals may leave after a switch from the high-quality level of monopoly to the lower-quality level of competition at R.

Other Quantity-Maximization Models. Still other models are possible. Hospitals may weight outputs by their prices, which leads to total revenue maximization, or

---

[5] "Toward a Theory of Nonprofit Institutions."

Figure 1

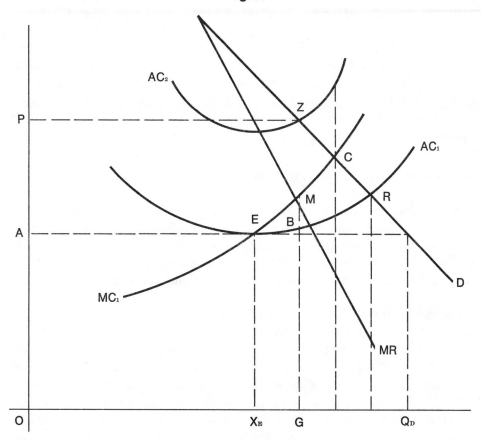

by their capital costs, or by other indexes. Or hospitals may maximize a utility function in which profits, output, staff, or "slack" all enter. In general, any of these models will be like the quantity-quality utility maximization one. Monopoly hospitals will tend not to produce that mix, type, or costliness level of care which consumers most desire. In effect, rather than taking monopoly profits in cash as does the profit-maximizing monopolist, they still charge a high price but convert the profits into types of cost which increase their utility. Price could, of course, go even higher than the profit-maximizing monopoly price.

Introduction of competition between a given number of firms will alter the price and the characteristics of output to accord more closely with consumer desires. Given a willingness of entrants to enter whenever they can produce some output and break even, price will be lowered until marginal cost equals minimum average cost. The result will be efficient in the sense of minimizing cost. The only qualification to this statement is the minor one that if suppliers of hospital services

151

prefer to take their income in the form of quality rather than cash, accounting costs may differ, though price will still equal social or opportunity costs.[6]

Conclusion. Competition is beneficial in these models. Only if there were some reason to suppose that consumers might choose too low quality (that is, a quality lower than that which a representative consumer would choose if he had full information) should one be distressed at the reduction in quality that competition might be expected to produce. To hash an aphorism, there can be too little of a good thing.

Models of the Hospital: Total Price Relevance

The price which is relevant to the demand for hospital services is now assumed to be the total price, the sum of the physician and hospital prices. The hospital's own price may still affect some aspects of care, especially amenity ones, such as additional hotel-type days for recuperation, but the important price which most affects the level of total expenditures is assumed to be the total price.

Perfectly Cooperative Physician-Income Maximization. Here I assume that physicians on the staff of a hospital cooperate perfectly. They all charge an agreed-upon price. The quantity of output produced by each physician, and his use of hospital inputs relative to his own input are mutually agreed upon. The level of each of these variables is that level which maximizes total physician income. I assume initially that the number of physicians on the staff of any hospital is fixed, that each physician is on the staff of at most one hospital, but additional physicians can be hired by any hospital at a constant supply price. Cooperation need not, of course, be explicit, nor need its enforcement be obvious. As Reuben Kessel has noted, denial or curtailment of staff privileges can keep price cutters (or overproducers) in line.[7]

Suppose there is a monopoly hospital. Ignore costs incurred by the physician in producing hospital output. Let AC_1 in Figure 1 be the hospital's cost curve, but let D now be the demand curve which relates *total* price (hospital plus physician price) to quantity demanded. The price will be set at OP and total output at OG. If physicians share output and incomes equally, each nonsalaried physician's output will be OG/Φ where Φ is the number of physicians, and his gross income will be $PZBA/\Phi$. As is obvious, this is the model of the "not-for-profit" hospital which

---

[6] For instance, suppose a hospital can borrow $1,000,000 net for expansion, or it can get $1,100,000 as a donation from me. I require it, however, to use $100,000 to place a bust of myself over the front door. Accounting costs would be higher in the second case, but would only represent income in kind to me, not waste.

[7] Reuben Kessel, "Price Discrimination in Medicine," *Journal of Law and Economics,* October 1958, pp. 20-53.

is most analogous to that of classical monopolistic profit maximization. The hospital still breaks even, charging a price equal to average cost. (Indeed, positive hospital profits reduce physician incomes.) Physicians replace stockholders as recipients of monopoly profits, and there may be some problems in specifying shares of those profits when not all physicians can produce equal shares of output. But, given some agreed-upon sharing scheme, the result is equivalent to profit maximization.

Now let competition between hospitals, which are really clubs of physicians, be introduced, but continue to assume that the number of physicians and the number of hospitals is constant. Price will be bid down, and output will expand. Again, the profit-maximizing competitor becomes the analogue, and the price tends to fall to C (or R if MC is less than AC where AC = D). Whether it will fall to C depends upon the opportunity cost of physician services.

The analogy with the profit-maximizing monopolist begins to break down if we permit the number of *staff* (not salaried) physicians to vary. Suppose there are more physicians in the community served by a monopoly hospital than that number which maximizes net income per physician, and that no physicians can be salaried. The hospital staff will only wish to expand up to the point at which average physician income (from hospital practice) is maximized. Some physicians will be kept off the closed staff, and will therefore be unable to perform hospital procedures; or perhaps they will be given only token privileges. There are many ways of justifying this situation. Since physicians obviously vary in qualifications, and since one qualification may be years of practice in the community, outsiders can be kept out. This can be fully in accord with the law if the hospital can show that addition of new physicians could, given its present bed size, cause it to be overcrowded. It is not required to show why it should not expand to accommodate the new physicians. This situation does pose a problem regarding the stability of the monopoly solution, since staff physicians would be willing to replace one of their number with a new physician who was willing to take a smaller income.

If there are several competing hospitals and if physicians can switch from one to the other, the process of adjustment to a competitive solution would be accelerated because a hospital staff which did not cut total prices would find its members eager to leave for other hospitals where incomes were higher.

New hospitals can enter only if they can attract physicians. Those physicians excluded from the staffs of existing hospitals would provide the staffs for the new ones. Price would fall until it just covered hospital costs and the opportunity cost of the physicians' time spent in rendering hospital services. If all physicians were already on the staffs of hospitals, no new hospitals could enter. Since the opportunity cost of hospital services is likely to be what the physician could earn in office practice, and since that is likely to vary inversely with the total number of physicians in an area, one would expect more new hospitals to enter, and the total price to sink lower, in such areas.

153

This observation also suggests an entry-preventing strategy for monopoly hospitals. It may admit more physicians to its staff than the number which maximizes average income in the absence of new entrants. If a sufficiently large number of physicians in an area are receiving sufficiently high incomes at the monopoly hospital, a new hospital may find itself unable to attract a sufficiently large staff, and so be unwilling to enter.

Normative conclusions regarding the desirability of monopoly must deal with the second-best problems alluded to earlier. For example, as Michael Crew has noted, it may be that monopoly will raise the gross price to such an extent that the net price paid by consumers with partial insurance will exactly equal marginal cost.[8] In such a case, monopoly with partial coverage insurance will be more efficient than competition with partial coverage insurance. But it should be noted that in this situation all of the efficiency gains accrue to physicians and none to consumers. In the absence of a special physicians' income tax we may want to continue to judge monopoly as inefficient from the viewpoint of consumers in general.

Imperfectly Cooperative Physician-Income Maximization. Now suppose that there is a single hospital, but there is no direct group control over prices and output, except via the capital and labor constraints provided by the limitations of hospital facilities. A physician cannot produce more output than that for which he can get hospital beds, but in this model he has no incentive to produce less. When acting as members of the hospital staff and deciding whether or not to favor adding beds, operating rooms, or nurses, staff physicians behave as a monopoly. Acting as solo practitioners, in deciding whether to use a bed, repair another hernia, or to cut prices, they all behave as competitors. Moreover, when they behave as a collective monopolist, they know they will behave as individual competitors.

The analysis now becomes a little (more) obscure. It seems likely that non-cooperation will lead to overuse of hospital capital and labor relative to the physician's labor. If a physician orders additional nursing care for one of his patients, it is likely to increase his net income, either because it raises the price he can charge or because it permits him to produce more output. The cost of his action is, under the average cost-pricing policies followed by most hospitals, spread over all other physicians' patients. The problem then becomes this: Given that overuse will occur, what is the second best ideal level of hospital inputs, that is, the level which maximizes average physician income? No precise answer can be given, though it seems likely that, since some vestige of monopoly control can be retained via group restraint on supply, the amount of capital and labor will be such as to yield an output smaller than the competitive output at C, even though the hospital cost

---

[8] Michael Crew, "Coinsurance and the Welfare Economics of Medical Care," *American Economic Review*, vol. 59, no. 5 (December 1969), pp. 906-908.

of producing that output is greater than AC because of the relative overuse of nonphysician inputs.

Price likewise will not be at the monopoly level. How low will it be cut? It clearly could fall to the opportunity cost of physicians' services. That is, it would be expected to fall until it just covered, at the margin, the opportunity cost of physicians services. Physicians will still earn infra-marginal rents, however. Even if hospital staff physicians compete, they can keep their incomes up by denying, through their collective control of the hospital, the use of hospital facilities to other physicians in the community, thus keeping both their prices and their incomes up.

If there are many hospitals, denial of staff privileges is less likely. In such a situation there is no locus for monopolistic collective decisions. So price would fall a little farther, and output expand more, than in the monopoly case. One might also suppose that there would be a greater incentive to minimize hospital costs, since physicians on the staffs of high-cost hospitals will have to charge less than physicians on the staffs of lower-cost hospitals in order not to lose their patients to them. This statement would not be technically correct, since cost minimization should also characterize the monopoly hospital. But if hospitals do not operate strictly to maximize physician incomes, competition between hospitals reduces the scope for such "slack," and provides a better indicator to physicians of whether or not their hospital really is a cost minimizer.

When the number of competitive hospitals is not fixed, as in the preceding paragraph, but entry is possible, then physician incomes will be bid down to the (low) level which just covers the opportunity cost of physician services, given both the number of physicians in the relevant market area and the costs of migration to it facing physicians earning smaller incomes in other areas. If entry is possible, every physician who can perform hospitalization services to the satisfaction of his patients will have access to hospital facilities. This will tend to reduce the prices, both relative (to out-of-hospital physician prices) and absolute, of hospital services. The distortion in relative prices potentially present in the previous two cases will be reduced. (Interestingly, this distortion is one which would lead to *too few* procedures being performed in hospitals.)

Not all implications of this model are obvious. What is certain is that the imperfectly cooperative monopoly will be closer to the competitive case than the perfectly cooperative one. There are at least two questions to which the answers are not clear. First, it may even be that competition between physicians is almost sufficient to achieve a competitive price and output, even if there is only one hospital. Imperfectly cooperative (or should we say perfectly competitive?) monopoly may be almost the same as simple perfect competition. The main difference is in the number of physicians who provide hospital services. Second, though imperfect competition leads to technical inefficiency in the sense of using too much hospital input relative to physician input, it is still not obvious that this result is inefficient in reality. Perfect cooperation, regardless of the degree of competition, may be im-

155

possible, and imperfect cooperation, because it is the best we can do actually, may be the best or most efficient, as I have argued elsewhere.[9] The characteristics of the physician's task may not make him a proper agent for direct control.

Conclusion. A true model of the hospital lies, in my opinion, somewhere between the alternatives of perfect cooperation and noncooperation. To the extent that co-operation on prices, outputs, and staffing can be achieved, monopoly is to be feared. To the extent that there is competition among physicians, even on the staff of a monopoly hospital, monopoly may not be so much different from competition. But, of course, the mere existence of a monopoly hospital provides what I would guess is a strong temptation to use it to enforce cooperative monopoly.

Implications of the Models

While it is obviously impossible to draw a single set of implications from five different models (for if they yielded identical implications they would be identical models), there are some important areas in which they all (or almost all) lead to the same conclusions.

Technical Efficiency. Regardless of the competitive setting, in almost all cases technical efficiency in the sense of maximum input for a given set of outputs is achieved. The one possible exception is the quantity-quality utility maximization model. Even there the hospital produces the level of quality it chooses in the most technically efficient way. But since patients may put no value on the extra inputs which go to provide higher "quality," the production process may be technically inefficient even though the hospital is minimizing costs.

Input Proportions. If we ignore the physician input, all of the quality-maximization models lead the hospital to choose combinations of inputs which, given their prices, minimize the cost of producing whatever output the hospital chooses to produce. (Of course, this combination will not yield the minimum cost of produc-ing some other, perhaps socially more desirable, type of output.) When we recog-nize that physicians do contribute something to producing hospital output and in-corporate their behavior into a model, then it is possible that there will be overuse of hospital labor and capital inputs relative to physician inputs, though it is diffi-cult to predict the influence of the degree of competition on this overuse.

Quality and Mix of Output. The general effect of competition in these models in which different qualities or mixes of outputs are possible is to induce the hospital

---

[9] Mark V. Pauly and Michael Redisch, "The Not-for-Profit Hospital as a Physicians' Co-oper-ative," *American Economic Review*, vol. 63, no. 1 (March 1973), pp. 87-99.

to provide a level of quality more consistent with consumer demands. Those demands reflect, presumably, not only evaluations of relative quality but also of relative prices. Theory cannot tell us whether quality produced under monopoly will be too high or too low, though intuition and casual empiricism would seem to suggest that it tends to be too high. Note that insurance increases quality demanded, and so reinforces the effects of monopoly. Here, even in a second-best sense, competition seems preferable to monopoly, since it prevents quality from being too high.

The physicians' monopoly model predicts that high-quality care will tend to be produced if production of such care yields higher physician incomes than lower-quality care. If the typical group of physicians makes more net income from the "big ticket" procedures than from a "low markup, high volume" strategy, and if the former procedures are called high quality, then competition will tend likewise to reduce quality.

If we are willing to trust consumer demands, informed by physician advice, this reduction in quality is not bad; it is positively desirable. Cost savings more than offset reductions in quality. If consumers are not informed, then perhaps we need not trust their judgment. But even here there are some problems: (1) If consumers are ignorant, they would seem to be as likely to choose too high a quality level as too low a level. (2) If consumer demands do not determine the level of quality to be provided, what will? Medical opinion, the usual answer, is not unanimous on quality definition or ranking, and in any case is useless as a guide to the value of these nonmedical goods and services which must be given up to provide "better" quality. Similar comments apply to using "consumer representatives" to make decisions. Perhaps a truly representative sample, chosen, not elected, might help, especially if it could be used to construct an artificial market. I would still be willing to try a strategy of providing information to consumers and letting them decide.

Insurance. The typical form of insurance, as noted above, can turn even a tolerable degree of competition into monopoly, in the sense that it produces similar results. Where insurance coverage of hospital services is widespread, the extent of ostensible competition among hospitals can be effective only for those few uninsured individuals, and it may not be very vigorous. Large numbers, free entry, and so forth may be immaterial in such cases. Regulation is one answer, and I suppose that it may be easier to regulate a few firms than many.

There are alternatives, however, which involve changing the form of insurance coverage. These include (1) larger deductibles and co-payments over ranges of expense which are not large relative to income[10] and (2) per unit indemnity insur-

---

[10] See Feldstein, "A New Approach to National Health Insurance" and Mark V. Pauly, *National Health Insurance: An Analysis* (Washington, D.C.: American Enterprise Institute, 1971).

ances, such as the variable cost insurance proposed by Joseph Newhouse and Vincent Taylor,[11] or episode-of-illness indemnities.[12]

In my analysis, I have generally assumed that there is still enough competition to make it worthwhile to study market prices. I believe this to be true generally, though I would probably exempt very-high-coverage states such as Rhode Island. I have ignored insurance coverage of physicians' services, since usually this is of an indemnity type. The spread of reasonable-and-customary-charge insurance on physician fees would be expected, again, to convert competition into monopoly and push prices up. I have also ignored the implications of monopoly or competition among insurers which, whether called insurance firms or health maintenance organizations, may be more effective than competition among providers.

Models of Bureaucracies

How might those who pass on applications for certificates of need, or who do health planning, be expected to behave? Is it reasonable to assume that they will, in fact, operate in consumers' interest? In what follows, I will outline briefly some models that have been suggested of how such organizations might be expected to behave. How they *will* behave depends in part on whether those who pass on certificate-of-need applications will be either hired, appointed, or elected.

Hired Bureaucrats. The appropriate level of demand to be satisfied is that level which would reflect the choices of fully informed consumers (or, in the case of externality, fully informed consumers and fully informed voter-taxpayers) who face prices which reflect true costs. It is not clear that hired officials, no matter how expert, could make this determination. For it would require not only that they would be able to evaluate and place a dollar measure on the benefits received from additional care (most of which affects psychological satisfaction, rather than health status), but also that they be able to evaluate costs in terms of what the value to individuals would have been of the goods and services that could have been produced with the resources devoted to medical care. When physicians do not even agree on appropriate amounts of medical care, it would hardly seem reasonable to trust to them, or to nonphysician experts, the determination of the comparative value of medical care versus better housing or better education or better rock music.

Given the actual motivation of bureaucrats, it is unlikely that appropriate choices will be made. For example, we might consider the model of the timid bu-

---

[11] Joseph P. Newhouse and Vincent Taylor, "A New Type of Hospital Insurance," *Journal of Risk and Insurance,* vol. 38, no. 4 (Summer 1971).

[12] Mark V. Pauly, "Indemnity Insurance for Health Services Efficiency," *Business and Economic Bulletin,* Fall 1971.

reaucrat. It has been noted in other connections that individuals working for salaries in government or quasi-government organizations tend to avoid making obvious mistakes. For an individual whose job is to approve or disapprove applications for certificates of need, permission to build the hospital which then stands half empty is certainly an obvious error. It is probably less obvious if a hospital is not built and demanders go away unsatisfied. This kind of motivation might be present even if the individual had all the appropriate information necessary for making the right decision.

Appointed Consumer Representatives. There are two problems with appointed consumer representatives. The first is that it is not clear what incentive they face to actually consider the preferences of those whom they purport to represent. Their decisions may well reflect only their own preferences and not those of consumers generally. It is also somewhat difficult to see what would happen in the case in which there is not a single consumer interest but in which different consumers have different interests. Some may prefer free care to the poor, while others may want the outpatient clinic expanded, while still others may want a renal dialysis unit installed. What is the "consumer interest" here that is to be satisfied, and how is it to be determined by an appointed individual?

The second difficulty involves the probable capture of such groups by the experts, those with access to information and experience in making the decisions being considered. Even if consumers are in numerical majority, I would not be surprised to find that if hospital administrators and other industry representatives are on the panels making planning decisions, they would tend to dominate those decisions. That is because they would tend to be better informed and would have a greater interest in seeing that decisions were made which benefit them. Little glory (or any other reward) comes to a consumer representative who makes a decision which helps consumers, but the hospital administrator who is able to get the body to make decisions which help his hospital will presumably get rewards from a number of sources.

Elected Consumer Representatives. We now suppose that consumer representatives are elected and actually represent a constituency. Here again there are two problems. The first is related to that mentioned in the preceding section. It is not reasonable to suppose that voters will pay much attention in choosing their consumer representatives. It is costly to obtain information about the state of the health care system; the benefits from getting one representative elected rather than another are likely to be small; and the effect that each voter foresees that he will have on the outcome is likely to be trifling. For all of these reasons, consumers are not likely to be very careful in choosing their consumer representatives; so it is equally unlikely that consumer representatives will try very hard to truly represent their constituencies. Although the total interest of consumers in health care arrangements may in some sense equal that of producers, the interest per consumer is certainly much less than the interest of any person who represents producers. Hence, we are likely to find that decisions will tend to be made in the interest of producers.

Moreover, even if consumer representatives do vote in the interests of their constituencies, decisions may not turn out right. It is probably true that any individual is most strongly concerned with that portion of the area-wide health care system that he uses most often. I care about the physicians in the suburb in which I live, and about the one hospital in that suburb which I usually use. I care much less about the other hospital or the physicians in the other end of town and care only very slightly (I might need an emergency or might wish to discourage outsiders' use of "my" hospital) about facilities in other parts of the urban area. This means that I would like my representative to favor expansion of facilities which I use and which yield me benefits, but to oppose using limited funds on facilities which yield benefits to others. Two outcomes are possible. It may be that each representative will vote only for projects which benefit his constituency and vote against projects which benefit others' constituencies; almost all projects will get turned down, even some which on balance would have been beneficial. An alternative outcome would occur if logrolling develops. A majority coalition could be formed which will favor projects in their constituencies and deny absolutely any projects and constituencies of those outside the majority. All funds would be diverted, as far as possible, toward projects favored by the majority.

Conclusion

Let me return to a theme with which I began and restate it in a slightly different way. If we had a generally agreed-upon model of the nonprofit hospital, the focus of this paper could have been much clearer. The only tasks would have been to describe the performance of the hospital under monopoly and competition, and to evaluate the efficiency, broadly defined, of that performance. But the first lesson of this paper is that predicted performance, and consequently the evaluation of that performance, is very sensitive to model specification. Alternative models with superficially equal appeal yield radically different conclusions.

Yet even in this theoretical vacuum, policy judgments must be made. My own judgment is that the best sort of model is that which explicitly incorporates physician behavior, and within that set I would lean toward the not perfectly cooperative form. Monopolization here has effects roughly similar to those it would have in an orthodox economic model. If it is true that economies of scale are not very important, appropriate social policy might involve limitation of expansion but not numbers of hospitals, within reasonable limits. Indeed, it would be better to see beds or facilities added in an area via a new competitor. The model also suggests that

160

regulation needs to look at the use physicians make of hospitals. I rather doubt that this use can be controlled directly, but indirect control is certainly possible.

Finally, the model suggests that hospital rates are not nearly so important as total prices. Keeping hospital rates down may only permit physicians to charge more, given a condition of excess demand. Indeed, it would probably be better to let hospitals raise prices if that permits improved service, because then consumers at least get something. Health planning cannot, in short, be done without reference to physicians and the prices they charge.

Planning and certificates of need, as controls via supply restriction or demand expansion, are not, of course, the ideal mechanism. Alternative insurance arrangements, coupled with free flow of information to consumers, could obviate the need for the planning apparatus. This is probably desirable, given the inherent imprecision of the planners' estimates of individual (let alone social) demand and of relative costs.

THE SUPPLY AND ALLOCATION OF MEDICAL RESOURCES: ALTERNATIVE CONTROL MECHANISMS

Judith R. Lave and Lester B. Lave *

Much has been written about the problems which plague the medical care system in the United States. The current system is characterized by escalating costs, by a maldistribution of services, by inefficient production of medical care, by patient dissatisfaction, and by growing financial pressure on health care institutions. Much research is being done to increase our understanding of the underlying problems; innumerable proposals have been put forth to solve them.

Some proposals, such as national health insurance, are directed primarily at the consumer. Others, such as the recommendations of the Carnegie Commission on Higher Education, are focused on physician supply and distribution. Some, such as President Nixon's original health maintenance organization (HMO) proposal, are aimed at increasing the efficiency with which health services are delivered. Finally, there are those that touch all areas, such as Senator Edward Kennedy's Health Security Plan. The proposals are offered from different vantage points and with different weights attached to such elusive concepts as freedom and equality.

In the next section we discuss some of the current problems in more detail. We go on to consider some of the principal control mechanisms which it is hoped can be used to ameliorate these problems. None of the current national proposals are considered in detail; rather some of their individual components are evaluated. We proceed to discuss some of the advantages of competition and the necessity of providing some level of choice in medical care. Finally we discuss the importance of incentives and propose an incentive reimbursement system which could be used to provide some controls while decentralizing part of the system. We focus particularly on hospitals in order to look at the single most important sector of the medical care industry, to provide concrete examples, and to keep the paper both short and relevant to the conference proceedings of which it is a part. Our narrow focus can be further justified by the importance of the hospital sector and because it also helps to shed some light on HMOs.

* This work was supported by grants from the R. K. Mellon Charitable Trusts and the National Center for Health Services Research and Development (PHS HS000592-01), Department of Health, Education, and Welfare. Any errors and opinions are those of the authors.

Some Current Problems

Rising Costs. Hospital costs have been increasing at about 15 percent per year since the passage of Medicare and Medicaid. All health expenditures have risen from about 5 percent of GNP to almost 8 percent of GNP during the last twenty-five years. Hospitals are characterized by bad location (in terms of proximity to the patients they serve), by excess capacity of expensive equipment, and by duplication of expensive services. The cost of a patient day has risen by five times in the last twenty years. These increased costs have resulted from factors such as rising salaries of hospital employees, changing case mix, new treatment methods, excess facilities and services, and badly structured incentives. Much current research is directed at sorting out these factors and determining the contribution of each to rising costs.[1]

Maldistribution of Medical Services. The problem of geographic maldistribution has been widely publicized.

> Figures from the American Medical Association show only one doctor for every 2,145 residents in the nation's most thinly populated counties; in the most densely populated, on the other hand, there is one doctor for every 442 residents. The AMA finds 132 counties without a single doctor practicing. While suburbia swims in specialists, many rural areas are better supplied with veterinarians than with family doctors. AMA data show that Los Angeles County alone has more active MDs (14,203) than the 13 states of Arkansas, Idaho, Maine, Montana, Nebraska, Nevada, New Hampshire, New Mexico, North Dakota, South Dakota, Utah, Wyoming and Vermont combined.[2]

In addition to geographic maldistribution, there is a training maldistribution.[3] In the last two decades, the absolute number of general practitioners has been falling, since over three-fourths of medical school graduates take specialty training of some sort. There is considered to be a maldistribution across specialties with, for example, too many general surgeons and too few pediatricians.

Inefficient Production of Medical Services. Observers have pointed out that much care which is given to people after they have been admitted to the hospital could have been given on an outpatient basis. There are too few ancillary personnel assisting the physician.[4] The physician is currently called upon to spend much of his time

---

[1] See, for example, the general bibliographies given in Martin S. Feldstein, *The Rising Cost of Hospital Care* (Washington, D.C.: Information Resources Press, 1971), and Anne R. Somers, *Health Care in Transition: Directions for the Future* (Chicago: Hospital Research and Educational Trust, 1971).

[2] James P. Gannon, "Missing M.D.s," *Wall Street Journal*, October 27, 1971.

[3] Somers, *Health Care in Transition*, Chapter 1.

[4] Uwe Reinhardt, "A Production Function for Physician Services," *The Review of Economics and Statistics*, vol. 54 (February 1972).

doing tasks which are far below the level of what he was trained to do, and which could easily be accomplished by people of lower skill.[5] There are also complaints that hospitals are plagued with unions and licensing restrictions that force them to hire unnecessary employees and to use them inefficiently.

Patient Dissatisfaction. The press has reported a growing feeling of patient dissatisfaction. The poor are calling for high-quality, dignified medical service as their right, while the middle classes complain that they are not getting the warm personal relationship with their family physician that they have been led to expect.[6] A number of recent motion pictures have satirized the modern hospital as a place where one is more likely to die than be made well. These and the publicity given to high Medicare and Medicaid payments to individual physicians may have tended to make the public somewhat cynical about the medical care system. Finally, one can look at the apparent support for sweeping federal legislation on health care delivery to see that people are dissatisfied with the current system and want some change.

Increasing Financial Pressure on Health Care Institutions. The Blue Cross, Medicare, and Medicaid programs that helped hospitals so much in the past are now the nub of the financial problem. The first two programs reimburse on a cost basis, with some expenses excluded from the cost base as not reimbursable (such as bad debts and free care). Medicaid generally pays less than cost. In spite of the public programs, the hospital still gives some free care. These excluded costs must be covered through self-paying, or commercially insured, patients and through philanthropy. The latter becomes a much smaller component of hospital revenues as the size of the hospital budget rises into the tens of millions of dollars annually. Attempting to cover these excluded costs by charging self-paying patients significantly more than cost has become less possible as the number of these patients has dropped. Many western Pennsylvania hospitals, for example, find themselves with at least 5 percent of their budget as excluded costs or some sort of free care; they also have fewer than 10 percent of their patients in the self-paying, or commercially insured, category. This means that these patients would have to be charged at least 50 percent more than cost (what is charged Blue Cross patients) in order for the hospital to cover its expenses.

The Health Services and Mental Health Administration of HEW recently reminded hospitals which have received Hill-Burton funds of their obligation to give free care to the indigent. A regulation was proposed that hospitals would have to give a reasonable amount of free care before they would be reimbursed by any federal program. Presumptive compliance required 5 percent of patient care to be

---

[5] Judith R. Lave, Lester B. Lave and Thomas Morton, "The Physician's Assistant: Exploration of the Concept," *Hospitals,* June 1, 1971.
[6] Somers, *Health Care in Transition,* Chapter 2.

given free. Many hospitals regard this regulation as impossible to meet without bankruptcy.

There has been a great deal of discussion about financial pressure on other health care institutions, such as medical schools. At the same time that our expenditures on medical care have been increasing at a record rate, we find greater financial pressure on our health care institutions.

Proposals for Government Intervention

Many proposals have been announced to increase government intervention in the health care industry in order to alleviate these problems. We will discuss five of the individual control mechanisms (which are basic to many plans). This list is far from exhaustive, since we have included neither proposals to handle the maldistribution of physicians nor the introduction of physician assistants, among other proposals.

Improved Financing of Medical Care. Within the last few years, organized labor, the American Medical Association, the Nixon administration, and others have sponsored bills to change the financing of medical care. Proposals range from the relatively mild one for catastrophic insurance to universal coverage for everyone. The question, as Eveline Burns states, is "Health Insurance: Not If, or When, But What Kind?" [7]

Some of the proposals have provisions to reform the medical care system at the same time, but we consider only aspects of the financial proposals here. It is widely accepted that financial considerations should not deter a person from receiving needed medical care, but there is little agreement on what level of care is "needed." It is also argued that individuals should not have to face bankruptcy or seriously deplete their assets to secure medical care.

The effects of past changes in the financing of medical care are illustrated by Medicare and Medicaid. One could predict that lowering the cost of medical care would lead to an increase in demand. One could predict that supplementing what consumers are willing to spend on medical care would increase the demand and, where supply is relatively inelastic (incapable of responding to the increased demand), would cause prices to rise rapidly.[8] These have been precisely the results of Medicare and Medicaid.

---

[7] Eveline M. Burns, "Health Insurance: Not If, or When, But What Kind?" *American Journal of Public Health,* vol. 61 (November 1971).

[8] There are many people who argue that people receive care when they need it independent of the cost of receiving care. If this were true, it is a tautology that no one would be deterred from seeking care for financial considerations—one of the pressing reasons given for health insurance. Arguments denying the importance of financial incentives for the consumer can be found in C. P. Hardwick, L. Schuman and S. Barnoon, "Effect of Hospital Insurance on Hospital Utilization," *Health Services Research,* vol. 7 (Spring 1972). For arguments stressing the

Lowering the price of care to the consumer is *intended* to increase his demand for services. Some of the additional care will be productive in discovering cancer, hypertension, and other problems for which early medical intervention would be highly effective. Most of the care, however, will not affect an individual's medical problems and, at best, may serve only to reduce his anxiety. Catastrophic insurance might have the effect of concentrating our medical resources on the last weeks of terminal illness, with little or no offsetting benefits. To complicate the problem, some of the additional care will be dysfunctional since people will be subjected to additional drugs and x-rays which harm them. Note that in addition to the cost of the medical care itself, there would be a considerable cost in the time lost from work or leisure and the transportation cost to obtain care.

If there is a dramatic increase in demand, and if supply continues to be inelastic, some way must be found to ration existing resources. Prices can rise or nonmarket (nonprice) methods of allocating will have to be found. Care could be rationed by extending the wait before getting an appointment, by increasing waiting time in the physician's office, or by forcing some group (such as physicians) to decide who is worthy of care. We doubt that physicians would relish extending some of the current, informal rationing mechanisms. The alternative of letting prices rise is not likely to produce more acceptable results. In a free market, rising prices would induce an increase in supply which would bring down the price; since the supply of physicians is controlled by state licensing, the size of medical schools, and entrance into specialty training, there is little room for rapid supply adjustment. Hence, there is increased interest in restructuring the medical industry to increase the efficiency with which current resources are used.

Restructuring the System for Delivering Care. Reorganizing physicians from their current solo or small group practice into HMOs is the best known of such proposals. The underlying assumption is that solo practice is inefficient and thus that current resources can be utilized much more effectively by establishing prepaid group practice. It hardly seems believable that a concept which has been so stoutly resisted as akin to socialized medicine should now be proposed by a Republican president.

It is argued that in prepaid group practices the incentives facing the physician are improved, and hence that he will be led to make more "economic" decisions and that intensive peer review will keep quality high.[9] However, prepaid groups have not been studied in enough detail for us to be sure that we know all their effects. It has been shown that (1) the hospitalization rate is lower than for comparable groups under fee-for-service, (2) physician visits are about the same, and

importance of incentives, see R. S. Kaplan and Lester B. Lave, "Patient Incentives and Hospital Insurance," *Health Services Research,* vol. 6 (Winter 1971).
[9] Ernest W. Saward and Merwyn R. Greenlick, "Health Policy and the HMO," *Milbank Memorial Fund Quarterly,* vol. 50, part 1 (April 1972), pp. 147-177.

(3) the quality of care is high, as measured by such indices as unnecessary surgery.[10] It is entirely plausible that unneeded medical care would not be given in such a setting, since physicians are actually penalized (both by the greater cost, and hence lower salary, and by peer review) rather than financially rewarded for this behavior. However, some of the efficiency characteristics found for the Kaiser Foundation health plans seem to be absent in other group practice.[11]

There is a range of reactions to prepaid group practice, both among patients and physicians. While some really love it, others cannot stand it. The Kaiser plan has recognized the difficulty by insisting on a trial period for new physicians and by insisting that consumers have a choice of at least one other alternative in choosing Kaiser. Furthermore, even those liking the Kaiser plan often use other medical services when they find Kaiser inconvenient or unattractive. One suspects that some patients whose requests are refused by Kaiser go to other physicians to secure prescriptions or services (such as a tonsillectomy). Some patients leave Kaiser to seek a physician more to their tastes. One can only speculate at the trouble that would arise if there were *no* alternative physician (in the event that all had been put into HMOs).[12]

Comprehensive Planning. The past thirty years have seen the establishment of numerous area-wide planning agencies. Some were established to help their participants coordinate efforts, while others served to screen proposals for local philanthropists. While the planners themselves have generally stated modest goals for these agencies, they have been criticized for not eliminating the duplication of services and generally making delivery of medical care more efficient. In spite of the criticism, the federal government has supplied funds for, and local groups have cooperated in setting up, many more planning agencies. One of the basic problems of the agencies has been a lack of power. The agencies served to get concerned parties together to exchange views. Without enforcement power, however, it seems that they can hardly eliminate excess capacity, relocate hospitals, and rationalize the location of specialized services. A limited amount of power has been given the planning agencies by federal legislation requiring that federal construction funds be given only to facilities which are approved by the planning agencies. This control is limited for two reasons: The first is that federal funds meet only a small portion of the capital needs of hospitals. The other is that some hospitals would be prepared to spend their own funds, even if the government paid for all approved con-

---

[10] George N. Monsma, "Marginal Revenue and the Demand for Physicians' Services," in Herbert E. Klarman, ed., *Empirical Studies in Health Economics* (Baltimore: The Johns Hopkins Press, 1970).

[11] Richard M. Bailey, "Economies of Scale in Group Practice," in Klarman, ed., *Empirical Studies in Health Economics,* and Joseph P. Newhouse, *The Economics of Group Practice* (Santa Monica, Calif.: The Rand Corporation, 1971).

[12] Saward and Greenlick, in "Health Policy and the HMO," consider in detail some of the problems that may arise if the HMO were blithely extended for all citizens.

struction. Philanthropists or determined hospital boards are not always going to agree with a planning agency and they have the capability to ignore them if they wish.[13]

Certificate-of-Need Legislation. One proposal to strengthen planning agencies would require proponents of any new health facility or modification of an existing one to secure a "certificate of need." [14] The proposal would give a planning agency still greater control by having it investigate each proposal to determine if it were needed and if it were in accord with a master plan. Review generally takes place in a local planning agency, a state agency, and some office of state government, or in all three (or more). The legislation would make it illegal for construction or renovation to take place without such a certificate. Thus, the planning agency would have absolute control over new facilities or renovation, although it could do nothing about existing facilities or about the way in which facilities are operated.

One problem with this legislation is that the exemption for "small" renovation is as small as $10,000 in some states. (The average exemption is $130,000.) [15] This means that it probably costs more to review whether to grant a small request than it does to make the renovation. We wonder whether current planning agencies are suited to this review task. They were established during a period when the emphasis was on getting parties to reason together, so they represent the current establishment. They are not likely to exercise control over one of their number and are likely to react badly to proposed innovations. Thus, the effect may be to endorse officially many of the current practices and to shut off innovation and new entry by "outsiders."

Licensure. Potentially, more comprehensive control than certificate-of-need legislation is inherent in governmental powers to license. The effect of the previous two proposals could be incorporated into licensure, if there were a requirement that an operating license had to be secured in advance of any construction or renovation. In addition to this absolute control over facilities, licensure could be extended to control all of health manpower. Conceivably it could be extended to the point where a physician would be refused a license if he wanted to practice in an area that already had "enough" physicians. If this power were used broadly, it would give government the power to eliminate all duplication of facilities and

---

[13] Somers, in *Health Care in Transition,* Chapter 7, considers some of these aspects of planning. See also Cyril Roseman, "Problems and Prospects for Comprehensive Health Planning," *American Journal of Public Health,* January 1972.

[14] For a review of certificate-of-need legislation, see Peter J. Elsasser and Thomas P. Galinski, "Certificate of Need, Status of State Legislation," *Hospitals,* vol. 45 (December 16, 1971).

[15] Ibid., p. 56.

personnel.[16] Licensure could be exercised to assign each provider a geographic area, or "franchise," which may carry monopolistic privileges as well as responsibilities.

While the potential power is great, there are many questions about the wisdom of using licensure or franchising to gain complete control of the medical care system. What planning agency or other agency is wise enough to exercise such tight control? What would be the reaction of the medical care system to such proposed control? Is there a loss in accountability when a preferred market position and a total or partial exemption from competition is "conferred?" What checks on efficiency, responsiveness, and quality can be maintained?

Such direct control would require an immense amount of data collection and analysis. The agency would have to learn the preferences of consumers and health professionals, and learn about economies of scale in medical facilities. It would have to arbitrate conflicting desires and decide how to weigh preferences of various consumers, towns, and health professionals. As argued in the next several sections, it does not seem likely that the benefits of such control would offset the very great costs.

Planning in Practice

As the problems in medical care delivery have mounted, there has been increasing pressure for government involvement and direct control of the medical care system. No one can seriously doubt that government involvement will increase, but it is important that government add to the solution rather than to the problem. This is not so easy as some critics make out, since actions have unanticipated consequences at unexpected places. As Saward and Greenlick point out, "Forecasting the result of any policy decision is quite difficult. It was certainly not perceived that the laudable Flexner reform of medical education, aided and implemented by the support of medical education through research funds from the federal government, would ultimately create a crisis in the access to primary medical care." [17]

The medical care system is an extremely large and complicated one. We do not have a good understanding of its structure, and so we seek symptomatic relief, rather than attempting to cure the problem. For example, the duplication of hospital facilities has been attributed to the lack of effective planning [18] and to the lack of incentive reimbursement programs (or rather to the presence of cost-plus reim-

---

[16] Some aspects of this type of power are incorporated in the contract negotiated between Blue Cross and hospitals in Philadelphia. The new contract states that a quasi-public hospital survey committee will in the future determine the actual need of the community for specific services and will order the shutdown of facilities and services deemed in excess of that need. See *Medical Care Review*, vol. 29 (January 1972), pp. 44-45.

[17] Saward and Greenlick, "Health Policy and the HMO."

[18] Elsasser and Galinski, "Certificate of Need."

bursement programs).[19] Either effective planning or incentive reimbursement could eliminate the problem, if there were sufficient control. The crux of the argument, however, is whether current planning methods are likely to help or whether incentive reimbursement is likely to have an effect quickly enough to do some good.

Voluntary planning agencies seek to get the parties together to share their plans. Thus, planning can prevent hospitals from duplicating facilities through lack of knowledge. However, if hospitals decide to go ahead even after they are informed of the duplication, there is little that planning can do unless the certificate-of-need or licensing proposals we discussed above are adopted. We doubt that ignorance was a major cause of duplication of facilities and services. Instead, we attribute this duplication to the hospital's ability to afford the new facility and to pass along the cost to patients. We believe that this problem is most effectively tackled at the reimbursement level. This is not to deny the importance of planning of large-scale projects, particularly since 37 percent of the funds for medical care come from government.[20] Government would be shirking its responsibility if it allocated tens of billions of dollars to medical care annually, but did not ensure that the monies were well spent.

The futility of simple solutions to rising hospital costs is evident from comparing the medical care system in various countries. Most are more centrally planned and controlled than those in the United States, but it is not evident that they have solved their cost problems better (although most would agree that their distribution of medical services is more equitable). Rapidly rising hospital costs appear to be endemic to modern medical care. Odin Anderson and Duncan Neuhauser studied the costs of hospitalization in the United States, Sweden, and Great Britain and found the same dramatic increases in expenditures, apparently for the same fundamental reasons, regardless of ownership of facilities, sources and control of funds, and staffing arrangements.[21] Ronald Andersen and John Hill compared hospital costs in the United States and Canada from 1950 to 1967 and found that costs rose more rapidly in Canada, in spite of the tighter control of the number of hospital beds and often strict budget review.[22] Swiss hospitals experienced a 10 percent annual increase in hospital cost per patient day from 1947 to

---

[19] This has been widely argued. See, for example, Gerald Rosenthal, "The Public Pays the Bill," *The Atlantic*, July 1966, and Herman M. Somers and Anne R. Somers, *Medicare and the Hospitals* (Washington, D.C.: The Brookings Institution, 1967).

[20] B. S. Cooper and William L. Worthington, "National Health Expenditures, Fiscal Year 1971," *Research and Statistics Note of the U.S. Department of Health, Education and Welfare*, vol. 35 (November 19, 1971).

[21] Odin W. Anderson and Duncan Neuhauser, "Rising Costs Are Inherent in Modern Health Care Systems," *Hospitals*, vol. 43 (February 16, 1969).

[22] Ronald Andersen and John Hill, "Hospital Utilization and Cost Trends in Canada and the United States," *Health Services Research*, vol. 4 (Fall 1969).

1969, a rate almost comparable to that of the U.S.[23] Thus, neither various forms of planning nor various sorts of national control and financing abated the increase in hospital costs over this period. One must look elsewhere for the solution.

The Role of Incentives

There are three good reasons for not using a siege gun to kill a gnat. First, to do so is expensive; second, there are undesirable spillover effects; and third, doing so often makes it difficult to use a more appropriate tool in the future. Even if direct, detailed government control were theoretically efficacious and practically possible, there are good reasons for not using it. First, it would be enormously expensive, since extensive data would have to be gathered and analyzed. Elaborate orders would have to be given and ways found to motivate the actors in the system to obey the orders.

Second, it is difficult to determine how to stop government control. Should the control be confined to institutions with billings of more than $10 million per year? Should the appropriate number be $250,000 per year, $25,000 per year, or $500 per year? The first figure would cause regulation only of large hospitals and group practices. The second would regulate any hospital or group practice with more than a few physicians. The third would regulate all physicians and dentists, while the fourth would include everything. There is also the question of who delivers health care. Surely hospitals and physicians do. Does a dentist? A podiatrist? An oculist? A private registered nurse? An orthopedic shoe store? A plumber? What is the boundary of the health care industry? Illinois has proposed a definition that would include all of the above, as well as grocery stores and other facilities.[24] Are we talking about government control of the entire economy, under the guise of control of the health system?

Third, extensive government control tends to destroy the ability of the system to function without central direction. If hospital administrators are made to follow orders, they will tend to lose the ability to think of the implications of their actions.

An alternative to this sort of intervention is to structure the incentives in the system so that providers are motivated to act in desirable ways. In particular, the incentives could be structured so that providers are motivated to use their initiative to find ways to deliver better care, cheaper care, or to satisfy patients better. (This of course is what the HMO movement is all about.) We will present evidence below that providers do respond to current incentives. In fact, it is precisely their

---

[23] P. Bischofberger and E. Desax, "Developments in Hospital Expenditure," as reported in *Hospital Abstracts*, February 1972, pp. 540-544.
[24] IBM, "Total Health Information System," a report submitted to the state of Illinois (1970).

172

response to current perverse incentives that has created many of the current problems in health care delivery. For now, we will characterize the relevant actors and types of incentives.

Three types of actors might be categorized: physicians, patients, and institutions, such as hospitals. What factors affect how hard a physician will work, what type of treatment he gives patients, and the quality of his care? Important factors include his training, his professional outlook, peer review, professional standards, and financial rewards. Surveys reveal that physicians work longer hours than comparable professionals. There is a difference between physicians in solo practice and those in prepaid group practice. At least one reason why the solo physician works long hours is the fact that every additional hour brings in additional income. This is not true for prepaid group practice, and not so directly true for group practice. Who doubts that the implementation of Medicare and Medicaid caused physicians to shift their practice in favor of treating more of the aged and poor (and fewer of the middle class)? Was this shift caused by a sudden worsening of the health of these groups? Was it even caused by a sudden realization that these groups needed more health care? Hardly. It seems evident that physicians found themselves reimbursed for treating these patients; patients found that care was less costly. The result was that these groups sought more care and physicians were happy to provide it.

What factors affect how much care will be sought by an individual? Important factors include the individual's health status and beliefs about the efficacy of medical care, the payment he must make to the provider, the time and cost of getting to the provider, loss of income in being absent from his job (or having to hire a babysitter), and psychological factors in finding a physician. When an individual must pay the full cost of his care, the provider payment is an extremely important factor in determining how much care he will seek. An opposite extreme is one where the provider payment is zero, such as in some prepaid group practices, or for hospitalization under most Blue Cross plans. In such cases, factors other than the financial incentive of the provider payment must ration care.

The final actor, which will be the focus of attention, is the health care corporation. Hospitals have been under great financial pressure in the last twenty years. They have had to make sure their patients paid their bills, and have had to tailor their operations to new government programs. If anyone doubts that hospitals respond to incentives, he need only look at how many hospitals had utilization review committees and tissue committees before Medicare. Since hospitals could not afford to exist without these funds, they tailored their accounting, medical reviews, and management to the dictates of government. The more subtle adjustment to Blue Cross reimbursement policies will be discussed in the next section.

In a later section, we will present detailed evidence of the effects of financial incentives on hospitals, particularly the effects of incentive reimbursement, and will

173

present a plan for using incentives, particularly financial ones, to help restructure the hospital end of the health care delivery system. But first we wish to emphasize the incentives that are generated by allowing consumer choice.

How Much Choice Is There at Present?

Many people view the medical care system as monolithic: the patient enters, puts himself totally in the hands of a physician, and eventually is discharged without having made a further decision. We, however, see a great deal of individual choice. The patient first selects his physician. Then he decides whether to accept his physician's advice or to seek a consultation, whether to leave the physician and seek another one or to seek no additional medical care; he decides whether to stay with the treatment regime; he generally has a choice about which hospital to enter (since most physicians have multiple staff privileges) and about which specialist to go to. Patients choose their health insurance, and choose whether to pay their bills and whether to sue for malpractice. The patient even has the choice of when to discharge himself from the hospital.

These choices are not strictly hypothetical ones. Many people change physicians until they find one that is acceptable. Apparently, over half of all prescriptions are never filled; of those filled, most are not taken as prescribed. We would not argue that consumers currently make these choices rationally. It is almost impossible for them to be rational because it is so difficult for them to get information. However, they do make choices, and it would be better if they had better information. Victor R. Fuchs has pointed out that it is easier to get information on the quality of beef than it is on the quality of medical care.[25]

There is no agreement on the meaning of choice with regard to medical care. Friedman argues that an individual ought to have the widest possible range of choices, including witch doctors and faith healers.[26] Anne Somers argues for a very limited range of choice, where the patient could not be hurt by making one choice versus another.[27] It is not obvious how much choice an individual should have. The answer depends on the extent to which he recognizes his own needs and problems, the extent to which he recognizes what each health resource has to offer, the extent to which he knows what is best for himself and wants to take responsibility, and the extent to which policy makers view him as being responsible. These individual responses obviously depend on the general level of education about medical care. We argue in the next section that individuals have quite different desires for the medical care they seek. We think it essential to provide a range of choices.

---

[25] Victor R. Fuchs, "Health Care in the United States Economic System," *Milbank Memorial Fund Quarterly*, vol. 50, part 1 (April 1972).
[26] Milton Friedman, *Capitalism and Freedom* (Chicago: University of Chicago Press, 1962).
[27] Somers, *Health Care in Transition*, Chapter 8.

Where choice is available, people use it. While the majority of all Kaiser enrollees report themselves happy with the plan, 44 percent of the subscribers to the Southern California Plan had used other doctors or other services outside the plan.[28] About 10 percent of subscribers in Kaiser Portland annually used outside services.[29] In Great Britain there are still many people who buy some or all of their medical care outside the National Health Service (NHS).[30] These people are a vocal minority whom it would be difficult to satisfy within the system. It takes a great deal of pressure off the NHS to have these people exercise their choice of a private physician when they become dissatisfied with the government service. Even in Russia there has been a plea for the establishment of nursing homes and hospitals which would charge patients;[31] the justification is the overcrowding of free facilities, which results in some degradation in care. Reasons for preferring private physicians in countries with a national health service include ideology (a personal opposition to government-controlled medicine), status (getting a personal service different from that available to most people), and, most important, the ability to arrange appointments to fit one's convenience and to eliminate waiting.

Choice is also important for the physician. Kaiser reports that 12½ percent of nonpartner physicians and 5 percent of partner physicians leave the plan each year.[32] Kaiser insists that any company offering prepaid group practice as a benefit also offer at least one alternative plan. Denying choice by assigning patient or physician to an HMO would have the undesirable effects of stifling competition and forcing an individual to stay within an organization he disliked. The HMO would have no way of dealing with malcontents, nor would it have to worry about satisfying them beyond the point of preventing rebellion. Even an administrator with the best intentions would learn that he could not please everyone, nor would there be any reason to try. After all, individuals could not leave the organization. Not only would it be undesirable to freeze consumers and providers in an HMO, but also patients should be able to choose between the HMO and fee-for-service practice and should not be unnecessarily confined in their choice of hospital or other facility. It is astonishing that as of February 1972 more than twenty states had legal bars to prepaid group practice;[33] furthermore, franchising and certificate-of-need laws may restrict choice unduly. In the next section we stress the importance of competition and of choice.

---

[28] Greer Williams, *Kaiser-Permanente Health Plan: Why It Works* (Oakland, Calif.: The Henry J. Kaiser Foundation, 1971), p. 38.

[29] Saward and Greenlick, "Health Policy and the HMO," p. 165.

[30] Samuel Mencher, *British Private Medical Practice and the National Health Service* (Pittsburgh: University of Pittsburgh Press, 1968).

[31] Harry Schwartz, *An Introduction to the Soviet Economy* (Columbus, Ohio: Charles E. Merrill, 1968).

[32] "Differing Group MDs Agree on HMO Go-Slow Approach," *Medical Group News,* November 1971, as reported in *Medical Care Review,* vol. 29 (January 1972), p. 13.

[33] "Over Twenty States Have Legal Bars to Group Practice," *Group Health and Welfare News,* February 1972, as reported in *Medical Care Review,* vol. 29 (March 1972).

Why Competition in Health Care?

The idea of fostering competition among physicians or health care institutions is anathema to most health care experts. They view health care delivery as outside the competitive arena and have worked to eliminate competition to the greatest extent possible. Rather than stress the differences among physicians or among health care institutions, they have emphasized the similarity. All medical schools are first class, and all physicians are highly qualified professionals. If they were not, they would not be licensed. All hospitals are first class, or they would not have been certified by their state. One might view the prohibition of advertising as a way of keeping competition to a minimum.

In opposition to this conventional wisdom, we see three principal advantages to competition in health care: (1) people desire different sorts of medical care, and competition would help people fill their needs better; (2) competition would motivate providers to adjust to patient demands and to promote patient satisfaction; and (3) the competition provided by an HMO, with its more efficient organization and better control over utilization of resources, would induce health insurers and fee-for-service providers to take measures to keep the cost of their insurance policies and services down. We discuss each of these briefly.

Rather than wanting some uniform standard of medical care, consumers evidently have vastly different preferences. Some desire a warm, friendly, personal physician (or community hospital) while others want an aloof, coldly competent physician (or university-affiliated hospital). Some demand and would pay for luxurious furnishings and surroundings when they seek medical care, while others care nothing for the physical setting. Finally, some demand a vast number of medical services, including the latest tests (which they learn about from popular medical articles), while others prefer to have as few x-rays, lab tests, and medications as possible. Pretending that these differences do not exist can only lead to patient unhappiness.

Competition among providers also helps to stimulate innovation. Surely the rash of innovative programs we currently see being developed has something to do with the competition for public funds. No one would deny that it was competition that led to the dramatic decrease in price for abortions in New York.

Cost controls in the fee-for-service sector (mostly by the hospital utilization-review committees mandated by Medicare) have been only slightly effective to date. They could be expected to strengthen, however, if HMO enrollment fees should begin to undercut insurance premiums significantly. Such competition would prompt intensified claims for review by foundations for medical care or health insurers, significantly reducing demands on health resources. Real relief from inflationary pressures could be expected from the shift in incentives that such competition would produce.

Incentive Reimbursement of Hospitals

We briefly discussed the role of incentives above, arguing that properly structured incentives can call forth both efficiency and innovation. In this section we (1) review specific evidence that hospitals react to current incentives, (2) present a proposal for incentive reimbursement by insurers and funding agencies in the fee-for-service sector, and (3) then discuss the implications of such a proposal.[34]

Do Hospitals React to Financial Incentives? Since most hospitals are nonprofit organizations, dedicated to serving patients, one might conjecture that financial incentives will not affect their behavior. But, of course, even nonprofit hospitals must have adequate financial resources to serve their patients. What further evidence is there that hospitals do react to financial incentives?

We have examined the behavior of western Pennsylvania hospitals since 1967. At that time, a new reimbursement contract was put into effect wherein hospitals were divided into nine groups (defined by three levels of teaching service and three locational factors) and reimbursed by Blue Cross on a cost basis, subject to a ceiling which was 10 percent above the mean for the relevant group. After studying this reimbursement plan, we formulated two hypotheses. The first was that this plan would do nothing to slow the general rate of cost increase, and that western Pennsylvania hospitals would experience cost increases comparable to those of similar groups nationally. The second was that individual hospitals would respond to the incentive in such a way that those with costs below the group mean would rise most rapidly and those with costs above the mean would rise more slowly. We tested these hypotheses and confirmed them. Thus, nonprofit hospitals do react to financial incentives in a predictable way.

A Proposed Incentive Reimbursement Plan. The per diem costs of a hospital are hypothesized to vary with its size, location, teaching status, occupancy rate, case mix, and severity of case mix. We have gathered information on each of these factors and estimated a cost function for sixty-five western Pennsylvania hospitals for the period 1966-68. We have tested the estimated function in a number of ways and believe that it reflects the influence of each of these factors on the cost per case. These are factors which most observers believe affect the variation of costs among hospitals.

We would argue that such an estimated relation can be used as a formula to reimburse hospitals for patients they have treated. Instead of either paying the patient bill (and therefore charges set by the hospital in an uncompetitive environment) or paying the hospitals their costs, we propose applying such a formula

---

[34] This section is based on Judith R. Lave, Lester B. Lave and Lester P. Silverman, "A Proposal for Incentive Reimbursement for Hospitals," *Medical Care,* vol. 11 (March-April 1973), p. 79.

to determine reimbursement. Recognizing the importance of inflation, we would argue that a negotiated, built-in inflation rate should be put into the formula.

The formula accounts for many of the factors that affect hospital costs and in a given year is independent of an individual hospital's performance. If the case mix became more expensive, reimbursement would automatically be increased. The necessary data for such a system are being systematically collected by most hospitals. The primary advantage of such a system is that it allows for decentralized control at the operating level. Since reimbursement would not be on a cost basis, hospitals would not be motivated to purchase unnecessary equipment or to open duplicate facilities which would be underused. Administrators would be required to exercise more of their management functions in order to control more of the activities going on in the facility.

The Effects of Incentive Reimbursement. No one can propose incentive reimbursement for hospitals without facing the issue of the consequence of paying hospitals either more or less than current costs. Both are difficult issues. If a hospital is paid more than current costs, this can serve to promote inefficiency. For example, the hospital might use the surplus to purchase unneeded equipment or luxuries, or to hire excess staff. The result of such actions would be that the hospital would be put in a difficult position in subsequent periods and might be forced to curtail necessary services. One would have to depend on the hospital's foresight in using the surplus to accomplish things that improve patient care, but could not be financed by normal means, for example, research in health care delivery, additional training for staff, community programs, or appropriate expansion.

Undercompensating the hospital puts it in the position where it must either raise funds from other sources or go bankrupt. For small or temporary deficits, the hospital can get funds from philanthropy or loans. If the hospital continues to be undercompensated (because it is inefficiently managed or underutilized), it must close. Presumably, this means that "necessary" services will no longer be available. It means that employees will lose their jobs, physicians will lose their staff privileges, and patients will have to travel greater distances to receive hospital care. The bankruptcy of some hospitals is almost certain if an incentive reimbursement system is to work. Purchase or reorganization may serve to minimize the losses associated with bankruptcy and to permit continued operation under new management.

What is the effect of incentive reimbursement? There are two beneficial effects. The first is that hospitals will be motivated to increase efficiency and to react more rapidly to changing demands. If people are moving from an area with hospitals to one without hospital services (as in moving from city to suburb), existing hospitals will discover that they must accommodate or close. They must get rid of excess beds, follow the population shift, or react in some way to curtail costs or increase utilization. (It is anticipated that low-income groups will be provided with

178

health insurance and hence the problem of leaving low-income areas without facilities will not occur.) As shown in the previous section, hospitals do react to financial incentives, and one can expect that the vast majority of hospitals which are of below average efficiency will improve.

For those hospitals which are incapable of improving, there may be no alternative to closure. In the long run, the system will be better without these hospitals. To assess short-run costs, one must examine what is lost when a hospital closes. Obviously, the plant and equipment will become useless (although much of the equipment can be sold). There is the cost imposed on employees of finding a new job. There is the problem for physicians of finding staff privileges elsewhere (if they can). Finally, there is the cost of the organization closing, in terms of trustees, volunteers, and fund raisers.

In assessing these costs, one must differentiate between a hospital closing in an area where there is an excess number of beds and one closing because it is hopelessly inefficient. Where there is overcapacity, the social cost of keeping even an efficiently managed hospital open is very great. Some way must be found to reduce the number of beds; efficiency and patient demand are good criteria for deciding which hospitals to close. When a hospital closes because it is hopelessly inefficient, there is social waste. If the hospital management and practices had changed, society would have saved all of these costs. Indeed, the board of trustees will be motivated to change management and save the hospital. If they cannot or will not react, there seems no alternative to closing the hospital and incurring the consequent costs. Keeping the hospital open and operating in an inefficient fashion is an expensive alternative for society.

The final problem that must be raised is, what about the hospital whose costs are too high because the quality of care it renders is higher than the average? We would argue that it is incumbent upon a hospital to justify its claim for higher quality in terms of *output* performance, rather than the quality of its inputs. Quality is an elusive concept, but, given its importance, much is hidden under the guise of quality.

Conclusion

We have described an extraordinary complicated system with a number of prominent faults. The public, as well as health care experts and government officials, are concerned with rising costs, maldistribution of medical services, inefficient production of medical services, patient dissatisfaction, and the increasing financial pressure on health care institutions. A number of attempts have been made in the last decade to deal with these problems. Medicare and Medicaid have done much to equalize access to medical care, but they have also increased the cost of care significantly and raised false hopes among many people. While we would not want to argue that these programs have done more harm than good, we would note that they have been disruptive.

To a large extent, government is now part of the problem and must take special care that its efforts accomplish objectives with a minimum amount of disruption. Common sense, goodwill, and good intentions are not sufficient to guarantee that attempts to solve these problems will not lead to new, even worse problems. It is important that we proceed carefully, attempting to ensure that proposals will be beneficial and that disruption is controlled.

Five basic proposals for government intervention in medical care delivery were discussed—improved financing of medical care as a means of ensuring equality of access, restructuring the delivery system in order to increase the efficiency with which care is produced, comprehensive planning with a view to reducing redundant facilities and services and coordinating providers, and certificate-of-need legislation and licensing as ways to increase the power of planning agencies or government to control the production and delivery of health care. Each of these tools can be used to improve the delivery of care, but in view of the complexity of the system each is fraught with difficulties and dangers in application. We conclude that planning has a very important but limited role in improving the delivery of health care.

There has been increasing pressure for government involvement in medical care delivery. Giving more power to planning agencies, restructuring the current delivery system, and increasing government control and financing are but three illustrations of this pressure. Centralization of control is fraught with difficulties. To control effectively, enormous quantities of data must be collected and analyzed, and much of the imagination and drive of local professionals would be subjugated to the centralized authority.

While recognizing that some increased centralization is inevitable, we stress the advantages of decentralization, of choice, and of competition. Properly structured incentives constitute a preferable solution to central control. If incentives can be structured correctly, there is much less need for extensive data collection and analysis, and one can put the intelligence and imagination of individual professionals to work in solving problems. We noted that incentives have tended to be perverse in the past, with cost-plus reimbursement for hospitals and with physicians paid for doing unnecessary surgery. Much more effort should be devoted to restructuring incentives.

The amount of current choice in the system and the role of competition were analyzed. We see a great deal of choice by the individual, a wide variety of preferences concerning the kind of services desired, and a tailoring of the current system to these preferences. We would advocate modifying the current range of choices by improving information to the consumer and by eliminating all legal impediments to prepaid group practice.

180

As a particular illustration of restructuring incentives, we focused on hospitals and proposed a system of incentive reimbursement. It was shown that hospitals adjust to current financial incentives, so the problem is one of devising a means of reimbursement that will meet a hospital's financial needs but not lead it to incur useless expenses by permitting duplication of services and facilities. We made use of an estimated cost function to construct an incentive reimbursement plan that would reward hospitals for efficiency. While increasing the efficiency of hospital operations is important, our plan would not be effective in dealing with the problem of hospital location. Questions of that sort would be better solved by planning.

Although we caution that the medical care system is a complicated one and that government intervention is as likely to cause disruption as to be helpful, our recommendations are not negative. Rather, we emphasize the role of incentives in harnessing the information, imagination, and energy of health professionals. Controlling some part of the system centrally is expensive and unlikely to be suited to local problems. We view the HMO as a way of restructuring incentives for physicians so that they become more interested in improving health at the lowest cost. Incentives for institutions and patients must also be restructured to motivate them to achieve the same ends. Political decisions have to be made concerning the level of funding. A proposed incentive reimbursement plan was argued to restructure incentives for hospitals correctly. A restructuring of incentives is likely to be the most productive way of reforming the medical care delivery system.

THE LEGAL ACCOUNTABILITY OF NONPROFIT HOSPITALS

Laurens H. Silver

The subject of my paper will be accountability of not-for-profit hospitals.[1] Before analyzing the factors bearing on accountability, I should note that I have been actively involved for the last three years in an OEO-funded, legal services backup center which has provided legal assistance to local groups of indigents and indigent individuals in cooperation with local legal services programs on matters pertaining to the health care delivery system as it affects the poor. It is in the context of this advocacy effort that I wish to describe to you today several significant developments with regard to the law affecting not-for-profit hospitals and their accountability that have resulted from the efforts of public interest attorneys spearheaded by the National Health and Environmental Law Program (NHELP) at the University of California, Los Angeles, during the last few years. I shall attempt to analyze the reasons for, and significance of, such developments.

We have all addressed ourselves during the course of the conference to the problems which result when decision makers, whether they be hospital administrators or doctors, perceive themselves immediately answerable to their professional colleagues rather than to the interests of patients. In such a situation, the hospital is viewed as the doctor's workshop and the task of the administrator is seen as being to provide appropriate tools, as demanded by the customers (the doctors of the workshop).[2] Yet it is difficult for the administrator to be sensitive to the patients' interests, as there is no organized, patient counter-constituency to the medical staff which is able to affect the decision-making process. We do not have an organized, broad-based consumers' movement in health care. However, an organization such as the National Welfare Rights Organization (NWRO), whose membership is composed of welfare recipients throughout the country, has expressed considerable interest in recent years in health as well as welfare issues on behalf of its membership. Organized consumer constituencies such as labor unions which

---

[1] Competitive factors which may produce accountability in decision making have been described ably by Professor Havighurst in his article on "Health Maintenance Organizations and the Market for Health Services," *Law and Contemporary Problems*, vol. 35, no. 4 (Autumn 1971), p. 716. Such competitive influences, to the extent that any currently exist, will not be analyzed in this paper.
[2] See Morton Creditor, "If Doctors Owned the Hospitals," *New England Journal of Medicine*, January 21, 1971, p. 134.

purchase health care plans have not used their potential countervailing power to affect decision making by health care providers. When the National Health and Environmental Law Program began operating three years ago, there was no organized consumer constituency and certainly no organized poor people's constituency with the exception of NWRO.

Two problems became manifest—two problems which it has been the task of the NHELP to focus upon during its first several years of operation. These are the problems which I wish to discuss here.

Access to Care for the Medically Indigent

The first problem is the question of accountability of health care institutions to the poor, primarily in terms of access. Although there have been few systematic studies chronicling access problems of the poor to health care institutions, legal services attorneys, working with client groups and with individual poor people throughout the United States, immediately began reporting to us the significant number of instances in which their clients have complained of being refused admission on an elective and emergency basis at hospitals in various parts of the country, in both rural and urban areas. One study of patient geographical origins in Chicago has revealed that indigent patients come from all over Cook County to apply for services at Cook County Hospital, bypassing local hospitals.[3] The author, Pierre DeVise, speculates that these patterns may be due to a number of factors, one of which is the failure of not-for-profit hospitals throughout the Cook County area to offer services both to Medicaid eligibles and to the so-called noncategorically related medically indigent (those individuals not eligible for Medicare and Medicaid). Though again I emphasize that there are no firm data, I would speculate on the basis of the reports to our project from legal services programs throughout the country that, in many areas, (1) there is channelization of indigent patients who present themselves for treatment at private, not-for-profit hospital emergency rooms to municipal and county hospitals; (2) there is a pattern and practice in many communities of hospitals requiring substantial deposits as a condition to entry, or proof of third-party source of payment as a condition of rendering emergency and/or elective services; and (3) such nonpublic hospitals do not provide a significant amount of free or below-cost patient services.

---

[3] Pierre DeVise, *Slum Medicine: Chicago's Apartheid Health System* (Chicago: Community and Family Study Center, University of Chicago, 1969), pp. 17-38. For a generally helpful appraisal of the difficulties faced by the poor in getting services from the medical care system, see Strauss, "Medical Organization, Medical Care and Lower Income Groups," *Social Science and Medicine,* 1969, pp. 143-177. See also Gibson, Bugbee, and Anderson, *Emergency Medical Services in the Chicago Area* (Chicago: Center for Health Administration Studies, University of Chicago, 1971), pp. 232-254.

Thus in the early stage of our existence as an organization we identified a problem of significance to the poor: entry barriers to access to adequate health services. As lawyers acting on behalf of clients with an actual grievance, we then began examining the relevant laws which might bear on a hospital's obligation to care for the poor. Among the statutes which we examined was the Hill-Burton Act which, since its enactment in 1946, had provided loans and grants for the construction and renovation of hospitals.[4] In analyzing that statute, we found that it provided for a reasonable amount of free or below-cost patient care to be provided by grantee hospitals unless there was an explicit waiver of this provision based on financial hardship of the grantee institution.[5] Moreover, we discovered that virtually all hospitals had signed a contractual agreement that they would provide a reasonable amount of free or below-cost patient care as a condition of receiving Hill-Burton grants. No hospital to our knowledge has ever been granted a waiver of this requirement. This legal requirement, it seemed to us, had perhaps been ignored during the previous twenty-five-year period of dispensation of federal grants. Having identified a possible legal theory upon which to base an obligation to serve the poor, we then had to consider the consequences of use of such a theory. We knew that there was no adequate federal or state funding available to subsidize the care of the noncategorically related, medically indigent although, since 1965, federal matching had been available through Medicaid to provide reasonable cost reimbursement to hospitals providing services to the categorically needy.[6] Therefore, enforcement of the Hill-Burton contractual commitment could, in the absence of subsidization from the public sector, result in imposition of the entire financial burden for caring for such patients on provider institutions.

As lawyers faced with counseling clients who would be injured by reason of the failure of hospitals in their local communities to care for them, we were confronted with few alternatives. It had become obvious to public interest lawyers, particularly legal services lawyers, that in dealing with the Department of Health, Education, and Welfare with regard to the categorical assistance programs, many administrators in the agency looked to a constituency of state welfare administrators.[7] Likewise it was surmised that the administration of the Hill-Burton program would not be responsive to consumer interests, not because of complicity or conspiracy but simply because providers have the greatest awareness of program problems and communicated rapidly, frequently, and often intimately with program

---

[4] U.S.C. 291 et seq.
[5] 42 U.S.C. 291 (c); 42 C.F.R. 53.11.
[6] The categorically needy are individuals eligible for money payments in the federally financed public assistance programs, Aid to the Disabled, Old Age Assistance, Aid to the Blind, and Aid to Families with Dependent Children. The noncategorically related medically needy are individuals who are not eligible for such programs because they do not have the requisite attributes for eligibility in any of the aforementioned public assistance programs.
[7] See Winifred Bell, *Aid to Dependent Children* (New York: Columbia University Press, 1965), *passim*.

administrators. We also knew that the Hill-Burton contractual obligation to provide a reasonable amount of free or below-cost patient care was an obligation that, at least in our knowledge, had not been enforced during the twenty-five years of the administration of the program. Therefore, it appeared likely that a simple appeal to the administration to enforce the contractual pledge would be met with stiff resistance or, more likely, apathy and/or procrastination.

We believed that we had identified a significant problem which required resolution through litigation. Only after litigation had been commenced could anything ever be accomplished administratively. It also appeared unlikely at that time that adequate forces could be mustered to amend the Hill-Burton legislation in a manner which would require greater accountability on the part of not-for-profit hospitals with regard to the plight of the noncategorically related, medically indigent. Moreover, there already were adequate mechanisms in the law, as it appeared that Congress had clearly intended in enacting Hill-Burton that not-for-profit hospitals receiving public monies under the Hill-Burton program would, as a quid pro quo, be required to provide a reasonable amount of free or below-cost patient care.

Faced with individual client complaints concerning the inaccessibility of hospital services and the nonaccountability of the not-for-profit sector to the health care needs of a significant consumer class, we undertook to develop a coordinated, litigative strategy whereby legal services programs throughout the country could start actions to enforce the commitment prescribed by the Hill-Burton Act. It was hoped that the commitment, appropriately framed as a legal issue on behalf of an appropriate plaintiff, could inspire a court order implementing and defining more precisely the Hill-Burton commitment, since the administrative agency charged by Congress with enforcing the act had egregiously failed to do so.

During the last year and a half there have been a number of actions alleging Hill-Burton causes of action brought in different parts of the country, including Florida, rural Colorado, West Virginia, Kansas, Louisiana, New York, and the District of Columbia.[8] These affirmative actions have been brought in federal district court on behalf of predominantly noncategorically related, medically indigent individuals who have alleged that they were refused hospital admission because of an admission policy requiring proof of third-party source of payment or a deposit. The legal theory of these actions was essentially that the hospital had signed a binding, contractual commitment to undertake a reasonable amount of free or below-cost patient care. This promise made by the hospitals at the time they had received the Hill-Burton grants could be enforced by plaintiffs suing in federal dis-

---

[8] Cook v. Ochsner Foundation Hospital, Civ. Act. No. 70-1969 (E.D. La.); Euresti v. Stenner, Civ. Act. No. C-2462 (D. Colo.); O.M.I.C.A. v. James Archer Smith Hospital, Civ. Act. No. 70-1794 (S.D. Fla.); Perry et al v. Greater Southeast Washington Community Hospital, Civ. Act. No. 725-71 (D. D.C.); United Appalachian Poor People v. Webster Hospital, Civ. Act. No. 71-207 (S.D. W.Va.); Corum v. Beth Israel Hospital, Civ. Act. No. 72-2674 (S.D. N.Y.); Johnson v. Storemont General Hospital, Civ. Act. T-5154 (D. Kan.).

trict court. Plaintiffs were alleging that they were beneficiaries of the promise made by the hospital to the state agency and federal government and that this pledge conferred upon them legal standing for seeking redress from the court. Seeking such redress is a slow, expensive process. A federal district court decision does not necessarily create binding precedent throughout the United States. Thus it was with some considerable trepidation and risk that a strategy of litigation was undertaken. It was hoped that the accumulation of favorable precedents and the articulation by some federal district judges of what a reasonable amount of free or below-cost patient care meant would generate enough pressure upon the Hill-Burton administrators in the Department of Health, Education, and Welfare to cause them to promulgate an administrative policy defining the free and below-cost requirement that would be of universal applicability throughout the United States.

One of the most significant cases, *Cook* v. *Ochsner Memorial Hospital,* was commenced in New Orleans in the early part of 1970.[9] This case named as defendants virtually all of the private not-for-profit hospitals in New Orleans, and alleged that all such hospitals were acting in violation of their Hill-Burton commitment by engaging in a pattern and practice of refusing services to indigent individuals on both an elective and emergency basis and by referring them to the Charity Hospital of New Orleans. I shall not describe for you the difficulties of the individuals named as plaintiffs in other cases; nor shall I chronicle differences in the allegations raised in the various jurisdictions. Suffice it to say that since the commencement of these cases several favorable court opinions have emerged. All have dealt with preliminary issues without making a final determination on the merits of the controversy.[10]

Thus there has been no determination by a court of what constitutes a reasonable amount of free or below-cost patient care nor has there been a determination as to the extent of the community service obligation of a hospital.[11] However, in anticipation of a court ruling (and perhaps concerned about a court's taking upon itself the definition of what constitutes a reasonable amount of free or be-

---

[9] See note 8 above.

[10] See Cook et al. v. Ochsner Foundation Hospital, 319 F. Supp. 603 (1970); O.M.I.C.A. v. James Archer Smith Hospital, 325 F. Supp. 268 (1971); and Euresti v. Stenner, 458 F.2d 1115 (1972).

[11] See 42 U.S.C. 291(c). The extent to which a hospital owes a legal obligation under the community service clause to provide services to the Title 19 categorically needy was litigated in Perry et al. v. Greater Southwest Washington Community Hospital and Cook et al. v. Ochsner et al., see note 8 above. In an oral opinion dismissing the *Perry* case, District Judge Gesell ruled that the trial court could not define the community service obligation; to do so would be performing the function of the Department of Health, Education and Welfare. However, Judge Comiskey in *Cook* disagreed with Judge Gesell, and held that the Department of Health, Education and Welfare had violated its obligation to enforce the community service commitments of seven New Orleans Hill-Burton hospitals which refused to participate in Medicaid (Slip Opinion, May 29, 1973). The Department of Health, Education and Welfare has informed the Court, in compliance with that finding and order, that it intends to promulgate a regulation covering this situation.

low-cost patient care) a few weeks after the decision of the Tenth Circuit Court of Appeals in *Euresti* v. *Stenner* [12] (which held that a migrant laborer had legal standing to sue as a beneficiary of the Hill-Burton contractual obligation to provide free or below-cost services), the Department of Health, Education, and Welfare promulgated proposed standards defining administratively the extent of the obligation. [13] These proposed standards would require hospitals receiving Hill-Burton grants to provide 5 percent of their operating costs (after deduction of costs atributable to Medicare or Medicaid patients) in care for the poor and near poor. The 5 percent level is a presumptive compliance level, and there is latitude for the state agencies charged with administering the state Hill-Burton program to set a lower (or higher) percentage depending upon the needs of the area served by the hospital. Two further points should be noted about the proposed regulations. First, the requirement of providing free patient care may be waived by HEW if the hospital proves it is not financially feasible. Second, the proposal establishes a mechanism whereby consumer groups may appeal a determination by the state agency that a hospital is to provide a certain percentage of free or below-cost patient care. This appeal may first be made to the state agency and then to the Department of Health, Education, and Welfare. The state agency is required to publish the percentage requirements which it imposes upon respective hospitals.

The American Hospital Association vigorously reacted to the proposed regulation. [14] Requesting additional time in which to prepare its comments and to amass data on the financial incapability of hospitals to satisfy the requirement, the AHA board of trustees resolved to resist final enactment of the proposal with all the forces at its command. In response to the outcry of the hospitals, HEW considerably modified the proposed regulations and considerably lightened the obligation proposed in the earlier form of the regulation. The principal modification was to set the presumptive compliance level at 3 percent of operating costs or 10 percent of all Hill-Burton grants, whichever was the lesser. [15] The state agency could not establish a higher obligation to serve the indigent.

Let us now reexamine the original strategy. It seemed unlikely that presenting to Congress the plight of clients who were alleging the denial of hospital services would result in legislation providing the noncategorically related, medically indigent with a third-party source of payment through federal subsidy. The resolution of the problem of the noncategorically related, medically indigent would probably come only in the context of national health insurance—a legislative issue that might take years to resolve. Without pressure exerted first by litigation, pressure upon the Hill-Burton administration would not be likely to result in any more pre-

---

[12] See note 10 above.
[13] 37 Fed. Reg. 7632 (April 1972).
[14] See William J. Curran, "Medical Charity for the Poor," *New England Journal of Medicine*, vol. 287 (September 7, 1972), p. 498.
[15] 37 Fed. Reg. 14719 (July 22, 1972).

cise definition of the existing requirement that hospitals provide a reasonable amount of free or below-cost patient care; nor would it result in enforcement of that requirement. Thus, as noted previously, the lawyers perceived a "right" arising from the Hill-Burton contractual undertaking; the task was to translate that right into an identifiable and enforceable quantum of services. How the hospitals might be able to absorb the additional expense was not, in legal terms, a compelling consideration, for as the lawyers reasoned, the legislative history of the law had made it clear that Congress had required a quid pro quo from hospitals in exchange for their eligibility for Hill-Burton grants.[16] The quid pro quo was to provide a reasonable amount of free or below-cost patient care.

A further strategy lurked in the background and was a factor in the decision-making process. Legal theories provided a tool for court enforcement of the existing commitments; having undertaken such a commitment, hospitals were vulnerable to pressures from the courts which might enforce such a commitment. Court rulings might propel administrative enforcement and articulation of the Hill-Burton requirement. Administrative definition of the requirement would force hospitals to make an appraisal—perhaps an agonizing one—of their relationship to the community and their obligations vis-à-vis the indigent. It was recognized that imposition of a rigorously enforced Hill-Burton requirement on the hospitals might even foster a fiscal crisis, and might, in some measure at least, shift the financial burden for care for such patients to the third-party insurers and private patients. It was hoped, however, that the financial crisis of the hospitals might cause the hospitals to focus their political energy on addressing immediately and adequately, through legislative redress, the problem of adequate financing of care of the categorically related, medically indigent. The litigative strategy might thus have an ultimately political end—namely legislative attention to the problem of the noncategorically related, medically indigent.

We have been recognizing—sometimes belatedly and sorrowfully—that courts may not be the appropriate forums for achieving widesweeping social change; assuredly courts cannot legislate a solution to the problem of financing the medical care of the noncategorically related, medically indigent. Yet we have seen the use of the courts—in dealing with the nonresponsiveness and nonaccountability of monopolistic enterprises and governmental agencies—to prod, push, and shove vulnerable parts of the sytem. Then the vulnerable parts of the system—the hospitals—can rethink new solutions to a systemic problem. Where other avenues of insuring accountability do not work, where there are no mechanisms of restraint imposed upon the system by competitive forces,[17] the courts can perform a useful function

---

[16] For a discussion of the legislative history see Marilyn Rose, "The Duty of Publicly Funded Hospital to Provide Services to the Medically Indigent," *Clearinghouse Review,* vol. 3 (February 1970), p. 254.

[17] Havighurst, "Health Maintenance Organizations and the Market for Health Services," *passim.*

in making hospital officials honor the commitment which they perhaps heedlessly made to provide free or below-cost services to the indigent.[18] To the extent that hospital administrators are captives of the medical staff in the decision-making process with respect to investment in capital equipment, the scrutiny of the decision-making process afforded by litigation can be effective in making the executive officer of the hospital responsive to countervailing forces to provide a greater quantum of direct patient services before he succumbs to the importunities of the medical staff to invest in capital equipment which might produce very few immediate patient services. In facing demands of the medical staff, a hospital administrator can say that he is legally obligated to take into account the needs of another constituency in his budget planning and that investment in another piece of medical equipment, possibly duplicative of other such equipment in the community, cannot be made in view of the Hill-Burton commitment to provide a certain quantum of services, compliance with which may be subject to judicial scrutiny.

Thus in the absence of market forces, and faced with unorganized applicants for services without a source of payment and without the capacity to go elsewhere for hospital services, hospital administrators can make decisions without being fully accountable to community needs. The hospital administrator and board of directors have one or two principal constituencies—the medical staff and also the increasingly organized hospital nonprofessional employee staff. In the absence of an organized consumer constituency, in the absence of countervailing pressures from the health insurance industry, decisions will be made that are not fully in the consumer interest. Thus there are appropriate instances where pressures directed toward insuring access to hospitals should be exerted through the courts despite the expense and time-consuming nature of litigation. The courts, in this instance, are only enforcing an allocative decision made by the Congress in enacting Hill-Burton. Congress imposed on hospitals a legal obligation, as a condition of receiving Hill-Burton funds, to allocate a certain proportion of revenues to free or below-cost patient care rather than to investment in substantial capital equipment acquisitions.

Accreditation and the Provider-Dominated Joint Commission on Accreditation of Hospitals

Having discussed the role of the courts in monitoring accountability of health care institutions and having examined the role of lawyers in articulating strategies to deal with nonaccountability, I would like to examine another more dramatic mode of approaching the issue of accountability. Early in the history of legal services activity in the health care area, in 1970, it became obvious that the Joint Commis-

---

[18] It may be conjectured that some hospital officials thought of the free or below-cost care requirement as a legal "boiler-plate" which could be disregarded.

sion on Accreditation of Hospitals (JCAH) occupied a critical role in the regulation of the quality of health care. This standard-setting and standard-enforcing body is comprised of representatives from the American Hospital Association, the American Medical Association, the American College of Physicians, and the American College of Surgeons. The organization is charged with the task of developing standards for hospital accreditation. The JCAH, however, may be regarded as more than a voluntary accreditation body.[19] Its standards of accreditation are actively intermeshed with the legal qualifications which providers must satisfy to establish eligibility to be a certified provider under Title 18, Medicare. If a hospital is JCAH-accredited and meets the utilization review requirements of Title 18, it is conclusively presumed to meet the secretary's conditions of participation to be a provider under Medicare. Further, the secretary cannot prescribe higher standards than comparable JCAH standards for hospitals that choose to be certified as providers for Title 18 purposes but which are not JCAH-accredited.[20] JCAH is thus a provider-dominated body which de facto both "legislates" and "enforces" standards which allow an institution to satisfy Title 18 participation requirements.

Historically, the early part of 1970 was a critical stage in the development of new standards of hospital accreditation. A draft dated October 1, 1969, had recently been prepared by the commission. On examination of the standards, it became obvious that the commission had given little or no attention to concerns which were especially patient problems. For example, the proposed draft did not include a provision that hospitals have appropriate devices for the communication of needs by patients to nursing staff; hospitals were not required to obtain the consent of the transferee institution prior to transferring or referring a patient; hospitals were not required, when they had appropriate means for treatment, to treat patients presenting themselves for treatment at hospital emergency rooms. Moreover, no attention was given to such matters as assuring patient privacy in examining rooms or in wards, protecting the confidentiality of disclosures to physicians, disclosing fully the identity of all physicians having responsibility for the care of the patient, insuring adequate communication with patients, particularly where such patients did not speak English, and assuring that accommodations were not denied patients for any reason unrelated to medical care needs or the physical capability of the institution.

These are just some of the concerns ignored; many more omissions were noted. By virtue of the composition of the commission, it was thought unlikely that the JCAH would respond to a simple request for inclusion of the matters men-

---

[19] For a more detailed discussion of the JCAH, see William Worthington and Laurens H. Silver, "Regulation of Quality of Care in Hospitals: The Need for Change," *Law and Contemporary Problems*, vol. 35 (1970), pp. 304, 310-327.

[20] If the states choose to establish higher standards for Title 18 providers, such standards must be applied by the secretary upon notification by the state that the secretary is requested to apply such higher standards. 42 U.S.C. 1395(z).

tioned above in their proposed standards. There was further a suspicion that an articulation of standards by a group of providers might, no matter how ardent the protestations of disinterestedness on the part of the group, be improperly affected by collateral considerations arising from the economic self-interest of the group. One such consideration might well have been the warning set forth in the celebrated case of *Darling* v. *Charleston Memorial Hospital.*[21] In that case, the Illinois Supreme Court held that joint commission standards could be introduced into evidence to prove the standard of medical care pertinent for a determination of negligence by the jury. This case, decided in 1965, certainly was not unknown to the joint commission as it was developing its new standards. Could not one surmise that hovering in the background would be a concern that the standards developed by the commission could become the basis, in light of *Darling,* for malpractice actions against doctors and hospitals? Such a concern would militate a cautious approach in articulating standards. That such a speculation is not unwarranted, perhaps, may be supported by the fact that the very standard at issue in the *Darling* case, pertaining to the requirement of consultation between doctors under certain circumstances (such as the circumstances of *Darling,* where the patient suffered complications from the improper application of a cast to a leg fracture), was deleted from the 1969 draft (and remains omitted to this day).[22]

Realizing the critical role of the JCAH in developing and applying standards and in Title 18 certification, we were again confronted with a question of tactics in counseling client groups which were interested in health issues. The most immediate task seemed twofold. First, it was critical to attempt to present to the commission and suggestions of health care consumers which could be incorporated into the standards; second, it was thought that a mechanism should be developed whereby there could be consumer input into the accreditation process itself during the course of the visit of JCAH surveyors to a hospital. With regard to the input into the standards, the National Welfare Rights Organization developed a set of some twenty-six principles, which covered subjects ranging from admissions policies of the hospital to consumer representation on the board of directors of hospitals.[23]

The next question was the one of tactics. Since JCAH had no formal petitioning procedure whereby outside groups could submit proposed standards, submit evidence on their behalf, and be assured as a matter of right of some response to such petition, it was decided that the only means of insuring access to the appropriate decision makers would be to request a meeting with the JCAH board of directors and to present the proposed standards at a regular quarterly meeting of the board.

---

21 211 N.E. 2d 253 (1965).
22 Worthington and Silver, "Regulation of Quality of Care in Hospitals," p. 311.
23 These are set forth in ibid, p. 328. For an interesting account of the activities of consumer groups in the medical care arena, see "The Surge of Community Involvement," *Medical World News,* May 19, 1972, pp. 51-63.

We should pause at this moment to note that the JCAH had taken the position that it had consulted with a number of groups prior to the preparation of the October 1969 draft and that it had sponsored conferences and other gatherings which had considered in depth the new standards. However, these conferences and workshops had been composed almost exclusively of provider groups with special competencies in medical care administration. To the best of my knowledge, there was no real attempt to involve nonprovider groups which might have had an interest in commenting upon the standards.

In any event, whatever the bona fide attempts of the commission to elicit a variety of views on the proposed standards prior to the 1969 draft, our analysis in December of 1969 revealed glaring deficiencies, and we so advised a number of "consumer" groups, such as NWRO and the National Council of Senior Citizens, which had preexisting client-attorney relationships with legal services programs. It was the decision of these groups to press certain points with the commission, to meet with the commission to explain these points, and otherwise to insist that the aforementioned list of "principles" be presented to the joint commission board meeting in January 1970.

I need not document here the history of the reception of the demands; suffice it to say that the encounter had the classic outlines of the "confrontation" politics of the late 1960s. First, there was the refusal of the JCAH to entertain a "consumer" delegation at the board of directors' meeting and an assertion that work on a final version of the standards would be seriously retarded if a new set of modifications were to be put forward. Next there was a telegram from several consumer-based organizations such as NWRO indicating that they were sending spokesmen to the board of directors' meeting anyway. JCAH countered that the board of directors' meetings were closed to the public, but that the board could vote as to whether or not to receive the delegation. On the day of the board meeting the delegation arrived without an invitation and reiterated its "demand" to meet with the board. This demand was conveyed to the board which duly voted that they would make an exception to their rules to hear from the group on that day.

The "confrontation," which continued in some form for a number of months, involved a number of skillfully executed parries and thrusts on both sides with the advantage of "uncertainty" and "unpredictability" being on the side of the consumer coalition. JCAH leadership was vexed and uncertain about how to institutionalize the new input. I believe they also perceived the situation as threatening to the functioning of their decision-making process and the acceptability of the 1969 draft standards; moreover, they feared possible disruption of their meetings. That JCAH was concerned about its public image and its capacity to deal with what was perceived as a threat from consumer groups (the most vocal of which was primarily composed of minority members) was illustrated soon thereafter by its appointment of a minority associate director—ostensibly its first—to deal directly with the consumer "assault."

To summarize, faced with a nonaccountable, provider-dominated organization charged with the critical function of developing quality of care standards applicable in a broad variety of contexts, including qualification of hospitals as Title 18 providers, consumer groups were forced into a model of confrontation, engaging in an intricate pirouette of confrontation and cooperation. Such ploys are not the best means for the conduct of rational discourse between reasonable men, but they can be effective in sealing the foundation for formal channels for input in the future.

The coalition "demonstration" or "presentation" at the January 1970 meeting of the JCAH board was directly responsible for producing (after months of further dialogue, including a four-hour session with the commission's standards committee) the following important modifications or additions in the standards (a list not meant in any way to be exhaustive):

Emergency Services

Standard I (Interpretation). Inherent in this action is the understanding that no patient should arbitrarily be transferred if the hospital where he was initially seen has means for adequate care of his problem. The patient may not be transferred until the receiving institution has consented to accept that patient. A reasonable record of the immediate medical problem must accompany the patient.

Standard II (Interpretation). If laboratory procedures are indicated and ordered, due regard must be given to promptness in carrying them out.

Governing Body and Management

Standard I (Interpretation). The governing body or Advisory Board should include a broad representation of the community served by the hospital.

Environmental Services

Standard II (Interpretation). Each patient shall be provided with a readily available and functioning nurse call system.

The entire preamble to the new standards was also based upon the NWRO demands. The preamble, which had no predecessor whatsoever in earlier versions of the standards, reads as follows:

The objective of clinicians and of the institutions in which they work always has been to implement the findings of research in the natural sciences and to bring their fruits to the direct and immediate service of the sick, the injured, the disabled, and the handicapped. Their concern with continuing improvement in patient care led to the formulation of the original standards for the accreditation of hospitals. For some fifty years, the standards have faithfully reflected the emphasis upon developments in the support of clinical care which have characterized the pursuit of excellence in medicine.

It seems appropriate at the outset to call attention to a shift in emphasis over the years within the body of the standards. The new standards are free of all direct demands upon the physician's clinical judgment and decision. Current standards relate entirely to the supporting elements of hospital life and the environment of medical practice.

Environmental factors, physical and other, serve to create the climate within which patient care takes place. Further, it has long been recognized that the patient's perception of and his response to his environment are important factors in his progress and recovery. Environmental considerations are reflected in the standards in certain general principles which may be said to represent a set of rights accruing to the patient, the consumer of health care services, the protection of which is one of the goals of the Joint Commission.

Equitable and humane treatment at all times and under all circumstances is such a right. This principle entails an obligation on the part of all those involved in the care of the patient to recognize and to respect his individuality and his dignity. This means creating and fostering relationships founded on mutual acceptance and trust. In practical terms, it means that no person should be denied impartial access to treatment or accommodations which are available and medically indicated, on the basis of such considerations as race, color, creed, national origin or the nature of the source of payment for his care.

Every individual who enters a hospital or other health facility for treatment retains certain rights to privacy, which should be protected by the hospital without respect to the patient's economic status or the source of payment for his care. Thus, representatives of agencies not connected with the hospital, and who are not directly or indirectly involved in the patient's care, should not be permitted access to the patient for the purpose of interviewing, interrogating or observing him, without his express consent given on each occasion when such access is sought. This protection should be provided in the emergency department and outpatient facilities as well as on the floors of the hospital. The hospital, like the church of old, must impart at least some sense of sanctuary.

The individual's dignity is reflected in the respect accorded by others to his need to maintain the privacy of his body. To the extent possible, given the inescapable exposure entailed in the provision of needed care, the patient should be aided in maintaining this privacy. The design and furnishings of examination and treatment areas, in the emergency department and outpatient facilities, as well as in other parts of the hospital, should be so planned as to facilitate the maintenance of the patient's privacy, and, as far as possible, to shield him from the view of others.

Another important aspect of the patient's right to privacy relates to the preservation of the confidentiality of his disclosures. The setting in which the patient's history is taken, for example, should be such that he can communicate with the physician in confidence. This is true of the emergency department as well as of other parts of the hospital.

In many teaching hospitals, and particularly in those which are closely affiliated with medical schools, all patients, regardless of their economic status, may be expected to participate to some extent in clinical training programs or in the gathering of data for research purposes. For all patients, regardless of the source of payment for their care, this should be a voluntary matter. The level of the patient's participation in such activities should in no way be related to the nature of the source of payment for his care.

In many large hospitals, the patient may be seen by several physicians during the course of his treatment. He has the right to know the identity of the physician who is primarily responsible for his care. In addition, the patient has the right to be informed as to the nature and purpose of any technical procedures which are to be performed upon him, as well as to know by whom such procedures are to be carried out.

The patient has the right to communicate with those responsible for his care, and to receive from them adequate information concerning the nature and extent of his medical problem, the planned course of treatment and the prognosis. In addition, he has a right to expect adequate instruction in self care in the interim between visits to the hospital or to the physician. In the matter of communication, ethnic and cultural considerations are highly significant, and should be taken into account by providing interpreters where language barriers are a continuing problem.

It should also be borne in mind that, even among people who ostensibly speak the same language, cultural variations may have the effect of obstructing effective communication. Where this a likely possibility, the hospital should employ individuals who will be able to facilitate meaningful communication among hospital staff and patients.

What has been said of the obligation of the hospital, its personnel and its physicians, to observe the human rights of the individual patient is equally true of their obligation to all patients, to the community served. Communication, mutual respect and trust, a matching of achievable resources to observable needs, all of these are inherent in the attitude and spirit of the true hospital. Whatever its community, the hospital is there to serve it, governed by scientific rule and logic, but imbued primarily with the sense of service, of compassion, of the fellowship of man.

The spirit and intent expressed in this preamble relative to the hospital patient's rights and needs and the observance of these in practice will be considered as a persuasive factor in the determination of a hospital's accreditation, in the same manner as are any of the standards of this volume.

It is my opinion that these changes in the standards are significant, especially in light of the doctrine of the *Darling* case, whereby JCAH standards could be introduced into evidence in malpractice cases to prove the appropriate standard of medical practice in a community for measuring negligence. The emergency room provisions, relating to transfer and treatment, should be especially noted in this regard. Under that section, hospitals may not "dump" an indigent patient who presents himself for treatment on another hospital without the consent of the transferee institution. A hospital which persists in such conduct may be subject to liability under *Darling* if injury ensues from its actions.

One other critical facet of the demands made by the coalition of consumer groups was that the joint commission allow participation by patient groups and by members of the hospital staff, including residents and interns and other allied health personnel, in the accreditation survey procedure. It was thought that the accreditation survey procedure, which had generally been a dialogue between administrators and surveyors, should be opened up to allow for greater participation on the part of physicians and representatives of patients who wish to report about conditions in the hospital. This was resisted by the joint commission since it was felt that the commission surveyors could evaluate the hospital on the basis of interviews with key members of the staff. The origin of the demand concerning representation and a hearing before the surveying team accrediting a hospital arose out of difficulties in the District of Columbia, where a coalition of senior citizens groups and the residents and interns association of the D.C. General Hospital undertook to examine in some detail the problems of the hospital. These problems ranged from inadequate record keeping to inadequacy of drug supplies, purchasing procedure problems, and x-ray and laboratory information retrieval difficulties.

The question was how to rectify such conditions at a hospital run by the government of the District of Columbia. One of the numerous tactics considered was to prepare systematically a report of problems in the hospital from the point of view of the residents and interns who practice daily within the hospital setting. It was thought that the joint commission survey procedure might be a convenient forum for preparation and presentation of this kind of report.

The needs of the group in the District of Columbia were conveyed to the Joint Commission on Accreditation of Hospitals in January 1970 as part of the consumer "demands." The joint commission, during the four or five months subsequent to the presentation of the demands by the coalition of consumer groups, acceded to the basic point that there should be a mechanism of presentations to the surveyors by consumer groups and/or by groups of residents and interns or other staff physicians. While the joint commission refers to the procedure as an "interview" and we have referred to the procedure established as an informal "hearing," the joint commission has established formal procedures whereby a hospital whose accreditation is being reviewed must upon request make the time available for a hearing at which grievances against the hospital concerning the quality of care in that hospital can be ventilated. This hearing procedure, since its inception, has been used on a number of occasions, most notably in the USC-County Hospital in Los Angeles, San Francisco General Hospital in San Francisco, and in D.C. General Hospital. In at least one instance, that of the Los Angeles County Hospital, a very detailed document chronicling serious deficiencies at the hospital was submitted to the joint commission. Such a report would otherwise not have been available to the surveying team.

Although the hearing procedure is inadequate in that no formal record of it is prepared, no formal response is made by the commission to the facts presented there, and no appeal procedure is available if the joint commission chooses to ignore the facts presented at the hearing,[24] the hearing procedure has made a difference in the care with which joint commission surveying teams conduct surveys. Perhaps the true significance of the hearing procedure may be that it gives the medical staff of the institution, particularly the residents and interns, a convenient forum for ventilating grievances which could potentially affect the accreditation status of the hospital. For example, USC-County Hospital residents and interns in a general medicine ward who were concerned about the allocation of manpower and equipment in their ward relative to the resources that seemed available in more specialized services used the mechanism of the accreditation interview to bring pressure on the hospital administrator to allocate more resources to the general medicine services. Thus the hearing process, although initially conceived as a forum for the ventilation of consumer grievances, becomes another mechanism useful in the delicate interplay of power constellations operative in the hospital setting. The survey interview becomes a convenient mechanism for residents and interns operating in administratively neglected areas of the hospital, areas which may not be of intense teaching interest, such as the general medicine ward, to present their case for a greater quantum of capital or human assets to be invested in their service. To the extent that the information presented may jeopardize the continued accreditation of the hospital, the use of the hearing procedure may be a convenient mechanism for challenging a hospital administrator reluctant to allocate sufficient resources to nonteaching-related patient care needs.

Conclusions

We concluded earlier that the Hill-Burton litigation could result in some reordering of decision-making priorities in a hospital setting. A hospital administrator would, under law, be answerable to another constituency and might be obliged to omit in the hospital budget sums of money for the acquisition of new capital equipment for specialized research needs in favor of a greater allocation of resources to provide primary care in the emergency room. Likewise, we have seen that a strategy to make the accreditation survey procedure more responsive to the concerns of patients has resulted in a forum useful for the exertion of countervailing power by doctors in less well-endowed services of the hospital against the specialized interests of specific departmental chairmen. We have thus seen examples of two very different kinds of strategies, one a litigative strategy and the other a political strategy, a "lobbying" strategy. Both of them have in some way affected not-for-profit

---

[24] These alleged deficiencies are the subject of pending litigation. See Self-Help for the Elderly v. Richardson, Civ. Act. No. 2016-71 (D. D.C.).

hospitals occupying an oligopolistic or monopolistic position in the community with regard to the provision of medical services.

While these strategies were formulated on behalf of the indigent, they could have been equally well applied to all medical care consumers. The litigation strategy is unpredictable in outcome; it invariably requires the investment of a great deal of lawyer time; and it involves the courts in judgments with policy implications that they may not be the most appropriate forum to make. Yet litigation under some circumstances, particularly where market forces are not at work and where patients have no effective alternative mechanism for making institutions responsive to the law that exists, may be effective as a device for focusing pressure on health care institutions to more adequately address the existing realities and problems of medical care for the indigent. The Hill-Burton litigation has focused attention effectively on the problems created by the failure of our society to provide adequate financing for medical services for the noncategorically related, medically indigent. The other strategy, the strategy of a more direct "confrontation" approach to a standard-setting organization composed exclusively of providers, all of whom exercise monopolistic powers in their respective domain, involved a delicate interchange of mutual suspicions, antagonisms, and pressure. Perhaps it was the sheer fear of consumer demonstrations and of a new kind of input into joint commission decision-making procedures that dictated the response of the joint commission to avert possible difficulties and unpleasantness. Perhaps the joint commission was vulnerable precisely by virtue of its isolation and its previous failure to take into account consumer concerns in the articulation of accreditation standards. But whatever the reasons, a confederation of groups with essentially consumer health care interests did bring about substantial changes in the Joint Commission on Hospital Accreditation Standards. Further, this approach brought about a potentially significant change altering the power relationships of junior medical staff to the administration. It is too early to know at this point what either strategy will ultimately yield and whether the substantial investment of resources, time, effort, and patience have been warranted.

We must acknowledge that we cannot rely on the courts as the principal forces for assuring accountability. The courts can fashion legal obligations from existing law, but cannot ordinarily fashion new rights and responsibilities where the legislature has not acted. Nor are courts the appropriate vehicle for allocating social priorities in the health care field.[25]

The confrontation approach also has its limits once the gambits are discerned, once the essential impotence of the consumer is exposed (except the power to disrupt and to become a nuisance). Perhaps the only long-term answer becomes the

---

[25] See Geoffrey Hazard, *Social Justice Through Civil Justice* (Chicago: American Bar Foundation, 1969), and Geoffrey Hazard, *Law Reforming in the Anti-Poverty Effort* (Chicago: American Bar Foundation, 1970).

fostering of market influences on the health care economy that would enable consumers more effectively to exercise options concerning delivery systems. This must be coupled with the effective enfranchisement of individuals to exercise such a choice by making available to all a third-party source of payment. To the end of enabling the consumer to have freedom of choice, we must direct our policy to encouraging health maintenance organizations and other new institutional forms for the delivery of medical care.[26] Decisions concerning investment in capital assets and allocation of manpower resources should be made by hospital administrators and board of directors under some market constraints. Accountability will be fostered where decision making is not solely responsive to medical staff pressure to make certain investments and changes.

The victories of consumer movements may be short-lived where there are no consistent, continued pressures against vital centers of the systems. This pressure is unlikely to be sustained because of the limited resources, both in people and money, of the consumer movement. Moreover, the public-interest lawyer resources heretofore available to the consumer movement may prove to be an exhaustible asset, both in energies of the individuals involved and in funding sources available. I am not optimistic, then, that strategies of confrontation and litigation will ultimately be productive of long-term solutions to the problem of accountability in health care institution decision making.

---

[26] See Richard A. Posner, "Regulatory Aspects of National Health Insurance," *University of Chicago Law Review*, vol. 39, no. 1 (Fall 1971), p. 1, and Mark V. Pauly, *National Health Insurance: An Analysis* (Washington, D.C.: American Enterprise Institute, 1971).

COMMENTARY ON THE PAPERS

David Mechanic

It would be extremely useful to have effective models of hospitals, physician behavior, and the changing demand for medical care of different types. I am unconvinced that the models presented here are particularly useful. The value of any model depends upon the extent to which its assumptions correspond to reality, and I would feel more comfortable if the assumptions in these models about the manner in which patients and physicians behave had a sounder empirical basis. Too many administrative solutions fail because they have not taken account of the multitude of human factors that intervene between planning and behavior.

I must also admit a certain prejudice that has grown as I have sat through this conference. I am increasingly impatient with such statements as "most of the care will not affect an individual's medical problems and, at best, may serve to reduce his anxiety." Or, in speaking of hospitals, "For those hospitals which are incapable of improving, there is no alternative to closure." I am similarly impatient with claims that the provision of more information will necessarily affect the character of the services bought by consumers or the manner in which the health care system operates. Although such possibilities are worthy of careful examination, I find such assertions too frequently based on theoretical prejudices rather than on any serious understanding of how patients and physicians see medical care or the factors affecting their behavior.

Although I have heard some discussion here about the possibility that planners are underrepresented at this meeting, I think it is more evident that the group obviously missing is the physicians. While I would agree that medical care is both too important and too expensive to be left to physicians, it is evident that planning without the involvement of those who actually provide the services is equally faulty. The absence of physicians may have contributed to the failure to appreciate that providing medical care is a highly personalized service and, even for Mr. Pauly, is somewhat different from purchasing a camera. Consideration of the factors that induce persons to seek medical care would reveal that seeking care is motivated not only by objective symptoms, but also by psychological distress and social and cultural factors. Physicians and their counterparts existed in society well before medicine could demonstrate any effectiveness, and much of the medical effort today is concerned not with cure but with the alleviation of pain and discomfort. The reduction of distress and the provision of support for the afflicted is not a piddling outcome, but rather a fundamental aspect of medical care.

It is perhaps ironic that individuals' estimates of their physical health are highly influenced by their levels of psychological distress and problems in their lives, but nevertheless it is the reality. Similarly, although the development of trust and adequate communication between physician and patient may not appear to be an efficient use of the physician's time, the probability that the patient will follow the physician's advice is likely to depend on such factors. There is danger in becoming too process-oriented, for medical care comes to naught if after a careful workup and diagnostic judgment the patient ignores whatever advice he is given. The probability of effective implementation of medical care depends upon our ability to see medicine as a human institution as well as a technical or economic activity. Given this perspective, I would like to approach some of the issues raised by Pauly and the Laves, but more from the viewpoint of what we actually know about how providers and consumers behave.

I cannot imagine that anyone would disagree with the contention of the Laves that incentives are important. The issue, of course, concerns what particular incentives are involved, how they come to be perceived, and how they affect behavior. The Laves are extremely vague and one-dimensional in their concept of appropriate incentives; in emphasizing the single dimension of cost, they neglect such factors as distribution, quality of medical and social management, and a variety of other matters central to medical care. If one's only concern is to control costs, this is not, technically, a difficult matter. What makes the issue difficult is the desire to control costs without damaging whatever quality and effectiveness that medical care has achieved. Although the Laves have many interesting points to make, and although I share their diagnosis of the crisis, they leave me unconvinced on the solutions. For example, they have not made a convincing case that hospitals can effectively control the behavior of physicians, that communities would allow hospitals to close, that the reimbursement scheme they offer would not exacerbate the process of case selection, that quality of care would be preserved, and that peer review would actually work as visualized, among other matters. Although they discuss a complex reimbursement formula in general terms, I would emphasize that it is extremely difficult to develop such formulas realistically without communicating to providers incentives and disincentives you never intended to provide. The task is not an impossible one, but I suggest that it is more difficult than meets the eye.

There is also a tendency on the part of the Laves to offer rather weak criticisms of policies which are in disfavor with them. I find their objections to federal planning in health—that data would be necessary, that it is difficult to define what should be regulated, and that following orders is bad for people—to be for the most part nonreasons. At this meeting there has been a strong bias that planning is an impossible activity, but I would suggest that we have considerable experience in such efforts both here and abroad and that we might benefit from looking beyond our own biases. Having made these preliminary remarks, let me now suggest a somewhat different perspective which, I believe, has more relevance to providing equity and which is more responsive to the needs of patients and doctors.

Every survey I have seen on consumers' views of physicians suggests that consumers seek a physician who is "competent" and "interested in them." When consumers are asked what they mean by "interest" they indicate that they refer not only to the demeanor of the physician but also to his accessibility when he is needed. Different dimensions of the physician's service seem to be important depending on the situation. For example, for routine needs consumers frequently seek a physician sufficiently accessible to minimize the consumer's costs of time and effort in obtaining the necessary service. For illnesses of a life-threatening character, or for those which have a high element of fear such as impending surgery, the patient's confidence in the physician plays a larger part, as may be reflected in the high rate of use of surgical services outside prepaid health plans by members of such plans.

In short, when an illness is threatening, consumers appear to be willing to pay a high price for alleged competence. When patients purchase medical care from a physician under such circumstances they purchase an entire package of care, including the physician's services, his judgment about additional necessary care, and his hospital and colleague affiliations. Once the basic choice of a physician is made, consumers have relatively little to say about the purchase of additional services, the use of one or another hospital (unless the physician offers a choice on the basis of amenities, assuming he has such a choice to offer), or the ultimate cost of a particular illness. Professor Pauly has suggested that since physicians are uncertain about quality, perhaps the consumer ought to decide. He ought to consider the possibility, however, that it is precisely because there is uncertainty that the consumer cannot decide. If quality of care could be objectively formulated and precisely stated, it would be relatively simple to give consumers a choice. Choice becomes impossible when a person under stress faces uncertainties that physicians themselves have difficulty resolving.

It is in this aspect of the discussion where I believe some economists have created confusions about the purchase of health care, although others have explicitly recognized how profoundly the medical care market departs from traditional economic assumptions.[1] On the assumption that consumers make relatively detailed choices, many economists have put emphasis on deductibles and coinsurance as mechanisms to limit "unreasonable demand." But since consumers primarily only make the judgment to seek initial health care or to reject further health care, coinsurance and deductibles have the effect of excluding both trivial and important incidents of illness from the health care system. For example, a study of changes

---

[1] See Victor R. Fuchs, "Health Care and the United States Economic System: An Essay in Abnormal Physiology," *Milbank Memorial Fund Quarterly,* vol. 50 (April 1972), pp. 211-237.

in prescription charges in the National Health Service showed that this affected the rate of prscriptions for both serious and trivial illness and did not function to filter off only unnecessary or less important care. Moreover, access to physicians is a relatively inexpensive component of medical care costs, and this is the aspect of medical services that consumers are presently most disturbed about.

The costs of medical care depend largely on the decisions the physician makes once the patient has made contact with him, and it is here that cost controls, if they are to exist, must be implemented. Here I would like to make two points that lead in a direction somewhat different from Professor Pauly's assumptions. First, the amount of work physicians do, and their income, is relatively insensitive to the total number of doctors available in the community, unless of course the total number of physicians is very large. Physicians, because they are gatekeepers of an elaborate technological system, have considerable choice in what measures they take to detect illness, to provide care, to maintain surveillance, and so on, and their ability to elaborate services is considerable. As Pauly notes, this is particularly the case as a greater proportion of medical costs are paid through insurance, since this eliminates whatever pressures may exist to cut costs and, indeed, may lead to pressures toward more elaborate work. Second, the character of medical work generated will tend to be related to the types of specialists and facilities available. For example, the availability of surgical talents, hospital beds, psychiatrists, or whatever, will lead to a distribution of work more or less consistent with it. Although these tendencies are not well understood, it is reasonable to assume that they result in large part from the uncertainty of medical care itself and the difficulty of specifying which of several alternatives is the best to follow. Surgeons and internists facing comparable problems favor different paths of care. Under conditions of uncertainty, decisions are likely to follow the professional predispositions and needs of the physicians who make them. Another mode of adapting to insufficient demand of a particular kind is to maintain sufficiently high prices to make it unnecessary to generate "excessive work." Basically, surgical fees are of this character; they allow general surgeons, for example, to support themselves on a modest amount of surgery supplemented by other kinds of patient care.

I would argue that the issue of whether hospitals should be competitive or monopolistic in the public interest sidesteps many important issues about the functions of health care and the behavior of physicians. As I already indicated, two crucial aspects affecting costs are the types of physicians we have and the nature of the decisions they make. As long as the physician is a paid agent of the patient, and as long as third parties pay the costs of care, physicians are unlikely to limit expensive decisions which in their judgment yield any benefits to the patient. Therefore, any uncontrolled voucher system is likely to increase demand and be highly inflationary. One way of getting around the issue is to make it personally costly for physicians to provide marginal increments of aileged quality to the care

204

provided as profit-type HMOs allegedly would do. But putting the patient's and physician's interests in conflict might produce pressures toward insufficient care and unwillingness to undertake expensive life-saving measures; it also might increase mutual suspiciousness between doctor and patient as well as patients' insecurities.

I think there is danger in speculating about the role of greater competition in health services since there are so many relevant but uncontrolled factors. Although nonprofit hospitals are not competitive in the economic sense, one of their pathologies is the extent to which they are competitive in a professional or sectarian way. Much of the duplication of facilities, services, and specialized personnel stems from a competitive spirit which is not entirely unrelated to attracting demand and earning income. We should not neglect the possibility that greater competition in hospital care may bring down price *but increase total cost* by generating all sorts of unnecessary work to make it economically feasible to maintain competitive facilities. For-profit firms may learn to provide many health care services using less expensive personnel and facilities, and thus reduce price in a competitive situation; but I also fear that such a competitive situation would generate a pathology of work and considerable iatrogenic illness as well. They may cut the intangibles, and the intangibles may be crucial to good health care.

In the last analysis, the issue *is not price but total cost,* and the crucial question concerns the mechanism through which demand is controlled (since every system of medical care must in some fashion control demand). For reasons I have suggested, I regard competition a particularly poor mechanism to control cost, and price a particularly bad mechanism to control demand. I believe that such mechanisms will inevitably increase the disparities in care among different social groups and formalize two classes of medical care. Assuming that third-party payments for care will increase rather than diminish, I would also anticipate continuing efforts on the part of competitors to increase the total volume of medical services provided, and in an irrational way (as in the drug industry, for example).

If my assumptions are correct—that is, that consumers are not in a position to make reasonable decisions about hospital care and necessary medical procedures and that it is destructive to introduce significant barriers to patients entering care or physicians providing care they deem necessary—how is demand to be reasonably regulated? The notion that decisions can be left to consumers, since quality is difficult for physicians to measure, is clearly wrongheaded. Precisely because quality is difficult to specify, it is necessary to maximize the opportunity for physicians to make professional judgments without intrusion of their own self-interest (although there are certain limitations which I will later specify). In my view, the best mechanism for doing this is to require professionals to work with a reasonable but specified budget and to plan necessary services within it. Also, by holding health professionals responsible for the health needs of a specified population, it is easier to plan reasonably, to monitor needs and performance, and to deal with special problems that arise. I believe that a health service organized in terms of population areas is the most reasonable way to provide services in a fashion that is truly responsive to the needs of the entire population. I doubt that we shall have such services in the foreseeable future, but since we are talking about equally obscure possibilities at this conference, I see no reason to exclude this one.

Obviously there are problems however you organize health services, and national systems have their share of them. Since such systems must ration services by planning, which is an uncertain process, such planning must involve certain guidelines. It is my view that such systems must begin by insuring everyone a minimal, but reasonable, guaranteed level of service. In circumstances where quality is established and generally agreed upon, guidelines would serve as restraints within which physician decisions would take place. For example, tonsillectomy is the most frequently performed surgical procedure in the United States, and constitutes the main cause of hospitalization of children. A rational system of health care would minimize these procedures, which have been shown to be of dubious value and dangerous as well. Within the broad context of care where the proper management remains uncertain, professional judgment would have to be maximized but under conditions where priorities must be weighed (that is, a fixed budget). In short, my view is that government must establish general restraints, but not contaminate the physician's work with a lot of petty restrictions and controls.

I think that an American system of health care which is national must insure a relatively high level of service to be acceptable. Certain amenities can, of course, be purchased outside the national system, and one must assume that a fairly robust private sector would continue to exist; but if the national system provided a decent level of care, I doubt that a private market would be destructive, and it might even help keep the national system up to par. One important function of a national system could be to insure an appropriate allocation of tasks among the specialties, and between physicians and other health workers.

What problems do national systems create? First, it is often assumed that a national system would greatly increase unnecessary demand. On the contrary, it seems more likely that the pressures would be toward restricting expenditures and unnecessary service; in contrast it is primarily the competitive system which would create and respond to irrational demand. Second, it is assumed that physicians would not work so hard in a salaried system as in a fee-for-service one, and there is considerable evidence to support this. It seems to me, however, that it would not be especially difficult to develop incentives for hard work within a national system, and incentives more consistent with patient need than presently exist. From my standpoint, the most damaging criticism against systems of care of a monopoly nature is the diminution of consumer controls and the tendency for physicians and hospitals to treat patients impersonally and without adequate consideration for

206

their overall needs. I think there are a variety of solutions to such problems, but none well investigated.

I share many of Mr. Silver's concerns regarding the failures of hospitals and health professionals to give adequate attention to the needs of consumers, particularly those most disadvantaged, and I commend his efforts in this regard. But I also share his reservations, and I am skeptical that the types of confrontations he describes can have pervasive or long-term effects on the functioning of health institutions. Bureaucracies have enormous advantage in contrast to consumer groups and they can co-opt them, deplete their resources, and tire them without themselves having to undergo fundamental change. Although advocacy groups can create temporary discomfort, it is difficult to maintain momentum and gains are often ephemeral. I have somewhat more enthusiasm for the litigation approach, but even here the path is tortuous and frequently ineffective. In the final analysis, hospital and patient care depend on the resources and priorities that the community is willing to assign to these activities, and legal decisions without resources to implement them can be empty vessels. I would like to believe that Mr. Silver is correct in his belief that consumer litigation creates leverage for different administrative allocations of resources, but I would like to see more direct evidence that this is indeed the case.

If we pursue the course of limiting market entry, and I believe this is the proper one to follow, the resulting monopolies, whether nationalized or not, must themselves be diversified, offering choice to consumers and encouraging competition within constructive limits. To some extent, the British have succeeded in encouraging excellence among consultant specialists through a merit incentive system, and I think much more along these lines can be developed. Although some of my colleagues have maintained that there is no fundamental difference between nonprofit and profit-oriented organizations in that personnel in both pursue their self-interest, I would maintain that there is an important distinction. Nonprofit enterprises allow much greater direction over the nature of the competitive process and can thus facilitate a more constructive form of competition. In any case, we have few models in health care that are informative in this regard, and experiences in other countries have limited value in that they have not had to deal with a populace as affluent and demanding as our own.

In sum I believe that planning and control on market entry are necessary precisely because quality is intangible and consumers are ignorant and helpless. I share Professor Pauly's wish that consumers would be sophisticated enough to make effective judgments, but I think that everything we know about patient reactions under stress and about the character of medical care requires the patient to yield a considerable amount of decisional control to the physician. That the physician behaves humanely and in a fashion which informs the patient, to the extent possible, is a wish we all have.

Anne R. Somers

I was very much interested in reading these three papers—although at times I admit I was confused as to the central theme of this session. I could not even find any common agreement on the meaning of "nonprofit" or "monopoly," either in their purely descriptive or value judgment sense. However, there was certainly one common theme: that this creature which we call the "nonprofit hospital" is today operating unsatisfactorily and that there is need for some fundamental change in its operations. Beyond that, it seemed to me that the authors' criticisms and their approaches to reform were almost diametrically opposed. On the one hand, there was the view that hospitals should be more competitive and more businesslike; on the other, the view that they should be less businesslike, more humane, and more concerned with nonfinancial considerations.

Actually, I think Clark Havighurst deserves real credit for this somewhat anomalous program. I do not know whether it was accidental or not, but it seems to me that this "trichotomy" illustrates very well the spectrum of criticism to which the nonprofit hospital is subjected today. This inconsistent criticism is not confined to academic meetings such as this, but fills the media and public debate constantly and is frequently translated into public law and public policy.

The result is an ever-increasing volume—a tremendous amount, more than any of us realizes—of hospital law and regulation at all levels of government. This body of law and regulation is uncoordinated, inconsistent, and often very contradictory. It is a major source of rising costs. It contributes not to efficiency or managerial strength and leadership on the part of hospital administration but, in many cases, to a growing sense of demoralization verging on fatalism. If continued much longer, this situation could lead in many cases to near paralysis of hospital management. For example, the problems, confronting the hospital administrator in New York City today are enough to drive him to the edge of insanity.

In short, this situation underscores, as strongly as anything could, the desperate need for a coherent and consistent national hospital policy. Again, I congratulate Clark Havighurst and the American Enterprise Institute for sponsoring a conference of this sort at this very crucial time. Since I have just a few minutes at my disposal, rather than to go into any detailed criticism of the three papers, it might be more useful to try to summarize my own point of view on these complex issues. For the sake of brevity, I will do this more didactically than under more leisurely circumstances. There are six major points.

(1) First, there obviously has to be what is now so evidently lacking (all three papers underscore this), some meaningful discipline on hospital costs—in which I include both price and utilization or volume—as well as discipline on quality. Where is this discipline to come from? The marketplace or government regulation?

(2) Considering the marketplace as a means of discipline, I have to conclude that however desirable it is in theory (I agree fully with those who say it is desirable) it is not now and will not in the foreseeable future be effective. I assume that you have already discussed the reasons for this at considerable length, but I will just enumerate a few of the most obvious.

The first, of course, is the effect of third-party coverage. As Lester Lave pointed out, in Pittsburgh, for example, only 10 percent of the patients pay their own hospital bills or have commercial, indemnity-type insurance. In other words, for 90 percent of the patients, the hospital is reimbursed by a third-party payer in accordance with a formula about which the recipient of care has virtually nothing to say. This situation will not only continue but will probably become more nearly universal. It seems to me indisputable that we will have some sort of national health insurance within the decade.

Second, there is the generally recognized lack of information that would allow consumers to exercise anything approaching cost-effective, meaningful choice with respect to hospital services.

Third, of course, there is the well-known fact that it is almost always the doctor who determines the use of the hospital and the length of stay of the patient, not the patient himself.

Fourth, a point that is not so widely recognized is the extent to which the hospital today is expected to carry on various activities which affect its costs and therefore its rates or its reimbursement but which may not involve the patient directly. I think, for example, of educational programs both at the graduate and, increasingly today, the undergraduate level. Medical schools are turning increasingly to community hospitals for education of their undergraduate medical students in the clinical years. This has to be paid for in one way or another. Many people feel that the community hospital is also the logical place for development of programs of consumer health education directed both to patients and to nonpatients, people who live in the community or in the area of the hospital. This has to be paid for in some way.

There is also the whole question that Mr. Silver so ably raises, the question of "free care." Personally, I do not like the term. I do not even like the concept "free care." I think that it still tends to be synonymous with second-class care. Nevertheless, until there is some sort of national health insurance, we know that there is going to be a certain percentage of the population which cannot pay and which has no third party to pay for them. Whether it is 3 percent or 5 percent or somewhat more or less, there is "x" percent which has to be accounted for in one way or another. A related point that you are all aware of is that hospital services are necessary in ghettos and other areas which are not attractive to profit-maximizers.

Finally, a point that would take a whole conference in itself is the effect of collective bargaining, which is still rather new in the hospital industry but seems to be coming pretty fast now and has hit some communities very hard. What effect is this going to have on comparative hospital costs and rates?

For all these reasons, I have had to conclude, reluctantly, that the market-place and free competition are not going to provide an effective discipline on hospital costs.

(3) Therefore, regulation, however distasteful it may be, is inevitable and, indeed, is already a fact. The amount of existing regulation is, as I indicated earlier, not generally recognized. It is tremendous. The Phase II federal price controls are just the latest example. It is significant that when the administration announced that controls would be lifted from significant portions of the economy, it emphasized not only that this did not apply to the health care industry but also that such controls were likely to be increased. The realistic issue, therefore, is not should there or should there not be regulation, but what kind of regulation.

(4) I agree with the Laves as to the danger of overly centralized regulation. Personally I oppose direct federal regulation for many reasons. I do not have to identify them to this audience. I also agree that much state regulation has proved inadequate for various reasons. I also want to preserve the maximum possible degree of institutional autonomy and even competition where appropriate.

The solution that seems most promising involves the middle road somewhere between these extremes. I think most knowledgeable students of the industry are tending in this direction as a pragmatic matter, no matter what their ideological biases may be.

(5) The best term I can find to describe this approach is the "public utility." I don't particularly like the term, but I use it for lack of a better one. To me it involves a state franchise, mandating a range of services to defined populations, to be administered by the state governments under federal/state guidelines.

I recognize the drawbacks in this formulation. I know that the very term "public utility" bothers many people, including myself. Anyone who read my 1969 book, *Hospital Regulation,* will recall that I resisted use of the term for various reasons. But this is 1972, and I now find myself using it more and more because it comes closest to saying, in the conventional vocabulary of public policy, what I have in mind.

I am not suggesting that we apply traditional public utility regulation. It is too negative and too narrow. I agree with Mark Pauly's concern that we have to consider the doctor and other professionals, as well as the hospital, in approaching this new problem. Perhaps this conference can suggest a better term, but the important thing, as I see it, is that we want to preserve a privately owned and a privately operated enterprise but with clearly defined, statutory, public accountability and public responsibility.

(6) Even with agreement on this broad philosophical concept, there obviously remains a world of defining to do, defining and refining as to the form, the nature, and the scope of regulation.

210

Last week I had the privilege of spending a couple of days in Madison, Wisconsin, working on this problem with the Governor's Task Force on Hospital and Health Care. There are many states that are working on this today. There are many states that want help, and there are several that have had enough experience to be helpful to others. We badly need a clearinghouse where we can pool this sort of information so that everybody will not have to rediscover the wheel again.

Here are a few of the problems that we will want to look at:

(a) Should the legislation apply to hospitals only? Should it cover hospitals and all other institutional providers? Hospitals and providers except MDs in their private office practice? This is what it says now in our New Jersey certificate-of-need law. Or should it cover all providers including MDs?

(b) What should be the relation of planning to regulation? Should they be separate or tied together? If tied together, how? Should the existing "a" and "b" agencies be incorporated into the regulatory mechanism? What should be the role of the "b" agency, the regional medical programs, and so forth?

(c) What should be the conditions for obtaining a certificate of need or franchise, and what should be the conditions for its revocation? How do you define "need"? Should there be a lower limit or dollar floor on programs or equipment requiring approval? The Laves in their paper point out the drawbacks of having too low a limit, the waste of money and time. How long should the franchise be valid?

Here is the crux of the problem that many of us are concerned with here today: How do we avoid "status-quoism" or "bureaucratic arteriosclerosis" or the suppression of innovation, and yet still provide the necessary controls? How do you avoid that and still have the necessary planning and regulation to make sure on the one hand that needed hospital beds and other facilities do get into the ghettos where no profits are available and on the other, that you do not sustain the overbedding that we now have in many suburban areas?

(d) What about quality controls? What should be the relationship between licensing, franchising, Medicare certification, JCAH accreditation, and so on? What is the relationship of personnel licensing to institutional licensing? This is an increasing problem today as we develop the new occupations of physicians' assistants, medics, and so forth. Are we going to have just that many more guilds and make the whole enterprise just that much more rigid and nonresponsive, or are the new developments really going to help?

How do you strengthen hospital peer review? Although peer review is working imperfectly in many institutions, it does provide a framework for quality controls—a framework that is accepted by the medical profession and accepted in the common law. What should be the relation of hospital peer review to medical "foundations"?

(e) Under cost controls we are developing a surprising amount of experience. Is it enough to have rate disclosure? Do you want to have state rate or budget review, or is rate setting necessary?

If we are going to have rate setting, on what basis? Should it be on the basis of budget approval? If so, on all elements of cost or just some? Should there be prospective rates with no retroactivity at the end of the accounting period, or are you going to have retroactive cost reimbursement, as in the Medicare and, frequently, Blue Cross formulas today? What are you going to include in "costs"? Capital costs as well as operating costs? Are you going to include the new educational costs which are not necessarily patient-related? If not, can you devise a viable method of separating them? Who is going to pay for them?

If you are going to have rate setting, should it be on the basis of the individual institution's own experience or on the basis of groups or categories, as in the Blue Cross contracts in Pittsburgh and in southern New York? Do you want it to be based on per diem costs, which is the traditional way, or on per case costs, or some combination of the two?

You can see that there are all sorts of possible combinations and permutations. There's enough research needed to keep everybody in this room busy for the next ten years, if we could just get on with studying these specific problems.

I like the Laves' suggestion for a new approach to incentive reimbursement. They accept the cost concept, I gather, but want some incentive built into it. This is fine. I'm not sure that I understand their formula completely. It was not very fully developed in the paper, but this kind of approach certainly should be pursued. To do so effectively, however, we have to have some sort of viable regulatory framework which would enable us to evaluate the results.

(f) What should be done about the administrative structure to avoid some of the rigidities that Mark Pauly refers to? Also, what about its relation to federal authority and penalties for noncompliance and so on?

(g) Another question that is just beginning to come up is the relationship of hospital regulation to the new bonding and lending authorities. Many states are now developing such authorities to make available capital funds to hospitals at lower than commercial interest rates. Should this, or should it not, be tied into the franchising mechanism and the rate-review mechanism?

I hope this suggests the range of unanswered problems that are crying out for study and for rather prompt answering.

In conclusion, let me repeat that these papers were useful. You will gather, without my having to go into detail, that there are many points in each with which I do not agree fully. But I still think the net contribution was considerable. I neglected to make some kudos in the direction of Laurens Silver. Despite the fact that I do not like the concept of "free care," I think what Mr. Silver and his associates have done in calling attention to some of the problems of the poor has been great.

212

Finally, it is my conviction that the hospital industry today is not averse to constructive criticism; indeed, it is anxious for assistance in solving its mammoth problems, which are clearly not entirely of its own making. Groups such as this, if they will take the trouble to understand the industry and approach its problems in a nondoctrinaire fashion, can be very helpful. But any attempt to distort the realities of health care to fit a procrustean bed of free market economics is inevitably doomed to failure.

PART FOUR

National Health Policy Directions: The Future of Certificate-of-Need Laws and Health Planning

REPORTER'S NOTE: It was inevitable from the beginning of the conference that the narrow issue of certificate-of-need laws would not be long confined, and in the final two sessions it broke out into a broad range of big problems, going to the heart of the question of what kind of health care system we want to have. In addition to adding interesting new dimensions to the discussion, this development illustrated the considerable implications of certificate-of-need legislation, suggesting that the design and enactment of such laws are not to be taken lightly.

In this final session, certificate-of-need proposals were still central to the discussion, but major efforts were made to fit them into other health policy developments and to show how directional shifts might not only obviate certificate-of-need laws but turn them into serious obstacles to realization of health policy objectives. Current federal proposals on health care financing and on health maintenance organizations were reviewed, and substantial proposals for narrowing the scope of certificate-of-need laws were advanced. Proposals such as that of the American Hospital Association for extending entry restrictions to health maintenance organizations were strongly condemned.

The role of proprietary institutions is explored extensively in these papers. The arguments for application of certificate-of-need laws to proprietary hospitals are analyzed and differentiated from the somewhat easier case for covering nonprofit institutions, which turns in part on their relative unresponsiveness to market incentives. The influences of proprietaries on pricing and services in the health care system are also examined, and special attention is paid to the proprietary health maintenance organization.

The future of health planning remained a central concern of the conference participants, and the final paper looks ahead to possibilities for restructuring the federal comprehensive health planning legislation when it expires.

COMPULSORY HEALTH PLANNING LAWS AND NATIONAL HEALTH INSURANCE

Joseph P. Newhouse and Jan P. Acton *

Introduction

This paper discusses the relationships between national health insurance and compulsory health planning. Compulsory health planning is taken to mean restriction of the entry of capital into the medical services industry, particularly into hospitals and other facilities providing overnight care. This paper will argue that the reasons for the increasing advocacy of planning stem from the spread of reimbursement insurance, especially for hospital services.[1] We argue that the effect of reimbursement insurance has been to increase demand for care and may have been to increase the costliness of the care produced. Both these factors have led to unacceptable expenditure levels. To reduce expenditures, capital restrictions are now proposed.

National health insurance would probably increase insurance coverage, but since a large proportion of the hospital bill is already paid by reimbursement insurance, the increase in the case of hospital services might not be large. However —and this is critical—national health insurance need not be of reimbursement form. Hence, national health insurance weakens the case for compulsory planning laws.

The paper also discusses an argument which is frequently made for restriction of entry, namely, that if freedom of entry is permitted, for-profit or other hospitals will enter and "skim the cream"—that is, service "profitable" patients. The remaining hospitals will then lose money. It is argued, in effect, that hospitals can only break even by overcharging certain cases to pay for others. We take the position that this argument is also seriously weakened if national health insurance is passed. Since such insurance is likely to have high limits, if any, there would be no reason to lose money on any patient.

---

* Any views expressed in this paper are those of the authors. They should not be interpreted as reflecting the views of The Rand Corporation or the official opinion or policy of any of its governmental or private research sponsors. The authors wish to thank Charles Phelps and Kip Viscusi for comments upon an earlier draft of this paper.
[1] Reimbursement insurance means that the amount of the insurance payment depends upon the total expenditure incurred.

Hospital Insurance and the Demand for Services

In this section we point out that reimbursement insurance has caused a significant increase in the demand for services and has caused hospitals to upgrade their product. Both factors have led to increased expenditures and to a growing concern over the efficiency with which services are produced. As a result of this concern, some have advocated compulsory planning.

For the past twenty-five years the spread of insurance for hospitalization has been extraordinarily rapid. In 1949-50 only 57.6 percent of hospital bills were covered by third parties; in 1970-71 the percentage had risen to 85.8 percent.[2] Thus, at the present time the majority of expenditures are covered by third parties. Under most national health insurance plans, this percentage would rise further.

The structure of hospital insurance is also important. Hospital insurance today is overwhelmingly of two sorts, which are analytically similar. The first is a policy with service benefits; the second is a comprehensive, major medical type policy, under which consumers are responsible for a fraction of any additional services. Both of these types we call reimbursement insurance. Medicare is an example of such insurance; the consumer must pay $17 per day after he has remained in the hospital for sixty days. These types of insurance are similar, since the first is a limiting form of the second; the portion paid by the consumer is simply zero.

The fraction of additional expenditures for which consumers are responsible is seldom more than thirty percent. Over 99 percent of the policies of large groups in force in 1970 with positive coinsurance rates had a rate between 10 and 30 percent.[3] With service benefits, of course, the rate is zero. This means that in most cases the consumer will have to pay at most a small fraction of the cost of staying an additional day in the hospital or of using various capital equipment of the hospital. This is the consequence of reimbursement insurance.

This is important because for many decisions it is the marginal price which is relevant for choice—that is, the price to the consumer of an extra unit of service. The consumer generally does not make the choice to use the service, of course; that is left to the physician. But the evidence we have collected to date shows that, regardless of who makes the decision, observed demand responds systematically to prices.[4] Thus, the decision on whether to stay an extra day in the hospital depends

[2] This calculation excludes expenditures in federal hospitals. Data are from Dorothy P. Rice and Barbara Cooper, "National Health Expenditures, 1929-1971," *Social Security Bulletin,* vol. 35, no. 1, pp. 3-18, and American Hospital Association, *Hospitals: 1972 Annual Guide Issue.*

[3] Health Insurance Association of America, *A Current Profile of Group Medical Insurance in Force in 1970* (New York: 1972), pp. 9 and 12. See also Louis Reed and William Carr, *The Benefit Structure of Private Health Insurance* (Washington, D. C.: Government Printing Office, 1970).

[4] The theory and empirical work underlying the estimates presented here are outlined more

upon the cost of that day. Similarly, the cost of the hospital selected depends upon the cost to the consumer of choosing one hospital rather than another, where the relevant price is the price net of insurance payments. For decisions on admission to the hospital, however, the relevant price is probably the total expected price of a stay in the hospital, since admission has more of an all-or-nothing character about it than the other decisions just discussed.[5]

Demand for hospital services will thus tend to be raised by insurance. We estimate that the price elasticity of demand for hospital services (patient days) with respect to coinsurance rate changes (arc elasticity) in the 0 to 25 percent range is probably on the order of 0.1, possibly smaller. This means that the difference in demand between 0 and 25 percent coinsurance is on the order of 20 percent or somewhat less. This calculation refers to a once-and-for-all charge, but the steady increase in the percentage covered by insurance and the level of its coverage is causing steadily increasing demand.

This increase in demand is not the end of the matter, however. There also may well be some autonomous response on the part of hospitals to the change in demand which they are facing. Specifically, they may on their own decide to expand their plant or increase their capital in other ways "because the market will support it." This, of course, tends to raise expenditures still further. One of the authors has analyzed this phenomenon in formal terms in a previous paper.[6]

The third-party payers (chiefly insurance companies and the federal government) have found themselves in the position of paying for these capital outlays through the reimbursement mechanism. Although some insurance companies, notably Blue Cross, claim to seek to keep charges down by excluding unnecessary and inappropriate capital charges, there is in fact no evidence that they have had significant impact on costs.[7] The effect on insurance premiums in the long run is obvious.

As a consequence of this rising demand and willingness to pay for additional capital expenditures, a number of persons have become concerned over efficiency

fully in Charles E. Phelps and Joseph P. Newhouse, *Coinsurance and the Demand for Medical Services* (Santa Monica, Calif.: The Rand Corporation, 1973).

[5] These arguments have been developed more fully in three articles by Joseph P. Newhouse and Vincent Taylor, "The Subsidy Problem in Hospital Insurance," *Journal of Business*, vol. 43, no. 4 (October 1970), pp. 452-456; "How Shall We Pay for Hospital Care?" *Public Interest*, vol. 23 (Winter 1971), pp. 78-92; and "A New Type of Hospital Insurance," *Journal of Risk and Insurance*, vol. 38, no. 4 (Summer 1971). An empirical model embodying the above assumptions is currently being estimated by Joseph P. Newhouse and Charles E. Phelps, *Price and Income Elasticities for Medical Care Services* (Santa Monica, Calif.: The Rand Corporation, 1973).

[6] Joseph P. Newhouse, "Toward a Theory of Non-Profit Institutions," *American Economic Review*, vol. 60, no. 1 (March 1970), pp. 64-74. In effect, the trade-off curve postulated in this paper shifts out, and this leads to a rise in quality and costs beyond the rise in expenditure due to quantity change.

[7] Mark V. Pauly and David Drake, "Effect of Third-Party Methods of Reimbursement on Hospital Performance," in Herbert Klarman, ed., *Empirical Studies in Health Economics* (Baltimore: Johns Hopkins University Press, 1970).

in the production of health services. There are charges of "unnecessary duplication" of facilities and equipment, leading to idle capacity and higher coverage costs in those facilities. It is this concern that has led a number of critics to call for regulation or compulsory planning for hospitals. Before we discuss the merits of this approach, let us briefly consider why reimbursement insurance has spread. This is not an easy question to answer. It is probable, however, that such policies are preferable to insurance which consists of purely lump-sum transfers. ("Lump sum" means the payment is made independent of the amount of expenditure so that the consumer pays the full marginal cost.) Since health status cannot be precisely defined, a purely lump-sum transfer is either very expensive or leaves a consumer exposed to risk. That is, one does not write a policy which agrees to give the consumer $X if he has an appendectomy of a certain severity, but $X + $300 if it is of somewhat greater severity, since severity cannot be well measured. One solution to the problem has been reimbursement insurance.

Thus, we have a situation where the introduction of reimbursement insurance has caused apparently unacceptable levels of expenditure. This does not mean that medical insurance is undesirable. On the contrary, medical insurance helps reduce the risk of large expenditures if one becomes ill. The problem is that while becoming ill can be thought of as a random event, actions taken to correct that illness are not a random event and are influenced by prices. This creates a dilemma between the desirable goals of risk-spreading and optimal allocation of resources.[8] National health insurance would further increase coverage, which would appear to make the dilemma more acute, but this need not be true. Exactly how national health insurance would be structured could make a considerable difference in the demand that would be expressed as well as the autonomous supply response. We return to this below after we consider compulsory planning.

Health Planning and Health Costs

In this section we consider the potential of certificates of need or other compulsory health planning for dealing with the problems which would be raised by national health insurance. We argued in the last section that national health insurance would probably increase the demand for services. In this section we point out that the magnitude of the demand increase is uncertain; we then consider the likelihood that planning agencies would successfully adapt to it.

There is considerable uncertainty about the size of the demand increase in response to national health insurance.[9] For example, the Social Security Administra-

---

[8] For more formal analyses of this problem, see Richard J. Zeckhauser, "Medical Insurance: A Case Study of the Tradeoff Between Risk Spreading and Appropriate Incentives," *Journal of Economic Theory*, vol. 2, no. 1 (March 1970), pp. 10-26, and Charles E. Phelps, *The Demand for Health Insurance* (Santa Monica, Calif.: The Rand Corporation, 1973).

[9] Since prices of outpatient services may fall relative to inpatient services, it is possible that

tion (SSA) has estimated that without legislation, national health expenditures would be \$105.4 billion in fiscal year 1974,[10] while the bill introduced by Senator Edward Kennedy would cost \$113.8 billion. This implies a small difference, 8 percent, between total utilization under the two plans. Other estimates of the difference are considerably larger. While we have significant reservations about the amounts, reputable scholars have estimated own-price elasticities to be -0.5 and even higher.[11] If -0.5 is the arc elasticity over the range of 20 percent coinsurance to zero—and no legislation represents a plan on average with 20 percent coinsurance and the Kennedy bill represents a plan with none (ignoring the changes in the delivery system the Kennedy bill calls for, as does the SSA)—the difference in demand under the two plans would be 100 percent which is very much at variance with the SSA estimates. And while we are confident of the general size of the elasticities we have estimated and cited above (around -0.1), there still must remain considerable uncertainty about the exact amount by which national health insurance would cause demand to change.

The additional demand generated by a national health insurance plan would, in all likelihood, require additional capital to enter in order to produce services to meet the demand efficiently. Since demand would change by an uncertain amount over an uncertain time horizon, it is obvious that the supply system must have some flexibility.[12] Thus, any planning agency will continuously be faced with the question of whether entry of capital is too large.

At the heart of the matter is the issue of whether a centralized or decentralized system is more likely to make less serious mistakes in adjusting to the changed demands. Because this is a difficult and often prejudged question, it may be easiest to approach it by considering some examples.

The present decentralized system is often berated for being a nonsystem, a cottage industry. Undeniably it produces its share of mistakes. Grossly underused surgery units in hospitals across the street from each other are difficult to rationalize, as are some other investments in very expensive equipment. But there are equally illuminating (or equally beclouding) examples to show the contrary. Agri-

---

national health insurance would lead to a decrease in the demand for inpatient services. For this to happen, cross-price elasticities would have to be large relative to own-price elasticities. At this time we have no good evidence on the magnitude of cross-price elasticities. It seems unlikely, however, that the cross-price effect would outweigh the own-price effect. See Charles E. Lewis and Harold W. Keairnes, "Controlling Costs of Medical Care by Expanding Insurance Coverage," *New England Journal of Medicine,* vol. 282 (June 1970), pp. 1405-1412.

[10] Social Security Administration, "A Study of National Health Insurance Proposals Introduced in the 92nd Congress," mimeographed, July 1971.

[11] Martin S. Feldstein, "Hospital Cost Inflation: A Study of Nonprofit Price Dynamics," *American Economic Review,* vol. 61, no. 5 (December 1971), pp. 853-872. See also Karen Davis and Louise Russell, "The Substitution of Hospital Outpatient Care for Inpatient Care: Comment," *Review of Economics and Statistics,* vol. 54, no. 2 (May 1972), pp. 109-120.

[12] Jan P. Acton and Robert A. Levine, *State Health Manpower Planning: A Policy Overview* (Santa Monica, Calif.: The Rand Corporation, 1971).

culture is a nonsystem, but no one questions its efficiency; indeed, its very efficiency created opposite kinds of problems in the recent past.

Centralized medical planning can also produce mistakes. Consider, for example, the case of the Willink Committee in Great Britain. In the late 1950s the Willink Committee recommended that admissions to British medical schools be reduced by about 10 percent.[13] This recommendation was duly carried out, but in the early 1960s it became apparent that the decision had been based on incorrect assumptions concerning population growth and the rate of retirement from the medical profession, among other things. Medical school admissions, which had fallen off by approximately 5 to 10 percent, were increased.

The point of this example is, of course, not the Willink Committee's methodology. Rather, it is that centralized planning is fallible, a point which seems trivial, but which nevertheless seems ignored in many discussions of planning. Planning is a process, not a solution. It is generally intended to correct for some kind of market failure—that is, some situation in which decentralized decision makers face inappropriate incentives. In such a situation one may attempt to change the incentives or centralize the decision process. There is no presumption a priori that either is better.

Examples are always inconclusive, and it pays to consider the problem analytically. If decentralized decision makers face the correct incentives, the law of large numbers can be used to support the proposition that a decentralized system will, on average, make fewer serious mistakes.[14] But the assumption of correct incentives does not hold in the health area, as argued above. In a later section we will consider how national health insurance might change these incentives, so that this consideration becomes more relevant. In the remainder of this section, we consider analytically the effects of entry restrictions imposed by the planning agency. We assume that the restrictions are effective. If the restrictions are not effective, of course, the planning agency does not change the outcome. In the next section we consider whether it is reasonable to suppose that the constraints are effective.

If restrictions are effective, entry of capital is less than it otherwise would be. If hospitals are cost minimizers, it means that suppliers must meet demand in less than optimal fashion—that is, they must use more labor-intensive methods than they would otherwise choose. This will make hospital care more expensive than it otherwise would be. In more popular terms, one would argue that entry restrictions are hindering the introduction of labor-saving (and presumably cost-saving) investments. In addition, nonprice rationing of some services may be instituted.

---

[13] See Ivor Jones, *Health Services Financing* (St. Albans: Fisher, Knight and Co., Ltd., 1970), and François Lafitte and John Squire, "Second Thoughts on the Willink Report," *The Lancet,* September 3, 1960.

[14] The law of large numbers guarantees that the variance in results produced by many similar decision makers will be less than that produced by one decision maker. Implicit is a nonlinear loss function which values such a reduction.

Persons may be forced to wait longer for treatment; hospitals may restrict the number of physicians with admitting privileges; or only certain patients may be treated (for example, kidney dialysis machines are rationed in such a fashion). Nonprice rationing always opens the possibility of accompanying monopoly rent (for example, doctors with admitting privileges may charge more).

But many would not agree with the assumption that hospitals minimize cost. Or, even if hospitals produced what they did produce at least cost, they may gold-plate their production. That is, they may produce an inappropriate product mix, by choosing to produce hospital care in a very capital-intensive fashion.[15] Indeed, this presumed overutilization of capital is a rationale for compulsory planning laws.[16]

Therefore, it appears important to know if hospitals are cost minimizers. But in the presence of insurance which reimburses hospitals for costs (such as Blue Cross), it is impossible to tell whether or not hospitals are truly cost minimizers because their incentives are distorted by the insurance. Most notably, hospital administrators may try to increase their "slack" to ease pressures. (In a later section, we discuss how incentives to minimize cost can be strengthened.) Whether hospitals are cost minimizers is, however, unimportant in appraising the merits of health planning if entry and capital restrictions are not effective. In the next section we argue that this may well be the case.

Effectiveness of Regulation

In this section we discuss some effects of regulation. In general, the conclusion from the literature appears to be that the effect of regulation is, if anything, perverse. If so, compulsory health planning probably would not be a very successful solution to the problems it is intended to resolve.

There are three studies we are aware of that deal directly with regulation of hospitals. One is a study by Robert Evans of Ontario hospitals.[17] The Ontario Hospital Services Commission (OHSC) is a third-party purchaser of hospital services and reimburses Ontario hospitals for over 75 percent of their budget.

---

[15] We might note a related argument to the gold-plating argument. It is maintained that "planning with teeth" will limit the spread of "toys." For instance, cobalt machines may seem necessary to attract a radiologist to practice in a given hospital. The cost is then amortized over all patients (or over all radiology patients) even though few patients need the cobalt machine per se. This is really a problem in cost accounting. It says that we have mispriced the radiologist's services. On equity and efficiency grounds, it would be more appropriate to charge all users of the radiologist's time the true opportunity cost of attracting the radiologist to practice in that hospital, and not choose selected diseases or procedures for bearing that cost.

[16] Note the similar conclusion to the famous Averch-Johnson effect in Harvey Averch and Leland L. Johnson, "The Firm Under Regulatory Constraint," *American Economic Review*, vol. 53, no. 5 (December 1962), pp. 1052-1069.

[17] Robert G. Evans, "Efficiency Incentives in Hospital Reimbursement" (Ph.D. dissertation, Harvard University, 1970).

The hospital submits a prospective budget which is approved by the OHSC; in theory the OHSC has the authority to disallow overruns, but in practice this is seldom used.[18] Evans examines the relationships among the submitted budget, the approved budget, and the actual cost figure. In general, he finds that while the submitted budget is systematically reduced by the OHSC, the approved budget is regularly overrun. He concludes that regulation appears to have little net effect. This conclusion depends on the tenuous assumption that the hospitals do not anticipate the OHSC's behavior when submitting a budget. If they do anticipate, one cannot really conclude anything from the available evidence. Since all hospitals are subject to regulation, it is difficult to use these data to establish the effect of regulation.

A second study which bears on the effect of regulation of hospital bed supply was Rosenthal's study of demand for hospital care.[19] The major point of Rosenthal's study was that it was inappropriate to base Hill-Burton allocations solely on population and income. Rather, demand for hospital beds had to be more systematically considered, since an empty hospital was a waste of resources and one artificially filled with patients who did not need to be there was a health hazard.

The Hill-Burton Act, of course, was "negative regulation"; entry was encouraged rather than discouraged. The point of citing Rosenthal's study is not to show that regulation is ineffective in changing the outcome—most would agree that hospital supply in rural areas is greater than what it would have been in the absence of the act—but that the planning agency based its decisions on a rather crude methodology. In particular, there is nothing about this example that gives one confidence that entry restrictions, even if desirable, would be carried out in the appropriate fashion.

In the third study, Joel May examined the effects of several hospital planning agencies.[20] The agencies had the nominal objective of reducing "unnecessary" capital expenditures. May found, in general, no significant differences stemming from regulation and, in some cases, he found the opposite impact from what one would expect. Agencies that had been in existence the longest seemed the least effective.

These are the only studies we know which bear directly on the question of hospital regulation. There are a number of studies of the economics of regulation which support the conclusion that regulation has no effect in an industry with substantial market power from its previous structure (such as public utilities) and a perverse effect in industries without substantial market power (such as freight car-

---

[18] Basing our judgments on Evans's data, we estimate that around 10 percent of all overruns were disallowed in 1967.

[19] Gerald Rosenthal, *The Demand for General Hospital Facilities* (Chicago: The American Hospital Association, 1964).

[20] J. Joel May, *Health Planning: Its Past and Potential* (Chicago: Center for Health Administration Studies, University of Chicago, 1967).

riers).[21] Hospitals in most areas probably resemble most of the latter category. George Stigler and Claire Friedland found no significant effect of state regulatory commissions on prices charged for electric power after other variables which could be expected to affect cost (cost of coal, availability of hydroelectric power, for example) were accounted for. William A. Jordan, using evidence from interstate California airlines that are not subject to CAB regulation, finds that fares are 32 to 47 percent lower than they would be with CAB regulation.[22] Richard N. Farmer finds exempt agricultural motor carriers had rates which were 41 percent lower than those of common carriers handling special freight and 58 percent lower than common carriers handling general freight. When regulation of truck transportation of poultry and frozen foods was terminated, prices of these products fell substantially.[23] James Sloss finds that rates in Canadian provinces which do not regulate motor carriers are around 10 percent lower than rates in provinces which do regulate carriers.[24] These findings are all the more disturbing since the hospital industry, on the whole, appears to have a market structure similar to these industries.

While we do not pretend to have made a complete survey of the literature on the economics of regulation, we do believe that there are justifiable grounds for skepticism concerning the ability of regulatory agencies to achieve their nominal objectives. If that is true, there are problems which either are not being resolved or are being exacerbated. Further, regulatory commissions are not free goods. We now turn to the possibility that there are more effective solutions to the problem and the relationships these solutions might have to national health insurance.

Alternative Solutions

We have found that reimbursement insurance causes significant problems. National health insurance, however, would not need to utilize reimbursement insurance. At

---

[21] See especially George J. Stigler and Claire Friedland, "What Can Regulators Regulate? The Case of Electricity," *Journal of Law and Economics,* vol. 5 (October 1962), pp. 1-16. Also Paul W. MacAvoy, "The Effectiveness of the Federal Power Commission," *Bell Journal of Economics and Management Science,* vol. 1, no. 2 (Autumn 1970), pp. 271-303, and his "The Formal Work-Product of the Federal Power Commissioners," *Bell Journal of Economics and Management Science,* vol. 2, no. 1 (Spring 1971), pp. 379-395; George J. Stigler, "The Theory of Economic Regulation," *Bell Journal of Economics and Management Science,* vol. 2, no. 1 (Spring 1971), pp. 3-21; and George W. Hilton, "The Basic Behavior of Regulatory Commissions," *American Economic Review Proceedings,* vol. 62, no. 2 (May 1972), pp. 47-54.

[22] William A. Jordan, "Producer Protection, Prior Market Structure and the Effects of Government Regulation," *Journal of Law and Economics,* vol. 15 (April 1972), pp. 151-176.

[23] Richard N. Farmer, "The Case for Unregulated Truck Transportation," *Journal of Farm Economics,* vol. 46 (1964), p. 398, cited in ibid.

[24] James Sloss, "Regulation of Motor Freight Transportation: A Quantitative Evaluation of Policy," *Bell Journal of Economics and Management Science,* vol. 1 (Autumn 1970), p. 327.

least three alternatives have been proposed: major risk insurance (MRI), variable cost insurance (VCI), and health maintenance organizations (HMOs).

Major risk insurance has been proposed by Martin Feldstein.[25] The basic idea of MRI is to utilize deductibles which are a fraction of income, so that for middle and upper classes they represent substantial amounts. This would retain access for the poor, but introduce cost-consciousness and restrain demand for the middle and upper classes.

The principal defect of this proposal with respect to making hospitals increasingly cost conscious is that most consumers with hospital stays will still face a low or zero price at the margin, unless the deductible is an extraordinarily large fraction of income, in which case the risk borne would be quite large. Note that the present distribution of hospital expenditures is not sufficient to determine what fraction of those in the hospital will face a small marginal price, since that distribution may change. Specifically, consumers may anticipate satisfying the deductible and so consume services into the range of the deductible.[26] For hospital demands which reflect considerations at the margin such as length of stay and choice of hospital, MRI is not completely satisfactory. For choices concerning admission and small expenditure cases, it is an improvement.

Variable cost insurance has been proposed by Newhouse and Taylor.[27] VCI would give hospitals an expense rating. An individual would be asked to choose a hospital or hospitals for insurance calculations, and his premium would be determined by the costliness of the hospital he chose. He would be free to go to a more costly hospital at time of utilization, but he would bear the full marginal cost. Whether he would receive money for going to a cheaper hospital than the one he originally chose would remain to be determined. A number of individuals in the insurance industry are opposed to money payments to the individual conditional on hospitalization, since it strengthens his incentive to be hospitalized. Income support plans that pay cash per day in the hospital, however, are exactly this kind of insurance. The principal advantage of VCI is that it would tend to force hospitals to produce efficiently the quality level of care for which consumers are willing to pay. Thus, what has been termed "x"-inefficiency should be reduced, and a mix of quality levels would appear based on what consumers would be willing to pay for.

---

[25] Martin S. Feldstein, "A New Approach to National Health Insurance," *Public Interest*, vol. 23 (Spring 1971), pp. 93-105.

[26] In technical terms a deductible represents a kink in the price line so that there are two local maxima. Anticipation of satisfying the deductible can be thought of as choosing a global maximum. For a further discussion of this point, see Emmett Keeler, Charles E. Phelps and Joseph P. Newhouse, *The Theory of a Consumer Facing a Variable Price Schedule Under Uncertainty* (forthcoming).

[27] Newhouse and Taylor, "The Subsidy Problem in Hospital Insurance," "How Shall We Pay for Hospital Care?" and "A New Type of Hospital Insurance." See also Morton Schnabel, "The Subsidy Problem in Hospital Insurance: Comment," *Journal of Business*, vol. 45, no. 2 (April 1972), pp. 302-304.

This last outcome is a disadvantage for some who feel that all should be entitled to the highest quality care. But we would suggest that it is precisely this attitude which has led to concern for hospital expenditures and overutilization of capital. Giving the highest quality of care to all may be good rhetoric, but it probably does not represent the best allocation of resources.[28]

A problem which VCI does not solve is the expansion in demand which results from lowering the price for additional days in the hospital (additional length of stay) and the low total cost of going to the hospital if one stays within the expense class specified in one's policy (additional admissions). MRI, as we pointed out, generally does not solve the first problem either. One could, of course, use a deductible in connection with a VCI-type policy if overadmission to the hospital proved to be a problem.

The third alternative, health maintenance organizations, is in effect an extension of the principle of VCI into comprehensive care. The consumer's insurance premium would depend upon the costliness of the HMO he selected; there is the difference that in general he would be restricted to the HMO he selected for care. It has been frequently pointed out that HMOs have an incentive to dilute quality of care; the usual answer is that to avoid this there would have to be competition among HMOs and between HMOs and other types of providers, with the consumer free to change. Whether an HMO market structure would be conducive to good performance in this industry is thus an empirical question which cannot be well answered a priori.

The empirical evidence available, however, suggests that HMOs may well be a solution to the problems which have led some to support compulsory health planning laws. The Kaiser-Permanente Medical Foundation, for example, runs a prepaid group practice with half the beds per capita of similarly located California hospitals.[29] One can ask whether Kaiser has too few beds, but the presumption of those arguing for health planning laws is that the voluntary system has too many. Without answering this possibly unanswerable question, we can point out that if HMOs are as effective as their backers hope, there is less rationale for compulsory health planning organizations.

When the consumer purchases his care from an HMO, he effectively votes for the capital which that HMO is using. To refuse to permit an HMO to obtain capital then is to suspend consumer sovereignty. If competition is effective, the argument that HMOs are not cost minimizers is difficult to sustain; thus that rationale for planning disappears. There is now a strong impetus from many quarters to de-

---

[28] Some have argued for one quality of care for all (not necessarily the highest). We regard this outcome as a practically unattainable goal (providers are inherently different in quality) and probably a misallocation of resources (on the assumption of consumer sovereignty, externalities would have to exist of exactly the right magnitude).

[29] National Advisory Commission on Health Manpower, *Report* (Washington, D.C.: U.S. Government Printing Office, 1967), Appendix 4.

velop prepaid health care or HMOs. Indeed, to do so is part of many proposals for national health insurance. This aspect of national health insurance, then, should lessen the need for compulsory health planning.

We started with a question as to whether there were alternatives to compulsory planning as a solution to the problems posed by reimbursement insurance and whether those alternatives could be incorporated into national health insurance. The answer to both questions is yes. Moreover, given the past apparent lack of effectiveness of agencies similar to health planning agencies, these may be more effective solutions than compulsory health planning.

The "Skimming" Argument

The prospect of national health insurance also reduces the importance of a familiar argument for control of entry—the "cream-skimming" argument. The basic skimming argument is that voluntaries and public hospitals are engaging in charity medicine and need the profitable hospital business to offset the charity business. Proprietary hospitals, if permitted free entry, will take only the most profitable business and leave the less profitable and losing business to the voluntaries and public hospitals. The most profitable business is generally either (1) inexpensive, high-unit-profit procedures (simple surgery or more routine laboratory or x-ray work, and so forth), or (2) services performed on patients who pay their bills (usually they have generous third-party coverage). The business left for the voluntaries, teaching hospitals, and public hospitals is difficult, requires expensive equipment (which is kept standing idle much of the time), is longer term, and is performed on persons from whom payment is less likely. If we limit the number of proprietaries, patients with simpler cases and those more likely to pay their bills have to go to the same hospitals with patients who have difficult cases or are less likely to pay. Thus, the first category of patients will be contributing to the revenue pool of the hospital to help offset the losses of the second category. Restricting entry hinders cream skimming, since a hospital can be obligated to accept all patients as a condition of entry. Moreover, by limiting the capital investment in exotic equipment, the hospital can keep down the amount of excess loss generated by an unprofitable service and everybody's hospital bill can be thereby reduced.

In considering the skimming argument we raise three questions: (1) What is the extent of charity medicine? (2) What are the merits of using revenues from the treatment of some diseases to offset the cost of treatment of other diseases? (3) What are the merits of using the higher collection rates from some types of patients to offset the losses in treating other patients?

First, how widespread is the practice of charity medicine? Very little charity medicine is actually practiced—in part because of the passage of Medicare and Medicaid. In 1970 $385 million of expenditures for hospital care were attributed

228

to "philanthropy." This was slightly over 2 percent of the $17 billion total expenditures on nongovernmental hospitals and less than 1½ percent of the $28 billion on all hospitals. Clearly philanthropy is not large in a percentage sense.[30] If national health insurance were to be relatively complete, particularly if it were to cover catastrophic cases and the care of the poor, charity care might vanish completely. Therefore, the argument that planning or regulation is necessary to ensure the continuation of charity medicine is weakened by national health insurance.

A chief argument for restricting the number of hospitals has been that it was necessary to have profitable procedures (for example, simple x-rays) performed in the hospital to offset unprofitable procedures (for example, cobalt therapy). In fact, the argument seems to extend to include a desire to have "profitable" diseases (simple surgery such as tonsillectomies and adenoidectomies) treated in the same hospital with "unprofitable" diseases (cardiac surgery, perhaps). This argument is hard to justify on a priori grounds. Why should some categories of ill persons subsidize other ill persons? If there are externalities in having certain diseases treated, the recipients of these externalities seem to be the logical financiers. It is hard to imagine that recipients of T and As and routine hysterectomies are the chief recipients of externalities generated by vascular surgery. This is the sort of problem we expect the political process to resolve, not the comptroller of the hospital.[31] There is a second reason for concern about the inter-illness subsidy of care—it distorts prices. By raising the price of treating some diseases so that the price of treating other diseases can be lowered, we may create an incentive to treat fewer of the first category and more of the second category of disease.[32] The case for doing so has not been persuasively made, although one could make an argument that there are excessive amounts of routine surgery and that to lower prices would only increase it. We must leave this question for the future.

The other skimming argument advanced was that it was necessary to combine in the same facilities those who paid their bills and those less likely to pay. The same sort of objection can be raised to this position as was discussed for inter-illness subsidies. Those who benefit from having bad debtors receive treatment should appropriately make reimbursement for bad debts. Since the beneficiary is

---

[30] Barbara Cooper and Nancy Worthington, *Research and Statistics Notes,* no. 1 (Washington, D.C.: Social Security Administration, 1972), Table 4. Furthermore, philanthropy has been declining for several years. In 1950, 2.9 percent of personal health care expenditures were financed by "other," which is the residual after taking account of direct payments, insurance benefits, and government payment; Ibid., Table 5. Just before Medicare and Medicaid, it was down to 2 percent and in 1970, to 1.5 percent.

[31] Further, it is not clear that subsidizing "unprofitable" procedures benefits the poor, a frequently voiced justification for the subsidy. Unless insurance is complete, some very expensive procedures may be completely beyond the resources of the poor, so the reduction in price caused by the subsidy does not induce greater purchases among the poor.

[32] There is no evidence that such substitution takes place.

more likely to be society as a whole, and not just those who are hospitalized, this argues for reimbursement from general revenues.[33]

Conclusion

We have argued that the chief reason that compulsory planning or regulation is advocated stems from the consequences of reimbursement insurance. The two chief results of reimbursement insurance have been (1) to significantly increase the demand for health care and (2) to cause hospitals to upgrade their product. As a consequence, we have experienced significantly rising expenditures and concerns over the efficiency with which health services are produced. This has led a number of people to call for compulsory planning or regulation. We reviewed evidence on regulation in other industries which leads us to skepticism concerning its impact on efficiency.

Some type of national health insurance now appears likely. Paradoxically, this weakens the case for compulsory health planning. An increase in demand can be anticipated which argues for flexibility in response. Otherwise, the increased demand may have to be met with more costly factor proportions than would be optimal. More importantly, national health insurance need not be of the reimbursement form which has characterized almost all insurance and which we think has generated the demand for compulsory planning. We considered major risk insurance, variable cost insurance, and health maintenance organizations as alternative approaches. There is reason to believe that these approaches—by changing the incentives facing medical decision makers directly (HMOs) or indirectly by changing the incentives facing consumers (MRI and VCI)—will contribute to improving efficiency in health services production. Finally, we considered the cream-skimming argument for planning and found that charity medicine now constitutes a very small amount of the hospitals' activities. Any national health insurance proposal should eliminate the need for any significant amount of philanthropy.

In criticizing regulation, we are not arguing for know-nothingness in the health sector. Information is essential to successful adaptation to changes in demand, whether in a centralized or a decentralized system. And formulation of intelligent public policy requires a sophisticated notion of how insurance interacts with prices, income, and other socio-demographic factors in determining the demand for medical care and type of provider chosen. In fact, it is appallingly difficult to find some simple but crucial facts about the health insurance coverage and utilization of our population. While preparing the administration's employer-mandated health insur-

---

[33] This is not to condone lax collection procedures on the part of hospitals. If some hospitals are just sloppy in billing, it is difficult to argue even for reimbursement from general revenues, and it is even more difficult to justify forcing all hospitalized persons to receive their care at such a hospital.

ance plan, HEW officials found to their surprise that the best available information on current insurance coverage in the population came from a survey conducted in 1963. No more recent surveys were available. In a $70 billion industry this fundamental ignorance is inexcusable. To the extent that health planning bodies collect and disseminate such information, they are performing an important function.

THE FUTURE OF PROPRIETARIES IN AMERICAN HEALTH SERVICES

Duncan Neuhauser *

What should be the future of for-profit hospitals and for-profit health maintenance organizations (HMOs)? Asking what the future of the proprietaries should or will be is like asking what is to be the future of the left forepaw of the (health care) dog. In order to understand the paw, you have to spend most of your time talking about the dog. To answer this requires (1) defining what society's goals are for the health service industry, (2) a theoretical framework for understanding how this industry works, (3) a theory of what proprietaries are, and (4) an ideology. Therefore we must take the long route around before coming to the question we started with. In the current academic jargon this is called the systems approach.

Social Goals of Health Services

What does society ask of health services? Several things: (1) quality of care, that is, high quality of output per dollar of input; (2) efficiency, or low cost for a standardized unit of output; (3) accessibility, including transportation costs;[1] (4) pooling of risk; (5) innovation, that is, adaptation or progressiveness; (6) redistribution of income, meaning health care to all regardless of ability to pay; and (7) choice, freedom, and protection from fraud.[2]

The Hypothesis of the Missing Means-Ends Constraint

This hypothesis illustrated in Figure 1 states that the production function for direct health care (hospitals, doctors, drugs) is horizontal and unclear in the relevant range.[3] Or, stated another way, at the margin plus or minus 30 percent, the provision of direct health services has no measurable effect on the health of the popula-

* Critical comments by Ralph Berry, Connie Evashwick, Charles Hays, and others have been appreciated.

[1] Millard Long and Paul Feldstein, "Economics of Hospital Systems: Peak Loads and Regional Coordination," *American Economic Review*, vol. 57, no. 2 (May 1967), pp. 119-129.

[2] Adapted from Howard R. Bowen and James R. Jeffers, *The Economics of Health Services* (New York: General Learning Press, 1971), p. 24.

[3] The production function is hypothesized to be horizontal, and this is unclear to most people; thus this superficially paradoxical proposal that it is both horizontal and unclear.

233

Figure 1

RELATIONSHIP BETWEEN DIRECT HEALTH CARE AND HEALTH

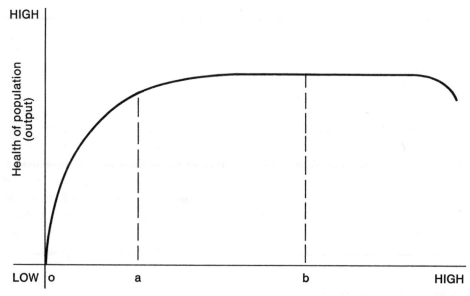

Volume of direct health care per person (input) *

Notes:

* includes doctors, hospitals, drugs.

a = present location: assumes that other things, such as income, sanitary conditions, education, housing, climate, living habits, age and sex distribution, and the state of medical technology, are held constant.

b = the point on the curve where it becomes indistinguishable from horizontal. To the left of *b*, health care might be viewed as a necessity, to the right of *b* a luxury. Point *b* might also be viewed as about the point at which the marginal ratio of output to input falls below that obtainable in other sectors of the economy.

The *o* point on the vertical axis does not represent zero life expectancy (health level) but, rather, the life expectancy that would prevail in the absence of all direct health care.

tion served. Or, simply, input-output relationships are unclear in the health care industry.

At the left of the graph in Figure 1, errors of omission predominate; on the right, errors of commission increase in importance as the average skill level of the provider falls and as there is increasing use of marginally useful forms of treatment. Although there is no single empirical study that can definitively demonstrate this, there is a large volume of empirical evidence which is consistent with this theory and which would be difficult to explain in other ways.

The recent great inflation in health care costs without much associated increase in life expectancy has made this kind of theorizing more acceptable today. Prior to

1910, it is argued, medical care had little or no effect on improving the level of health.[4] By 1910, it is stated, the patient for the first time had a fifty-fifty chance of benefiting from health care.[5] Today, there are some health care inputs which are very effective and quite a few of doubtful effectiveness. In fact, those patients who can readily be helped often leave the health services system while those who are not helped keep coming back.

The Evidence. Stepwise multiple regression production functions for health care using data for the states demonstrate that after the demographic variables like per capita income and education are entered in, the health input variables like hospital and physician use do not have a significant impact on health level measures such as life expectancy.[6] However, there are major statistical problems with these studies.

About 25 percent of hospital admissions are for patients over the age of sixty-five. Yet between 1900 and 1970, we have been unable to increase the life expectancy of people aged sixty-five by more than a year or two.[7]

Querido, in a study of patients discharged from a Dutch hospital, concluded that only 40.5 percent actually benefitted by the care they received. And data of Robert Brook and other for Baltimore City Hospital discharges show that only 41 percent of these patients had improved health levels six months later.[8]

Expert estimates of the number of patients who do not need to be in general hospitals have ranged from a conservative 7 percent to a high of 50 percent. A vivid example of what can be done occurred in 1939 when the British government ordered hospitals to empty 100,000 beds to prepare for possible massive civilian victims of pending German air raids. In fact, the hospitals were able to clear 140,000 beds or an estimated 40 to 50 percent of the inpatients.[9]

---

[4] Thomas McKeown, *Medicine in Modern Society* (London: George Allen and Unwin, Ltd., 1965), Chapters 1 and 2. Also see Rene Dubos, *Mirage of Health* (New York: Anchor Books, 1959).

[5] Kenneth Boulding, "Ecology and Environment," *Trans-Action*, March 1970, p. 38.

[6] See Joseph P. Newhouse, "Toward a Rational Allocation of Resources in Medical Care" (Ph.D dissertation, Harvard University, 1968). See also Richard Auster, Irving Leveson, and Deborah Sarachek, "The Production of Health: An Exploratory Study," *The Journal of Human Resources*, vol. 4, no. 4 (Fall 1969), pp. 411-436.

[7] U.S. Department of Health, Education, and Welfare, *Toward A Social Report* (Washington, D.C.: U.S. Government Printing Office, 1969), Chapter 1. See also Bowen and Jeffers, *The Economics of Health Services*.

[8] See Robert Brook, Francis Appel, Charles Avery, Morton Orman, and Robert Stevenson, "Effectiveness of Inpatient Follow-up Care," *New England Journal of Medicine*, vol. 285, no. 27 (December 30, 1971), pp. 1509-1514; and R. H. Brook and D. S. Stevenson, "Effectiveness of Patient Care in an Emergency Room," *New England Journal of Medicine*, October 1970. See also A. Querido, *The Efficiency of Medical Care* (Lieden, Holland: H. E. Stenfert Kroese, N.V., 1963), p. 252.

[9] Richard M. Titmuss, *Problems of Social Policy* (London: Her Majesty's Stationery Office, Longmans Green, 1950), p. 193, cited in Odin W. Anderson and Paul B. Sheatsley, *Hospital Use*, Research Series No. 24 (Chicago: Center for Health Administration Studies, University of Chicago, 1967), p. 113.

There are major differences in hospital admission rates by region, which as far as is known, are unassociated with differences in health levels or patient satisfaction. Admissions to general hospitals per 1,000 population in the United States are 136, in Sweden 135, in Great Britain 96, and in Saskatchewan 218.[10] The Kaiser plan hospitals had an age-adjusted annual hospital cost per person equal to 53 percent of that of the nonenrolled California population in 1965.[11] On the other side of the coin there is some evidence to suggest that simply building more beds will lead to increased utilization.

In Enoch Powell's blunt words,

Common thought and parlance tend to conceal or deny the fact that demand [for health services in the British National Health Service] for all practical purposes *is* unlimited. The vulgar assumption is that there is a definable amount of medical care "needed" and that if that "need" is met no more will be demanded. This is absurd . . . there is virtually no limit to the amount of medical care an individual is capable of absorbing.[12]

For further support of this hypothesis one can look at the evidence illness by illness. Nearly all American babies are born in hospitals attended by physicians, while in the Netherlands in 1963 70 percent of the babies were born at home and 35 percent were delivered by midwives. These differences are not inconsistent with lower infant mortality in the Netherlands.[13] The benefit of that most frequent surgical operation, the tonsillectomy, is questionable. The effect of various types of treatment of mental illness remains debatable. The Soviet Union for ideological reasons in 1959 had 0.84 psychiatric beds per 1,000 population compared to 4.3 in the United States with apparently the same level of mental illness in the population.[14] Now in the United States there is increasing use of less costly care

---

[10] Odin W. Anderson, "Comparative Tables Relating to Health Care," mimeographed, April 1971. See also Ronald Andersen and John Hull, "Hospital Utilization and Cost Trends in Canada and the United States," *Health Services Research,* Fall 1969, p. 216.

[11] Walter J. McNerney, "Implications of Increasing Hospital Use of Prepayment Plans," in *Where is Hospital Use Headed?* (Proceedings of the Fifth Annual Symposium on Hospital Affairs, Graduate Program in Hospital Administration, University of Chicago, 1962).

[12] J. Enoch Powell, Minister of Health, 1960-1963, British National Health Service, *Medicine and Politics* (London: Pitman Medical Publishing Co., 1966), Chapter 4.

[13] J. H. de Haas-Posthuma, *Infant Loss in the Netherlands,* Vital and Health Statistics Analytical Studies, series 3, no. 11 (Washington, D.C.: Department of Health, Education, and Welfare, National Center for Health Statistics, August 1968), p. 20; "Do It Yourself Childbirth is a Dutch Way of Life," *Medical World News,* June 13, 1969, pp. 58-59. In fact the high cost of obstetricians in the U.S. may lead to increased use of induced deliveries which may lead to increased prematurity which in turn increases the infant mortality. See articles by William C. Kettel, Lawrence Hester, and Kenneth Niswander on "Elective Induction of Labor," in Duncan E. Reid and T. C. Barton, eds., *Controversy in Obstetrics, Gynecology* (Philadelphia: W. B. Saunders Co., 1969), pp. 107-133.

[14] World Health Organization, "Traveling Seminar on Public Health Administration in the U.S.S.R." (Copenhagen: Regional Office for Europe, 1961); U.S. Department of Health, Edu-

for the mentally ill compared with high-cost-per-case, long-term custodial care—if it could even be called "care." The effectiveness of annual physical exams is also debatable, as is the value of varying nurse staffing ratios in general hospitals, the treatment of most acute myocardial infarctions in hospitals, treatment of the terminally ill patient, the care of the retarded and the care of the elderly in nursing homes.

Perhaps this is belaboring a well-known phenomenon, but one does frequently see statements that more direct health care inputs are needed and, by implication, will improve health. How does one interpret the idea of "the health care crisis" in the context of this hypothesis?

A.L. Cochrane in his brilliant review of these issues argues that the absence of randomized clinical trials in medical care, as a result of inertia, cost, and ethical considerations, allows dubious methods of treatment to persist.[15] Once "the experts" are convinced that a treatment is essential and once this treatment is in widespread use, ethics thereafter forbid randomized clinical trials and there is never another chance to find out whether the treatment is beneficial or not. In this context, Cochrane's challenge that "all *effective* treatment must be free" is an interesting proposal. In the terms of Figure 1, one implication is that all care to the left of "b" should be paid for by the government, and anything beyond that should be paid for by the consumer.

Behavioral Implications. This hypothesis of the absence of a means-ends constraint allows us to understand some of the important characteristics of health services. For example, there are persistent differences in treatment methods for similar patients; there are particularly major regional variations in the amount of surgery performed, in average length of stay, and in physician/population ratios. It leads to understanding why almost simultaneously various articles can appear suggesting that we need (1) fewer doctors, (2) more doctors, or (3) just the number we now have.[16]

---

cation, and Welfare, Public Health Service, "Hospital Services in the U.S.S.R." (Washington, D.C.: U.S. Government Printing Office, 1966).

[15] A. L. Cochrane, *Effectiveness and Efficiency* (London: The Nuffield Provincial Hospital Trust, 1972).

[16] Charles E. Lewis, "Variations in Incidence of Surgery," *New England Journal of Medicine*, vol. 281, no. 16 (October 16, 1969), p. 880; M. A. Heasman, "How Long in Hospital?" *Lancet*, September 12, 1964, p. 539; R. W. Revans, *Moral and Effectiveness of General Hospitals: Problems and Progress in Medical Care* (London: Oxford University Press, 1964); J. Simpson et al., *Custom and Practice in Medical Care* (London: Oxford University Press, 1968); S. Halter, *Factors Affecting the Length of Stay in Hospital* (Strasbourg: Council of Europe, European Public Health Committee, 1968); Carl M. Stevens, "Physician Supply and National Health Care Goals," *Industrial Relations*, vol. 10, no. 2 (May 1971), pp. 119-144; Henry R. Mason, "Manpower Needs By Specialty," *Journal of the American Medical Association*, vol. 219, no. 12 (March 20, 1972), pp. 1621-1626, and "Are There Too Many General Surgeons?" ibid., p. 1627; Hyman K. Schonfeld, Jean F. Heston, and Isidore S. Falk, "Numbers of Physicians Required for Primary Medical Care," *New England Journal of Medicine*,

In the absence of a means-ends constraint, what does define the health services system? Laws, bureaucratic controls, the marketplace, professional dominance, historical events, production technology, and ideology are some of the constraints.

Ideological Implications. This theory is consistent with at least four widely differing policy prescriptions which have different implications for the proprietaries:

(1) Close down 30 percent of hospital beds now. If we were to do this which beds would be closed? Would the proprietaries be the first to go, or would it be the high-cost, large teaching hospitals?

(2) Since the means-ends are unclear, do nothing radical. The trend toward certificate of need (which is freezing the status quo) and our bureaucratic tendency toward incremental decision making suggest this will be the route we go. This approach may abruptly halt the further growth of the proprietary hospital.

Or, as a variant of (2): While maintaining the status quo, let us encourage health maintenance organizations with their lower utilization.[17] In this connection, what is the prospect for proprietary HMOs?

(3) The Marxist interpretation is that health services are the new opiate of the working classes: The health care crisis is really the crisis of the capitalist order; the only way to substantially change the health of the workers is to change the means of production and the associated class structure; anyone who advocates that health can be improved by direct health care is as much a toady to the imperialist-capitalist elite as the Pentagon generals are; the parallel current failures of housing programs, education, and prisons support this interpretation. It appears that some senior government officials have accepted this diagnosis, but, because they ignore the Marxist therapy, it is labeled "rampant pessimism." This rampant pessimism suggests a general cutback in federal health funds in the absence of clearly demonstrable results. From the Marxist viewpoint, the proprietaries will end up on the scrap heap of history.

(4) The free-market, consumer sovereignty interpretation: The relationship between health and health care is irrelevant. The health services industry should respond to consumer demand (whatever that might be) in a competitive market. This ideology would probably benefit the proprietaries. It is consistent with encouraging a choice between HMOs at the left of the production curve shown in Figure 1 and traditional fee-for-service at the right of the curve.

---

vol. 286, no. 11 (March 16, 1972), pp. 571-576; and "Lettters to the Editor," *New England Journal of Medicine*, May 25, 1972, pp. 1164-1165.

[17] For our purposes here an HMO is a self-contained corporate entity which provides comprehensive doctor and hospital care to a defined subscriber population which pays a periodic premium for this coverage regardless of use. Thus the plan has a fixed income from which all care must be paid. When this arrangement includes salaried or retained doctors and the ownership of hospitals, as the Kaiser health plan does, it appears to result in substantially lower utilization of services.

The Ideology of the Expert

Since the reason nonprofit hospitals predominate appears to be professional and public predilections or taste, it is useful to ask why this preference occurs. The professional ideology assumes that the professional is an expert as a result of his years of education and learning. Since he knows more about his area he should tell others what they "need." Consistent with this is the idea that the public is unwise and unknowing. This is in contrast to the idea of consumer sovereignty where the consumer is the best judge of his own desires. Physicians have tended toward the former ideology and businessmen and economists toward the latter. But in the last analysis, until the day comes when we can plant electrodes in peoples' skulls to measure utilities, this must remain an ideological assumption.

One rationale for the professional ideology is in the placebo effect, where the less the patient knows the more he will benefit by the treatment.[18] As far as I know, there has yet to be a good economic analysis of the welfare implications of the placebo effect. An interesting case can be made for saying that the current peculiarities in the market for physician services is consistent with maximizing the placebo effect, including the physician's high status in terms of social class, income, and education, the rituals, the fancy scientific equipment, the religious overtones, and the nonprofit hospital.

Paralleling the ideology of the expert is the expert's demand for more resources: more quality, more education, more personnel, more research, more buildings, and more money. An extreme example of this is the amount of intensive psychotherapy some experts think this country "needs." Professionalism seems to have a preference for the high-cost, high-quality option leaving a gap in the low-cost, low-quality sector to be filled by for-profit firms.[19] Given the absence of a known input-output relationship, given extensive insurance coverage, and given the influence of the ideology of the expert, it is not surprising that we are not to the left of the horizontal part of the production curve.

One can argue that the professional ideology and the independent nonprofit organization are associated with each other. Professionalism is strong in universities, religion, and health care, and these are the bastions of nonprofit organiza-

---

[18] "The effect of placebos has been shown by randomized clinical trials to be very large. Their use in the correct place is to be encouraged. What is inefficient is the use of relatively expensive drugs as placebos. It is a pity some enterprising drug company does not produce a wide range of cheap, brightly colored, nontoxic placebos." See Cochrane, *Effectiveness and Efficiency*, p. 31.

[19] There is nothing inconsistent with high quality care and the profit motive as Ernest Amory Codman's "End Result Hospital" indicates. In 1911 he quit the Massachusetts General Hospital and founded his own proprietary hospital because he was disgusted with the lack of quality control at the MGH. Ernest A. Codman, *A Study in Hospital Efficiency* (Boston: Privately printed, 1916 or 1917), and Ernest A. Codman, *The Shoulder* (Boston: Thomas Todd and Co., 1934), Introduction and Epilogue.

tions, which allow the professionals to be relatively free from market forces, if not in fact at least in ideological terms.

Nonprofit hospitals have been relatively free to charge some patients more and some less than the services cost. Thus the rich sick pay for the poor sick, and the "appendectomies" pay for the "open heart surgery." In the absence of any government health insurance, this may have been an appropriate way of redistributing wealth, but it is certainly nonoptimal. If proprietary hospitals come in and equate charges to costs and only accept those patients whose costs are covered, this increases competitive pricing in the hospital field. In the short run, this may be painful, but in the long run it is probably beneficial in that it may compel the government to provide a payment system which is consistent with society's goals for the health services industry.

It is only fair to point out that "cream-skimming" is probably far greater within the voluntary sector. The hospital room rate is a "loss leader," the loss to be made up by high profits in radiology, pathology, and pharmacy. The "interesting cases" are fought for, while the "crocks," "vegetables," and "gorks" are "dumped" whenever possible. The suburban community hospitals avoid the poor, who are left to the urban community hospitals which, in turn, struggle for survival or save their money in order to move. The voluntary teaching hospitals prefer if they can to take the "interesting cases" and send everyone else to the city or county hospital. When these hospitals don't find the patient interesting, he is finally sent to the municipal chronic disease hospital. In short, cream-skimming is a way of life in the entire hospital field.

There is almost no hope of devising a low-cost, easy way to itemize patient bills so that they exactly reflect both the hospital's dollar costs and its preference for particular types of patients. It is estimated that we now spend nationwide about $2 billion a year processing itemized patient bills, costs which do not exist at all in the British National Health Service or need not exist in an HMO. Unless we are willing to let the third-party payer auction off each patient to the hospitals for care, cream-skimming is built into our system and is something we have to live with in some measure.

Uncertainty, Planning, and Proprietaries. The unpredictable nature of health care costs leads to pooling of risk through health insurance or prepayment. This alone is not a sufficient justification for planning; however, combining this with the absence of a means-ends constraint means that if the people in Los Angeles consume a large amount of care, then I, in Boston, am affected by their behavior through my participation in Social Security. If there were a precisely definable finite need for health care, then there would be much less need for planning.[20]

---

[20] By planning I refer here to imposing restrictions on the construction of hospitals. In the absence of a means-ends constraint, the easiest way of controlling use is to control the vol-

In the absence of externalities, why should you or I care if people in Los Angeles use 218 or 400 admissions per 1,000 population and have idle cobalt therapy equipment in every thirty-bed hospital? Planning beyond the limits of externalities is an unnecessary interference with personal liberties. The absence of an accepted means-end constraint and externalities beyond the limits of planning is an invitation to overuse and abuse. One of the intriguing things about HMOs is that they have the potential of equating planning, control, and externalities.[21]

As Bruce Steinwald and I have demonstrated, a case can be made for saying that from 1880 to the 1960s proprietary hospitals in the United States have played a useful role in rapidly adapting to fluctuations and growth in "paying" demand for hospital services.[22] They have sprung up in the absence of voluntary hospitals to meet the needs of local practitioners. As demand stabilized, they either went out of business or became voluntary. From at least 1928 until the last two years proprietary hospitals have held a declining share of the hospital market, from 36 percent in 1928 to 11 percent in 1968. Apparently this is due to a public and professional preference for voluntary hospitals. This role as the "cutting edge" is consistent with the proprietary's small size, low capital costs, and short half-life.

This role was entirely appropriate until the advent of extensive health insurance coverage. Now the unfettered growth of proprietary, or for that matter voluntary, hospitals is no longer appropriate. However, the problem is that health planning in the U.S. has yet to demonstrate its effectiveness.[23]

The Characteristics of the Proprietary Hospital

One can say a great deal about the differences today in the U.S. between for-profit and voluntary hospitals. The proprietaries are smaller, offer a narrower range of

---

ume of available services. To demonstrate, imagine what would happen to Medicare costs if there were no physician licensure and anyone could call himself a doctor and collect for the services he performed.

[21] For example, in Massachusetts state planners pass on whether the hospitals in Worcester should build more beds. But whether Worcester builds more beds or not does not affect my experience-rated group in Boston and therefore it is none of my business what Worcester does. It is my group's concern, however, that planning provides the special options that we want. Yet my group cannot now do this. Perhaps the state commissioner of insurance should have all experience-rated groups of larger than fifty people elect representatives who would design the benefit options that the group may choose, thus equating planning, control, and externalities to a greater degree than now exists. Experience rating allows externalities to be limited to the group involved, while community rating makes us all busybodies. Given the goal that all effective health care be free, then perhaps the federal government should provide coverage up to point "b" in Figure 1, and if I want more than this, then I individually or as a group member should pay for it. From this point of view community rating is an evil to be avoided.

[22] Bruce Steinwald and Duncan Neuhauser, "The Role of the Proprietary Hospital," *Law and Contemporary Problems,* Autumn 1970, pp. 817-838.

[23] J. Joel May, "Health Planning—Its Past and Potential," Health Administration Perspectives No. A5 (Chicago: Center for Health Administration Studies, University of Chicago, 1967), Appendix; and John Carr, "Central Planning Versus Evolutionary Development," in Klarman, ed., *Empirical Studies in Health Economics,* p. 195.

services, have shorter lengths of stay and lower costs, and are concentrated in a few states. According to physician opinion they do not offer the quality of care found in the large, famous teaching hospitals.[24]

But on deeper reflection all these characteristics are specific to 1970 and to the United States. The characteristics of proprietary hospitals in France or the Philippines may be quite different. Perhaps there is only one characteristic which distinguishes proprietaries and that is their ability to rapidly adapt to changes in "paying" demand for hospital care. If the paying public wanted and could not otherwise get longer stays, more expensive and higher-quality hospital care, then we would expect the characteristics of proprietaries to be very different. For example, now there are almost no proprietary hospitals serving the poor. If the government were willing to subsidize care of the poor sufficiently to make it profitable then this would no doubt change.

The Efficiency of Proprietary Hospitals. In spite of the glowing reports from the Wall Street press, which confuse profitability with efficiency, it is, in my opinion, still unclear whether proprietaries are more efficient than voluntary hospitals. Apparently proprietary hospital costs have been rising about as fast as voluntary hospitals so they do not seem to be an answer to this problem. Moreover, anyone who wishes to praise the profit motive throughout the health field must contend with Richard M. Titmuss's devastating attack on proprietary blood banking and paid blood donors. However, it is debatable how applicable his findings are beyond the market for blood.

It is not inconceivable that there might be a substantial amount of "excess capacity" or "duplication of services" among for-profit firms in competitive markets —witness the relatively low occupancy of gas stations and hotels.

Apparently there is little problem in running a hospital with a substantial "excess revenue" and more than a few voluntary hospitals do so. The formula is simple: (1) locate in an affluent suburb; (2) be from 200 to 400 beds in size; (3) refer poor patients elsewhere; (4) attract patients with commercial insurance and avoid Blue Cross, Medicare, and Medicaid patients; (5) do not get involved in education or research; (6) negotiate tight contracts with the pathologists and radiologists; and (7) eliminate those services which do not pay their own way. I

[24] See Milton I. Roemer, A. Taher Moustafa, and Carl E. Hopkins, "A Proposed Hospital Quality Index: Hospital Death Rates Adjusted for Case Severity," *Health Services Research,* Summer 1968, pp. 96-118; Duncan Neuhauser and Fernand Turcotte, "Costs and Quality of Care in Different Types of Hospitals," *The Annals of the American Academy of Political and Social Science,* January 1972, pp. 50-61; Milton C. Maloney, Ray E. Trussel, and Jack Elinson, "Physicians Choose Medical Care: A Sociometric Approach to Quality Appraisal," *Journal of the American Public Health Association,* vol. 50, no. 11 (November 1960), p. 1678; and Herbert Bynder, "Doctors as Patients," *Medical Care,* vol. 6, no. 2 (March/April 1968), p. 157.

knew of one voluntary hospital which by following these rules had a "profit" of 20 percent on invested capital per year. It does not even take brilliant management to do this. What part of this behavior can be called efficiency and what part is just using the loopholes in the present system is debatable.

It seems likely that economies of scale at the hospital plant level occur up to 250 beds and perhaps beyond.[25] Only a few proprietaries are as large as this, and therefore most are not in the efficient plant size range, although the for-profit chains may be achieving economies of scale at the firm level. Furthermore, it is not clear that the savings from efficiency in proprietaries are returned to the patients in lower charges. The chain proprietaries have reported lowered costs and high profits after takeover of existing hospitals. However, it should be remembered that with one or two exceptions these have been takeovers of other proprietary hospitals and therefore have no relevance to the question at hand.

The potential for efficiency gains does exist. In a study of medium-size voluntary Chicago hospitals which I did recently, a substantial number lacked such basic management techniques as budgets, position controls, job descriptions, and adequate management information systems.[26] In this study it was estimated that improved management would lower standardized costs by 15 percent. Although this saving is substantial it is dwarfed by the potential saving that would result from the lower hospital admission rates found in HMOs.

Quality of Care. There is growing evidence if one controls for hospital size and scope of services that good management is directly associated with good quality of care. With respect to the hospital's medical staff, good management includes participatory decision making, good information systems, active staff committees, and enforced regulations. A cohesive medical staff can reinforce the physician's desire for quality long after his training, while a poorly organized medical staff can destroy these aspirations. If one is willing to assume a cause and effect relationship, then good management can save lives, and bad management kills. Many seem convinced that there are incentives for management to be efficient in proprietaries, but what about quality control?

---

[25] Ralph Berry, "Returns to Scale in the Production of Hospital Services," *Health Services Research,* Summer 1967, pp. 123-139; Thomas R. Hefty, "Returns to Scale in Hospitals: A Critical Review of Recent Research," *Health Services Research,* Winter 1969, pp. 267-280; Donald Yett and J. Mann, "An Analysis of Hospital Costs: A Review Article," *The Journal of Business,* vol. 41, no. 2 (April 1968), pp. 191-202; Judith R. Lave, "A Review of Methods Used to Study Hospital Costs," *Inquiry,* vol. 3, no. 2 (May 1966), pp. 57-81; and John Carr and Paul J. Feldstein, "The Relationship of Cost to Hospital Size," *Inquiry,* June 1967, pp. 45-65.

[26] Duncan Neuhauser, *The Relationshp Between Administrative Activities and Hospital Performance,* Research Series No. 28 (Chicago: Center for Health Administration Studies, University of Chicago, 1971), Chapter 6.

Proprietary HMOs. If the major savings are to be had in lower utilization, then there may be a doubtful future for proprietary hospitals but perhaps a great one for proprietary HMOs.[27]

It is argued that what is slowing the growth of HMOs is management and money, both of which the proprietary chains have in abundance along with an ability to move quickly in response to changing demands. It seems like a perfect match, but, as Bierig and Kovachy point out, there is the AMA's distaste for having nonphysicians extract any of the monopoly profits from the market for physician services under the banner of "the corporate practice of medicine." [28] But to have doctors own the HMOs is to close out access to stock market capital and to discourage the aggressive young business school graduates who are looking for ownership. If this battle is joined, it will be fascinating to watch because the chains with their size, their ideology of efficiency, and powerful political constituency on Wall Street may give the AMA a run for its money.[29] On the other hand, this might be avoided by having the proprietary own the hospital and having the doctors form a separate corporation to provide the medical care in the way that the Kaiser hospitals are separate from the Permanente medical groups.[30]

Once the demand for HMOs stabilizes, then the special benefits of the proprietaries will no longer offset the public's and professionals' preference for voluntary organizations. Other things being equal, physicians would prefer to work for a medical school HMO rather than for one run by a labor union like the UAW or a publicly held conglomerate. How does one promote the transition from proprietary HMOs into voluntary HMOs in the same way that proprietary hospitals have traditionally gone voluntary? Perhaps what is needed in this era of "future shock"

---

[27] Perhaps fifty years from now historians will view this single-minded passion for HMOs as a myopic aberration. They will point out that the major effect of the HMO is to lower utilization of services perhaps at the price of an increase in impersonality in the doctor-patient relationship. They might say that lowering utilization could be obtained in many other ways; for example, having doctors personally pay for their patients' unnecessary hospital care as in the recent Philadelphia case. See Ralph Thurlow, "You Admitted Her, Doc—You Pay the Hospital Bill!" *Medical Economics,* May 22, 1972, pp. 101-116. For another way of controlling use see Earl Brian, "Government Control of Hospital Utilization: A California Experience," *New England Journal of Medicine,* vol. 286, no. 25 (June 22, 1972), p. 1340. Perhaps if the AMA wishes to fend off the HMOs and perpetuate solo fee-for-service it entered the wrong side of this case. Perhaps the AMA should urge this liability for the cost of unnecessary hospital care on the part of doctors to lower utilization and to fend off the HMO movement, thus saving those benefits that are supposed to accrue from having a fee-for-service family doctor. By not taking this stand, the AMA has forced the growth of HMOs and forced into existence a "countervailing power" which may destroy the AMA's power.

[28] Jack R. Bierig and Edward M. Kovachy, Jr., "The Case for For-Profit Health Maintenance Organizations" (unpublished paper, Harvard University, April 1972).

[29] Apparently the AMA is now willing to allow the development of proprietary HMOs on an experimental basis. See American Medical Association, "Statement before the Subcommittee on Health of the Labor and Public Welfare Committee," U.S. Senate, June 2, 1972, mimeographed.

[30] Anne Somers, ed., *The Kaiser-Permanente Medical Care Program* (New York: The Commonwealth Fund, 1971).

244

and permanent change are holding corporations which have both for-profit and voluntary components shifting in importance as demand fluctuates or stabilizes.

Conversely, there should be legal arrangements by which inefficient, sluggish, unresponsive voluntary hospitals can be bought out by proprietary interests who can revitalize them and return them to voluntary status. The certificate-of-need legislation may have the unintended consequence of perpetuating these sluggish voluntaries indefinitely.

We have all witnessed the disastrous effects of lavish federal funding of start-up costs for voluntary health services which then must continue with heavy federal funding or die. The market test used by the proprietaries seems to have its advantages by comparison.

Proposals for the Future

I would like to see the following: growth of HMOs so that 90 percent of the population has the option of joining one or not. Then their share of the market will stabilize at substantially less than 100 percent of the market. Consumers will have available to them high- and low-cost options in terms of premiums analogous to points *a* and *b* on Figure 1. The federal government will provide universal health insurance coverage at the lower level (point *b*) consistent with the philosophy that "all effective treatment must be free." If the consumer or his experience-rated group wants the luxury of a higher cost option he or it can pay the difference. Providing low- and high-cost options will take the political "heat" out of the issue of rising health care costs. Then, if the people in Los Angeles want 218 hospital admissions per 1,000 population they can have it, and I will not be affected by their behavior. If they want all proprietary providers or none, it is up to them.

As HMOs grow rapidly, proprietaries will take over a larger share of this market. As demand stabilizes, the proprietary's share will begin to decline again to wait in the wings for the next major shift in demand.

One type of HMO I could envision is, as an entirely hypothetical example, one for Spanish-Americans in greater Chicago. They might have Catholic hospitals where Spanish is the first language and the primary culture. The population served may well spread beyond the bounds of existing planning agencies. This group will have the political clout and will have captured the externalities so that they can ignore the regional planners and build however many hospital beds they wish; they can also defy the licensing boards by initially importing plane loads of Spanish-speaking doctors who do not know enough English to pass the proficiency exam. Perhaps they will then send out local youths to Guadalajara for medical education there or open up a night medical school in Chicago. Perhaps these doctors would not be allowed to practice outside this HMO. Thus, regulation through licensure and regional planning will be limited to the non-HMO sector.

Although in starting this HMO the group might greatly appreciate having a for-profit hospital chain provide the initial capital and managerial skill, such a permanent arrangement would be intolerable. The membership would view it as a form of imperialism and exploitation. The members would want eventual ownership and control for themselves. Perhaps the for-profit chain would be delighted to sell out to a nonprofit member-owned corporation, particularly if they saw a potential threat of a membership revolt if they failed to do so.

There will always be some role for the proprietary hospitals or HMOs. How big this role is depends in part on the volatility of demand for hospital services, the extent of loopholes in the reimbursement system which can profitably be exploited, and in part on ideology and politics. The proprietary role also depends on the degree of public and professional preference for the voluntary system. The proprietaries must tend to their image, marketing, and politicking to define their future. Perhaps this for-profit/not-for-profit dichotomy will disappear as complex corporate structures evolve which contain both.

In the present U.S. context there is a good case for saying that the unregulated growth of hospitals whether voluntary or proprietary is inappropriate.

The current balance between proprietaries and voluntaries does not seem to call for major externally imposed readjustments. Allowing a shifting equilibrium between the two seems appropriate. Apparently some states like Tennessee have legally sanctioned the existence of proprietary HMOs. To a researcher, the fact that some states have approved proprietary HMOs and other states have forbidden them provides an interesting natural experiment to see if this will make a difference. Allowing variation in state law is also consistent with regional variations in preferences for proprietaries.

Some think that in the absence of proprietary HMOs the federal government will have to provide the start-up funds for voluntary HMOs.[31] Much of the capital costs of HMOs comes in connection with the construction of hospitals. To have the government pay HMOs to build their own hospital beds so that they can reduce hospital utilization, which will result in emptying existing hospitals, is a marvelous folly. The other major use of start-up funds is to pay for the initial idle capacity until the plan reaches the break-even volume of business. This is to argue substantial indivisibilities and therefore economies of scale in the provision of HMO care. I wonder if the indivisibilities would exist in the absence of legislation prescribing minimum HMO characteristics.

---

[31] John Valiante, Office of the Secretary of Health, Education, and Welfare, unpublished memorandum, no date. Also, Ronald Klar, "Differential Patterns of the Generation and Investment of Capital by Non-Federal, Short-Term General Hospitals," mimeographed (Harvard School of Public Health, May 1972).

246

It is customary for the experts to urgently recommend that something must be done because it makes them feel important and keeps them employed. As my contribution to the health care crisis I recommend that nothing be done about the proprietaries. There are more important things to do.

SPECULATIONS ON THE MARKET'S FUTURE IN HEALTH CARE

Clark C. Havighurst

Introduction

My remarks are directed to the market's potential role in organizing and animating the health care system of the future. I argue that providers of health care can reasonably be expected to do an acceptable job of controlling costs while maintaining the quality and attractiveness of their services if, and only if, they face meaningful market competition from prepaid providers. Though I despair of ever achieving acceptable cost control by direct regulatory measures, I do not question the possible desirability of regulation directed to other aspects of the system, particularly the quality of care. Government intervention is also needed to provide a comprehensive and fully funded health plan for the poor, a program that, for reasons I shall develop, must be adopted before substantially increased reliance on market incentives can be a realistic goal of health policy. Thus, in addition to being politically inevitable, a substantial degree of government involvement in health care is essential to achieving a market, as well as a nonmarket, solution to the industry's problems. Fortunately, it is possible to design such involvement to improve, or at least to be compatible with, the operation of market incentives and consumer freedom to choose among available providers.

Because a market solution to the health care crisis is basically quite attractive and is less difficult to bring about than most people believe, I think it must be considered a viable candidate for the job of straightening out the health care industry. Congress, however, may be insufficiently courageous, or perhaps just not single-minded enough, to depart from a depressing course of regulatory incrementalism in favor of a market solution. My hope, nevertheless, is that the case can be made persuasively enough to engage congressional interest and that then some of the current and popular legislative proposals on health maintenance organizations, which are really not so far from bringing things right, can be reviewed with an eye to preserving and increasing competitive forces and the desirable incentives they generate.

My paper is meant to be more about the market than about comprehensive certificate-of-need laws, but I will lead off each of the two main subdivisions with one of the main arguments supporting limitation of competition in the rendering of hospital care. I shall show (1) that these arguments have validity only if we accept as given the health care and financing systems we now have and (2) that the

249

real issue presented by protectionist certificate-of-need laws [1] is therefore not so much whether they make sense as things now stand but whether they are inevitable or are the best way of meeting the problems that exist. Although my main purpose is to demonstrate that relatively simple changes in the method of supporting care for nonpaying patients and in the functioning of the market would not only obviate anticompetitive entry restrictions but solve other problems as well, I shall nevertheless propose an alternative type of certificate-of-need law. My proposal would preserve the benefits of health planning and give due weight to the validity and urgency of the arguments supporting such laws; but it would also reduce the risk of locking the system permanently into a policy of needless protectionism. I will also offer a surprisingly short list of conditions that must be met before the market can be safely relied upon to promote substantially better performance by this industry. I shall conclude with some reflections on whether the market as I visualize it would be ethically or socially objectionable.

The Cream-Skimming Argument for Entry Restrictions:
Will National Health Insurance Foreclose a Market Solution?

I begin with the observation that the cream-skimming argument for legislative protection of health care providers against competition, although not unpersuasive, is based on expediency. It seizes upon the presence of price discrimination, itself a symptom of monopoly, and argues for the strengthening of monopoly power to preserve an intricate system of subsidization of one hospital service by the users of another service, and of one class of hospital users by another class. The cream-skimming argument presupposes two things: first, that those services which cannot support themselves when priced in accordance with their costs are nevertheless desirable to have and, second, that financial support for the subsidized services or classes cannot be obtained from other sources and must therefore be supplied by preserving providers' ability to set monopoly prices. While these premises would be difficult to establish theoretically, they may not be untenable as things currently stand. But what interests me more is that the conditions on which these arguments

---

[1] Note the emphasis on the word "protectionist." I develop later in the paper the distinction between competition-limiting certificate-of-need laws, which I take to be controls on private, profit-motivated investments in health facilities, and laws imposing supervisory controls over the investments of nonprofit and governmental entities. Laws of the latter type find their justification in the relative unresponsiveness of decision makers in nonprofit enterprises and bureaucracies to market signals and their tendency to overinvest in health facilities for prestige or other essentially irrelevent reasons. See generally William A. Niskanen, *Bureaucracy and Representative Government* (Chicago: Aldine-Atherton, 1971). My concern in the early portions of this paper is only with entry restrictions designed to limit competition for its own sake. I recognize, however, that planning solely for the purpose of improving the quality of decision making in governmental and private nonprofit institutions might also easily result in the suppression of desirable competition among providers of these types.

depend are not immutable and that, with certain changes in the underlying conditions, the cream-skimming argument could totally collapse.

The odds are beginning to seem good that sometime in the next several years Congress will enact some kind of improved health insurance system emphasizing subsidization of the purchasing power of disadvantaged consumers. If this insurance scheme were to mandate payment of amounts commensurate with the cost of each service rendered (or the competitive price thereof) and also full government backing for those who cannot themselves afford to pay, it would eliminate the need for internal cross-subsidization by providers. Because of the imminence of congressional action on an improved health insurance system, one might have expected a go-slow attitude toward the enactment of protectionist certificate-of-need laws, but in fact the pressure for legislative action has increased. The result is that protectionism may complete its conquest of the states at almost the precise instant that one of its chief justifications is largely removed. I trust we all know that, once these laws are on the books, a change in the conditions that prompted their enactment will not necessarily result in their quick repeal.

In suggesting the impending collapse of the foundation of the cream-skimming argument for protectionism, I have assumed, of course, that the national health insurance scheme to be enacted will come reasonably close to paying the full cost of caring for the nonpaying patient. Realism compels a recognition, however, that underfinancing is very likely to plague any new system of health insurance for the poor and medically indigent, just as it has plagued Medicaid. If Congress were to elect not to provide adequate funds, it would also probably wish to preserve all the supplementary revenue sources that providers now use to make up the deficiency between what the government provides and what the services in fact cost. It would be reasonable in these circumstances to expect federal law to mandate entry restrictions as a means of protecting hospitals' monopoly revenues.

There are numerous reasons, mostly political, why Congress may prove unwilling to adopt a health insurance scheme having benefits adequate enough to destroy the cream-skimming argument for entry restrictions. First, we all know there is a tremendous shortage of money for this kind of project anyway, even where its political appeal is great. Of course, some funds might be diverted from direct provider subsidies with pro-competitive effects, and the appropriation might be seen, in the spirit of revenue-sharing, as providing financial relief to state and local governments. But money is still short, and past experience may have bred a reluctance to subsidize new demand too heavily or too suddenly.

Second, we have already witnessed at both the state and federal levels a tendency to underestimate costs of health programs at the time when the laws enacting them are passed, and then to cut back on coverage, benefits, and reimbursement formulas when fiscal crises occur.

Third, government has not in the past seemed uncomfortable that providers, and ultimately their private patients, must bear some of the burdens. Thus, we have seen the creeping institutionalization of what I call the "monopolistic charity" approach to the provision of hospital services. When HEW recently proposed to order all hospitals that have ever received Hill-Burton funds to dedicate a minimum percentage of their gross revenues or net income to providing free care,[2] it extended a little farther the somewhat jarring principle of "compulsory charity" that originally appeared in connection with tax exemptions for health care providers. The principle at work here is very much of a piece with Galbraithian fatalism about the inevitability of monopoly and the consequent need to bully business firms into essentially charitable undertakings. As we witness the increasing popularity of the idea of the "social responsibility" of business, it seems to follow that hospitals particularly have an obligation to dispense charity. Hospitals more than other businesses have been quick to embrace public responsibilities but then have based a claim to legislative protection on the quasi-public status thus achieved.

A fourth reason that Congress is unlikely to adopt a health insurance plan that provides adequate coverage for those unable to pay is that it is politically easier to do it the cut-rate way, perhaps with federally mandated entry restrictions to make it effective. Although it should be clear that the true cost is no lower, and indeed is probably higher, the political cost of a system relying on provider monopolies is much less. Thus, rather than levy taxes itself and appropriate federal money to pay medical bills in full, Congress can appear to accomplish the same humanitarian result by conferring monopolies on hospitals and then forcing them to use their extra revenues in caring for the poor. To get some sense of the hypocrisy involved in a legislature's use of entry restrictions to protect hospitals' ability to tax their patients for this public purpose, ask youself how many legislators would vote in favor of a heavy excise tax, say $10 a day, on the occupancy of hospital beds. Yet most would have to agree that such a tax is preferable, from the standpoint of equity as well as honesty, to a system allowing each tax collector to decide what the tax rate should be and, to a large extent, what use should be made of the proceeds. Of course, subterfuges of this kind may permit more to be done in the way of wealth redistribution to the poor than a majority of the voters would approve if they had the facts, and the price of some sacrifices in the organization and efficiency of the health care industry may be deemed worth paying. Congress is of course free to make just this choice, but it should at least recognize that alternatives are available and that certain substantial costs may be incurred in adopting the monopolistic charity mode of attack on health care problems.

Finally, it is important to recognize that the political power of neither the poor themselves nor the providers who serve them is being exerted to obtain a broadening of insurance coverage to the point where 100 percent of the cost of indigent care would be paid by the government. Both groups seem instead to be quite content to lobby for conditions that will allow the needed supplementary re-

---

[2] See Proposed Regulations, 37 Fed. Reg. 7632 (April 18, 1972).

252

sources to be obtained from paying patients by monopolistic overcharges. Consumer groups, though they often complain about monopolistic providers, have generally supported the providers in their pursuit of a protected market position, perhaps recognizing that fully adequate financing at the federal level would be hard to get and would reveal to taxpayers too plainly the full burden that the health needs of the poor impose. Spokesmen for the poor have rested their hopes not on the restoration of a competitive marketplace with subsidized insurance and freedom to organize cooperatives, but on their ability in time to impose themselves politically on the management of the health care institutions with which they deal. On balance, the strategy may be a wise one. But it is based on a view of the world exclusively in terms of power relationships, and a hospital run on political principles may in the long run fail to contain costs or to maintain quality. Moreover, the paying patients on whom fiscal reliance is to be placed may, with the help of their doctors, find other accommodations where the tax rate is not so high. In any event, it may be instructive that, even though representatives of the poor and of the institutions serving the poor agree in favoring a policy of strong entry restrictions, alternatives are available that might leave the poor themselves, though perhaps not their representatives, better off, indeed with some access to the so-called mainstream of American medical care.

I have just advanced some powerful political reasons—none of them having anything notable to do with the merits of the issue—as to why national health insurance, when it comes, is likely to complete the institutionalization of the monopolistic charity model for delivering health care to the poor. If this occurs, the poor, though they might increase their political involvement, would find themselves trapped in a highly segregated system, ultimately dependent on appropriations by federal, state, and local governments, on compulsory charity, and on the perhaps tenuous willingness of some professionals to forgo better financial opportunities to fulfill a perceived social or professional obligation. For the better providers, the financial and other incentives would all point away from serving the beneficiaries of the public program, perhaps necessitating direct provider subsidies that would raise the overall cost. Inadequate funding of such a health insurance scheme would affect more than just the poor, of course, since it would set in motion the chain of events culminating in strict certificate-of-need laws and hospital monopoly. Because of the lack of market incentives, the costs of care and health insurance would be higher for everyone, and opportunities for choosing among providers would be restricted. Most important, the philosophy of relying on the good faith of nonprofit providers and on the government's ability to correct their failings will carry over into the health maintenance organization sector in numerous ways, all of them destructive of the functioning of a market that, as I shall show, is much more vital than the market for hospital services.

This seems to be the way we are going. To overcome the political realities and to counteract the momentum already built up may require more than a convincing argument, which is all I have to offer. Nevertheless, let us look at what the market could do if given a chance.

The Duplication-of-Facilities Arguments for Entry Restrictions:
Can Costs and Utilization be Otherwise Controlled?

In getting into broader questions about the working of a market-oriented health care system, it is convenient to begin by addressing the other main argument advanced in support of certificate-of-need laws, namely, the high cost to the public of the duplication of facilities. The argument is both more particularized and more persuasive than the general inefficiency arguments, based on scale economies and natural monopoly, which are advanced in support of the use of "certificates of public convenience and necessity" in public utility law. It has essentially two parts. The first involves the process by which the capital costs of hospitals are borne, and the second focuses on the added variable costs that are allegedly incurred in keeping "unneeded" hospital beds filled by patients who do not need to be there. Both arguments merely call our attention once again to the weakness of cost-consciousness in a system of fee-for-service institutional care that is prescribed by doctors and financed primarily by third-party payments based on cost. If preservation of this system in its present form is inevitable, then entry restrictions, and perhaps more far-reaching controls, may be essential.

In the rest of the economy, where excess plant capacity appears, prices fall and investors suffer. The market thus provides a strong deterrent to duplicative private investments except where significant efficiency gains accompany them. Where efficiency appears, inefficient plants are forced to close and, though their owners suffer losses, the new entrant prospers. If a county hospital is forced to operate at a loss or to close a wing by the entry of a more efficient proprietary institution, I see no problem just because the county taxpayers must then pay off the hospital bonds; the county should not be entitled to any greater protection for its investments than any other entrepreneur. Nevertheless, there is still a problem. It lies in the often relatively riskless nature of the investment in the new hospital. Investors in the new proprietary hospital seem to me to be excessively protected against having to bear any losses associated with the excess hospital capacity they help to create. Because of two imperfections in the system, these costs are "externalized," that is, borne not by investors but by the public. Thus, duplicative investments are insufficiently deterred by the market as things now stand, providing a justification for certificate-of-need laws.

The first peculiarity of the system contributing to the externalization of risks has to do with the prevalence of third-party insurance. Although it is not inevitable that it should be so, third-party payments for institutional care are related almost exclusively to costs, including capital costs. Payments are usually made on the basis of cost without regard to whether a competitive price for the service might be lower because of excess capacity in the market. Thus, the county hospital, writing off its capital investment as a loss, could set its price well below the proprietary hospital's price, but insurers would still pay the proprietary hospital its full costs. For this reason the new entrant need not fear that it will not get at least a compensatory price for every bed that is filled. In other words, competition will not force it to lower its price below cost.

The second market imperfection contributing to insulating investors from risk of loss in an overstocked market for hospital beds is the considerable control exercised by physicians over the patient's choice of hospital. In many cases this assures a supply of paying patients. This is particularly true if physicians themselves control the new entrant, but it may be true in other circumstances as well, such as where there are special inducements to the medical staff. Where the physicians have a preference, even a substantially lower price set by the county hospital is unlikely to lure many patients back. With reasonable assurance that their beds will be filled, the potential proprietors of a new hospital are not much deterred from entry by the risks of creating costly excess capacity.

The phenomenon of doctor control over hospital admissions and discharges also accounts for the assertion that overbedding in a community breeds overutilization. This proposition is said to be supported by experience, and it forms the basis for the second part of the duplication-of-facilities argument for entry restrictions on hospitals. Very roughly, this argument says that hospital administrators have ways of keeping beds filled unnecessarily, and, to the extent that the value of the care thus rendered is exceeded by its cost, there is an additional inefficiency associated with excess bed capacity. The source of the problem, however, is once again the lack of internal cost constraints bearing on fee-for-service doctors with insured patients.

As we found in the case of the cream-skimming argument, the duplication argument for certificate-of-need laws seems to be valid but expedient, an attempt to address the symptoms of the problem rather than the market failure that is its cause. My emphasis in the rest of this paper is on the market's ability to get at the cause of the problem, which is the relative unresponsiveness of fee-for-service providers to cost considerations in their use of health resources. The key to my argument is unrestricted market entry for health maintenance organizations (HMOs). The competition provided by HMOs would in due course, in my judgment, generate spontaneous utilization and cost controls that would go very far toward solving not only the cost and overutilization problems associated with overbedding but other problems as well. Note that I am now shifting the emphasis from the conditions affecting market entry by hospitals to the very important consequences of HMO entry. In the next paper, Rick Carlson and Patrick O'Donoghue will discuss the prospects for preserving entry opportunities for HMOs. To my mind this is the *sine qua non* of a market solution.

The Impact of HMOs on Utilization and Costs. The HMO can inject into the health care marketplace a more significant element of price competition than it has ever seen before. HMOs are likely to find ways to cut costs dramatically, primarily by curbing unnecessary services and finding least-cost methods of promoting health. Their charges will therefore almost certainly be significantly lower that the premiums of conventional health insurance for the same coverage. Although we can anticipate that widespread government or employer financing will remove the consumer from the actual purchase transaction itself, HMOs will be able to offer consumers many extra inducements for enrollment, such as broader benefits or lower deductibles, and this kind of competition is just as meaningful and effective as direct price competition. Of course, we need a law that would accord all consumers, including Medicare and Medicaid beneficiaries and members of insured employment groups, a choice between insured fee-for-service medicine and HMO-type care, as well as choice among available HMOs. But once we have such a law, the market, through the standard mechanism of marginal shifts in consumer loyalties, will reflect all the tradeoffs that consumers may wish to make. Each consumer's calculus will embrace the elements of cost, convenience, personal rapport, amenities, and even quality of care insofar as the consumer can evaluate it on the basis of his own experience, hearsay, and information that might be obtained as a result of advertising or regulatory disclosure requirements.

I think it is remarkable how poorly understood is the possibility that HMOs, by adding new competitive dimensions to the health care marketplace, would fundamentally reorder incentives. Most discussions of HMO proposals tend to dwell on such issues as whether preventive care can really make much difference, whether substantial efficiencies are really possible, whether the HMOs' apparently better performance records result primarily from the lower-risk populations being served, or whether the incentive to underserve the enrolled population may produce serious abuses. While all these are questions deserving attention, the assumption underlying them seems to be that the benefits derivable from HMOs will accrue only to their enrollees or to those paying for their care. Even enthusiastic proponents of HMOs often focus their praise only on the cost and quality of care that HMOs render to their enrollees, again as if this were the only place where benefits might be found. What is not observed, except occasionally in passing references to the bare fact that HMOs will compete with the fee-for-service sector, is that HMOs have the potential for dramatically affecting the *entire* health care system top to bottom.

It should be obvious, once you think about it, that, if HMOs should start selling their services aggressively at prices well below health insurance costs, the fee-for-service sector, which is in large measure supported by health insurance of the conventional kind, will have little choice but to find some way to lower the cost or increase the value of that insurance. The result can only be new and gradually strengthening cost, utilization, and quality controls imposed in some way by the insured fee-for-service sector on itself. These controls, when they appear, will be totally unlike the window dressing that has been set up to curb overutilization under Medicare and Medicaid. Instead, they will be both effective in reducing costs and efficient in not impairing quality, because providers will recognize that the competitive position of fee-for-service medicine will be hanging in the balance. All peer review proposals to date have suffered from the drawback that reliance is placed primarily on the good faith of the professionally nominated reviewers and secondarily on the ability of government to enforce a minimally acceptable level of performance. Controls emerging from a provider consensus that costs must be reduced for competitive reasons would be a vast improvement over such mandatory schemes, and consumers' otherwise legitimate fears about peer review would be to a large degree obviated by the complete reversal of incentives that had occurred.

Foundations for Medical Care: Spontaneous Cost and Utilization Controls. Fortunately, I do not have to confine myself to sheer speculation about what would happen if HMOs should someday appear in the marketplace. I think that what I am predicting for the future has to some extent happened already as the result merely of the appearance of HMOs on the horizon. My main item of evidence is the development of the so-called foundations for medical care, which I shall call FMCs. These are, of course, prepayment plans sponsored by local medical societies as a sort of second-generation Blue Shield plan, and their main feature is that they incorporate controls stricter than those of Blue Shield on the utilization practices and charges of the fee-for-service doctors who participate in them. The last year and a half or so has seen a substantially heightened interest in the organization of FMCs, and some portion of this interest seems traceable to the appearance of the HMO threat. Of course, FMCs are also in some measure a response to the threat of expanded federal intervention in the health care system, and it is clearly impossible finally to disentangle this impetus from fear of potential HMO competition as the motivating force behind the FMC movement. Nevertheless, just about every published description of the famous San Joaquin Foundation for Medical Care includes a statement that it was originally formed for the purpose of keeping the Kaiser plan from invading San Joaquin County; moreover, editorializing about foundations by medical societies throughout the country indicates that an important thrust is toward moving fee-for-service doctors into cost control as quickly as possible so as to preclude the development of plans less subject to control by the organized profession.

Some of you may be aware that I have said some harsh things about FMCs in an article in *Law and Contemporary Problems*.[3] Indeed, I said I thought they

---

[3] Clark C. Havighurst, "Health Maintenance Organizations and the Market for Health Services," *Law and Contemporary Problems,* vol. 35 (1971), pp. 716, 767-76.

might easily be found to violate the Sherman Act because they represented a combination of independent economic units—namely, fee-for-service doctors—to keep a competitive form of medical practice—namely, HMOs—out of the market. I said that, in my view, such a combination might be in restraint of trade even if its object was merely to curb universally recognized abuses such as high charges and overutilization. This conclusion follows because such activity by a trade association of competitors is prompted by a desire to lessen the attractiveness of new entry into the marketplace and thus to stifle future competition, which might be more beneficial to consumers in the long run than is the self-regulatory activity. The antitrust case would, of course, be even easier if, in the absence of mandatory freedom of choice for consumers among available HMOs, the FMC signed up employment groups in such a way that independent HMOs were unfairly foreclosed from needed customers. I suggested that because of the risk of such entry-limiting behavior, FMCs might easily be found to be "per se"—that is, automatic—violations of the Sherman Act. As a less drastic position, I suggested that FMCs might be judged to be illegal unless they were specifically shown not to have prevented HMOs from getting established. Now I would like to say some more things about FMCs and the terms on which they may be safely accepted as elements in the health care system of the future.

FMCs seem capable of moving in either of two directions depending upon the market circumstances in which they find themselves. The FMC which exists to the exclusion of other HMOs will probably limit its enrollment to those groups most likely to sign up with new HMO entrants. These groups will include the poor, the Medicaid population, who might otherwise find their way into HMOs under contracts with cost-conscious state governments. Similarly, large employers might be sold the FMC plan as a way of keeping their employees tied to the fee-for-service sector. But FMCs being operated defensively against HMO entry are unlikely to recruit new members outside these groups, and, insofar as the poor are exclusively served in this manner, a system of second-class care could develop. It is noteworthy that the Medi-Cal program has contracted with FMCs but has sought to find FMCs which have other enrollees besides the poor and has sought to do business with independent HMOs as well. Other states doing business with FMCs under Medicaid have been less attuned to their anticompetitive side, allowing the FMC to obtain a dominant position vis-à-vis potential HMO entrants.

In a competitive market setting with HMOs present, the FMC would probably have a different line of development. Rather than narrowing its coverage, it would probably broaden it. The tendency would be toward taking over the present system of conventional health insurance by providing a program of effective cost controls. Monopolization of insured fee-for-service medicine would be a possible result, particularly since insurers facing excessive costs might actively seek to bring their beneficiaries under the FMC umbrella; but monopoly might be avoided if insurers were not inhibited from initiating cost-control plans of their own.

258

Thus, although I think the appearance of FMCs helps to prove my argument that HMO competition will induce responsive change in the entire health care system, I see two reasons to be fearful. The first is that the FMC might monopolize prepaid HMO-type care, excluding independent HMOs much as the San Joaquin foundation appeared to do in California. The second is that the FMC might monopolize fee-for-service care, a possibility I shall soon discuss further. These two monopolistic dangers are great enough that only unusual circumstances would prevent the FMC from violating antitrust principles. For these reasons, my position on the antitrust issue remains approximately what it was when I wrote the article in *Law and Contemporary Problems*. In the absence of either (1) meaningful competition from the active operation of an independent HMO in the market or (2) some reason to think an HMO could not support itself, FMCs should be held (at least after passage of a reasonable amount of time) to violate both Section 1 and Section 2 of the Sherman Act. Where such meaningful HMO competition is present, I think an FMC should still be deemed presumptively illegal but should be subject to redemption if it can establish that it is an essential mechanism in the preservation of insured fee-for-service medicine. If this defense can be made out, I would willingly endorse the restraints implicit in the FMC as ancillary to a legitimate and ultimately pro-competitive, overriding purpose, namely, the preservation of a time-honored kind of medical practice that particularly emphasizes quality and personalized attention to patient needs and provides important incentives for physician productivity. But, since Blue Cross, Blue Shield, and commercial health insurers may ultimately be the better and more competitive vehicles for introducing meaningful cost controls through spontaneous peer review and other mechanisms, an essential item of proof in establishing the antitrust defense of the FMC is a showing that insurers are unable or unwilling to take on this job.

Establishing that health insurers cannot or will not control costs may not be difficult. Proof might consist of evidence that health insurers are plunging into HMO formation and are therefore relatively indifferent whether fee-for-service medicine survives or not. Also the absence of community-rating and open-enrollment requirements applicable to health insurers may be shown to have directed the competitive efforts of insurers toward risk selection and assiduity in negotiation of rate increases rather than toward cost control over providers. Legal impediments to cost control efforts by commercial insurers, and perhaps by Blue Cross and Blue Shield as well, would also be particularly relevant and persuasive evidence. However, the historical failure of insurers to impose cost controls is not persuasive in itself since that failure was largely brought about by the health industry itself, through its adamant concerted refusals to cooperate, and by establishment of Blue Shield plans. As is revealed by the record in the Oregon State Medical Society case,[4] the industry actively discouraged insurer cost-control measures by pointing

---

[4] United States v. Oregon State Medical Society, 343 U.S. 326 (1952).

to Blue Shield as an "ethical" alternative to insurers who violated canons against interference in the doctor's essentially monopolistic relationship with his patient. Nevertheless, although the health industry assisted in preventing insurers from imposing cost controls, the result of an extended inquiry might well be a finding that, at least as things now stand, FMCs are the only real hope for bringing the fee-for-service sector under internal cost controls.

In a perfect world, of course, each competing health insurer would wish to reduce the level of its premium through cost controls and would actively seek ways of implementing them. By judicious use of such devices as lists of participating physicians, each insurer would be able to offer prospective policy holders an attractive combination of low cost and access to competent doctors practicing in the community. Excessive emphasis on cost, however, would result in nonparticipation by doctors, reduced choice, lower quality, and deterrence of purchasers. The medical profession has, of course, always bridled at the suggestion of insurer-initiated cost controls and, where necessary, has used the device of refusing to accept direct payment from any insurer who asserted a right to implement such controls. But as the threat of HMO competition becomes more palpable, doctors will be more willing than they are today to subscribe to cost-controlled plans initiated by insurers. Medical societies, recognizing the magnitude of the competitive threat and perhaps being barred from taking direct action themselves under antitrust principles, will be less likely to interfere. Each doctor subscribing to an insurer's plan would have the insurer's beneficiaries available to him as patients, and the insurer with the plan best combining the elements of low cost and acceptability to doctors (widening consumer choice) would achieve the most commercial success. But consumers could still elect among a variety of plans with different combinations of price, available services, amenities, and so forth. In such a world, health insurance plans would be harder to distinguish from HMOs, since most would offer only a closed panel of doctors, and many would gravitate toward integration and centralization of services—becoming HMOs in fact. Consumers would have a wide range of choice.

There are several reasons why the model of a fee-for-service sector featuring a multiplicity of insurers each with its own cost-control plan might be deemed preferable to the FMC model. Most important, if the FMC has not monopolized prepaid HMO-type care as a means of protecting the fee-for-service sector against aggressive HMO competition, it may be inclined to monopolize fee-for-service care instead. If the FMC should become the sole cost-control mechanism in fee-for-service medicine—as it might by undertaking claims review for the Blues and all commercial insurers, for example—it would be motivated to cause the reduction of prices only down to the monopolist's profit-maximizing level and not to the level that would prevail under competition among insurers operating independent cost-control plans. Moreover, even though the FMC might ostensibly be engaged only in controlling maximum prices—an activity which, incidentally, presents serious antitrust problems in itself—it would be hard for it to avoid inducing individual doctors to raise their prices toward the prescribed maximum; this in turn has an additional price-increasing effect. The striking thing is that the higher prices maintained under a monopolistic FMC would cause consumers to buy less fee-for-service care and to elect HMO care in greater numbers. Should that happen, we would wonder at the irony of the FMC device, which is now billed as the savior and preserver of fee-for-service medicine, being used to reduce artificially the amount of fee-for-service care delivered. Let there be no mistake about it: an FMC monopoly over fee-for-service care would not be preserving the institution of fee-for-service medicine but only the profits of its practitioners. Ultimately, monopolization of fee-for-service medicine under the FMC device can only reduce its importance in the American health care system.

People who are truly dedicated to fee-for-service medicine as an institution and who would like to maximize the output of fee-for-service care in the health system of the future should be exploring ways of helping insurers individually to bring down the price of the insurance they sell. Indeed, one important strength of a competitive system featuring insurer-initiated cost controls is that it would place a greater premium on finding the most efficient, effective, and acceptable cost-control techniques, a challenge that calls for much experimentation and competitive development. Obviously professional involvement is necessary if the right balance of cost control and quality is to be obtained, and a variety of plans striking different balances would be desirable. Insurers should also have an incentive, using professional help, to seek and realize available organizational efficiencies, perhaps integrating and centralizing in varying degrees the services offered in particular communities. The blurring of the line between insured fee-for-service medicine and HMO schemes would increase the range of choice for both consumers and providers.

Now, even though I might prefer a system under which health insurance companies were competing in their cost-control and quality-maintenance efforts, it may be that insurers are unlikely enough, for reasons I have indicated, to embark aggressively along these lines that I must embrace the FMC model as the only way to implement the needed controls. I might even be persuaded ultimately that, as most of the noneconomists in this audience are probably inclined to believe, FMCs are a *better* mechanism than health insurers for achieving fee-for-service cost controls in a market featuring active HMO competition. For one thing, in some markets at least, insurers might exercise an excessive amount of buying power—economists call it monopsony power—and might use it to exploit physicians unfairly. Moreover, I myself am still enough of a noneconomist not to be totally indifferent as to whether we err on the side of too much cost control rather than too little; moreover, I recognize that FMCs might be more responsive than health insurers to quality considerations and more vigorous in preventing unwarranted lay interference with the rendering of care. Indeed, to achieve the proper balance between cost and quality, I would be quite content to rely fully on the competitive tensions and the offsetting incentives not to skimp in either department that are provided by the presence of prepaid and postpaid providers in a competitive marketplace. Monopolization of the fee-for-service sector by an FMC still strikes me as a serious danger, but perhaps the continued presence of Blue Cross and Blue Shield, increasingly subject to consumer pressure to move independently into cost control, would prevent monopoly from occurring. And of course I would continue to advocate an absolute prohibition against FMCs unless the condition that there be active competition is satisfied. The antitrust laws seem to me to provide an adequate mechanism for meeting this condition or for dealing with the situation where it is not met.

PSRO: The Risk of Monopoly through Cost and Utilization Controls. A line of development closely related to FMCs is that likely to result in legislation recognizing Professional Standards Review Organizations (PSRO). Although PSROs are designed to provide a monitoring system only for care rendered under government programs, they have the potential to become the mechanism for imposing cost discipline on the entire fee-for-service sector. Indeed, as FMCs are likely to be designated PSROs in many areas, the PSRO model may simply be a device for adding teeth to the FMC's efforts. Already, in such states as California, New Mexico, Colorado, Georgia, and Illinois, the FMC model has been adapted for use in controlling Medicaid costs, in most cases not as a risk-bearer but as a reviewing agency. One might expect that, if effective HMO competition should develop on a wide scale, fee-for-service providers would seek to have PSRO review extended to all care, not just that financed by government. Professional support for PSROs reflects primarily a recognition of the inevitability of cost controls in the subsidized sector, but there is (1) increasing recognition that cost controls will tend to extend themselves in a variety of ways and (2) a spreading conviction that such controls must be kept in professional hands. For reasons somewhat paralleling my concerns about FMCs, I must conclude that the PSRO's monopolistic potential is too great to warrant its adoption.

A major concern of mine is Senator Wallace F. Bennett's intention to include HMOs within the regulatory jurisdiction of the PSRO. Viewing the matter as I do, I think this would be a serious—indeed, a calamitous—mistake. A PSRO with such broad powers would offer an unfortunate forum for the negotiation of treaties between the two competing sectors, allowing them to fix prices, divide the market, regulate practices in mutually agreeable ways, and generally repress desirable kinds of competition. The suppression of cartel behavior is difficult enough without having the government actively encouraging the parties to meet together under conditions where anticompetitive tendencies would be manifested. Moreover, the PSRO would put governmental sanctions behind the cartel's decisions, thus improving its effectiveness in stamping out competitive impulses. I am fearful that the encouragement which the PSRO notion has received from many professional sources may in part reflect their sense that it will provide the opportunity whereby they can monitor, guide, and generally slow down the development of effective, efficient HMO models. Given the power to regulate HMOs, the PSRO would be nothing but a device for monopolizing the provision of medical care.

But even if Senator Bennett's proposal provided for PSRO jurisdiction only over fee-for-service care, it would still be objectionable because it would create the monopoly over fee-for-service medicine about which I have already expressed my concern. It is impossible to believe that the PSRO would not behave like so many other regulatory and self-regulatory agencies, including the CAB, the ICC, the Maritime Commission, and the New York Stock Exchange, in adopting a regulatory program similar to that which an industry-wide cartel would adopt if it could. Although the most obvious abuses might be eliminated to divert the most telling criticisms, the price of fee-for-service care would be higher than it would be under competition, and the quantity of fee-for-service care delivered would be lower. In a world where the price of fee-for-service medicine was not subject to independent control by health insurers, FMCs, or market competition, the PSRO's cost-control efforts could be expected to cease when a profit-maximizing price was reached. Since the PSRO idea seems to have been conceived to head off or weaken other controls on fee-for-service doctors, it is reasonable to expect that such monopoly behavior would occur and that the volume of fee-for-service care would be significantly less than it would otherwise be.

Conditions of a Market Solution

The minimum conditions that must be met in order to achieve a market solution to the organizational and allocational problems of the health care industry are not many.

In the area of financing, I have already spoken of the need for a better and more direct subsidy mechanism for helping the poor to obtain care. An extension of this requirement is the need for supplying the public generally with better financial protection against a medical catastrophe. Professor Martin Feldstein's proposal for major risk insurance [5] and Professor Mark Pauly's similar proposal [6] are extremely attractive means not only of supplying this need but of reintroducing market forces generally. Perhaps these proposals, if they were acted on, would generate a better market than the one I have been discussing. But they appear to impose on consumers a considerable burden of controlling costs without much knowledge, whereas vigorous HMO competition leaves the day-to-day technical

---

[5] Martin Feldstein, "A New Approach to National Health Insurance," *Public Interest,* Spring 1971, p. 93.
[6] Mark V. Pauly, *National Health Insurance: An Analysis* (Washington, D.C.: American Enterprise Institute, 1971).

decisions in professional hands. At any rate, the political prospects of major risk insurance and variable subsidy insurance do not seem good at the moment. It is for this reason that I have concentrated on the less radical HMO proposals in exploring the prospects for introducing market forces.

Aside from financing changes needed to implement a market solution, unrestricted entry for HMOs is the main requirement. This means that for-profit HMOs, HMOs with only a handful of physicians, HMOs practicing fee-for-service medicine on the side, HMOs purchasing substantial amounts of specialists' services in the fee-for-service sector, and perhaps HMOs practicing pediatrics only, all should be allowed a great deal of freedom, subject only to quality regulation not inconsistent with market functioning. Most of the current legislative proposals overdefine the term "HMO" to fit some well-intentioned liberal's model of the ideal delivery system. Because of their exclusionary tendency and large capital and enrollment requirements, these legal requirements would be fundamentally destructive of entry prospects. The inclusion of HMOs' outpatient facilities under certificate-of-need requirements, which will be discussed in the next paper, seems to me the quickest way of all to lose the ball game, although restrictions on hospital construction might prove a positive benefit by providing an occasion for obtaining commitments from existing hospitals to make their facilities available to the HMO on nondiscriminatory terms. Federal legislation overriding state entry restrictions of all kinds has been proposed and would be helpful in making unrestricted entry a reality; whether liberalization at the state level can be relied upon remains to be seen.

Other conditions are no more difficult to meet. Some freedom to advertise must be granted to all elements of the health care system, and I am attracted by Senator Edmund Muskie's idea of a federal corporation having as one function the education of the public about the HMO concept generally, thus relieving individual plans of the cost of such education. Regulatory attention must also be given to prescribing a set of benefit packages to be offered by both HMOs and health insurers; this would facilitate consumer comparison of prices and coverage. Various other disclosure requirements would similarly help consumers, particularly in assessing quality.

Particular measures would be required to minimize the impact of the propensity of HMOs and health insurers to sign up healthier populations. Open enrollment requirements for insurers as well as HMOs, a requirement of some kind of community rating perhaps with supplemental government payments for enrolling the elderly, the poor, the disabled or other high-risk individuals, and mandatory HMO options for all members of insured groups are all important steps in meeting these problems, but additional regulation may also be needed.

Government subsidies to particular HMOs must not be lavish and should perhaps not be provided at all because of the competitive advantage necessarily conferred by them. Much the wiser government policy would be to concentrate, perhaps through a public corporation such as the one proposed by Senator Muskie, on investments in training HMO administrators, in providing technical and management consulting services to all HMO applicants, in the development of private capital resources, and in education of the public on provider prepayment and such other things as the functions of paraprofessionals.

A final condition seems to me to be antitrust enforcement, even against non-profit and public institutions, to prevent restrictive practices and the development of an undue amount of unchecked monopoly power. In the *Law and Contemporary Problems* article, I discussed the various ways in which competition can be undermined by private action but concluded that free entry plus antitrust would yield adequately competitive conditions.

The foregoing conditions must be met before a "workably" competitive health care system can emerge. Compromises on any of the principles suggested, such as are so likely to occur in the legislative process, would undermine the market's functioning and render the outcome less attractive than it might easily be—and even perhaps wholly unsatisfactory. Still, this is not a long list or one particularly difficult to realize in practice if the will is found. The administration's legislative proposals embody a great deal of what I suggest, and Congress should not be incapable of understanding what is at stake or what needs to be done to accomplish the objective. At the moment, I see no reason to despair though I cannot pretend to be encouraged.

A Modified Certificate-of-Need Law

You will note that I did not include repeal of protectionist hospital certificate-of-need laws among the essential conditions for realizing a market solution. I have argued not that anticompetitive entry restrictions on hospitals stand in the way of restoring market incentives in the system as a whole, but only that they would be unnecessary at such time as (1) a sound health plan has been developed for the poor and (2) HMOs have appeared in sufficient numbers and under the right conditions to stimulate greater cost-consciousness on the part of all providers. Since the restrictive laws would probably not be repealed even if the arguments for restricted entry should collapse, I want to propose an amendment to be enacted as part of any new certificate-of-need laws. I think this proposal would meet both immediate necessities and future eventualities.

Although there are different ways of accomplishing the result I seek, I propose simply adding to the pending bills a proviso to the effect that certificate-of-need requirements will become automatically inapplicable to all new private investments in hospital facilities on the effective date of any federal law providing a substantial increase in financial support of health care for persons unable to pay. With such a proviso, the law would produce a moratorium rather than a permanent prohibition on unapproved, private hospital construction. It would therefore require the legislature to reexamine the need for entry restrictions under the new conditions prevailing after Congress had finally acted, at which time it would be possible to determine with greater accuracy (1) whether HMO competition was developing satisfactorily and (2) whether the monopolistic charity model of the hospital had been endorsed or repudiated. In the meantime, the planners would have had the power they claim to need, and the agencies' performance could be evaluated to determine if changes in their mandate or in their constitution would be desirable. Such laws would also challenge Congress to face the ultimate issues a bit more squarely.

You will note that I would relieve only "private" investments from certificate-of-need laws. While the term "private" might be defined to refer to all so-called private hospitals, I would propose a narrower meaning, encompassing only proprietary institutions; I would leave voluntary hospitals subject to continuing certificate-of-need requirements. The reason for this choice is that the voluntary hospital sector has in the past seemed particularly needful of outside review, since it is subject to few external constraints on its investment decisions and is often unduly influenced by empire-building impulses or the wishes of the hospital's medical staff. Although I have confidence that a restoration of cost-consciousness will occur if a market solution is adopted—and that such cost-consciousness would greatly strengthen the external constraints on nonprofit providers—hospitals will often have monopoly power that will shelter decision makers unduly from the adverse consequences of investment mistakes. Even though, in the absence of certificate-of-need laws, elements of the newly cost-conscious, insured fee-for-service sector would probably impose private sanctions against high-cost hospitals, measures to put teeth into planning decisions would assist the forging of new links in the cost-control network. Indeed, competition from unregulated proprietaries and strengthened support for cost control from the fee-for-service sector would sharpen the performance of the planners.

The most important objective seems to me to be the freeing of proprietaries from anticompetitive regulation in a system relying fundamentally on the market to mediate the unavoidable conflicts among the cost, quantity, and quality of care. I have tried to cast my proposal so as to obscure its appearance as a special concession to proprietary hospitals, for as long as it has this aspect it will have rough political sledding in the medical world. Still, the scope of a certificate-of-need law should be tailored to the need, and I hope I have persuaded you that, under the conditions I visualize, the need will not extend to proprietaries. If, however, even apparent favoritism for proprietaries renders my proposal untenable, then I would prefer to exempt all private institutions and to rely instead on emerging cost-consciousness for curbing wasteful investments. Earlier discussion indicated how insurers might alter payment policies to bring home the consequences of excess capacity.

The Obstacle of Antimarket Attitudes

The greatest obstacle to the adoption of a market solution is the inbred sense of many observers that the market as an instrument of social control carries with it certain values that are incompatible with the proper care of human health. Talking someone out of this persuasion is difficult, of course, partly because it is deeply ingrained in liberal philosophy and particularly because it is seemingly confirmed by the generally poor reputation which proprietary institutions have earned in this industry. For another thing, most of the costs attributable to an excess of commercialism are identifiable, whereas the costs of repressing market forces are generally hidden, both in higher dollar costs and in a spreading tendency to take patients for granted and to de-emphasize their human concerns and preferences. Yet these adverse consequences must be counted in some way, and they have ethical dimensions no less important than those underlying qualms about commercialism.

Just as nonprofit educational institutions are now charged with neglecting their students, nonprofit institutions in health care are widely accused of rendering their services in impersonal ways and according higher priority to scientific and educational pursuits than to patient care. Against this background, a strong ethical case for the market can be constructed, starting from the premise that, in a matter so intensely personal, consumers rather than providers have the better claim to occupy the driver's seat. Given market choices and information he has long been denied, the consumer would probably reject the most commercialized providers and reward only those providers who appeared to meet his total needs most fully. Providers' humanitarian impulses would thus be rewarded to the extent they are appreciated by the beneficiaries, but no special privileges would flow from representing one's self as being charitable. I find less reason to object ethically to such a system than to one ostensibly dependent on altruism but reduced to coercing it by free-care requirements or subsidizing it by tax incentives, guaranteed loans, direct grants, and protectionist legislation. To the extent that consumers are thought incapable of evaluating medical services and thus of protecting their own interests, regulatory intervention may be appropriate; but there is no ethical warrant for depriving persons of all choice or even of the greater part of the ultimate responsibility for their own well-being.

In bringing these remarks to a close, I want to refer to Professor Titmuss's book on blood, entitled *The Gift Relationship*.[7] The book seeks to demonstrate by a comparison of American and British experience that total reliance on donors'

---

[7] Richard M. Titmuss, *The Gift Relationship: From Human Blood to Social Policy* (New York: Pantheon Books, 1971).

altruism in collecting blood for medical uses produces better results than does the market and that partial reliance on market incentives dilutes and undercuts altruism, driving it from the field. Not only do Professor Titmuss's veiled efforts to generalize from this unique market fail, but the obvious and regrettable market failures he finds so significant appear readily correctable without rejecting the market as the primary organizing influence. For example, a legal rule imposing strict liability for hepatitis reactions on blood banks and on hospitals would have generated closer attention not only to blood collection methods and donor selection but also to the development of blood testing techniques and to alternatives to the use of blood in therapy. Such a legal rule, which is readily derivable from recent market-oriented scholarship in the field of torts, was adopted by a number of courts but subsequently rejected by numerous legislatures to whom the hospitals quickly appealed. Nevertheless, adoption of this legal solution of creating reasonably balanced market incentives for providers to find the least-cost solution to the problem might so change the conditions studied by Professor Titmuss that his conclusions would have to be, if not reversed, at least retracted. The lesson that Professor Titmuss should learn is the same one that the legal profession is now in the process of learning, and somewhat painfully, from economists—namely, that in the formulation of legal rules, the most satisfactory solutions, the solutions that provide the best balance of conflicting interests and the fewest untoward side effects, can usually be achieved by placing primary reliance on market forces and cost incentives, thus supplementing the market and correcting its failures rather than supplanting it. This is, of course, what I am proposing that we do in the field of health care.

Finally, a review of Professor Titmuss's book in the *Yale Law Journal* by economist Robert M. Solow comes about as close as anything I have seen to exploring the roots of the antimarket bias about which I have been speaking. Solow says in conclusion, speaking generally about money and its use in organizing human affairs:

> . . . though it has become less fashionable to say so, there are real *moral* as well as economic advantages in having an impersonal, universalistic way for people to express and exhibit the strength of their preferences. Prescription by authority or ascription by custom and status are not always attractive alternatives to the market registration of the sum of individual wishes.
> . . . *Given rough equality* [the condition which national health insurance could help us to meet], I should think the free market provides a tolerable and even preferable way of organizing a fairly large area of economic activity. One of the reasons Professor Titmuss disagrees—if, as I think, he does disagree—is that he seems to attribute somewhat less importance to the notion that individual preferences should count. There is a slight, rather typically Fabian, authoritarian streak in Titmuss; he seems to believe that ordinary people ought to be happy to have many

decisions made for them by professional experts who will, fortunately, often turn out to be moderately well-born Englishmen.[8]

I take it that elitism of the kind referred to is not unknown in the world of medicine.

---

[8] Robert M. Solow, "Blood and Thunder," *The Yale Law Journal*, vol. 80, no. 8 (July 1971), pp. 1696-1711.

HEALTH MAINTENANCE ORGANIZATIONS AND COMPREHENSIVE HEALTH PLANNING AGENCIES: ACTUAL AND POSSIBLE RELATIONSHIPS

Patrick O'Donoghue and Rick J. Carlson

The Applicability of Federal and State Planning Legislation to HMOs

Federal Law. Since the generic term "health maintenance organization" (HMO) is not used in existing federal health legislation, the application of federal law to such organizations is limited to the oblique recognition of prepaid health care plans in some existing laws and to prospective direct application under pending proposals. Regulations and guidelines promulgated for Titles 18 and 19 of the Social Security Act and the Federal Employees Health Benefit Program classify prepaid plans as providers, but do not address the issue of the application of planning legislation.[1] H.R. 1, now pending before both the House and Senate (and cumbersomely carried from chamber to chamber in a wheelbarrow), would be the first legislation to use and define the term "health maintenance organization."[2] It provides, in Section 221, for the applicability of planning authority to such entities.

The effect of Section 221 of H.R. 1 upon HMOs will probably be briefly as follows: if an HMO proposes a capital expenditure (defined in the legislation as an expenditure for nearly any purpose in excess of $100,000 or as one which alters the bed capacity, or substantially changes the service capacity, of a provider), it must first notify the designated planning agency of its proposal (in most cases an area-wide CHP "b" agency) and submit to review and comment in accordance with such plan or plans for capital development which shall have been developed for the area. If the decision of the planning agency is adverse, the provider may appeal to some "body" which is to be created at the state level and which is unspecified in the legislation. Final adverse decisions are certified to the secretary of health, education, and welfare, who then must deduct amounts "attributable to

---

[1] While this legislation accords recognition to health maintenance organizations, the modes of payment currently utilized under Medicare and Medicaid are inconsistent with the capitation financing arrangements of such organizations. This was the primary reason for proposing the HMO amendment to Medicare through H.R. 1.

[2] As noted earlier, H.R. 1 has subsequently been enacted, in substantially the form discussed here, as Public Law 92-603.

271

depreciation, interest on borrowed funds, a return on equity capital (in the case of proprietary facilities), or other expenses related to such capital expenditure" from reimbursement payments under Titles 5, 18 and 19 of the Public Health Service Act (Maternity and Child Health, Medicare, and Medicaid, respectively). In the case of HMOs the amount to be deducted must be calculated by the secretary as a "reasonable equivalent" of the amount which would be deducted if the payments were made on other than a capitation basis.

Notwithstanding the sweep of Section 221, paragraph (2) of subsection (d) of this section substantially softens the application of this section to HMOs:

> (2) If the Secretary, after submitting the matters involved to the advisory council established or designated under subsection (i), determines that an exclusion of expenses related to any capital expenditure of any health care facility or health maintenance organization would discourage the operation or expansion of such facility or organization, or of any facility of such organization, which has demonstrated to his satisfaction proof of capability to provide comprehensive health care services (including institutional services) efficiently, effectively, and economically, or would otherwise be inconsistent with the effective organization and delivery of health services or the effective administration of title V, XVIII, or XIX, he shall not exclude such expenses pursuant to paragraph (1).

If paragraph (2) is interpreted and applied with some sense of what an HMO is and how it behaves, the language seems sufficiently pointed to have the effect of exempting HMOs from the application of Section 221 in most, if not all, cases. Even a spongy legal mind or a hard-hearted planner would have difficulty arguing that "expansion" through adding beds or spending $100,000 plus on a capital plant would not be "discouraged" if a CHP agency ruled that it could not be done.

Assuming, however, that HMOs are at least theoretically subject to Section 221, there are at least two trouble spots worth noting. First, it is easy to apply the law to a hospital as an independent provider, but it is less clear in the case of an HMO to which part of its capital plant the law extends. If, for example, an HMO houses its physicians in an office building and wishes to expand or remodel it for a cost in excess of $100,000, would the legal constraint apply? Similarly, if an HMO alters its services by, for example, converting an outpatient facility to a crisis-intervention, drug and alcohol-related therapy unit, is such a change a "substantial change" in the "services" of the facility? Moreover, in the interests of parity, how would the same "capital developments" be treated if they were implemented by traditional providers? These questions suggest that Section 221 would extend health planning well beyond the narrow concern with the hospital bed supply and accord it a much wider role, which might not be desirable.

A second problem relates to the nature of administrative discretion to which we will return later. Thus, while the language in paragraph (2) of subsection (d) recited above is clearly a sop to the HMO lobby, its value is nevertheless dependent on the whims of the secretary of HEW at any time, or, as a practical matter, on the whims of one of his teeming minions who exercises his innumerable discretionary powers.

State Law. For a change, the states are ahead (or behind, depending on your point of view) of the federal government. Starting with New York in 1966, twenty-one states had enacted legislation with somewhat the same intent as the pending federal law by late 1972. The level of state legislative activity, as measured by bills introduced, makes health planning as controversial as abortion reform, if not necessarily so volatile. In late 1972, legislative activity on the issue was reported in seven additional states according to the American Hospital Association.[3]

The state legislation in question is generally classified under the rubric "certificate-of-need" legislation, although it has also been referred to as "franchising" law. The generalizable impact of the legislation is that no new construction and/or other capital expenditure and/or alteration in service capacity can be undertaken by an institutional provider unless approval or "certification of need" is first obtained from a designated health planning agency, again in most instances a CHP agency. Since Professor Curran covered this legislation in detail in his paper, our treatment will be mercifully brief.

In this paper our specific interest is the application of this species of law to HMOs. Although the laws differ to some extent and some are silent as to HMOs, what can be said is this: in general, the laws apply to HMOs as to any other institutionally based provider, at least to the extent of requiring compliance with certification requirements if the HMO desires to construct a new inpatient facility or to increase the number of beds in an existing facility. To a lesser extent, some states might require certification in the event that an HMO desires to reduce bed capacity, purchase an existing facility, or make significant changes in its service program. Of the first twenty-one states which have passed certification legislation, only Kentucky and New Jersey have expressly mentioned HMOs in their statutory definitions of covered health care facilities, while Rhode Island has reached substantially the same result by use of the term "ambulatory care facility." Florida has a need requirement built into separate HMO enabling legislation.

The bulk of the certificate-of-need statutes fails to differentiate between HMOs and more conventional health care delivery systems. This "benign neglect" of HMOs in the statutory language is accentuated by the fact that the bulk of the statutes specify broad general criteria for consideration by the planning agency in reaching certification decisions, without providing any express statutory provisions forcing recognition of the unique criteria necessary to evaluate the "need" for HMOs. For example, the New Jersey statute states:

---

[3] American Hospital Association, "Status of State Certification-of-Need Legislation," December 15, 1972.

No certificate of need shall be issued unless the action proposed in the application for such certificate is necessary to provide required health care in the area to be served, can be economically accomplished and maintained, and will contribute to the orderly development of adequate and effective health care services. In making such determinations there shall be taken into consideration (a) the availability of facilities or services which may serve as alternatives or substitutes, (b) the need for special equipment and services in the area, (c) the possible economies and improvement in services to be anticipated from the operation of joint central services, (d) the adequacy of financial resources and sources of present and future revenues, (e) the availability of sufficient manpower in the several professional disciplines, and (f) such other factors as may be established by regulation.[4]

Nevertheless, while the term "health maintenance organization" has not been expressly used in most certification statutes, it is clear from the peculiar phraseology in the law of a few states that HMO promoters have exerted an influence. For example, the certification legislation in the state of Washington contains the following criteria (with selected passages italicized for emphasis):

A certificate of need shall be issued only where the proposed construction is reasonably necessary to provide health care *to the defined population served or to be served* as economically as practicable, consistent with high quality standards and in such a manner as to encourage orderly, coherent, timely and economic developments of adequate and effective health services in the area, region and state. In making such determinations, the Secretary shall take into consideration:

(1) Recommendations of the regional planning agency and, if provided, recommendations of the state planning agency.

(2) The *comprehensive health plans and development for the area,* region and state, and the relationship of the proposal to such plans and development.

(3) *The need for health care services in the area and/or the requirements of the defined population.*

(4) The availability and adequacy of health care services in the facilities which are currently *serving the defined population* and which conform to federal and state standards.

(5) The need for special equipment and services in the area which are not reasonably and economically accessible *to the defined population.*

(6) The need for research and educational facilities.

(7) The probable economics and improvement in services that may be derived from the operation of joint central services or from joint, cooperative, or shared health resources which are accessible to the defined population.

(8) The availability of sufficient manpower in the professional disciplines required for the facility.

---

[4] Laws of New Jersey, 1971, Section 8, Chapter 136, "Health Care Facilities Planning Act," S. No. 2088.

(9) *The plans for and development of comprehensive health services and facilities for the defined population to be served.* Such services may be either direct or indirect through formal affiliation with other health programs in the area, and shall include preventive, diagnostic, treatment and rehabilitation services.

(10) Whether or not the applicant has obtained all relevant approvals, licenses or consents required by law for its incorporation or establishment.

(11) Relevant information from interested persons and agencies.

(12) *The needs of members, subscribers and/or enrollees of institutions and health care plans which operate or support particular hospitals for the purpose of rendering health care to such members, subscribers and/or enrollees.*[5]

Legislation in Oregon and California contains comparable language. The effect of this language is to compel the planning agency to consider the needs of a "defined" or "enrolled" population, that is, of HMO subscribers, when reviewing a proposed capital development or expansion, as distinguished from the needs of the community-at-large. Presumably reflection by the planner upon such delicately phrased criteria will deter him from disapproving the expansion plans of an HMO, possibly at the price of litigation.

The laws of several states (Arizona, Connecticut, Kansas, Kentucky, Massachusetts, New Jersey, New York, Rhode Island, and South Carolina, for example) seem to go well beyond the concern with the possibly excessive supply of hospital beds and to seek control over outpatient facilities, perhaps including those which an HMO might construct. Similarly, the AHA model bill would require specific approval of all significant capital investments, including those for an outpatient clinic; it would thus give regulatory authorities the power to prevent or constrain HMO entry or to favor the kinds with greater political backing. Several of the enacted laws, however (for example, Arizona and Kentucky), make specific exceptions for outpatient facilities, primarily to make sure that doctors' offices receive the benefit of these exemptions. It should be noted that Section 221 of H.R. 1 appears not to differentiate one kind of capital investment from another, even though the primary impetus behind the legislative trend was a concern about utilization of hospital beds.

In summary, state legislative activity manifests two trends: first, increasing acceptance of the certificate-of-need concept with increasingly broad coverage of health care facilities and, second, recognition by a distinct minority of states (not coincidentally those in which established HMOs are located) that certificate-of-need legislation not only may frustrate the growth of HMOs if rigorously applied but seeks to regulate behavior—that is, inefficient investment by HMOs—which it is unlikely to find.

---

[5] Laws of Washington, 1971, Section 15, App. 70. 198 X.

Past Relationships between HMOs and CHP Agencies:
Are the HMO Lobbyists Telling the Truth?

In order to get some feel for the actual relationships between CHP agencies and HMOs, we conducted a quick, relatively superficial, but reasonably complete survey. Letters were sent or telephone contacts were made with twenty-five HMOs. Three specific questions were asked of the organizations surveyed:

(1) What have been your experiences (if any) with CHP approval of capital expansion by your organization? Such capital expansion could naturally take a variety of forms including the construction of a new hospital, the renovation of existing hospital facilities, or the purchase of new equipment.

(2) What have been your experiences or contacts (if any) with CHP agencies in other substantive areas? Examples might be grants from a CHP agency to develop a special program or the receipt of technical assistance from a CHP agency in putting together an HMO.

(3) Do you own your own hospital? If so, did you build it from scratch or did you purchase an existing facility? Or do you contract for or otherwise purchase hospital services from hospitals in your community? If the latter, have you found such contracting arrangements satisfactory? Have you had any specific problems which are worth noting?

In addition to asking the three questions specified above, we also attempted to solicit information on respondents' experiences generally with CHP agencies.

Of the twenty-five contacts initiated, twenty responses, representing all of the major HMOs, were obtained. The responses and the respondents are summarized in Table 1.

As to question (1), eleven of the twenty respondents (55 percent) have had literally no experience with CHP intervention with respect to capital expansion; six respondents (30 percent) have had either "warm endorsement" or approval of capital expansion by a CHP agency. These latter respondents reported they obtained such approval with no special problems. Three programs (15 percent) encountered substantial, but not insurmountable, difficulties.

Eight (40 percent) of the respondents, in answer to question (2), indicated a generally favorable relationship with CHP agencies. However, in most instances the relationship did not derive from the substantive areas specified in the question, but rather from informal contacts, frequently growing out of serving on joint committees, et cetera.

Seven programs (35 percent) indicated they have had no other experiences with CHP agencies. Four respondents (20 percent) had problems with CHP agencies in areas other than capital expansion—generally relating to program areas into which the HMO wished to expand. One respondent thought it likely that problems could well arise in the future.

276

Five (25 percent) of the respondent organizations own their own hospitals. Nine (45 percent) of the programs contract for hospital services. Only one of the latter programs has experienced difficulty in the contractual relationship. The remaining six respondents do not yet provide hospital services, or provide such services but do not contract for them, or gave no response to this question.

Although relatively superficial, this survey does, however, demonstrate that the clear majority of contacts between HMOs and CHP agencies have not been prejudicial to HMOs. Three types of relationships seem to obtain. The clear preponderance of contacts appears to have been routine with approval of HMO plans procured with no demonstrable prejudice or hassle. A second set of contacts, while few in number, appears to have been marked by measurable (or at least palpable) hostility on the part of the planners. Finally, a third set of contacts represents that capacious category of mutual indifference.

The relationships of the increasingly far-flung Kaiser-Permanente plan with CHP agencies embrace the full range of possibilities. In California, where Kaiser is presumably a formidable political force, three Kaiser plans have been approved by CHP agencies in southern California, while two plans (although one by an 11-9 vote) have been approved in northern California. Hostility or at least labored circumspection has surfaced in Oregon (despite favorable legislation). Kaiser is currently processing plans for construction of a new hospital on appeal to the state CHP agency from an adverse county planning decision (11-1), in turn reversed by the area-wide CHP (9-7). Kaiser's Hawaii and Colorado experience thus far fills out the spectrum—no CHP interaction—but in the case of Colorado, problems are anticipated.

The gravamen of some recent political theorists, Theodore Lowi, Grant McCannel and Kenneth Culp Davis—to name the most acclaimed—has been the dangers of unbridled, or at least uncanalized, discretion. The CHP experience, as recent and slender as it is, illustrates what planners, or for that matter any group of bureaucrats, are likely to do with vague statutory guidelines. The impact of CHP activity on HMO development appears to vary markedly with the peculiar attitudes, or animus, of the planners or planning body in question. No pattern emerges to explain conflict in one setting, equanimity in another, and indifference in yet another. Thus, while HMO apologists may overstate the general case for blanket HMO exemption from CHP planning mandates, there appears to be some grounds for the concern that, in the absence of concrete guidelines to the contrary, HMO development could be significantly retarded or misshapen by CHP activity.

A Possible New Role for CHP Agencies

As Havighurst and Newhouse and Acton have pointed out in their papers in this volume, the HMO model is a market-oriented approach which relies upon the

Table 1

BRIEF TABULATION OF RESPONSES

Location of HMOs	Question 1 What have been your experiences (if any) with CHP approval of capital expansion by your organization?	Question 2 What have been your experiences or contacts (if any) with CHP agencies in other substantive areas?	Question 3 Do you own your own hospital? Or do you contract for or otherwise purchase hospital services from hospitals in your community? If the latter, have you found such contracting arrangements satisfactory?
California	See text	See text	Has own hospital
Connecticut	Built and equipped health center; had warm endorsement of two CHPs	Good relationship with CHP agencies regarding grant and contract applications	No hospital; have affiliation agreements
District of Columbia	No experience	Two "a" agencies signed off on grant requests to feds	No hospital
District of Columbia	Have had problems	Has had problems with CHP agency in neighboring state	No response
Maryland	Obtained certificate-of-need approval from "b" agency with no problem	No other experience	Has hospital; no problems with contractual relationships for referral services
Massachusetts	No experience	Little experience; indicated there may be problems	Contract for hospital
Michigan	No experience	No experience	Contract for hospital; no problems
Michigan	Obtained approval for purchase of one hospital and expansion of another; no problems	Minimal other contracts which have been favorable	Owns two hospitals and several neighborhood health centers; contract for some services; no problems
Minnesota	No experience	No other experience	No response
Minnesota	No experience	Has grant with CHP to provide technical assistance	Contract for hospital
Minnesota	No experience	Few relationships; generally favorable	Contract for hospital; no problem
Missouri (employee)	No experience	No other experience	No response
New York	No experience	No other experience	No response
New York	Obtained approval for ambulatory care center with no problem	Good relationship	No hospital

Location of HMOs	Question 1	Question 2	Question 3
	What have been your experiences (if any) with CHP approval of capital expansion by your organization?	What have been your experiences or contacts (if any) with CHP agencies in other substantive areas?	Do you own your own hospital? Or do you contract for or otherwise purchase hospital services from hospitals in your community? If the latter, have you found such contracting arrangements satisfactory?
Ohio	No experience	Minimal other experience	No hospital; have had problems with contractual relationships regarding obtaining privileges
Texas (employee)	No experience	No other experience	Owned hospital but sold it; contracts now; no problems
Utah	Many problems with "b" agency regarding location of facility	Has experienced problems in getting program areas approved	No problems with contractual relationships
Washington	Was instrumental in getting new certificate-of-need legislation passed; had problems regarding hospital approval	Has had problems	Has own hospital
Wisconsin	No problem with approval	No other experience	Has own hospital
Wisconsin	No experience; pilot project in state just going through now	Formal organizational contacts favorable	Partnership agreement for hospital; no problems

Note: In some instances, more than one program existed in one state.

stimulating and pruning effects of competition among HMOs and between HMOs and other providers. The HMO approach thus stands in distinct contrast to the fully articulated planning model in which resources and services are allocated through a centralized, bureaucratic process. Many of the papers presented at this conference have focused on the advantages and disadvantages of this latter model, and we will not discuss those arguments again in detail here. However, we will briefly summarize the reasons why we think a well-functioning market has important advantages as compared to the bureaucratic process. These comparative advantages are outlined below.

(1) The actual costs of the allocation process itself are lower for a market than they are for central planning or similar bureaucratic processes.[6]

---

[6] The efficiencies of the so-called "invisible hand" have been repeatedly stressed by economists and others for a number of years.

279

(2) A market takes into account the preferences of *individual* consumers and producers, whereas, judging from past experience in this and other countries, the bureaucratic process is likely to be dominated by a combination of providers and government administrators, who can, at best, only assume what individual consumers desire.[7] On the other hand, a market takes as a given the existing distribution of income. Hence, allocation of resources by a market may be unsatisfactory since those individuals with relatively little income may, at least in the eyes of some, have too little influence in the market (for example, perhaps health care at present). However, assuming a more even distribution of income is desirable, as we think it is, this objective can be achieved in the health care market through a variety of alternatives ranging from direct cash transfers through federal subsidization of the health care of the poor and near-poor to a broader program of national health insurance with uniform benefits for all. Hence, as Havighurst and Newhouse and Acton point out, a program of broader federal health insurance, far from being incompatible with the market-oriented HMO model, may actually enhance the effectiveness and equity of this model.[8]

(3) Evidence has increasingly accumulated during recent years that public monopolies are at least as inefficient and as unresponsive to consumers as private ones.[9]

(4) The decentralized decision-making process of a market encourages innovation and at the same time forces most innovative developments to be tested on a relatively small scale so that major "mistakes" in resource allocation are less likely to occur than they are with a more centralized decision-making process.[10]

---

[7] In his paper, Havighurst emphasizes this point with a discussion of Solow's review of Titmuss's recent book.

[8] This synergism between uniform health insurance benefits and the HMO model breaks down if the national health insurance program attempts to specify in detail all of the relevant variables. In other words, HMOs and other providers must be free to compete with each other on at least some important variables. For example, the national health insurance plan could give each consumer family a voucher which would purchase $600 of health care per year. Providers could then compete with each other over who could provide the largest benefit package for this $600 as well as on the quality, availability, and accessibility of the services provided. Or the national health insurance program could specify a minimum benefit package, and HMOs and other providers could then compete with each other on additional services provided (as well as on quality, availability, and accessibility).

[9] There is a good deal of indirect, circumstantial and anecdotal evidence which attests to this point. For example, see E. F. Savas, "Municipal Monopoly," *Harper's Magazine,* December 1971. However, relatively few studies have actually compared in depth the performance of similar private and public firms. Two that have are the following: (1) Roger Ahlbrandt, *Efficiency in the Provision of Fire Services* (Seattle: Institute for Economic Research, University of Washington, 1972), who compared the relative performance of public and private fire departments, and concluded that the private firm is considerably more efficient with no diminution in the quality of service; and (2) David G. Davies, "The Efficiency of Public vs. Private Firms: The Case of Australia's Two Airlines," *Journal of Law and Economics,* vol. 14 (April 1971), who found that Australia's heavily regulated private airline was more efficient with again no apparent lowering of quality than Australia's publicly owned airline.

[10] Newhouse and Acton point up this argument in their paper by using the activities of the Willink Committee in Great Britian as an example.

Thus, provided that we include sufficient safeguards to prevent an HMO or another provider from gaining monopolistic control of the health care industry in different regions of the country,[11] there are sound reasons for preferring the competitive HMO model to the central planning approach. Consequently, it seems unwise to give CHP agencies additional resource allocation authorities. At a minimum HMOs should be exempted from certificate-of-need laws.[12] Not only does the allocation of resources through bureaucratic planning impede the effective functioning of a market, but it is particularly inappropriate and unnecessary in this specific case because HMOs do not usually overutilize hospital beds, the prevention of which is the ostensible purpose of certificate-of-need legislation. In addition, some CHP agencies appear to be heavily influenced by traditional providers, which could thus use the power of certificate-of-need legislation to limit the entry of HMOs. Although our survey of past HMO experience does not indicate that this has been a significant problem as yet, the experience of a few HMOs indicates that it could well become so in the future.

There is, however, a second, at present less important, thrust to CHP legislation which should perhaps be strengthened—consumer involvement. This was an objective of the original legislation, manifested by the requirement that a majority of the members of the CHP boards must be consumer representatives. Is it possible to de-emphasize or remove the resource allocation responsibilities of CHP agencies and still retain this function of serving as a representative and as an advocate of consumers? Is such a step necessary and/or desirable?

The issue upon which this question turns is: can consumers register their preferences effectively in the medical care marketplace? Certainly they cannot if they are not reasonably knowledgeable about health care. Unfortunately, evidence on this crucial point is expectedly slim since it is difficult to measure public knowledge. However, several studies have been done which do shed some light on this issue. C.A. Metzner and his associates showed that, in their choice of health care plans, UAW members put most emphasis on a pragmatic evaluation of the specific attributes of the rival programs.[13] A. Thaer Moustafa, Carl E. Hopkins, and Bonnie Klein analyzed the choices made by UCLA employees among six different

---

[11] Clark C. Havighurst discusses in depth this question of monopolistic control of the health care industry in his paper, "Health Maintenance Organizations and the Market for Health Services," *Law and Contemporary Problems,* vol. 35, no. 4 (Autumn 1971).

[12] An alternative to flatly exempting HMOs from certificate-of-need laws is to allow a health planning agency to reject an HMO's application to construct new hospital beds only if it can show that appropriate beds are available for purchase by the HMO on nondiscriminatory terms.

[13] C. A. Metzner and R. L. Bashshur, "Factors Associated with Choice of Health Care Plans," *Journal of Health and Social Behavior,* vol. 8 (December 1967); and C.A. Metzner and A.B. Kaluzny, "Cognitive Balance in a Choice Situation Involving Two Health Care Plans," *Journal of Health and Social Behavior,* vol. 11 (June 1970). (Their studies are published in other journals and books as well.)

health care plans. They concluded that "consumer knowledge of details of plan characteristics is low, but their choices are compatible with plan realities." [14]

M. A. Kisch and Leo G. Reader found that the evaluation of physicians by a group of patients (in this case, welfare recipients) agreed overwhelmingly with the medical profession's usual standards of MD competence (that is, years of physician training, avoidance of excessive patient loads, and peer supervision by other physicians).[15] M. A. Morehead and associates compared the judgment of patients with that of physician experts. They found that three-quarters of those who had received less than optimal care in the eyes of the experts felt that they had received good care. On the other hand, five-sixths of those who said they had received poor care were also placed in that category by the experts. Hence, if this study is correct, the consumer may not always be able to determine if (s)he is receiving poor care, but if (s)he feels the quality of care is low (s)he may well be correct.[16]

Thus, as indicated earlier, the evidence about consumer knowledgeability is slender and somewhat mixed.[17] Nonetheless, the overwhelming opinion of observers of the current health scene is that except at the point of entry, physicians and other professionals have the predominant voice in determining how much and what kinds of health care will be provided to consumers. Are there reasons to expect that consumers in the setting of the fully developed HMO model would be able to function more effectively than consumers at present? The answer is yes. There are a number of reasons why we might expect consumers to register their preferences more effectively in the HMO setting.

First, in choosing an HMO, consumers make their choice when they are well rather than after they become sick, as they often do at present. Second, HMOs permit consumers to choose one provider whom they will almost certainly use

---

[14] A. Thaer Moustafa, Carl E. Hopkins, and Bonnie Klein, "Determinants of Choice and Change of Health Insurance Plans," *Medical Care*, vol. 9, no. 1 (January-February 1971).

[15] M. A. Kisch and Leo G. Reader, "Client Evaluation of Physician Performance," *Journal of Health and Human Behavior*, vol. 10 (March 1969).

[16] M. A. Morehead and others, *A Study of the Quality of Hospital Care Secured by a Sample of Teamster Families in New York City* (New York: Colombia University, School of Public Health and Administrative Medicine, 1964).

[17] Although the market can function tolerably as a mechanism of social control with substantially less than perfect consumer knowledge, because it is marginal shifts in consumer preferences which are felt by providers, inducing efforts which improve service to all, there is no easy or clear-cut way of prescribing the level of sophistication needed to obtain satisfactory market performance. Neither is it easy to assess the level of consumer understanding in the numerous geographic and product submarkets of the health care industry. Moreover, under conditions of widespread ignorance, marginal shifts may occur for the "wrong" reasons, as objectively assessed, inducing excessive attention to nonqualitative or even antiqualitative factors. Our judgment is that, although consumers can be counted on to induce better performance if given a choice, special attention should be given to improving information flow and to encouraging a variety of public and privately sponsored coalitions of consumers to improve their bargaining and information-collecting capabilities. Labor unions, employers, health insurers, cooperatives, neighborhood groups, and HMOs purchasing fee-for-service care are just some of the mechanisms which can perform useful services on behalf of consumers.

rather than requiring choices of the eight to twelve providers whose services they may require in the near future; this problem with solo practice may be ameliorated by the consumer's reliance on his primary physician to refer him to a specialist when needed. Third, the HMO model allows consumers who have joined together in groups (for example, employee groups, neighborhood groups, and so forth) to bargain collectively with the HMO over benefits, fees, and amenities, thus increasing the leverage of consumers in the marketplace. Fourth, it should be easier to provide consumers with pertinent information about a few large institutional providers than about numerous individual providers. It should also be less difficult for consumers to grasp information about a small number of institutional providers than about a large number of individual providers.

In addition, there are several steps that can and should be taken to increase the power of consumers in the competitive HMO model. First, consumers cannot make informed choices between health care providers if they are not routinely given information about those providers. Hence, the federal government should mandate and monitor the provision of information to consumers by providers about the following items: benefit packages and/or services offered; fees, prices, and/or capitation payments; the accessibility and availability of services (for example, location of facilities, hours of operation, amenities, and so forth); financial status; and an overall quality rating of providers (if such is available).[18]

Second, the federal government should mandate and monitor the establishment by providers of internal grievance systems to resolve relatively minor disputes between consumers and providers, with either party being able to appeal disputes unresolved by the internal grievance system to binding arbitration carried out by arbitrators mutually acceptable to both parties.

However, despite the advantages that consumers are expected to have in the setting of the fully developed HMO model as compared to the present system, despite a presumably much freer flow of information to consumers, and even if effective internal grievance/arbitration systems are established, there are reasons to suspect that the power of consumers may still be disproportionately low compared to that of providers. As Freidson thoroughly demonstrates, the tradition of professional dominance in the health care industry is strong and will not be overcome easily.[19] Medical care is a complex subject, and its intricacies will be understood by few consumers at best. HMOs will be large organizations, and it may be difficult for consumers to gain access to the decision points of such organizations even with effective internal grievance/arbitration systems. Finally, even if many consumers are organized in groups and even if antitrust vigilance is strong, it may still be

---

[18] In the future, as quality assessment systems become more sophisticated, it may be possible to provide consumers with more specific information about the quality of different components of the care dispensed by providers.

[19] Eliot Freidson, *Professional Dominance* (New York: Atherton Press, 1970). He points out that this professionalism is manifested by, among other things, a "lock" on information.

easier, because of variants of the "free rider" problem, for providers to register their preferences decisively than for consumers to do so.

For all of these reasons it seems desirable to us that there should be a publicly funded body in each medical market area whose primary function would be that of a consumer advocate. As indicated earlier, the theme of consumer representation is already partially interwoven into CHP legislation. Thus, such legislation might represent the best vehicle through which to establish this new kind of government body designed to explictly function as a consumer advocate.

How might CHP agencies be reconstituted in order to enable them to play this new role as consumer advocates? It would appear that the following steps represent some of the actions which might transform CHP agencies from their present status into effective consumer representatives:

(1) The CHP councils should be relatively small (perhaps seven to eleven members). At least two-thirds of the council members should be consumers not involved in the delivery of health care. The makeup of the council should broadly reflect the socioeconomic characteristics of the community but need not do so exactly. Instead, the council should be able to appoint advisory groups of consumers and/or health professionals to provide it with specific viewpoints or expertise.

(2) The CHP agency should have the following powers: (a) the authority to investigate and evaluate providers and delivery system arrangements within its jurisdiction; (b) the power to disclose information about providers as it sees fit (provided, however, that any provider may seek court relief if such disclosure is deceptive, fraudulent, or libelous); and (c) the power to sue (and be sued), to initiate class actions on behalf of consumers and consumer groups, to seek injunctions against specific practices, and to join other groups in litigation or other legal processes.

(3) The agency should possess the right to review and to comment on all applications for assistance under the Public Health Service Act originating from providers within its jurisdiction. The agency should be given a set period of time (perhaps forty-five or sixty days) in which to comment after receiving all the information pertinent to an application.[20] The agency should not be given veto power over any such application but may, of course, publicize its views in any manner it chooses. In addition, it might well be appropriate to extend this right of review and comment to the expenditure of state and local monies for health services.

(4) The agency should monitor the above-described internal grievance/arbitration systems (if created) of providers within its jurisdiction. If a system for the arbitration of medical malpractice suits is established, as now proposed in S. 3327, the agency should monitor that system as well.

---

[20] The agency should, however, be under no compulsion to comment at length (or at all) on each application.

(5) The agency should have a small amount of research and development money which it could use for such things as experimentation with delivery systems, consumer education, and consumer advocacy.

(6) The agency's purview should perhaps be broadened to include at least consideration of socio-environmental variables which strongly influence the health of the population in its area, such as housing, waste disposal, and pollution control programs.

(7) The agency should have a strong staff and sufficient funds to enable it to carry out the tasks outlined above.

The next and final section of our paper will amplify each of these points, indicating the apparent importance of each in enabling the reconstituted CHP agencies to function as effective consumer advocates.

Delineation of the Consumer Advocate Role

We have emphasized the advantages of a market-oriented approach to the delivery of health care services. However, we have also pointed out that despite the improved posture of consumers in the fully developed HMO model as compared to the present system, it is still likely that providers would wield disproportionate power in the medical care marketplace and that consequently a consumer advocate organization might significantly improve the functioning of the medical care market. We then suggested that CHP agencies in a reconstituted form [21] might be able to undertake this advocate function and outlined seven steps designed to enable them to do so effectively. We will now discuss each of these suggested changes in greater detail.

Size and Composition of CHP Agencies. Large committees seldom accomplish anything unless they are subdivided. Consequently, we think that CHP councils should have a relatively small number of members (perhaps seven to eleven). It seems to us that it is more important for such councils to be able to reach decisions at least somewhat expeditiously than to include in their membership all political factions in the area. In short, it seems prudent to us to trade off "representativeness" for expected effectiveness in decision making. In accordance with this approach, serious consideration should be given to making council membership either a full- or part-time position with compensation.

---

[21] At present, CHP agencies are forced to play the game of "accounting" with providers to determine whether a given capital development does or does not conform to a plan for capital development for the area in question. The result is a presumably consumer-controlled body dueling with providers using provider weapons—not only do providers possess the presumed expertise on questions of "need" for facilities, they also have the money to buy hired guns to make their arguments and to manipulate their numbers. CHP agencies are at a distinct disadvantage in this setting even if one assumes that they ought to be playing this role, which we do not.

On the other hand, the council, to some extent, should reflect the socio-economic characteristics of the community which it serves. A consumer council comprised only of "meeting specialists" from the middle class is not only likely to distort the views and misrepresent the interests of the poor, but also to be chary about seriously "rocking the boat."

A second argument arises from largely political considerations. With a large council, every consumer organization in the area is likely to seek a seat, rather than to bargain with other organizations and possibly to enter into consortiums for the placement of a person representing a congeries of organizations and viewpoints. We prefer this latter approach as one which is not only sufficiently representative but as one which also ensures a higher level of community participation in the long run.

Under current law, CHP agencies are required to have a majority of consumers. The difficulty is that the slender majority possessed by consumers is often eroded through lack of attendance by consumer representatives or their lack of understanding of many issues under discussion. Thus, as a practical matter, many CHP agencies are under the effective domination of providers who are both "committee-wise" and generally more knowledgeable about the issues. The agencies we propose should be clearly consumer controlled with providers participating largely in an advisory capacity. Thus, we suggest that at least two-thirds of the council members be consumers not directly or indirectly involved in the provision of health care. Councils may create advisory task forces of providers if desired, and could also concede some seats to providers. However, the enabling legislation should not prohibit councils made up entirely of consumers.

The councils should be empowered to spawn neighborhood councils of a similar charge and composition to feed findings, views, et cetera, to the larger area-wide council. Perhaps more important, such neighborhood councils could be delegated the responsibility to carry out specific projects as well as being used in an advisory capacity.

Powers of New CHP Agencies. These agencies should be given powers in the following three areas:

(1) Authority to investigate and evaluate. Under current law and regulations CHP agencies act largely as supine bodies "reacting" to matters put to them, including issues addressed to them in their capacity as a review and comment agency under state certificate-of-need legislation. We believe the agency should be not only capable of reacting to matters brought before it but should possess the authority to initiate investigations of providers and/or delivery system arrangements within its jurisdiction, including the performance of individual providers within its jurisdiction. For example, we envision that an agency might annually publish a "state of the area" health report which would discuss, among other things, changes in health

care delivery arrangements over the past year, evaluations of specific providers and delivery system arrangements, a set of socio-health indicators for the health status of the community, and recommendations for change. We also expect and hope that certain CHP agencies would develop the capacity to undertake intensive investigations of certain providers or delivery system arrangements which might be critical in nature, perhaps somewhat analogous to the "Nader Reports."

(2) Information disclosure. As noted earlier, we feel that a barrier on which a market-oriented approach to the delivery of health care services may founder is the lack of useful information available to consumers and the limited ability on the part of consumers to digest information which is provided. We sketchily suggested an information disclosure scheme. Not only should such a scheme require providers to disseminate information to consumers, but it should further require providers to disseminate information to the CHP agency. The CHP agency might then counter what it thought was misleading or inadequate information disclosure by publicizing what it felt was a more realistic appraisal.

More importantly, we envision the reconstituted CHP agency acting as a substantial force to increase both the flow and the digestibility of information about health care. The "state of the area" health report outlined above is an example of one kind of information disclosure. An intensive investigation of specific providers with subsequent disclosure of the findings and conclusions of that investigation represents yet another way in which pertinent information can be brought to the attention of consumers. Another hypothetical example would be full publication of the arguments, pro and con, for the construction of a new hospital in an agency's area. As we point out again later in this paper, CHP agencies should also explore and finance new approaches to increasing the comprehensibility of information about health care.

On the other hand, the CHP agency's powers of disclosure should be balanced by the right of a provider to obtain redress should that disclosure be deceptive or libelous.

(3) Litigation. While we do not expect that reconstituted CHP agencies will frequently resort to litigation, such agencies should be able to initiate class actions on behalf of consumers, consumer groups, and consortiums within the area they serve, and should have the power to obtain injunctive relief as well. If, for example, a public general hospital is proposing the construction of a large centralized facility and if the CHP agency concludes after investigation that a smaller downtown hospital with satellite outpatient clinics would better serve the community, the agency should have the power to seek injunctive relief should the local governmental authority attempt to proceed summarily with the construction of the hospital. This would not necessarily mean the CHP agency could permanently block the construction of the hospital, but it could at least force a hearing on the issue.

Litigation might also be resorted to where unsafe practices were thought to exist. For example, the oversight of such an agency might allow enactment of a broad delegation statute, allowing institutional providers [22] and perhaps even solo practitioners [23] to delegate functions freely to licensed or unlicensed personnel who they thought were qualified to perform them. Competing providers or consumers could complain about unsafe delegation practices, and the CHP agency might be given the power to litigate in such instances, if it concurred that such a step was warranted.

It is our intent that the legal process would be used sparingly by CHP agencies and that other tools available to them, including information disclosure and public hearings, would be used first in order to influence change.

Review and Comment on Applications for Assistance or for Coverage of Capital Expenditures. Under existing state certificate-of-need legislation (and potentially under federal law if Section 221 of H.R. 1 passes in roughly its current form), CHP agencies are granted the power to control capital investment within their jurisdiction. The primary impetus behind this development stems from the fact that in the current system there is little effective restraint on capital investment since demand can easily be simulated by providers and since capital investments in the health care field are largely insulated against loss by cost-plus reimbursement through the insurance mechanism. The remedy commonly proposed to redress this situation (control of at least capital resource allocation through the bureaucratic process) is only one of a series of remedies, including a progressive shift to prepayment through the formation of HMOs, and is a remedy which we are not yet ready to embrace. However, our suggestion that CHP agencies should review and comment upon all applications for federal assistance originating within their jurisdiction is not inconsistent with the point of view that primary reliance should be placed upon the marketplace to allocate resources in health care.

Our basic premise is that consumers should be given a larger, more active, and more informed role in that marketplace and that investing CHP agencies with a new and different kind of clout may be one way in which to achieve this objective. In the absence of information about what providers propose to do with public funds, an enlarged consumer role for CHPs could be largely illusory. Thus we propose that CHP agencies possess the right to review and comment on all applications for assistance under the Public Health Service Act and for coverage of capital expenditures under the Social Security Act. Once the information is made available, the agency should be given a specified period of time (perhaps forty-five or sixty days) in which to comment before the responsible public funding

---

[22] Rick J. Carlson, "Health Manpower Licensing and Emerging Institutional Responsibility for the Quality of Care," *Law and Contemporary Problems,* vol. 35 (1971), p. 949.
[23] Clark C. Havighurst, "Licensure and Its Alternatives," in *Proceedings of the Third Annual Duke University Conference on Physicians' Assistants* (1970), p. 21.

agency reaches a decision on the application. The CHP agency should not be given the power to prohibit capital development (as distinguished from some existing state certificate-of-need laws and Section 221 of H.R. 1), but rather should be allowed to bring public and consumer pressure to bear upon the plans of private and public actors. Further, the agency may find it desirable to decline to comment in certain instances so that it can concentrate on other cases.

We also feel that CHP agencies should have a similar right of review over the expenditure of state and local monies. It is not clear that federal legislation which would empower CHP agencies to review proposed assistance under the Public Health Service Act could readily extend that right to the expenditure of state and local monies. Hence, parallel legislation at the state and local level might be necessary to give CHP agencies such authority.

Monitoring Internal Grievance/Arbitration Systems. If providers of care establish internal grievance systems, with the right of appeal to arbitration, the consumer-oriented CHP agency should exercise surveillance of such systems. Consumers face an unequal balance of power in processing complaints through even well-functioning internal grievance systems. Providers possess the facts and also possess the power to exert subtle but effective pressures upon consumers to underutilize internal grievance machinery. If HMOs and perhaps other providers are required by federal law to establish internal grievance/arbitration systems, and if the operation of such systems is to be regulated by a federal agency, it could be quite costly for such a federal agency to monitor closely the activities of these internal grievance systems. Conversely, CHP agencies are favorably situated to do so. The monitoring of such systems should include the right to impose reporting requirements upon providers (to the extent federal law does not do so, or, if federal law does so, to an extent not inconsistent therewith) and the right to inspect the records of those systems whose performance is in doubt. Additionally, the agency should possess the authority to publish aggregate findings of internal grievance systems and to systematically publish the results of arbitration proceedings held upon appeal from decisions made through internal grievance procedures.

If a federalized system for arbitration of medical malpractice suits is established pursuant to federal law,[24] CHP agencies would again be appropriate choices to monitor the performance of such arbitration systems, to require reporting, and to disseminate information about arbitrated cases.

Research and Development. The "new" CHP agencies should be given some research and development funds in order to facilitate their exploration and promotion of projects in the health care sector which they feel are of particular importance. Such research and development projects might include aid to neigh-

---

[24] S. 3327, as currently written, would establish such a system.

borhood groups in establishing consumer advocate organizations, seed money for the formulation and implementation of innovative consumer health education programs, and partial support of the development of new information systems for dissemination of health and health-related information.

An issue of some concern which can perhaps be partially resolved with research and development funds stems from the fact that in many cases CHP agencies currently embrace large geographic areas. Under those circumstances it is unrealistic to assume that most consumers at the neighborhood level will be able to participate effectively in the program of a large area-wide CHP agency. For example, in a large urban area, two, three, or more counties may be within the jurisdiction of a CHP agency; a one-hour drive may be required to get to a meeting. The problem is compounded in rural areas where existing CHP "b" agency jurisdiction extends to many counties and many miles of terrain. Under such circumstances it is imperative that the process of consumer advocacy be brought down to a distinctly local neighborhood level through both programming and concrete delegation of authority. Perhaps the best way in which this can be accomplished is to stimulate the formation of localized consumer-oriented health bodies at the neighborhood level. One way to do this would be to give the area-wide CHP agency funds for the establishment of such programs on an experimental basis.

Scope of Jurisdiction. There is persuasive evidence that the delivery of personal health care services has a relatively moderate impact on health status, when contrasted with a host of socio-environmental factors such as housing, education, waste disposal, public welfare, air and water pollution, and so forth. The work of Rene Dubos, Eli Ginzberg, Allen Chase, and others has supported this thesis.[25]

Thus, it can be argued that one of the most important functions of the reconstituted CHP agencies would be to review those programs outside "health" which may have as great an impact on health status as personal health services. Accordingly, it might be desirable to give CHP agencies the authority to review and comment on the plans of public and private actors who propose to use public funds in "non-health" areas which nonetheless strongly affect health status.

On the other hand, it would be unwise to overwhelm the new agencies with too much responsibility too quickly. Hence, perhaps the best compromise solution is to begin by giving the agencies the authority to review and comment upon applications for public assistance in a limited number of "nonhealth" fields, such as perhaps housing and pollution control. In addition, the CHP agencies should have the power to review and comment on the plans of public health agencies within their jurisdiction.

---

[25] Rene Dubos, *Men, Medicine and Environment* (New York: Praeger Publishers, Inc., 1968), and *The Mirage of Health* (New York: Harper and Row, 1959); Eli Ginzberg, *Men, Money and Medicine* (New York: Columbia University Press, 1969); and Allen Chase, *The Biological Imperatives* (New York: Holt, Rinehart, and Winston, 1971).

Staff and Funds. As we indicated before, the new CHP agencies must be given sufficient funding if they are to effectively carry out the tasks which we have outlined. Although specification of exact funding levels is obviously premature, we think that the average area-wide CHP agency should have an annual budget of at least $300,000. Assuming an average of nine area-wide agencies per state when the program is fully developed and assuming that each state agency should also have a budget of approximately $300,000, this means that the total annual cost of this program, when fully developed, would be approximately $150 million (not including the cost of the federal component which we think should be small), or .2 percent of total health care expenditures. We do not think that this is an inordinate amount to spend in order to enhance the position of the consumer in the medical care marketplace and to make the medical care industry more responsive to consumer demands and expectations.

COMMENTARY ON THE PAPERS

REPORTER'S NOTE: Professor Somers's remarks were addressed to the Newhouse-Acton, Havighurst, and Carlson-O'Donoghue papers. To improve overall coherence, Professor Neuhauser's paper has been printed in this section although it was originally part of the second session. Professor Grad's remarks responding specifically to the Neuhauser paper have been incorporated in the general discussion.

Herman M. Somers

My remarks may appear somewhat contradictory, since while I support the general thrust or apparent objectives of this afternoon's papers (I was unable to read the O'Donoghue-Carlson paper in advance because it was unavailable, but I did read the Newhouse-Acton and Havighurst papers with care), I disagree with many of the claims advanced to support their themes.

As I understand the major thrusts of the papers, they are these:

(1) Competition and market incentives in health care should be fostered, encouraged, and maximized to the extent practicable. As my wife and I, in our writings and public lectures, have for many years been extolling the attractions of pluralism, my agreement is not likely to surprise anyone. I would, however, give more emphasis to the limitations on the practicability of significant competition in major sectors of this field. Moreover, I doubt that competition is the only conceivable way of maintaining quality of services or to contain costs, as has been alleged. If it is, large sections of the country appear doomed to grave difficulty.

(2) Health maintenance organizations are a highly desirable vehicle for creating and augmenting competition. My support goes even further. I regard the HMO—particularly in its prepaid group practice forms—as a meritorious structure for health care delivery even when the assets of competition are absent. However, I do not believe there is any substantial evidence to support the view that legislation or public administration has been the major restriction upon the emergence or growth of such organizations. More about that later.

(3) Legal restraints on free market entry (of hospitals, HMOs, or other health institutions) are unjustified and damaging when the motivation is simply restriction of competition. This, I would add, is particularly true when the form of restraint results in the curbing of innovation.

(4) Adding a significant consumer input into the decision-making apparatus, as O'Donoghue and Carlson emphasize, has my enthusiastic support, although the difficulties are multifold.

293

I trust these are correct interpretations of the main themes. I find the underlying principles relatively unassailable. But, as I have indicated, I am puzzled by some of the statements made in support of sound principles, some that appear to me to misrepresent important facts, and some blithe assumptions about the problems associated with building competition into this monopolistic field that tend to reduce complex issues to simplistic levels.

I dislike picking on allegations that seem to me quite unnecessary to support the basic themes. But I do think it is important that we be accurate about our facts and that we understand what the real problems are. There are enough of these without contriving false ones.

Let me illustrate with the argument about "certificates of need" because that phenomenon has been a central concern of these meetings. The notion and the allegations that "cream-skimming" (or "protectionism" as some call it) is a major, if not the major, justification advanced for certificates of need has been pervasive. In fact, the Newhouse-Acton paper this afternoon alleges that the only other justification is to limit the spread of "toys."

That, I submit, is an unfair and inaccurate representation of the position taken by certificate-of-need advocates. The skimming argument has been a rather minor one, even if it is periodically blurted out by frustrated hospital administrators. Its attraction to debating economists is that it is the easiest argument to demolish—thus we get an apparent magnification of a small point and the beclouding of issues.

Since the writers feel that certificate-of-need legislation is dangerous, it would seem that they ought to confront the real arguments of its advocates, whether correct or incorrect. Such arguments, therefore, seem to me worth listing, without necessarily taking sides. Such a recital may also throw some light on aspects of the industry that have been neglected in the discussions thus far.

(1) The impression has been given in several papers that certificate-of-need legislation has been aimed primarily, if not exclusively, at keeping out new institutions. This has certainly not been the case in the states with whose legislative history I am acquainted. The recent laws have been aimed primarily at containing the expansion of existing hospitals (and surely not at hindering HMOs as has been implied). The influx of relatively small new proprietaries was quite lively some three or four years ago, but the movement had slowed down before the legislation passed in most states. The tendency of existing hospitals to expand is ever present, and that is where the big threat of overbedding is. That threat should not be brushed aside by conventional economic arguments that oversupply will correct itself by bringing down prices and shutting down beds, arguments which have little empirical validity in this atypical industry.

(2) In contrast to the assumptions made in several of the papers, the advocates of certificates of need argue that overbedding or underoccupancy is very expensive for the entire community, not just for the hospitals directly affected. The

Laves' paper, for example, argues that in the event of substantial underoccupancy in hospitals, such facilities will go broke and out of business. I would argue that it would be desirable for some hospitals to go broke and out of business, but, unfortunately, for the most part that is highly unlikely. They will not go out of business because the community, or their special constituency, will not permit it. There are a great many one-hospital areas, where the market is so limited that competition is highly improbable—by the politics of the situation if not the economics—and the community will not let its hospital die even if it is losing money (sometimes an imprecise concept in hospital accounting).

More important, hospitals are not ordinary business enterprises. They go beyond the business of rendering medical care for a price. Very often they are symbols for constituent groups—religious symbols, fraternal symbols, prestige and status symbols for a community. For the Catholic church, Jewish communities, and Protestant denominations, their hospitals are matters with high institutional and emotional attributes that are far beyond the question of balancing the books. They symbolize the cohesion, the devotion, and the status of the constituent groups. This is also true of many small communities. They will find the money to keep "their" hospital solvent. (Parenthetically, such hospitals also answer a deep psychic need for many individuals; rendering free volunteer services is a way of getting a posthumous foot into the door of heaven.)

(3) The certificate-of-need advocates deny the assumption that excess supply is automatically self-eliminating—that is, that demand remains independent of supply. Empty beds will in fact be filled at great cost to the community. Hospitals and their medical staffs have impressive and demonstrated means of expanding or contracting so-called "demand," within broad limits, almost at will. By and large, people are not invited into hospitals; they are ordered. And they are not often asked to select their hospital, even if a choice were available, which frequently it is not. This is not necessarily due to "irresponsibility" by the medical staff. The twilight zone of those who need and those who do not need hospitalization is very broad. The availability of beds is inevitably a powerful determinant in physician decision making. Moreover, the hospital is the natural workshop of the doctor; he has a professonal interest in keeping it solvent.

(4) Probably most important to many of the proponents and, more cogently, to most of the legislators to whom I have talked is the issue of quality. As Professor Havighurst stated, proprietary institutions have somehow achieved a bad reputation on quality. The medical profession, by and large, is suspicious of them as money-grabbing rackets. Professor Lave has correctly pointed out that this is really a licensing problem. But in many states licensing authorities are considered slack and unreliable. Thus, in accordance with conventional American political practice, we undertake not to correct the licensing process (which, for many reasons, would face very special difficulties) but to pyramid it. In the eyes of many legislators, the

certificate of need supplements and strengthens the licensing procedure for quality purposes.

True, the authority to reject poor quality already exists in the licensing body of some states, and could be added in the others. But the existence of authority and its utilization are not the same. (We may well have the same experience with certificates of need. Lawyers and economists have a tendency to confuse formal authority with real practice. The certificate of need may turn out to be a paper tiger because of the realities of political power.)

A second aspect of the quality argument is the conviction that excess, or underutilized, facilities result in poor quality, quite aside from costs. The most common example is the superfluity of cardiovascular surgery facilities in many areas where few institutions have sufficient cases per month to maintain the relevant skills of the surgeons and other personnel. In short, slackness is not just an economic issue but also a quality problem.

A third feature of the quality concern is the widely held belief that wherever possible small institutions should be discouraged, that institutions with less than 200 beds (the precise number varies) cannot offer optimum care.

I do not claim that these arguments of the advocates, either individually or collectively, justify certificates of need. I suppose my mere recital of their case may cause you to assume that I am one of the advocates. In fact, I have considerable skepticism about certificates of need. I believe there is a persuasive case that can be made against them. But such a case should confront the real arguments, and "protectionism" is not prominent among them.

There appears to be in some of the certificate-of-need discussion an implicit assumption that we have been suffering a supply scarcity. It is, of course, quite natural for economists to assume that a rapid rise in prices is virtually synonymous with scarcity, and that theoretical assumption seems sturdy enough to withstand any amount of empirical evidence to the contrary. But most American communities have more beds than they can use effectively. Occupancy rates are, on average, low; in some places, very low. Most metropolitan areas have more technologically advanced equipment than they can keep in reasonably active use. Restrictions do not appear to have had much impact yet. Of course, surplus supply does not necessarily imply effective competition, and that is not what I am claiming. But it is useful to be straight on whether we are suffering from shortages.

A related point: the Newhouse-Acton paper places considerable emphasis on the allegation that "reimbursement insurance" has been a major cause (perhaps *the* major cause) of increased utilization and thus the increase of total expenditures to an unacceptable level. According to data recently published by the Social Security Administration (SSA)—and also the House Ways and Means Committee —this common impression may need some modification or at least further examination, particularly in the case of hospitals. The data indicate that increased utilization has been a relatively minor factor in the growth of total expenditures.

The studies by Dorothy Rice and her associates show that during the period 1950-70, 47 percent of the rise in personal health care expenditures was attributable to price increases, another 17 percent resulted from population growth, and the remaining 36 percent was due to "increased use of services and the introduction of new medical techniques." Since increased utilization is not separated from product change we can only say roughly that the former probably represented substantially less than one-third of causal influences, perhaps not more than 25 percent.

Even more interesting are the data for the period starting in 1966 when Medicare made its appearance and we had the most pronounced acceleration of reimbursement insurance. The SSA data show that of the total increase in expenditures for hospital care, 6.4 percent was attributable to population increase, 91 percent to price inflation, and only 2.6 percent to increased utilization and technological advances.

Supporting indicators can be found in the reports of the American Hospital Association which show that per capita use of hospitals has not been rising in the last three years, while prices continue to spiral. Fewer persons relative to population are entering hospitals; they are staying a bit longer, however, so overall utilization has remained about static.

All of which underlines the precaution that conventional demand-supply analysis is not very rewarding when applied to the idiosyncratic health care industry.

I was surprised to hear so much sharp criticism of Medicare and health insurance for causing increases in utilization. I should have thought that to remove financial barriers to access was one of their major purposes. Certainly Medicare was legislated on the justification that it would enable people who could not otherwise afford it to use more health services. Yes, seems to be the reply, but now they are using too much. How much is too much? In his monumental Michigan study some years ago, Walter McNerney showed that if you took the degree of overutilization and matched it against underutilization, insofar as these could be identified, you would emerge with a pretty close balance. The only convincing data we have indicate that utilization has in fact increased, but we have no evidence as to whether the increase is more or less than the amount medically necessary.

The central thesis of Professor Havighurst's paper is, I believe, that HMOs would change the cost and utilization picture without regulation if they are allowed to enter the market freely. He seems to believe that if they were only allowed to enter the market freely, they would rapidly proliferate through the nation. This seems an odd assumption in the light of history. The HMO idea (at least in its pure form as prepaid group practice) is an old one, having achieved wide national attention and discussion through the classic reports of the Committee on the Costs of Medical Care in the early 1930s. We have had considerable experience with such plans for some twenty-five years. They have not been growing or spreading proportionately. Why? It would have been useful if Havighurst had addressed himself to that question, as most of his case seems to rest on optimistic assumptions about the imminent prospects for HMOs.

What have been the barriers? Surely, certificate-of-need laws had nothing to do with the situation. They are a very recent development, and HMOs were showing no signs of national expansion before certificates of need were even thought of. Moreover, certificates of need, now that they exist in some states, are not aimed at HMOs but at hospitals. True, there is legislation restrictive of HMOs in some twenty-two states, but these laws long antedate certificates of need and are based on an entirely different principle, generally of the antiquated "corporate practice of medicine" vintage. Such laws ought to be abolished (a matter on which this administration has been waffling despite its alleged enthusiasm for HMOs). But the point here is that HMOs have not been developing in other states either.

Good HMOs are very expensive to develop, in capital costs and start-up costs. It has proved difficult to attract physicians to prepaid group practice for a variety of professional, ideological, and economic reasons. It has proved even more difficult to attract patients to enroll. Ordinarily, some 30,000 enrollees are required for a sound and viable plan. Those of us who have been close to many attempts to inaugurate HMOs know this is a formidable task, with failure far more common than success. In New Jersey, for example, groups of intelligent and dedicated men and women have been struggling for six years to get at least one HMO under way, and success has not yet crowned their efforts. I think such people would find some bitter irony in being told that if only certificates of need were eliminated their difficulties would disappear, when they know that the certificate process (which has been in operation only a few months) has nothing to do with their problems. A prominent medical editor said recently, "Everybody is for HMOs except providers and consumers!"

I cannot detail here the multiple barriers to rapid expansion of HMOs, but I do commend to your attention the excellent article by Ernest Saward and Merwyn Greenlick (both of whom have had many years experience in the operation of such institutions), "Health Policy and the HMO," which appears in the *Milbank Memorial Fund Quarterly* of April 1972. I see nothing on the horizon right now to offer any confidence that we could within the next ten years do any better than double the proportion of the population cared for by bona fide HMOs. That might bring us to 10 percent! How we might change that is the question that ought to concern us. I submit that preachments against certificates of need will not expedite HMOs.

Professor Havighurst tells that "it is remarkable how poorly understood is the possibility that HMOs, by adding new competitive dimensions to the health care marketplace, would reorder incentives fundamentally." I wish he were right. My hunch is that it may be understood too well, at least by the medical profession, and this has accounted for its resistance to HMOs for many years. If you will observe the congressional battle that is developing over federal support of HMOs,

298

you may note that the only formidable opposition is coming from the American Medical Association, and my guess is that the AMA will prevail in this session at least.

I so very much agree with Havighurst's desire to increase the spread of HMOs (although my definition of such institutions is somewhat narrower than his) that I wish he had made a stronger, or at least more comprehensive, case. The cost-containment argument (even if accepted at face value) is not the best available. The existing evidence on comparative costs is not definitive. The best of the HMOs have said that the Nixon administration in its Madison Avenue promotions of HMOs has greatly overstated their economic advantages. I believe the better and more important case to be made is that modern medicine can be more effectively delivered in a comprehensive, prepaid group practice plan, that better medical care is far more likely than under prevailing current forms of practice. In short, economy is likely to come from value received for our dollars rather than from the expenditure of fewer dollars.

Competition and economic incentives are highly desirable. They should be built into the health services economy wherever possible. But I believe that careful examination of health care institutions and behavior (devoid of the conventional "reasonable assumptions" that economists like to make when they are uncertain of the facts) will show that there are inherent limitations upon effective competition and that normal incentives have limited efficacy. Health care *is* a unique market, as I and other writers have demonstrated in many publications. With or without the augmentation of HMOs, we will, I believe, have to face up to the unpleasant necessity of regulation. We will be moving more rapidly towards rate regulation and quality controls. Any increase in effective competition may reduce the range of such regulation, but it seems quite improbable that they can be avoided altogether.

Such talk leads to ready accusation of an antimarket bias. As it happens, I have a rather strong pro-market bias in economics. But neither bias nor rhetoric can create effective competition where special factors militate to the contrary. The movement towards regulation did not develop from bias or ideology. It has emerged because of failure of the marketplace to operate according to the competitive model, with the resultant waste, injury, and public dismay that cause meetings like this to be held. Some of that failure was avoidable and is correctable. But a large part of the difficulty lies in the special technological and behavioral aspects of health care, about which economists must take the time and trouble to learn more before their very useful skills and tools can make their maximum contribution to curing the ills in this field.

DISCUSSION

On Professor Neuhauser's Paper

PROFESSOR GRAD: Professor Neuhauser's paper is a very fine job indeed, but there were times when I was not quite sure whether he was serious or just plain kidding. If I read his paper right, hardly anybody benefits from health care. There are all of these operations that do not produce anything; there are all of these old people in hospitals, and none of them survives those who are outside the hospital. Actually on the basis of his paper I have decided to stop going to the doctor.

He makes the point very strongly that more is not better. Well, the question I would like to ask is, is less better? And I am not at all convinced that less is better. Because basically what I get out of his paper—there are many very interesting data there—is that we should greatly maximize the placebo effects, that we could, indeed, cut down the cost of health care enormously by relying on placebos exclusively. I would gather from Professor Neuhauser's paper that it does not make a great deal of difference what you do for people anyway, since most of them are going to die around age seventy, regardless of whether you do tonsillectomies or give them an annual examination.

More seriously, I realize that Professor Neuhauser deals with the marginal effects of incremental costs, but I have trouble defining what is a marginal effect and what is a real need. I have a sense that some medical care must make a difference. I cannot for a moment conceive that all of you who are involved, after all, in the field of public health and in personal health services are so deluded that you would spend your entire life on an entirely fruitless effort. That being the case, it would seem to me that you yourselves believe that it must make more than a mere marginal difference.

Now, it seems to me that the free market and the lack of planning have led to the rather serious, unmet needs which are reflected in our Medicaid and Medicare efforts. Though it is asserted by some that Medicaid and Medicare created more problems than they solved and have done more harm than good, I suggest that we cannot blame all our problems on Medicaid and Medicare; indeed, I would suggest that these programs merely brought to the surface many problems that had long been comfortably submerged. To a seventy-year-old person who has had a long hospital stay with a degenerative disease, or to a "medically indigent" parent with a seriously ill child needing expensive care, it would be rather difficult to explain that Medicare and Medicaid do not address real problems. The reason I stress this is that there is a kind of comfortable assumption in this oft-repeated assertion that supply of health services creates its own demand, an assertion that is implicit in much of what has been said here today. In effect, it is asserted that even if we pour more and more funds, more and more effort, into the health services system, it is not going to make much difference in outcome.

Well, it may be true that expansion of services beyond a certain point may not be particularly useful, or may be only marginally useful. At the same time, if you were to project this in the other direction, does this mean that we simply do not have to have any growth at all? Does it mean that there are no real needs? If we say supply creates its own demand, the logical conclusion would be that no real needs exist, that all we must do to reduce the demand is to reduce the supply. In other words, this would lead to the contention that medical needs are essentially in the mind, that there is no such thing as a real need which must be met. I would contend that there are a great many real needs which must be met, that we have not met those needs and that, in order to meet those needs, we must have a considerable amount of planning.

Whether you go in the direction of HMOs, proprietaries, more voluntaries, a national health service, or national health insurance, whichever institutional system or system of delivery you are going to adopt, you will need planning to make it work to meet the needs—unless, of course, you believe that we have already reached a stage at which all needs are being met, and thus we can just sit tight and let free market forces take over. I, frankly, do not happen to believe this; I think that prior to Medicare there were a great many people over sixty-five who did not have their medical needs met, and who therefore simply died. To say that life is not being extended because the average life expectancy is not being extended overlooks a number of factors. We have had enormous increases in immigration of groups of people who have traditionally had a lower life expectancy, and there have been other movements of population; thus, if we can hold our own in terms of life expectancy, I rather suspect that the system has done a great deal to help that along. And perhaps life expectancy does not tell the whole story. Perhaps we have reduced an immeasurable amount of pain and discomfort of old age.

Now, talking about proprietary hospitals, I rather agree with Professor Neuhauser's conclusion that they do not seem to matter that much right now—or not so much that we ought to do anything very special to regulate them. I do think, however, that his discussion of the proprietary hospital tends to support entry regulations.

He did comment on the cream-skimming aspects of the private hospital industry, and he has a marvelous prescription on how to run a profitable proprietary hospital. (It is such a marvelous description that I would like to try it myself.) But the point he makes which I would like to emphasize is this: What we have in this field is not simply skimming by the proprietary hospitals, but double skimming; the proprietaries skim off that part which is truly profitable, and the voluntaries skim off that part which is truly interesting, leaving the public hospitals with the junk, which is exactly what the public hospitals have been getting all along. The question which we ought to ask ourselves is whether franchising can be used to prevent at least the worst abuses of skimming, and of double skimming, which have occurred in this field.

It seems to me that while the proprietaries may well be left alone, I would like to see entry regulations and construction controls to make sure that we do not get more of the less-needed facilities—drying-out places, for instance, which are enormously profitable—at the cost of underemphasizing some other aspects of the system which we may need more.

PROFESSOR NEUHAUSER: Of course health care does some good! [Laughter.] All I am questioning is the effectiveness of direct health care at the margin, not for all health services.

Replies to Professor Somers

MR. ACTON: I am left in an awkward position if Professor Somers actually said that he agrees with our conclusion but feels that the laws would not have been enacted if they were expected to be effective and that, anyway, even if the laws had been effective, the hospitals would not close down because the Jews are in a big race with the AFL-CIO to be the first to build a 1,000-bed hospital! So I am not really sure what I can say in response.

He made a point later in what he said about my paper, however, which touched on a subject that is worth expanding. There is a fundamental tradeoff we face between efficiency and equity; when you start raising barriers you start cutting back on utilization. That is just one of the intrinsic problems that rises to hound us whenever there are activities that generate externalities.

What I wanted to suggest though is that it is not essential to retain the same form of insurance as what we have had so far, that is, one in which the insurer pays a percentage of the bill, or perhaps all of it after some point. As Duncan Neuhauser emphasized, this produces a situation where people buy some services that they personally value much less than society values as resources.

One approach to the problem is major risk insurance. For instance, if you have a $400 deductible even for the poorest people and combine it with a $400 cash transfer, you guarantee that they have enough money to buy the care if they want to, but they pay a dollar for a dollar on every unit of service that they buy. Therefore they are required to think about the question, Is it really worth a dollar to me?, rather than, Is this "dollar's" worth of service worth twenty cents to me? It is alternatives of this type which I think we ought to explore in some detail.

PROFESSOR HAVIGHURST: I appreciate Professor Somers putting into the record as good a statement of the specific arguments for certificate-of-need laws as we have had in the conference, and I am sorry it has come so late. It seems to me we should have had it the first day. But insofar as that statement was offered in response to my paper, I think it is not responsive.

The arguments I was addressing were the arguments not as to certificate-of-need laws generally but as to their application specifically to prevent new competition from entering the marketplace and particularly competition from private sources, where there is no expenditure of public monies or of charitable and philanthropic funds, and where the empire-building problem does not exist—that is, where the AFL-CIO, or some other prestige-oriented group, is not spending money without being adequately responsive to market circumstances. But it seems to me that private, profit-seeking investments can still be considered to be, at least under the circumstances that I was trying to visualize, responsive to market pressures and to the deterrent effect of the market insofar as the possibility of duplication is concerned.

And I tried to make that distinction. I may not have said enough in my paper about the extent to which planning and certificate-of-need laws should in fact be used, but it seems to me that they do have an important role in curbing nonmarket-inspired expansion of the kind Professor Somers described. My own position is that control of this kind of investment is one question, and that the question of the anticompetitive impact of certificate-of-need laws is something else. I tried in each case to refer specifically to *protectionist* certificate-of-need laws, which seem to me to be those which go so far as to keep proprietaries out, to control the intensity of competition, and to protect discriminatory pricing, all in the name of trying to solve a problem generated by the much bigger problem of the third-party cost-reimbursement method of payment. And that is where I begin to have trouble.

Political Influence in the Certificate-of-Need Process

PROFESSOR LAVE: Will certificate-of-need legislation have any effect at all? I doubt that certificate-of-need legislation is going to prevent any group from building a facility they have the capital to build. These groups have the political power to force any CHP agency to let them go ahead. And as an economist I want to say I would not fight it. If your little community wants to have its own hospital, let it go ahead; if the Jews want to have their own hospital, let them go ahead—*as long as they are willing to pay the bill!*

The only thing I am against in the current situation is my paying for that community over there to have its own hospital when I do not get the benefit of it. If the people in that community want to raise the funds to subsidize the hospital, let them do it. But make sure the people who want it bear the cost.

PROFESSOR SOMERS: I agree.

DR. GERTMAN: Professor Somers, bearing in mind your remarks and Professor Lave's comment, would you suggest that CHPs go even further than denials and participate rather actively in a sort of institutional euthanasia—that is, have the authority to buy up, close down, and demolish hospitals and provide a sort of objective third party that, say, a marginal religious hospital could sell out to for demolition if such a need arose?

PROFESSOR SOMERS: I think in an ideal economic world you probably would not need that because if hospitals did act like normal business enterprises, we would have many mergers. Because most hospitals are too small to operate efficiently and much too small to hire professional managerial staff, we would therefore have combines. You might even have all the hospitals in one community under common management, and a lot of them would disappear; this consolidation would improve the health of the community considerably.

However, the same forces which prevent this from happening also prevent the CHP from performing institutional euthanasia, because, as Mr. Lave just pointed out, the people involved in the institutions in question have political muscle, which I think was the force of your point—that you cannot go and commit euthanasia on what is to many people their entrance to heaven.

In a community like mine the hospital does not just take care of sick people. A very short story illustrates this. A lady came around to raise funds for Princeton Hospital. They do this regularly; they have a big fete, go to a lot of trouble, and raise about $50,000. Now, $50,000 does not mean anything at all to Princeton Hospital. So why do they have these things? It is to create in the minds of the people the idea that this is something they are doing for virtue. And when I told this little old lady I was not going to contribute to the hospital because I thought additional capital to them would just increase operating costs and that they did not need it, she did not just think I was an old miser; it was more than that. I was attacking her fundamental vehicle for getting into heaven. That was the good thing she was doing; you cannot attack that sort of thing.

Now, on Lave's point, I quite agree with everything he said. And that is exactly why I am a little bewildered as to why so many of the people have been so worried about the certificate-of-need process. It is not going to have much effect.

PROFESSOR HAVIGHURST: However, proprietaries do not have that kind of political clout, at least not very often. And they are the ones who will be excluded.

PROFESSOR SOMERS: That is true. They are outside the process.

PROFESSOR HAVIGHURST: They are the ones for whom the certificate-of-need arguments seem to be the weakest, and yet they are the ones who are most likely to be excluded.

PROFESSOR SOMERS: Yes. That is true.

Prestige-Motivated Investments

PROFESSOR KESSEL: The implication of Professor Somers's position is that we should not have certificates of need. He contends that the analysis that we have undertaken has really been too shallow when we conclude that some hospitals are inefficient. In other words, if we take into account the community pride and these other factors, the hospital concerned is perfectly efficient, and it just looks inefficient to us because we do not fully understand its workings. Thus, an appropriate response to people who want certificates of need is to say, "You really do not understand the world, and your analysis is too simple. Those hospitals are there because people want them there, and they are willing to pay a price for them, even though, superficially, they look inefficient because you have left certain factors out of your analysis." Is that not your view?

PROFESSOR SOMERS: No, I do not think so. I think the CHPs can still be justified on the grounds that while they cannot do the whole job, they can do important things at the margin. The CHP agencies are important vehicles of information, and there are various degrees of inefficiency which they feel they can keep under control by having some moderating influence on this ever-rising growth. It is a question of degree, and I think all of these things have had a very important educational effect in the community generally.

Now, what is efficiency? We have been using that word a lot. But we have been using it exclusively in an economic sense, maximizing utility and uses of resources. That is not necessarily the only definition of efficiency. Efficiency is related to purpose, and we are assuming an economic purpose exclusively. The point I have been making is that the hospital, in its own eyes and in the eyes of its trustees, has an additional purpose going far beyond effective rendering of medical care; therefore, the fact that it satisfies certain social needs and desires in another way is part of efficiency. I mean, if you are satisfying what you set out to satisfy, that is to their way of thinking being efficient, even though it would not be by the usual economic analysis.

PROFESSOR KESSEL: I am accepting your analysis. I just thought it implied that we ought not to be fretting about what appears superficially to be excess capacity.

MR. SIEVERTS: I think Lester Lave is just dead wrong on one important point that he presented as a fact: the notion that if the little community next door wants to build a hospital and pay for it, that is up to them, that in fact it is not going to cost me anything, and so long as it does not cost me anything, why should I worry? All right, maybe that is not what you said, but I am allowed, just like Professor Kessel, to misquote people at will, I hope. Even if that is not what you said, that is what I prefer to respond to, and anyway, Professor Kessel implied as much in what he just said.

In fact, whether we like it or not, the vast majority of the dollars that go to operate hospitals are paid for out of area-wide insurance pools, or even national pools like Medicare. If the hospital is going to be built or expanded, it raises the costs of everybody who is contributing to the insurance pool. Incidentally, *new* hospitals just are not an issue in most American communities. In Pittsburgh we have had exactly one firm proposal to establish a new hospital in the last fifteen years. It is current right now. Six months ago, I would have said we have had none in the last fifteen years.

The issue is not new hospitals, but it is expansion and renovation and change. The same point counts, however, in terms of increased health care spending; we all pay, like it or not. The fact is that if the cost of operating a little town's hospital system goes up $10 million a year, those $10 million are not simply borne by the people who live in that neighborhood but by all of us in the area and even the nation.

We estimate, for example, that the proprietary hospital that is about to be built (if they get their way) in Pittsburgh will immediately result in an increase of about $1 to $1.50 per month for every Blue Cross subscriber in western Pennsylvania, whether or not they ever use the hospital. Now, that is not a reason not to build a hospital. Some costs are justifiable, of course. I am just saying it as a fact. To say that if a group wants to raise its own capital, we should allow it to do so because it is its own money overlooks that fact. You can take that point of view if you wish, but we *all* end up paying any expansion of health care expenditures. I think it is a very important point and one which is easily overlooked.

The Consumer's Role

MR. ACTON: I would like to pick up on the O'Donoghue-Carlson paper, particularly the last part. They had some very pragmatic suggestions, since the many comprehensive planning laws are up for re-enactment or modification next year. Specifically they had suggestions for the composition of the boards of the planning agencies.

I very much agree with them that consumer preferences have a role in the health sector. What I would like to point out is that there are several ways to get consumer preferences, one of which is to have "consumer representatives." However, the more I listened to them, the more I began worrying, because it started to sound more and more like the Illinois law where if you have a comprehensive board that really thinks about health, it has to worry about plumbing and grocery stores, too, before it is done. And I realized we have bodies that meet this description already; we call them legislatures. They already consider a whole broad range of the interests of society and enact laws and merge preferences and so forth.

Having sharpened my thinking further during the coffee break—especially in a conversation with Paul Gertman (although you should not assume that this reflects his point of view)—I now tentatively agree that these special CHP bodies might perform an important function by articulating consumer preferences that otherwise might not be articulated, even if you thought the consumers' preferences per se ought to have a different origin. For instance, I have a particular bias that the direct approach to consumers via surveys may be a feasible means of determining what some of their preferences, priorities, and utilities will be. It is unlikely, however, that a legislature would commission surveys of consumer preferences like this, whereas a comprehensive health planning body might.

RITA CAMPBELL: I agree with Dr. O'Donoghue and Mr. Carlson that consumers need to be better informed if they are to be more effective in the marketplace for resource allocation in health care. In this respect, the efforts of the insurance commissioner of Pennsylvania and the New York State Department of Health in publishing ratings or "grading" of health insurance plans are commendable. With the exception of health insurance plans which have a cost-benefit relationship built in, it is very difficult to rate health providers objectively unless one is exceedingly knowledgeable in the health care field. One basic problem is that medical care and health are not synonymous, and the healthier person with relatively poorer medical care may be more satisfied with his choice of medical care arrangements or rate them higher than individuals with poorer health and better medical care.

Health Maintenance Organizations

RITA CAMPBELL: Whether HMOs, as suggested by the paper of Dr. O'Donoghue and Mr. Carlson, can provide a better vehicle through which consumers can exercise judgment about the quality and form of delivery of medical care than existing third-party payers, government and private, I do not know. The major virtue of the HMO from the public point of view is that it permits more accurate advance budgeting for the cost of prospective medical care by whatever governments or third parties are paying for the individual's medical care. The third party is a major conduit through which the consumer's influence is made effective. In the private sector the consumer selects his insurer, often from those pre-selected by the company for which he works, at a time when he is well, not sick, and therefore his judgment is clearer. The HMO can be looked at not only as a provider but also as one of the several types of insurers among which the consumer chooses. The consumer, even without the proposals set forth, can influence a health care provider by his initial choice of an HMO or any other insurer-provider combination and by changing his choice if dissatisfied. Providing the consumer with the knowledge to make his choice wisely is to me a far preferable first step to be taken before even considering that the federal government "mandate and monitor" the many items listed in the O'Donoghue-Carlson paper in an industry with such a multiplicity and diversity of providers.

PROFESSOR HAVIGHURST: I hope it is clear that the argument in my paper that the market could solve many of the problems presented by third-party payment rests heavily on facilitating just that consumer choice to which Mrs. Campbell calls attention.

MR. SIEVERTS: I want to respond to some of the points made by the American Rehabilitation Foundation spokesmen regarding what they alleged in the way of bias in area-wide CHP agencies against HMOs. I note first the curious fact that one of the two HMOs that reported difficulty with a local CHP agency was in Washington, D.C., where there is no CHP agency. Maybe that was the problem.

The fact is that the large majority of CHP advisory councils and boards around the country are dominated by people who are very skeptical about the existing health care system and hence are very pro-HMO, whatever that means. And if there is any group of providers who could complain volubly that they are not getting a fair shake by local CHP agencies, it would be general hospitals and nursing homes. If one were to do a poll of the kind that O'Donoghue and Carlson did, with a representative sampling of hospital administrators in America, you would find that a large percentage of them feel that they are not getting a fair hearing in the kinds of programs that they want to develop. You must remember that it is upsetting to *any* agency to go through a review process.

DR. O'DONOGHUE: We agree with that. The survey, I think, showed there was much less problem then had been anticipated.

Deductibles and Coinsurance

MR. SIEVERTS: The economists' argument about deductibles and coinsurance which we have heard from time to time is based on sheer naivete. They do not have the effect that some of the theoreticians here suggest.

We have a Medicare program which was enacted six or seven years ago with deductibles and coinsurance built into it. Western Pennsylvania might be unique, but I do not think it is. Approximately 80 to 90 percent of the people over age sixty-five voluntarily and at their own expense bought additional insurance to fill up the deductibles and the co-pay risks. So where is this incentive for controlled use you are talking about? What the consumers have instead of one insurance policy to cover their health care is two: a Medicare policy and (usually) a Blue Cross-Blue Shield policy. If your intent is to have people restrict their own entry into the health care system because of their reluctance to pay deductibles, the people, the consumers, are going to fool you. They are going to immediately buy second coverage to eliminate that risk.

Very frequently liberals—who are notably in short supply at the speakers' table at this meeting—attack the President's proposal for health insurance standards on the ground that if we force employers to give everybody a health insurance package with deductibles and coinsurance this will unduly restrict the entry of consumers into the health care delivery system. I do not worry much about that. I would predict with total certainty that if the Health Insurance Standards Act passed and were made law, almost immediately virtually all employed consumers would buy a second coverage which would fill all those deductibles. In fact, I suspect that in the majority of industries the minimum standards would indeed be regarded as minimum, and that the fringe benefit coverages that people got would be comprehensive and not the partial insurance that the President, like so many of the speakers today, seems to think would reduce entry into health care.

APPENDIX

The Prospectus for the Conference

Part I: "Voluntary" Health Planning

(1) The Need for Planning. The oversight of redundant or extravagant investments in health facilities; the problem of decision making in the public and eleemosynary sectors; how "overbedding" generates overutilization; how third-party payment and the principle of cost-reimbursement translate excess capacity into higher costs to consumers; the external benefits not obtainable from reliance on market forces.

(2) The History and Appraisal of Voluntary Health Planning. The background with emphasis on the source of the impetus; selling the CHP notion to Congress; a summary of federal and state laws on voluntary planning; an appraisal of the results in U.S. and elsewhere; the beginnings of the move to put "teeth" in planning.

Part II: Health Planning with "Teeth"

(1) Legislative Developments and Proposals. A summary of the character and scope of state "franchising" laws and proposals; the H.R. 1 provisions on Medicare reimbursement for capital costs of unplanned facilities; the administration's and other proposals for more substantial sanctions.

(2) The Planning and Licensing Agencies. The performance, particularly with reference to competitive ventures; the character, membership, and staff; the likelihood of "capture" by the regulated industry or the voluntary hospital segment thereof; the role accorded consumers.

(3) Planning Versus Proprietary Facilities. The statutes' application to proprietaries and the rationale therefor; the vulnerability of full service hospitals to competition resulting from unremunerative services and charitable undertakings; the "cream-skimming" argument for protectionism.

(4) Precedents from Other Industries. The experience with "certificates of public convenience and necessity" in other fields; defining "need" in terms of impact on existing providers of the service; the experience with "skimming" arguments in other regulated fields.

311

Part III: Nonprofit Monopolies in Health Care

(1) Grounds for Concern. The origin in economies of scale, the competitive advantages of nonprofit status, and entry restrictions; behavior; comparison to monopolies of the profit-making variety; opportunities for diversion of "profits" for personal advantage; implications for resource allocation, efficiency, quality of care, and consumer interests; the issue of rate regulation.

(2) Benefits and Costs of an Unrestrictive Policy toward Entry. The possible confinement of planning to investments of the nonprofit and governmental sectors; the value of actual and potential competition; "cream-skimming" versus possible subsidization of competitive services by higher charges on monopoly services; allowing nonprofit institutions to "fail"; effect on overall costs and debt financing of new nonprofit facilities; quality-of-care considerations.

(3) A Consumer-Oriented View. The consequences of loss of consumer choice the "new medical elite" versus the consumer/patient; the monopolist's tendency to take its customers for granted; consumer pressure for participation in decision making as a manifestation of "countervailing power"; tax law, accreditation, and other means of enforcing charitable purposes and more responsive behavior.

Part IV: National Health Policy Directions and Implications for Health Planning

(1) Effect of National Health Insurance on Unremunerative Services. The nonprofit providers on a more businesslike and less charitable basis; benefit limits in public programs and the residual need for charity; catastrophic insurance proposals including Feldstein's "major risk insurance"; relevance of increased consumer self-sufficiency to policy on entry restrictions.

(2) Likely Future Status of the Market for Health Services. The opportunities for continued reliance on the market in the context of increased federal third-party payment; the role of HMOs; new utilization controls through medical care foundations and PSROs, particularly in response to HMO competition; planning's function in a market-oriented system; federal policy versus state planning legislation.

(3) HMOs and Health Planning. The application of H.R. 1 to planning affecting HMOs; state legislation applicable to hospital-based HMOs and perhaps others; the effect of entry restrictions on realization of the HMO concept; the relevance for planning of possible "skimming" by HMOs in selecting or attracting lower-risk populations.

312

LIST OF
CONFERENCE PARTICIPANTS

Acton, Jan P., *The Rand Corporation*

Altman, Stuart H., M.D., *Department of Health, Education, and Welfare*

Calabresi, Guido,* *The Yale Law School*

Campbell, Rita R., *The Hoover Institution*

Carlson, Rick J., *Health Services Research Center, Institute for Interdisciplinary Studies, American Rehabilitation Foundation*

Curran, William J.,* *School of Public Health, Harvard University*

Davis, Karen, *The Brookings Institution*

Feingold, Eugene, *School of Public Health, University of Michigan*

Galinski, Thomas P., *Division of Planning, American Hospital Association*

Gentry, John T., M.D., *School of Public Health, University of North Carolina*

Gertman, Paul M, M.D., *Office of Science and Technology, Executive Office of the President*

Gottlieb, Symond R., *Greater Detroit Area Hospital Council*

Grad, Frank P.,* *Legislative Drafting Research Fund, Columbia University School of Law*

Grosse, Robert N., *School of Public Health, University of Michigan*

Guthrie, Eugene H., M.D., *Maryland Comprehensive Health Planning Agency*

Havighurst, Clark C.,* *Duke University School of Law*

Kessel, Reuben A.,* *Graduate School of Business, University of Chicago*

Lave, Judith R. *School of Urban and Public Affairs, Carnegie-Mellon University*

Lave, Lester B., *Graduate School of Industrial Administration, Carnegie-Mellon University*

May, J. Joel, *Graduate Program in Hospital Administration, Center for Health Administration Studies, University of Chicago*

Mechanic, David,* *University of Wisconsin*

Neuhauser, Duncan, *School of Public Health, Harvard University*

Newhouse, Joseph P., *The Rand Corporation*

O'Donoghue, Patrick, M.D., *Health Services Research Center, Institute for Interdisciplinary Studies, American Rehabilitation Foundation*

Pauly, Mark V., *Northwestern University*

Pfeiffer, Eric, M.D.,* *Older American Resources and Services Program, Duke University Medical Center*

Posner, Richard A., *University of Chicago Law School*

---

* Member, Committee on Legal Issues in Health Care.

Sieverts, Steven, *Hospital Planning Association of Allegheny County, Pennsylvania*
Silver, Laurens H., *National Health and Environmental Law Program, School of Law, University of California, Los Angeles*
Somers, Anne R., *College of Medicine and Dentistry of New Jersey (Rutgers Medical School)*
Somers, Herman M., *Woodrow Wilson School of Public and International Affairs, Princeton University*
Stickel, Delford L., M.D.* *Duke University Medical Center*
Wright, Peter K., *Governor's Health Policy and Planning Task Force, Wisconsin*
Zwick, Daniel, *Department of Health, Education, and Welfare*

---

* Member, Committee on Legal Issues in Health Care.

Cover and book design: Pat Taylor